The self in social inquiry

Researching methods

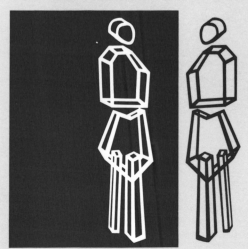

David N. Berg
Kenwyn K. Smith

The self in social inquiry

The editors and authors gratefully acknowledge the permission granted to reprint the following: The excerpts in Chapter 2, by Clayton P. Alderfer, are reprinted by permission of the University Press of Kansas from *The Life of a Psychologist: An Autobiography* by Fritz Heider, © 1983; and by permission of Random House, Inc., from *Methods of Research in Social Psychology* by J. M. Carlsmith, P. C. Ellsworth, and E. Aronson, © 1976. The excerpt in Chapter 11, by Philip H. Mirvis and Meryl Reis Louis, is from "Little Gidding" in *Four Quartets* by T. S. Eliot, copyright 1943 by T. S. Eliot; renewed 1971 by Esme Valerie Eliot. Reprinted by permission of Harcourt Brace Jovanovich, Inc.

For information address:

SAGE Publications, Inc.
2111 West Hillcrest Drive
Newbury Park, California 91320

SAGE Publications Inc.   SAGE Publications Ltd.
275 South Beverly Drive   28 Banner Street
Beverly Hills   London EC1Y 8QE
California 90212   England

SAGE PUBLICATIONS India Pvt. Ltd.
M-32 Market
Greater Kailash I
New Delhi 110 048 India

Printed in the United States of America

Library of Congress Cataloging-in-Publication Data

Main entry under title:

Exploring clinical methods for social research.
    The Self in social inquiry : researching methods / [edited by]
David N. Berg, Kenwyn K. Smith.
        p.   cm.
    Previously published as: Exploring clinical methods for social
research. c1985.
    Bibliography: p.
    ISBN 0-8039-3347-9 (pbk.)
    1. Social sciences—Research—Methodology.   2. Social sciences—
Field work.   3. Participant observation.   4. Clinical sociology.
I. Berg, David N., 1949-   . II. Smith, Kenwyn K.   III. Title.
H61.E97   1988   88-11320
300'.72—dc19   CIP

VI. December 26, 1945

IX. January 5, 1946

VII. December 28, 1945

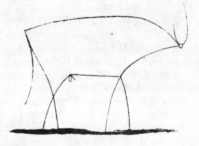

XI. January 17, 1946

CONTRIBUTORS

Contributors to this volume represent a number of disciplines, a diversity of institutions, and different stages of their academic careers. Between them they have published hundreds of journal articles and (co-)authored or (co-)edited scores of books, some of which are listed below.

Clayton P. Alderfer, Yale School of Organization and Management, *Existence, Relatedness, and Growth* (1972), *Learning from Changing* (1975), and *Advances in Experiential Social Processes* (1980).

David N. Berg, Yale School of Organization and Management, *Paradoxes of Group Life* (1987).

Cortlandt Cammann, Institute for Social Research, University of Michigan, *Assessing Organizational Change* (1983).

Marshall Edelson, Department of Psychiatry, Yale School of Medicine, *Language and Interpretation in Psychoanalysis* (1975) and *Hypothesis and Evidence in Psychoanalysis* (1984).

Jonathon H. Gillette, Yale School of Organization and Management, *Group Dynamics: Examining a Tradition of Experiential Education* (forthcoming).

J. Richard Hackman, Harvard University, *Behavior in Organizations* (1975), *Work Redesign* (1980), and *Groups That Work* (forthcoming).

A. Michael Huberman, University of Geneva, *Innovation up Close: How School Improvement Works* (1984) and *Qualitative Data Analysis* (1984).

Kathy E. Kram, Boston University School of Management, *Mentoring at Work* (1985).

Meryl Reis Louis, Boston University School of Management.

Rodney L. Lowman, North Texas State University.

Matthew B. Miles, Center for Policy Research, New York, *Whose School Is It Anyway?* (1981) and *Learning to Work in Groups* (1981).

Phillip B. Mirvis, Boston University School of Management, *Failures in Organizational Development and Change* (1977).

Helen Swick Perry, Cambridge, Massachusetts, *The Human Be-in* (1970) and *Psychiatrist of America: The Life of Harry Stack Sullivan* (1982).

Stewart Swick Perry, Cambridge, Massachusetts, *The Human Nature of Science* (1966).

Alan Peshkin, College of Education, University of Illinois, *Growing Up American* (1978) and *The Imperfect Union: School Consolidation and Community Conflict* (1982).

Schulamit Reinhartz, Brandeis University, *On Becoming a Social Scientist* (1979).

Susan J. Schurman, University of Michigan.

Valerie M. Simmons, University of California at Santa Cruz.

Kenwyn K. Smith, The Wharton School, University of Pennsylvania, *Groups in Conflict* (1982).

Robert I. Sutton, Stanford University, *Readings in Organizational Behavior* (forthcoming).

CONTENTS

PREFACE

It has always been hard for social investigators to know what to do with their selves. On the one hand there have been voices encouraging us to keep our selves out of our inquiry, to take postures that are distant. On the other hand there are those who suggest we become fully involved, to swim, as it were, in the streams whose currents we wish to know.

No matter what methods we use in our social investigations, we have to make a choice about where we will position our selves, at one of these extreme points or some place in between. Whatever our choice, the position we take is still a position. And what we look at, what we see, what we encode, what we make sense of, all are a function of that positioning.

There is an overwhelming burden and an immense liberation associated with this realization. The liberation comes from recognizing that no matter where we place ourselves, there are benefits and there are biases. Hence each social investigator can rest in the assurance that there are no ultimate rights and wrongs. The choice about how to relate to those being studied thus becomes one of the many craft skills each social scientist must develop, at the same level of importance as the craft of determining which analytic technique best unlocks the mysteries of a particular data set. The burden is that every piece of research, to be full and integritious, must constantly monitor the relationship between the researcher and the researched.

Given that we are human beings investigating human beings, it is logical to expect that whatever we conclude about those whom we research will be equally applicable to us, the researchers. Hence if our research teaches us that social relationships influence what we attend to, what falls into our blind spots, and the attributions we make, then it follows that the relationships we are involved in during the research will influence us in similar ways.

Instead of affirming which method is right, serious social science asks us to investigate ourselves while we are investigating others, so that we know about the tradeoffs being made as we apply the methods we have chosen. As social investigators, it is our responsibility to be researching our methods while we are applying them, just as it is to be asking whether our findings are valid, our measuring devices reliable, or our conclusions generalizable.

This places the scrutiny of self in the center stage of social inquiry. We have chosen to use the term *clinical* to apply to this aspect of research methods. This

9

choice is grounded in the conviction that the application of the principles of social research to the process of social research itself both enhances the quality of the inquiry and nourishes the vitality of the inquirers. It is a special use of the term that we believe comes to full life in the pages of this text. It should not be confused, however, with the way it is used in medicine or psychiatry, where it is tightly associated with therapeutic activity.

The earlier edition of this book was titled *Exploring Clinical Methods for Social Research*. For this edition we have changed the title because so many social scientists associate the term "clinical" exclusively with pathology and reparation. That was so far from our intent that to retain the original title would only continue to foster an understanding contrary to our purposes.

We knew of many compatible voices struggling to articulate the theme of this book, so we chose to craft an edited volume rather than to write it exclusively ourselves. In creating this volume, we asked individuals from a variety of fields to discuss aspects of their research that they would not normally scrutinize in a public forum. This was a difficult task for both authors and editors. The many iterations were painful, but the quality of the book and the relationships established were worth the effort.

As students learning research methods, we were grateful to an earlier generation of writers and teachers who explored the personal and relational work together with the intellectual demands inherent in social research. With this volume we seek to advance this tradition by encouraging all social investigators to reflect on what we do with our selves while we conduct our inquiry.

> The question is whether the validity of science depends on the achievement of a completely objective, noninvolved, nonprejudicial point of view, or whether the acknowledgement of the necessary relativity, subjectivity, and prejudice involved in any act of perception is, in fact, a truer and more scientific approach to knowledge.

(Susan A. Handelman, The Slayers of Moses)

Kenwyn K. Smith
David N. Berg
Philadelphia
March 1988

INTRODUCTION

Kenwyn K. Smith and David N. Berg

It is one of the contentions of this volume that when we use ourselves as instruments for studying human systems we take on a special responsibility. It is a responsibility to science and to the people with whom we work. We are obligated to struggle to understand the complex emotional and intellectual forces that influence the conduct of our inquiry. These forces are at once the source of our insight and our folly. We must apply the same systematic attention to our analysis of these forces as we do to our analysis of the topics we study. Especially as we move into the field and concentrate our research on the social problems that confront the cultures in which we live, it becomes increasingly important that we examine, describe, and scrutinize who we are, why we do research, how we create knowledge, and how the research process changes us.

This book is an attempt to focus attention on these issues. It is a book about the emotional and intellectual struggles that attend researchers as they formulate ideas, collect and interpret data, and build theory. The chapters in this volume describe struggles with concepts, with methods, with relationships, and with each individual researcher's quest to define his or her place in the social sciences. Not least of all, this book is the product of many individual struggles to *write* about these issues in the belief that both the writer and the reader will learn from such an undertaking.

WHY CREATE THIS BOOK?

All research activity, including fieldwork, laboratory experiments, published articles and books, seminars, and presentations, serves a variety of interests. In its simplest and perhaps most naive conception, the research endeavor serves our interest to know more about the world around us. It also serves the personal interests of the individual researcher and, in some cases, the interests of the individuals and organizations participating in the research. But research, like other human undertakings, is embedded in a society and enmeshed in the interests of that society. The concerns of a funding agency or supporting institution, the current directions of the profession or discipline, the pressures of career advancement, the subtle influences of class and culture all combine with the desire to know, to form a web of interests served by any research activity. These interests are not easily recognized by the researchers themselves. Some may not be able to see the ways in which their work serves interests other than their own. Others may choose not to see what interests are served because of the difficult questions raised by such an awareness.

Often the methods we choose to conduct research are, wittingly or unwittingly, an expression of the conflicting interests that are being served by the study. Whether in the lab or in the field, these conflicting interests affect our work. In the lab, conflicting interests between researchers and "subject" sometimes lead researchers to use their power to transform the subject's interests into their own interests. Required participation in psychology experiments in universities is an example of this transformation. In other circumstances this conflict has led researchers to lie about their objectives. In the case of field research, the conflict between the interests of science and the interests of the people participating in the study may lead some researchers to return to the controlled environment of the lab. It can also lead to the development of field methods that provide guidelines for accommodating the two sets of interests.

Especially since this volume is devoted to an examination of research methods, we think it is important to be as explicit as we can about the multiple and sometimes conflicting interests served by the creation of this book. In most cases we, like other researchers, do not openly discuss the interests being served by our research nor do we articulate them for others to consider as they think about our work. But since this volume is about research, we believe it is important that we try to convey our thoughts about the interests being served herein. The discussion of the historical, conceptual and personal interests being served by the book is intended also to function as an introduction to the ideas contained in the following pages.

Historical interests. There are many historical themes in the social sciences that the chapters in this volume might address. Over hundreds of years the development of the scientific method has brought with it an increasing separation between knowledge and methods of knowing. In the physical sciences this split served knowledge because scientists were too often and too easily influenced by the needs of their patrons, the dogma of the Church, or the power of their own beliefs. The standardization of a scientific method took a number of important decisions out of the domain of the individual and made them subject to the demands of specific rules of evidence, inference, and generalization. The development of the scientific method meant that a community of researchers could all work toward expanding the existing knowledge about the physical world by using a common language that, on the surface, did not require a common belief other than a belief in the utility of the language itself.

The growth of the social and behavioral sciences, as well as the increasing attention paid to social science by philosophers, has raised a number of important questions about the utility of a research method that is separated from the knowledge it creates. As we learn more about human behavior, as our behavioral science begins to yield fruit, it becomes increasingly clear that we must examine the implications of this knowledge for the research endeavor. In the social sciences, to maintain the split between what we know and how we know it is to handicap ourselves in the service of a belief that social and physical sciences should share the same research methods.

During the past century in particular, social scientists have struggled to integrate their knowledge of human beings with the human practice of research on social systems. Rather than act as if it were possible or advisable for us to step out of our humanity when we do research, these social scientists sought to develop methods that either took account of the researcher's humanity or used it to generate insight into the phenomenon at hand. To be sure, there were also many social scientists who continued to develop methods that took the researcher out of the process as much as possible, convinced then as now that the benefits of such a "removal" far outweigh the costs. It is our view that this separation places severe limitations on what we can learn about social systems precisely because the method itself denies what we already know: that human beings studying human beings are inevitably influenced in complex ways by a variety of social and psychological forces.

This volume attempts to continue the search for ways to integrate our knowledge about human beings with the methods we use to study human systems. We are taking what is usually treated as peripheral and making it central. The book is addressed to both those who have worked to remove the researcher from the research process and those who have attempted to reintegrate the two. The following chapters offer the former an explanation of the necessity of developing clinical methodologies and some examples of their usefulness, and the latter a statement about the need to bring what we know about the researcher out of the closet.

Conceptual interests. At this point it would probably be confusing to use the term *clinical* to describe those aspects of behavioral science research that acknowledge and utilize the special characteristics of human beings studying human systems. Part of this confusion originates in the current uses of the term, especially in medicine and psychology where *clinical* often refers to a therapeutic activity. Given its current usage in other fields one might ask why we have chosen to redefine this term for the behavioral sciences. There are at least four reasons.

First, especially in psychology, the clinical setting is an arena of professional practice or research in which understanding is sought in the systematic examination of the researcher and the research relationship as well as in an analysis of the human phenomenon being studied. Clinical psychologists in both practice and academe pay close attention to all three aspects in order to inform both their actions and their theories. Psychologists in other subdisciplines often scrutinize the researcher and the research relationship only to the extent that these variables affect what can be known about the psychological issue at hand and then seek to minimize, control, or eliminate their influence whenever possible.

Second, activities that take place in a clinical setting also involve a responsibility to others. Practitioners and researchers alike must struggle to balance the multiple responsibilities they carry. These responsibilities influence the choices they make and the work they do. As a result, much of current practice and theory represents the ways in which professionals have managed these responsibilities. It could be argued that all research in the behavioral sciences has this clinical aspect to it since all research involving human beings also brings with it responsibility whether or not the researcher chooses to attend to it.

A third reason for choosing the term *clinical* is that clinical research or practice necessarily involves the participation of other human beings. In clinical medicine, for example, the physician must learn to work with patients in both the diagnosis and treatment of illness. In the clinical setting it is not enough to know the physiology and chemistry of the human organism; the doctor must also know how to involve the patient. The less the doctor knows, the more he or she must rely on the patient's experience and ability (or willingness) to report that experience. Thus, new knowledge is directly connected to the quality of the doctor-patient relationship and, by implication, the various factors—personal, interpersonal, organizational, and cultural—that affect that relationship. As behavioral scientists move into the field to do their research or begin to conceptualize the laboratory as an organization, these clinical aspects of research become even more important than they already were. Freud's work is perhaps the best-known example of knowledge that can be created when systematic attention is paid to the information available in a clinical setting—information found not only in the research participant but in the researcher and the research relationship as well.

Finally, our frustration with the current polarization between quantitative and qualitative methods pushed us to seek a concept that would not carry with it the historical baggage born of this controversy. As will become evident, both quantitative and qualitative research can be either clinical or nonclinical, depending upon the stance taken by the researcher and his or her definition of relevant research data.

Our conceptual goal in the chapters that follow is to develop a definition of *clinical* and to explore its relevance for social science research. This will involve further discussions of the distinction between clinical and nonclinical research and an examination of the nature of validity in clinical research. In clinical research, for example, how does one know the difference between knowledge and idiosyncratic whim? How does one learn to trust one's own understanding and how does one evaluate the utility-validity of this understanding? Since we argue that almost all social science research has a clinical element to it, we believe these are important questions for all social scientists.

Personal interests. There are a number of personal interests served by the creation of this volume. Through this work we give further definition to our identities as social scientists. We differentiate ourselves from some in our field and identify with others. In putting forth the ideas in this book we are simultaneously seeking and affirming the worth of these ideas. In working on this jointly, we affirm the importance of our relationship to each other. This activity adds meaning to both our professional and personal lives, and represents one of the tangible products that remain after the work is completed.

We are also aware that this volume is an attempt to increase the legitimacy of a method and the kinds of knowledge it produces. Many of our traditionally trained colleagues come to us for guidance and help when confronted with difficult interpersonal, group, or organizational problems in both research and practice. We suspect that this is more than just colleagial goodwill and that these people find what we know about human behavior useful. In spite of the fact that *clinical* is often placed in opposition to *academic*, it is clear that clinical knowledge adds to our colleagues' understanding of a human system (and their role in it) and, in some cases, helps them act. In part we write this book to open up a professional conversation about what clinical understanding is and how it contributes to our knowledge about human systems. Whereas this now requires traditional social scientists to converse with colleagues who are often on the fringe of academic respectability, this volume seeks to make that conversation an important and more central part of research in the field.

ORGANIZATION OF THE BOOK

There are four sections to this volume. Each section opens with an introduction and concludes with a brief editorial commentary. The introduction describes the chapters included in the section and the commentary discusses some of the issues and themes raised by them.

Clinical Issues. The three chapters that make up the first section set the stage for the rest of the volume. These initial chapters both pose and seek to answer a number of questions about a clinical method in the behavioral sciences: What is it? What might we learn from such a method? What does it require of researchers who use it? How do we go about it? In this section issues are raised that are then addressed in the chapters that follow.

Clinical Understanding. The five chapters in the second section explore what can be learned from a clinical method and how this knowledge adds to our understanding of human behavior. The chapters range from an epistemological analysis of clinical methods to an examination of the cultural and political influences on what we know about human behavior to a discussion of the ways an action orientation changes how we understand the social world.

Clinical Involvement. The third section includes chapters that focus on the relationships that are part of a clinical method. Some of these chapters examine relationships among researchers and between researchers and the people they work with. Others explore the researcher's relationship with himself or herself during the research process, and still others look at the influence of intergroup relations in the surrounding culture on the relationship between the researcher and the social system being studied. This section takes a particularly hard look at the personal and emotional demands of clinical research.

Clinical Methods. The final chapters present the clinical side of various research methods including interviewing, participant observation, historical analysis, and qualitative data analysis. Through the description of specific cases, these chapters illustrate some of the dilemmas, challenges, and rewards of a clinical method taken into the field.

In summary, we have sought not only to identify some of the emotional and intellectual struggles in social research but to shed some light on them as well. We hope this volume will provide its readers with some thoughtful companionship as they struggle, inevitably, with some of the issues raised in this book. One's mind, thoughts and feelings, conscious and unconscious, with its links to family and culture, is nurtured by the company it keeps.

Clinical Issues

What is a clinical method? What does it require of the researcher? What is its role in social science? The three chapters in this first section address these questions and identify conceptual themes that are explored in subsequent chapters. Together they initiate a provocative dialogue on the meaning, importance, and challenge of clinical methods.

The first chapter proposes a definition of *clinical* for the behavioral sciences. The authors describe the potential contribution of a clinical method and point out the intellectual and emotional demands on the researcher who wants to use such a method. The coauthors of this chapter emphasize the importance of research relationships—between researchers and research participants, between researchers and their colleagues, and between the various internal "parts" of any individual researcher.

The second chapter struggles with the implications of the fact that researchers are themselves human beings. Using the vehicle of an ongoing conversation between the researcher as scientist and the researcher as self, Alderfer explores how aspects of the researcher as human being influence method development and theory building. Along the way he scrutinizes not only Sigmund Freud and Fritz Heider but himself as well. A clinical method, argues Alderfer, brings the often denied human aspects of the researcher into social research, thereby enhancing its validity and vitality.

The issue of validity is central to Edelson's chapter. He contends that a clinical method must adhere to scientific canons if we are to believe one explanation or hypothesis over another. He addresses the arguments sometimes put forth to exempt a clinical method from scientific standards of inference and concludes that such an exemption is both unwarranted and unwise. Edelson, a psychoanalyst, concludes that psychological phenomena (inside an individual, between researcher and patient, in the scientific community) can be the legitimate domain of a scientifically rigorous clinical method and suggests steps toward this end.

As you read these three chapters, you might reflect on the issues that are alive in your own research work. How do you fit yourself and your work into the social sciences? When do you think about the role of research relationships in the research process—at the beginning, whenever things go wrong, or as you explain unanticipated findings? What demands for rigor do you experience? How satisfied are you with what you are able to see with your current methodological approach? What forces do you struggle to control inside your self and inside your world, and what influence does this struggle have on your work and your life?

THE CLINICAL DEMANDS OF RESEARCH METHODS

David N. Berg and Kenwyn K. Smith

The arguments of this chapter are made upon the foundation of three firmly held beliefs. First, the nature and quality of social research findings are powerfully influenced by the relationship between the researcher and the researched. Second, this relationship should receive the same intense scrutiny as other methodological issues in the research process (such as the tools of statistical inference). Third, any system of investigating social reality must address the whole research process, including the research relationship as well as the formal procedures represented in our methodological canons.

The perspective that social science knowledge is developed in the context of a relationship has been acknowledged and discussed by people in many disciplines across many generations (Mannheim, 1936; Sullivan, 1953b; Devereux, 1967; Heron, 1981). Until recently (Morgan, 1983; Reason & Rowan, 1981) there has been little call for the inclusion of a systematic examination of these relationships in the research write-up. Except for a brief explanation of the power of the experimental manipulation or of the rapport developed with informants, it is entirely possible to read an article in psychology, sociology, or even anthropology without knowing much about the research relationships and their impact on the researcher. Important contextual information is therefore not available and we often are forced to supply our own.

Within an academic discipline, research relationships are often assumed to have similar characteristics across studies. In elementary chemistry, for example, standard temperature and pressure are often assumed when findings are reported, but one can easily imagine the confusion if this relationship were altered and not reported. In the social sciences, however, it is very difficult to assume a standard relationship between the researcher and the researched, given the complexity of this relationship. Even when we seek to standardize our research relationships, we are often unaware of the key characteristics of these relationships until we attempt to apply our findings to other settings. It is usually only then—when they do not fit—that we recognize the special features of our research relationships. To pursue the analogy, we discover that water does not always boil at 212°F when we try to cook an egg in Denver. To say that water boils at 212°F is to say "at sea level" simultaneously if implicitly. As we move to studying complex human phenomena, especially in field settings, we need to be more diligent in our attempts to describe, analyze, and understand the relationships in which we seek our knowledge of social systems.

What makes research relationships in the social sciences complex is the fact that both the researcher and the social system being studied contribute to creating the research relationship. In turn, the relationship has both emotional and intellectual consequences for both parties.

THE CENTRALITY OF RESEARCH RELATIONSHIPS

Research relationships are an important part of social research for several reasons. First, it can be maintained that virtually no information about a person, group, or social system exists without a relationship with that person or social system. Irrespective of whether social phenomena exist independent of our relationship to them, our knowledge of the social world is a consequence of our relationship with this world (in the laboratory, in the field, or in our own lives) or our exposure to the relationships of others (social science research, literature, history).

Sullivan (1953b) discusses this issue in the field of psychiatry, arguing that psychiatric understanding is rooted in the relationship between the psychiatrist and the patient rather than in "objective" data that exist somewhere independent of the psychiatric relationship. This does not preclude the discovery of psychiatric regularities across different relationships. These similarities may indicate a critical pattern in the individual disorders being examined. However, it may also be that these patterns reflect the reality that the doctor-patient relationships are consciously or unconsciously following contours prescribed by a culture or a particular setting.

There are real, not merely philosophical, ways in which our research relationships create what we see. When we examine the creations of a collection or generation of social researchers we can see regularities in both their research relationships and research findings. These patterns help us to develop our theories. But it is important to remember that different relationships will create different data in social research. Hence we may need to move away from an idealization of standardized relationships, replacing this with a commitment to report and describe the relationships we develop.

Second, research relationships are the vehicle through which the researcher comes to understand a social system. Whether one assumes that each research participant provides a glimpse of an objective social reality or one piece of a mosaic of subjective social realities, the researcher's relationship with the participants and their social systems is an extremely powerful determinant of the quality of the data. Mutual and respectful relationships are more likely to give birth to sensitive thoughts and feelings (in both the researcher and the research participant) than are mistrusting ones.

Third, a description of the research relationship provides the context necessary for interpreting what has been discovered. The mere process of separating the data from their context of origin diminishes the meaning of the data. Preserving as much of the context as possible is an investment in maintaining the meaning of the data.

Critical to the context are the circumstances under which the research was begun. Were participants coerced by authority figures, or by extra points in a college exam, or were mutual benefits established for all parties involved in the research? The reasons why research relationships get established and the interests served by such relationships can be deceptively complex. In its simplest form the relationship grows out of the researcher's desire to understand human behavior and the participants' desire to help or to learn about themselves. However, this simple form is rarely found. There are usually many additional factors that influence the creation of a research relationship and these issues emerge as the relationship develops, constantly shaping its character. Researchers, for example, may differ in their orientation to research, their preferred relationship with a participating individual or social system, their personal or cultural characteristics, and the intellectual or career interests being served by the research. Organizations too may be interested in the research because of its potential value to their primary task, because of their desire to be affiliated with a university, or because they expect the research to provide a rationale for change. As the two parties learn about each other through their interaction on the research, the relationship often changes as the people involved adjust their needs and expectations.

Perhaps the most complex situation is in field research, where many research relationships may exist simultaneously. The number of relationships is not limited by the number of participants since a social system also includes authority structures, work or social groups, and a variety of identity groups (e.g., race, gender, ethnicity, age). Each of these units in a social system (individual, group, organizational) will develop its own relationship with the researcher or research team depending upon the initial characteristics and interests of all people involved and the information collected along the way. As many researchers will attest, the complexity of managing research relationships is magnified by the fact that what happens in one relationship affects others and that skill and awareness in one relationship domain (e.g., individual relationships) do not necessarily carry over to other domains.

WHAT WE MEAN BY CLINICAL

The word *clinical* is an adjective formed from the word *clinic*, a setting where knowledge about a field of endeavor is pursued, accumulated, and applied to problems arising in that field (Morgan, 1984). The Greek word *clinicos* means bed or couch (from the verb *clino*—to cause to lean). In modern usage, an important element of the historical root of the word clinical has been maintained—namely, the delivery of therapeutic service to someone who is "bent over" or in bed. Clinical medicine, clinical psychology, psychiatry, social work, nursing, and most recently clinical sociology are all considered clinical fields because of the professional therapeutic activities involved. But the research aspect of the clinical setting—the role of the clinic in producing professional knowledge that can then be used for therapeutic purposes—has not only faded from view, but given way to a popular view that the clinical and research aspects of a profession are distinct and often conflicting endeavors. In fact, *Webster's New Collegiate Dictionary* (1975) defines *clinician* as "one qualified in the clinical practice of medicine, psychiatry or psychology as distinguished from one specializing in laboratory or research techniques."

In spite of the development of a definition that characterizes clinical as almost exclusively therapeutic and distinct from research, most of the social sciences use the term to refer to specific kinds of research methods. Glassner and Moreno (1982) quote Alfred M. Lee, a former president of the American Sociological Association, as describing participant observation as "a clinical study of social interaction." Like other social scientists, Lee seems to be using the term clinical to describe an approach to research rather than an application of research to a thera-peutic situation. In our experience as well, the term *clinical* is regularly used to refer to an approach to the study of social systems, a method with its own characteristics and its own demands.

We argue that all social research has its clinical aspects. However, these are ignored more often than not and hence the application of the term *clinical* seems inappropriate. In this book, we have chosen to use the term *clinical* for those aspects of research that have the following characteristics:

(1) direct involvement with and/or observation of human beings or social systems;
(2) commitment to a process of self-scrutiny by the researcher as he or she conducts the research;
(3) willingness to change theory or method in response to the research experience *during* the research itself;
(4) description of social systems that is dense or thick and favors depth over breadth in any single undertaking; and
(5) participation of the social system being studied, under the assumption that much of the information of interest is only accessible to or report-able by its members.

(1) The characteristic of direct involvement requires that the researcher have firsthand experience with the social system being studied. Clearly this excludes activities such as secondary analysis of questionnaire data. But what about observation through a one-way mirror, or structured field interviews for a national sample survey, or laboratory experiments with rigid experimenter protocols? With each of these situations there is some direct contact with other human beings; but is this direct involvement? Usually not, since each of these activities prescribes a role for the researcher that is intended to remove him or her from the emotional and unwanted intellectual aspects of the situation. When this psychological removal occurs, then the relationship can be viewed as being without direct involvement. To the extent that this removal does not occur—either because the role itself requires the researcher to examine his or her emotional and intellectual reactions while inside the role (e.g., psychoanalysis, participant observation, group relations training) or because the person in the role is unable (or unwilling) to practice this removal—there is a clinical aspect to the research at hand.

The type and extent of our involvement in social research varies with the project and the researcher, but all researchers have a stake in their research. This stake influences their involvement and brings a clinical dimension to most research. The involvement may be intense for any number of reasons: career imperatives, belief in the social utility of research findings, or the desire to leave a legacy to the society and culture. For virtually all of us research is seen as a process that informs a professional practice that is itself born of a set of values about progress, justice, fairness, health, happiness, or quality of life.

Direct involvement also implies responsibility. Since, at a minimum, involvement can be understood as the pursuit of the researcher's interests with either the acquiescence or active participation of a social system, the researcher takes on certain responsibilities: responsibilities toward the people participating in the research; and responsibility to behave in accordance with professional standards of ethics, in particular to consider the consequences of one's work for the people involved. For some researchers these responsibilities lead to the development of a contract with participants in which these issues are discussed and specific boundaries or guidelines are laid out including provisions for renegotiating the contract. For others, these issues are left implicit.

In sum, the characteristic of direct involvement includes (1) firsthand experience with the social system being studied; (2) the engagement of the researcher's interests above and beyond his or her interest in science and knowledge for its own sake; and (3) responsibility toward the people participating in the research. Almost all field research in the social sciences, and especially research that has action or policy implications or is part of an intervention designed to help the system involved, has this clinical aspect to it.

(2) The commitment to self-scrutiny on the part of the researcher follows as a direct consequence from the characteristic of direct involvement. As researchers live with other human beings or social systems in the process of doing research, they are inevitably influenced by the relationships. This influence may actually change the researchers, their understanding of the world, values, beliefs, feelings about individuals, groups, or cultures, or it may evoke reactions specific to the research relationship, such as sympathy, anger, pity, condescension, prejudice, love, or hate. In both cases the influence process may go unnoticed by researchers since the process may be slow and the researcher's reactions may be attributed to sources other than the research involvement, especially if involvement is viewed as something to be avoided.

When the influence of the researcher's involvement goes unnoticed, a wealth of information about the social system is lost because the researcher is not attending to the characteristics of the social system that are influencing his or her feelings or reactions and may also be ignoring the hypothesis that the social system is responding, in part, to the researcher's thoughts and actions. A researcher, for example, may find that he or she avoids certain members of the organization because they make the researcher uncomfortable or ask difficult questions about the researcher's role. This avoidance, in turn, may influence key research decisions.

Self-scrutiny is essential because of the researcher's many and often conflicting interests engaged by the research endeavor. Especially when social science trains its fledgling practitioners to believe that good science is interest free, neutral, and dispassionate, it is all too likely that the influence of the researcher's values, prejudices, gender, group affiliations, career interests, and so on will go purposefully unnoticed or unexamined. Too many of us are taught that our personal involvement in our research renders our work unscientific or illegitimate, as if there is a social scientist somewhere who has no personal involvement or whose involvement has no influence on his or her work. A clinical view of social research contends that this is a myth and that only through a commitment to periodic scrutiny of the researcher's involvement in the research process can the inevitable consequences of doing social research be described, examined, and understood.

Responsibility also brings with it a demand for self-scrutiny. Since what the researcher does not know about his or her own involvement in the research endeavor may affect other people, there is an implicit injunction that the researcher engage in systematic self-scrutiny. While few would argue with this premise, the proof is commitment to a process with this as its goal. Such a process must contend with the natural human tendency to avoid self-scrutiny for fear of learning something unpleasant or unsavory, or something that requires hard, painful decisions. The second characteristic of clinical research is precisely this commitment.

There are many other aspects of the self-scrutiny process, but we will hold our discussion of them until later in this chapter.

(3) The third characteristic of clinical research is *the willingness to change or adapt theory while involved in the research experience*. This does not mean that theory *must* change while the research is in progress, but rather that the researcher is *willing* to change a theory. This, in turn, might change action, data collection, or the type of involvement. This flies in the face of the traditional view that throughout the research process the relationship between data, method, and theory should remain strictly defined and unchanging.

The importance of this characteristic is underscored when viewed in light of the first two characteristics. Direct involvement coupled with a commitment to self-scrutiny by the researcher can result in the development of new hypotheses about both method and theory at unexpected times in the research process. It would be self-defeating for the researcher to ignore this information, rigidly adhering to the stipulated procedures in order to preserve uniformity at the price of diminished meaning. It is, in fact, easy to see that if one sought to remove oneself from the research experience by minimizing one's involvement or acting as if involvement were unimportant and, in turn, placing little value on self-scrutiny, then it would be logical to separate theory and experience, stipulating precisely the points at which data and experience influence theory development.

(4) Clinical research is predicated on *the preference for dense or "thick" description* (Geertz, 1973) and a choice in favor of *depth over breadth* in any single research undertaking. It is generally accepted that the process of standardization and aggregation sacrifices richness in the service of generalizability. The clinical perspective emphasizes that meaningful generalizations about human behavior in social systems cannot be generated without density of social phenomena. It can be argued, however, that many of the theories about human behavior that meet the standards of science are ultimately rather thin (not very useful or insightful) when confronted with the complexity of social behavior as it occurs in the world.

In clinical research the work of generalization comes after the difficult and time consuming work of description, fraught as it is with the perils of involvement and self-scrutiny. In some instances the process of abstraction may have to be done by people other than those who generate the data. In other instances, the task of theory building on a grand scale may come only in the middle or near the end of a long career in research.

(5) Clinical research emphasizes *the participation of the social system being studied*. As in clinical medicine, clinical research starts with the assumption that all cannot be known merely by an observation of the living system. Some things can be known only when the experience of the system can be conveyed to the clinician in enough detail and depth. Often this communication of detail and depth requires mutual participation in the process of uncovering and understanding the many facets of the system's experience. The system and the researcher must work together to define what is relevant (Torbert, 1983). This takes time, effort, and commitment since the individuals in the social system may not have a language for describing their collective experience and the researcher may not be able to understand the system without a significant depth of mutual involvement and participation.

Real participation occurs only when there has been a mutual exploration that satisfies all parties involved as to the goals, competence, purposes, and capacities of the people involved. In the case of medicine, for example, the doctor literally depends on the patient's participation for both diagnosis and treatment. The more complicated and rare the disease, the more the patient's participation is important. If the patient does not trust the doctor or the institution in which the doctor works, he or she may not be willing to participate actively in the diagnostic work. A wonderful example of this was Norman Cousins's (1979) participation in his own decisions about how to cure himself. He insisted on treatment that flew in the face of medical wisdom because, as he said, the "doctor latent within him" (lifting a phrase from Albert Schweitzer) told him what was needed for healing in his particular case. Cousins was also fortunate enough to have a doctor who took the research approach that maybe the information accessible to the patient via internal processes, but not confirmable from any external vantage point, might lead to wiser treatment choices.

Participation is particularly important in social research since the perceptions, thoughts, emotions, and beliefs of people constitute the primary subject matter for our investigations.

THE KEY QUESTION

Thus far in this chapter we have highlighted that all social research occurs in the context of a relationship and that there are certain critical characteristics that distinguish what we are labeling as clinical research. The key question that we are moving toward and with which we will conclude this chapter is the following: If clinical research is distinguished by these five characteristics, what kinds of understanding about social systems are likely to emerge from a process with these characteristics? To set the stage for our discussion of this issue, however, it is necessary to elaborate at greater length the role of self-scrutiny in clinical research.

THE ROLE OF SELF-SCRUTINY
IN CLINICAL RESEARCH

When a human system seeks out the assistance (or responds favorably to the overtures) of an applied researcher, it usually does so because it recognizes its need for help in self-reflecting—either on the relationship of its internal parts or on its external relationships with other entities in its ecosystem. Hence, the key work of the researcher involves establishing a way to assist the entity in developing additional insight into its behavior— providing, as it were, a system's analog to the self-observing ego in individual psychology (Smith, 1983b). Given that all systems have difficulty in developing self-reflecting perspectives that are not riddled with misattributions and faulty interpretations, the task of the researcher is both complex and rather tenuous. One of the great difficulties is to avoid having, as it were, the doctor suffering from the same disease that plagues the patient. That is, if the system has major difficulties in self-reflection, then if the researcher (or research team) has the same difficulty, we have the classic situation of the blind leading the blind. For this reason it is absolutely imperative that the skills of self-scrutiny in the researcher be highly developed.

When the research is being conducted by a group, there is a need for self-scrutiny to occur at the individual, interpersonal, and group levels. At each of these levels, the mechanisms for self-scrutiny may differ, but the basic processes are the same: a careful and systematic examination of the conscious and, when possible, unconscious activities of the research system. At the individual level this requires an ability to reflect on one's own experience with a willingness to embrace interpretations that might run counter to one's instincts. For example, if the researcher sees one group in the system as the "bad guys" it may be important to explore the possibility that they might be the "good guys" and then to ask the more difficult question—what is it about my relationship with them or the system as a whole that leads me to use these categories? If the research is being conducted by a group, self-scrutiny must involve attention to group-as-a-whole phenomena such as the dynamics around leadership, influence, authority, intimacy, race, gender, sexuality, power, and intergroup relations.

The value of self-scrutiny is twofold. First, it can help develop both an intellectual and emotional understanding of the dynamics inherent in a human system's struggle to learn about itself, especially those involved in confronting weaknesses, imperfections, failures and problems. Second, self-scrutiny can help uncover valuable information. The scrutiny may be directed at the researchers themselves or at their relationship with the social system. Since all research is approached with some intellectual presuppositions and a variety of emotional predispositions (sometimes called *biases*) it is absurd to act as if this were not the case. Addressing these inevitable influences in a systematic way provides the reader with some of the context in which the research was conducted, allowing others to make independent judgments concerning the role of these factors in the research.

Parallel processes. There is an even more important reason for a research system to have both the commitment to self-scrutiny and the skills to undertake this complex task. Under normal circumstances, the probability is very high that the processes operative within the researcher (individual or team) will be a playing through, in parallel form, of the key dynamics that are driving the system being researched. We refer to these alignments as parallel processes, defined as the tendency for two or more social systems that have significant contact with each other to show similar affects, behaviors, and cognitions (Alderfer, Brown, Kaplan, & Smith, in press).

An understanding of parallel processes has been part of the therapeutic world for a long time. In this field these processes are referred to as transference and countertransference—concepts that indicate the unconscious tendencies of both the client and the therapist to relate to each other in terms of a prior relationship, transferring to the other attributes of a previous significant individual with whom he or she has been identified (Lidz, 1968). There is a firmly established tradition in psychotherapy to keep a keen focus on countertransference reactions. If they go unnoticed or unexamined, the therapist's understanding of the patient's situation will become distorted, potentially jeopardizing the treatment. On the other hand, if the countertransference can be recognized and scrutinized, it can provide a special kind of insight into the patient's life. It has also been observed that in the supervision of psychotherapy, what transpires in the relationship of the supervisor and the therapist can be a parallel playing out of the therapist-client relationship and vice versa (Searles, 1955; Ekstein & Wallerstein, 1958; Sachs & Shapiro, 1976).

Parallel processes occur not only in interpersonal relationships. They can be found operating in interactions among groups or even at the organizational level. Understanding parallel processes and their impact requires a willingness to deal with emotional reactions that can be disturbing—both in others and in oneself. However, they are only accessible to our understanding if we are willing to do the hard work of self-scrutiny. Turning a blind eye to them does not make them go away; it merely drives them into those areas marked "error" or "the researcher's blind spots" (Berg, 1980; Smith & Crandell, 1984; Alderfer et al., in press).

In summary, the process of self-scrutiny is central to our definition of clinical research because it can yield information about the intellectual and emotional factors that inevitably influence the researchers' involvement and activity, and at the same time provide information about the dynamics of the individual or social system being studied. The self-scrutiny process is difficult and complex precisely because *both* the researcher and the "researched" are simultaneously influencing each other. Since this is occurring in ways that initially are out of the awareness of the parties involved, scrutiny is an absolutely necessary part of social science research.

WHAT UNDERSTANDINGS COME
FROM CLINICAL ACTIVITY?

The purpose of developing the clinical side of social research methods
is not to replace what is knowable using traditional approaches but
rather to augment it. Through clinical methods we see different aspects
of social reality and we look with differently calibrated eyes. Our clinical
engagement confronts us with thoughts, feelings, and information that
are not accessible under tightly controlled circumstances, and forces us
to expand our conceptual horizons beyond the boundaries of our prede-
fined theories.

As part of appreciating the special contribution of the clinical side of
research methods, one question we must understand is, What is it that is
usually not seen? Then we must move to the question of how new aspects
can be seen via clinical methods.

In all of our experience there exists simultaneously what we see and
what we do not see, what is known and what is not known. We cannot be
everywhere at once and we are incapable of seeing certain things while
looking at others. We know, however, that the unseen exists even if we
cannot see it because the Gestalt suggests such a side exists (as, for
example, in the case of an unfamiliar coin that rests on a table with one
side up). We have experience flipping things over, which also contributes to our belief that the underside exists even when we cannot see it.
Likewise, in social relationships certain issues, ideas, or emotions are
inaccessible. This may be because of implicit, shared agreements to keep
certain topics unspeakable. For example, each of us knows things about
ourselves, our family, the organization we work in, and the like that we
find hard to reveal except under special circumstances. Or it may be that
we have no way of really knowing.

We have a sense of the "other side" of physical objects because of our
existence as three-dimensional creatures in three-dimensional space.
Analogously, our perspective of what's on the other side of social
phenomena depends on our view of the structure of the social world and
how we interact with it. For example, those who are willing to descend
into the depths of Dante's inferno are likely to understand both the
manifest and the hidden sides of the human psyche differently than
those who have never chosen or been forced to take such a journey.

Perhaps one of the best ways to capture this issue is to illustrate a
similar choice point in the evolution of art.[1] When one thinks of a
traditional painting, such as a still life of a table, most of what is
captured is the top and whatever is placed on the surface. We do not see
what is underneath and, if there's a tablecloth, we may not even see the
legs. We are left to surmise about the underside, the hidden, extrapolat-

ing from that which is presented. In a way the artist is saying that only what meets the eye is of importance. Then along came cubism, a tradition suggesting everything is important and should be attended to, including the undersides. Even more important, each aspect should be given space within the painting to exist in a way that preserves its essentiality, not subordinating the core of any one element to any other element. In this way the cubists expanded the methods of the traditionalists, representing in two dimensions multiple sides with the goal of preserving a sense of the whole that did not depend on surface structure as the only system of integration. Some critics argued that in the process the artists violated the integrity of the scenes they sought to represent. To this the counterargument was offered that the cubists brought to life different relationships with the objects of their art, thereby expanding the world capable of being represented on canvas. Cubism did not replace anything; it added something.

Although this analogy to art may seem rather pretentious, given the incredible skill and sophistication of that craft, we consider the crossroads we face as social science researchers similar to that confronting artists when cubism had its birth. Are we going to move from being a science that seeks only to represent "reality," or will we become a discipline that makes explicit our interpretive sides and that attempts to represent data, method, and theory in a holistic way?

In this chapter we want to offer a glimpse of what we sense might become our heritage if we can develop adequate clinical sophistication. Again, we turn to art to make our point, and to Picasso. We illustrate with his lithographic work of the *Bull*.[2] If you look at the last photograph of this sequence you may well find yourself asking how a person took a pen, drew five lines, essential and universal, and produced a seemingly effortless distillation of a creature called a bull. In fact it did not happen this way, as the series reproduced here indicates. This bull is a lithograph created via the medium of a stone, and the final representation is the result of eleven iterations on the same stone.

Picasso began with a thick description of a bull, a straightforward image that captured a particular animal. A week later he returned to his lithographic stone and transformed the particular into an animal of brute mass and power. Then, after another week, he scraped the stone again, reducing the size of the bull and in the process leaving clear traces of the artist's personal interaction with his medium. At this stage the focus shifted from mass to surface as white lines were scratched across the body like divisions indicating cuts of meat, as one might find on a butcher's shop poster.

By the midpoint of his series, Picasso had given surface divisions increasing strength over the image. The lines were lengthened and connected across broader areas of the bull, forcing the body into simpler shapes, as parts were distended. Eventually the bull became centralized again. In portraying the bull, tension between mass, structure, texture, and the animal's individual characteristics was created as Picasso moved to simplify. All remaining hints of representational texture were let go as lines of structure became dominant. By the end the question seems to be how few lines can be used to represent the animal fully in the simplest geometric terms. The simplification to a tiny and empty head surmounted by enormous horns evokes the sense of the bull's unique characteristic—both the universal and the particular represented in the one form.

Picasso's work was the product of a long and complex relationship with both his subject matter and his medium. He was constantly experimenting with his medium and every experiment led to different forms of representation. For our purposes, we can almost imagine him asking a host of methodological questions such as, Where do I start? How do I know when I'm finished? What are the criteria by which I judge the product? How do I know if I have captured the essence of the phenomenon? Need I satisfy only myself? What exactly is the process? How do I conduct this conversation between subject and medium and translate what I learn into further action?

These are questions the clinical side of research evokes: What are the clinical aspects of social research? How do the actions of the researcher make clinical research occur? What are the hazards? What are the demands? What actually is added to our understanding when clinical methods are included in our research? What does it feel like and what are the emotional as well as intellectual signposts along the path of the clinical research process?

We are sure some of our critics will dismiss what we have to say here with the off-handed retort "Are you talking about art or science!" That is exactly our point. When we no longer can distinguish between art and science as separate processes but experience their holism we will have tapped the real meaning of the term *clinical*—knowledge through encounter, valid because it fits with experience, real because it touches the core, the universal and particular simultaneously.

NOTES

1. Our definition of cubism draws heavily upon French (1977).
2. The commentary on Picasso's *Bull* was provided by the National Gallery of Art.

TAKING OUR SELVES SERIOUSLY
AS RESEARCHERS

Clayton P. Alderfer

What becomes acceptable psychology accrues only when all observations, including those which a psychologist makes upon himself, are treated as though made upon "the other one." Thus, we make explicit the distinction between the experimenter and the thing observed. This distinction is obvious in physics, in psychology it is equally valid . . . .

Although a particular experimenter may himself become the object of study by another experimenter, and he in turn by still another, at some stage of such a regress an independent experimenter *must be* [emphasis in original] (i.e., is always) assumed. (S. S. Stevens, 1939, pp. 221-263)

I was attempting to describe some of the dangers of psychological analysis. It can lead to a certain presumption and arrogance when others are seen as mere puppets without freedom and human dignity. The psychologists who stand outside to observe and explain *their* [emphasis mine] mechanisms may feel himself the only exception, the only real person . . . . When I spoke to them [different people in the big city] I had the feeling that I lived; when I talked with psychologists, it was to speak about life but not to live it in the same way. (Fritz Heider, 1983, pp. 28, 47)

The serious problems in life, however, are never fully solved. If ever they should appear to be so it is a sure sign that something has been lost. The meaning and purpose of a problem seem to lie not in its solution but in our working at it incessantly. This alone preserves us from stultification and petrification. (Carl Jung, 1931, pp. 11-12)

Since becoming a social scientist nearly twenty years ago, I regularly have been impressed with what goes on at professional meetings—both inside and outside official sessions. Below are three episodes from the most recent professional meeting I attended. They illustrate the operation of "self effects" among social scientists and suggest that such phenomena readily appear wherever members of the profession gather and individuals decide to be attentive.

(1) Within the first hour of my arrival I was invited to dinner by two colleagues—one I know well enough to call a friend and the other was a new acquaintance. The two people knew each other reasonably well. One was male, the other female. We discussed three topics over dinner: the achievements and adventures of our children; the career movements of common friends coupled with the job openings at our respective universities; and finally, in the taxi on the way back to the meetings, which prominent female and male psychologists were sleeping together and whether they had gotten married yet.[1]

(2) During the conference itself, I gave a talk with the same title as this chapter. The audience was primarily composed of younger members of the profession who reacted positively when I suggested that the self-awareness of the profession—especially of the senior members—was not excessive, and perhaps we might have a more intellectually exciting and practically useful field if we paid more attention to our own consciousness and behavior. Riding in the elevator after the session ended, I was confronted by one of the senior members from the audience, a man senior to me, who said, "Aw, come on, Clay, you're part of the establishment now. You've got to cut this stuff out!"

(3) The final significant event of the conference was a panel of distinguished members who discussed career options for social scientists. Among the group were three men and a woman, whose organizational affiliations included a major university, a consulting firm, a financially successful corporation, and a research laboratory. Listening to these people describe the trials and rewards of their careers, I was suddenly taken with the thought that their organizations, however diverse they were, also had at least one major commonality: They represented the predominantly white male and economically secure sector of our society. I then asked the panel how they thought their organizational location affected their research work. The first person responded, "Just because we are in a wealthy corporation does not mean it is easy to get research money!" Another was unclear about my question. I rephrased it, "I was wondering what difference you think it would make if you had worked for the New Haven, Connecticut,

Welfare Department." Another panelist responded, "Oh, I know what stereotype you are coming from. Well, I served for years on the school board of [a wealthy suburb of a major New England City]. Working for major corporations does not mean you do not serve your communities."

The words "Our Selves" in the title of this chapter are printed correctly; the separate words were selected to indicate several meanings of the term *self*, which we might take more seriously in order to enhance the significance and the quality of social research. I believe these various "selves" are repressed and suppressed by the positivist approach to methodology that most of us are taught and accept. Although avoided and denied, the various aspects of our selves do not go away; instead they operate indirectly and covertly. Professional meetings, manifestly devoted to the sharing of scientific information, are settings where the full range of our personal and professional selves can be seen, if we choose to notice. The three episodes selected were described to illustrate the presence of those frequently unacknowledged and yet most important selves.

In this chapter I shall explore three senses of the term *self*, each taken from a well-developed theoretical position. The various meanings of the concept also have a significant similarity; each accepts and incorporates conscious and unconscious elements. The three theoretical positions are the following: (1) ego psychology (Erikson, 1956); (2) analytical psychology (Jung, 1963); and (3) intergroup theory (Alderfer, 1982).[2]

Ego psychology attends to the conscious and personal unconscious intermingling of the individual's sense of "Who am I?" The theory is concerned with changes in this sense of self induced internally by biological developments such as sexual maturation and aging, including their effects on significant interpersonal relationships, and, externally, by major historical events such as wars and economic transformations.

Analytical psychology focuses on universal symbols of the collective unconscious on their own terms and as a means to examine and illuminate the personal unconscious. *Self* in the language of analytical psychology refers to a favorable coming together of the ego (including the personal unconscious) and the collective unconscious. The collective unconscious includes symbols and myths that may be found across diverse cultures and historical periods.

Intergroup theory concerns the relations among groups taken as entities and the effects for individuals of memberships in interdependent groups. For individuals, selves are shaped by people serving as representatives of groups in relations with other groups. For groups, their internal dynamics and external relations are shaped by the diversity of group affiliations carried by members.

The idea of unconscious processes carries a number of related assumptions, regardless of the theory in which the construct arises. The key idea is that important material is out of awareness and can be brought into awareness. Unconscious material takes the form of symbols, metaphors, and myths. People become expert in understanding unconscious processes by examining their own experience, usually with the aid of a professional therapist or consultant who has developed a disciplined expertise in these matters. Legitimate expertise includes subjecting oneself to analysis before practicing on others. All of the theories include the concept of projection, whereby individuals initially "see" the unconscious material in other individuals or groups before they see it in themselves. All recognize the resistance of people to accepting unconscious dynamics, and all purport to value positively the process of a person taking ownership of her or his unconscious material. The Jungian term for this process is *withdrawing projections*.

I began this chapter with the three examples because they are rich with unconscious material. They would be even richer if I named the individuals involved, and the readers knew about their personal and professional lives. Without doing this, I can make only comparatively general connections between the three concepts of self and the examples.

Example 1. We all were working on our family identities, our fantasies about what men and women do at professional meetings, and our professional identities as receivers and givers of jobs at prestigious universities.

Example 2. As I challenged the old king (a mythological theme) by my words about changing the reigning paradigm of research methodology, I was reminded that I was already a member of the court, from which I could presumably be expelled if I did not "cut it out."

Example 3. A question whose aim was to explore the effects of membership in the white, middle to upper socioeconomic group evoked denial (because we are rich, it is not easy to get research money), avoidance (misunderstanding the question after someone had already answered it), and projection (attributing a "stereotype" to me while giving information that further affirmed the speaker's membership in the group whose membership I asked him to explore).

Professional meetings, of course, are not where research ususally gets done. (My sample of people who have agreed to fill out the JDI after engaging in sexual gossip is not large.) One might argue that professional meetings serve as a kind of outlet for material that is successfully suppressed while the main work of research is going on. Or, one might view professional meetings as a sort of microcosm of professional behavior in general. What occurs in the official sessions then parallels what shows up in research reports and journal articles, and what occurs in question-and-answer sessions inside and outside official sessions is similar to the unreported material associated with most research projects—no matter how rigorous or carefully controlled.

The remainder of this chapter explores the events around the actual conduct of research rather than professional meetings. The chief question is to what degree the various senses of self importantly influence research processes and products. Efforts to answer follow in four sections.

The first presents two dialogues: (1) Are researchers people when we do research? and (2) How, if at all, do professional organizations in social science affect the behavior and attitudes of their members? Patterned after the Socratic method, these discussions take readers through an example of self exploration by the writer. Readers also may be prodded to engage in similar conversations with themselves or with others.

The second gives biographical and autobiographical material from well-recognized psychologists to illustrate how the operation of "self" dynamics shapes highly regarded research products. Data illustrate all three meanings of the term *self*. In general, the phenomenon of well-known social scientists being subject to biographical or autobiographical study suggests growing awareness of self effects in research.

The third examines the social psychology laboratory as an organization. This major invention of social scientists has had some scrutiny for self effects with attention focused mainly on experimenter-subject relations. I propose to view the laboratory as an organization to identify systemic influences that shape research results without the awareness of the investigators.

Each of these sections provides data pertaining to one or more theories of self. Generally, a section emphasizes one kind of material about the self and includes information relevant to other meanings as well. From this point forward, the text treats readers as if they carried an "intellectual receiver" of three bands—one for each self theory—that is analogous to a radio capable of receiving three stations singly or in combination. The two dialogues focus primarily on the ego-identity of investigators. Secondarily, they attend to group-level issues within social science and between the profession and its publics. Next, the chapter turns to events from the lives of particular individuals. In the first case, self data emerge from the collective unconscious of the person. In the second instance, the data pertain to ego-identity struggles. Group-level influences are also observable in both accounts. Analysis of the social psychology laboratory leads with group-level effects and also includes information deriving from the ego-identity of investigators.

The fourth portion offers conclusions pertaining to the underlying philosophical issues in self analysis. It also presents the implications of untoward effects of inadvertent and covert self processes on social research and the creative possibilities of effectively harnessing self dynamics to produce more intellectually exciting and socially useful inquiry.

TWO DIALOGUES

The dialogues occur between two persons who may be alive in many of us. Scientist is the individual trained in rigorous methodology undergirded by logical positivist philosophy. He seeks objectivity and is concerned with avoiding bias and preventing loss of control. Self is the whole person speaking. She is sympathetic to critical philosophy and is attentive to avoiding illusion and deception, whether of oneself or of others.

Scientist and Self agree, "We meet to explore these questions: Are social scientists people when they do research? Do the laws and empirical generalizations that social researchers work so hard to develop pertain to themselves? When professional investigators do their work, are they subject to the same lawfulness of behavior and experience as those individuals they study? If not, why not? If so, what difference does it make? These questions may strike readers in a variety of ways."

> SELF: Yes, the answers are obvious! Of course social scientists are people!
>
> SCIENTIST: Maybe, but I think the answer should be more tentative. I suppose the "laws" of human behavior apply to social scientists, but we have to be careful about the limits of our findings. There have been comparatively few carefully controlled studies of social scientists.
>
> SELF: True, social scientists are a bit difficult to control—especially after they cease being students and most especially after they have tenure.
>
> SCIENTIST: I meant statistical control and laboratory control, not political or administrative control. You do know the difference, don't you?
>
> SELF: I believe I can recite the ideology of the scientific establishment, if that's what you mean.
>
> SCIENTIST: Would you stop this political innuendo? I am talking about the agreements social scientists make with each other in order to get on

with the business of doing research. These agreements are only political in the largest sense. They serve the aims of social science. Ideology is really an inflammatory word.

SELF: OK. It certainly upsets you a bit, doesn't it?

SCIENTIST: Well, ideology implies lack of objectivity. It suggests that emotional and group forces shape what individual investigators perceive and think.

SELF: That it does.

SCIENTIST: Well, I have difficulty with that. The scientific process is more complicated.

SELF: In what ways?

SCIENTIST: Competent, well-trained social scientists use sophisticated methodological and statistical controls to prevent their own feelings and behavior from influencing their findings in unknown or uncontrolled ways. Social scientists do not inadvertently influence what they study because they have a professional discipline that either prevents such artifacts from arising or permits an assessment of their effects.

SELF: Do you mean the feelings and behaviors of social scientists and their effects are artifacts?

SCIENTIST: Well, not quite. But you know the saying, "One person's artifact is another person's finding."

SELF: Perhaps you mean that the feelings and behavior of social scientists are artifactual when they do research.

SCIENTIST: I guess that's what I mean. But I must say, I experience you as leading me somewhere I am not at all sure I want to go.

SELF: I can understand that. The inevitable conclusion from what you say seems to be that social scientists basically are not people when they do research, except when there are artifactual effects that are unintended and should be corrected.

SCIENTIST: Right, right!! That's what I mean. You've got the idea.

SELF: Do you think the people who are subject to social scientists doing research experience them as people?

SCIENTIST: You mean, "Do our 'subjects' experience us as people?"

SELF: Right, that's what I mean.

SCIENTIST: Well, that is a good question. Perhaps we should study it.

SELF: You mean we should ask the people we study whether they experience us as people studying them?

SCIENTIST: That seems almost nonsensical, doesn't it? What do you think they'd say?

SELF: Of course they experience us as people. I'll bet they even experience us as certain kinds of people or at least as people with certain kinds of characteristics.

SCIENTIST: Well, that's another story. If we asked them what kinds of characteristics social researchers have, do you think we'd have to listen to their answers?

SELF: Why would we ask them if we didn't want to listen to their answers?

SCIENTIST: That's my point. I am not at all sure I want to listen to their answers.

SELF: Then you probaby shouldn't ask them.

SCIENTIST: Right, I think it would be a mistake. Suppose they said things that made us uncomfortable or implied we ought to change.

SELF: It could happen.

SCIENTIST: That settles it. Now I am sure we shouldn't ask. If people gave disturbing answers, I'd probably have an emotional reaction.

SELF: And then your objectivity for future work might be compromised?

SCIENTIST: Absolutely!! For, even after, I might approach the task of data collection with an eye toward how people perceive me; I might never be the same again.

SELF: Well, maybe, but I believe you are over-reacting a bit. Some people do learn to receive feedback about their own behavior with an open-minded attitude. Some even change their behavior in constructive ways.

SCIENTIST: Well, maybe, but then again, maybe not. You know how easy it is to lose one's objectivity if one becomes emotional!

SELF and SCIENTIST now shift their attention to the second question, "In what ways, if any, do professional organizations of social scientists affect the behavior and attitudes of their members?"

SELF: Will you give your answer to this question?

SCIENTIST: Of course, I am a scientist who is sympathetic to other scientists. I avoid no important scientific questions, none, do you hear me? I avoid no important scientific questions!

SELF: Oh, good, would you please answer the question?

SCIENTIST: What question was that?

SELF: In what ways, if any, do professional organizations of social scientists affect the behavior and attitudes of their members?

SCIENTIST: Right, I had forgotten the question. Now that you remind me, I am not sure why you ask.

SELF: I asked because I want to know your answer.

SCIENTIST: What are you, some kind of research person?

SELF: Will that affect your answer?

SCIENTIST: GOOD HEAVENS!! Can't you just answer my question? Answering a question makes me think you are either a research person or some kind of clinical shrink. Which is it?

SELF: Wait a minute! I asked you the question because I wanted to know your answer. PERIOD. That's all. We're colleagues, right?

SCIENTIST: OK! OK! What was the question again?

SELF The question was, "In what ways, if any, do professional organizations of social scientists affect the behavior and attitudes of their members?"

SCIENTIST: Yeah, yeah. Now I remember. Well, I guess I am not sure.

SELF: Isn't the social psychology of organizations built on the assumption that organizations affect the behavior and attitudes of their members? There are many journals, educational programs, research laboratories, divisions of professional organizations, certifications to practice professionally, etc.

SCIENTIST: It is an empirical science. Why don't you go out and collect some data?

SELF: Hold it! We're doing it again. I just want the opinion of a colleague on whether our professional organizations affect the behavior and attitudes of our members. Could you please tell me what you think?

SCIENTIST: All right! You've worn me down. I guess I think the organizations should affect the behavior and attitudes of our members.

SELF: Please wait a minute. I did not ask you what should happen; that's a normative question. I asked your opinion about what does happen; that's an empirical matter.

SCIENTIST: That settles it. I won't answer your question. I am a researcher. I study other people's organizations. That's it!

SELF: Well, what if our professional organizations affect our behavior when we study other people's organizations?

SCIENTIST: Well, what if they do?!? I already said I thought they should.

SELF: But doesn't that suggest we might improve the study of other people's organizations if we understood our own better?

SCIENTIST: Look, cut out this clinical stuff! We're scientists not clinicians. And that's the name of that tune. Because we are in charge, we decide what to study and how. Period. Do you know any real scientists who study their own organizations?

SELF: Thank you very much for not avoiding the question.

The dialogues end here. A reader may relate to them in several ways. First, they are personal material from this writer. They emerged from my self. They represent my internal dialogue with myself. I am both Self and Scientist. Their struggle is my struggle. Second, the dialogues also represent my relationship to the reigning paradigm in social research. With this orientation, I am Self, and Scientist is a representative of the reigning social consensus among well-established, highly respected social scientists. The point of view of Self is my own, and the responses of Scientist are my perceptions of how the dominant consensus consciously and unconsciously deals with questions of self-reflection. Third, the reader might take these dialogues as a stimulus for constructing her or his own. I do not believe I am alone with the conflict between Self and Scientist. The existence of this book testifies to that assertion. Later sections of this chapter provide additional material pertaining to others' relations with the conflict. A reader who at this time writes her or his own version of the dialogues might experience subsequent sections of this chapter more fully, but, then again, he might not. She probably would, unless she has identified with him excessively. Fourth, a person might relate to the dialogues by enacting them with a colleague. The most interesting results might occur if both people tried both parts for each question.

TWO INDIVIDUAL SELVES
AND THEIR CONCEPTUAL PRODUCTS

Social research as we think of it today is a comparatively recent addition to civilization. The social form was suggested in the early part of the nineteenth century by such writers as August Compte and actually achieved the roots of its present condition in the later 1800s through the publications of scholars such as Wundt, Le Bon, and Freud. From this perspective, the field is close to the end of its first century. During this period, there has been an increasing number of people whose careers have been "being social scientists." We are in a period now when the lives and careers of people born near the start of the twentieth century are drawing to a close. For a variety of reasons—both personal and collective—we see an increasing interest in the personal lives of distinguished social scientists. Some individuals prepare "intellectual autobiographies" as a way of ending their careers. Others, perhaps the more prominent, become the subjects of biographies. Whether stated explicitly or left unacknowledged, the fundamental question of these works is how the personal lives of the social scientists related to their intellectual work.[3]

In this section, I focus on two examples of relationships between selves and conceptual products. The particular people were selected for a variety of reasons. First, I wanted individuals whose contributions I genuinely respect. I did not want to be in the position of disparaging the scholarly work of a person by seeming to reduce it to "nothing more" than acting out of personal conflicts. Second, I wanted the people to be notably different in their preferred styles of working. As one friend put it, "Everyone knows personality theorists are a little bit nuts, but social psychologists, how could their personal lives affect their science?" Third, of course, there had to be material that either set the stage for relating person and concept or actually made the connection. Fourth, I wanted to examine people through the vehicle of both biographical and autobiographical reports. Sources of error are different in the two forms, and relying on both has the advantage of showing the sorts of associations that are possible from own and from others' data. Finally, I wanted people who represented different generations of behavioral scientists—one from the founding fathers of the 1890s and another from the second generation.

Fritz Heider, with his masterwork of *The Psychology of Interpersonal Relations* (1958), is the first example. The second is Sigmund Freud, with attention to factors that shaped his theoretical conflict about his own seduction theory (Balmary, 1979; Masson, 1984). Heider was a social psychologist not known for embracing depth psychology in his theoretical work. Freud was the founder of a professional movement based on understanding and utilizing unconscious processes.

HEIDER

My attention to Heider's autobiography was stimulated by Harold Kelley's (1984) review, entitled "The Impractical Theorist." Kelley's title was intended to contrast Heider's life and work with that of Kurt Lewin, who was a friend and mentor. Alfred Marrow wrote a biography of Lewin, which he entitled *The Practical Theorist.* Lewin died at a comparatively young age, wrote copiously, and is famous for saying, "Nothing is so practical as a good theory." Heider has lived into his eighties, wrote comparatively few published pieces, and focused his attention on mainly theoretical questions. Lewin is viewed by many as one of the most influential figures in the founding of modern laboratory social psychology and in the start up of action research. Kelley (1984, p. 455) assesses the influence of Heider's (1958) book, *The Psychology of Interpersonal Relations,* as having "enormous influence on modern social psychology, especially in the areas of 'balance' and 'attribution'— perhaps more influence than any other single person."

Kelley begins his review with a quotation from the final paragraph of Heider's autobiography. The full paragraph reads as follows:

Another happy event was being asked by Roger Barker whether I would consider coming to Kansas, just at the time when I most needed to make a change. That question brought us to this haven where we have made our home for thirty-some years and where our three sons grew up so comfortably. There were many more such turning points in this story that came at exactly the right moment to produce the end effect that seems so happy when I put it all together. As a matter of fact, If I were inclined to be superstitious, I could believe that a friendly spirit arranged the whole sequence of events in which the powers of fortune were so kind to me. (Heider, 1983, p. 190)

Among his numerous transitions, Heider clearly views the move to Kansas as of special significance. As things turned out, it was this change of location that brought the conditions that permitted him to finish his influential book. Kelley recognizes the importance of this transition by calling it "the most dramatic point in Heider's story." Yet Kelley's explanation of the event differs from the one I would give. He reported that Heider felt "cornered" and suffered anxiety attacks. He commented that Heider managed "cognitive restructuring," and it brought him relief. Heider's chief frustration in Kelley's mind was Heider's inability to obtain grant support for his "conceptual research."

Now listen to Heider's (1983, pp. 152-155) own words describing his experience at the time.

I was also frustrated with what I could do during the summer vacations to deal with the ideas about interpersonal relations that I was gradually developing. Somehow my brain does not seem to be very efficient organ. It generates some acceptable products, but only after periods of leisurely dreaming and inactive somnolence. I am not a person of great energy, and the thinking that goes on in my head often seems to be without my personal participation. Nietzsche's words—that one should say, "It thinks," not, "I think"—seems very much to fit my case, and the life I was leading did not seem to give "it" much opportunity.

Gradually, during this period, I developed the idea of writing a book on interpersonal relations, but if I was to do that, I needed more unbroken stretches of free time. I went to New York and to Washington to try to get support from foundations, but everywhere came the same answer: there was nothing available for "conceptual research." A few of the people I talked with said that they, personally, would favor it; the time would come when help would be available—perhaps in five years—but at present it would not be possible to persuade a committee to accept the kind of proposal that I was talking about.

The result of all this was that I felt cornered and became the victim of attacks of anxiety. It is true that they gave me some new insights and were perhaps worthwhile in a way, but on the whole it was a rather unpleasant way of learning about myself. These attacks always came on when I was lying down for an afternoon nap or for a night's sleep; therefore, even sleep was no longer an escape from what was troubling me. I often formulated my situation or my fate in a kind of picture, partly to realize more clearly what was happening, partly to exaggerate and make fun of it—a way of handling what is unpleasant in life perhaps. The picture accompaniment to the attacks of anxiety was taken from the old story of Prometheus, chained to a rock, with an eagle coming every day to feed on his liver. Though I did not really compare myself to this hero, there was always a ferocious bird that, when I lay down to sleep, came and hacked away at my heart and liver with great gusto. I am sure that this annoying image stemmed from the old Greek saga. I tried to fight the bird off in different ways, but it was very persistent and merciless. It even seemed to me that the more I struggled to repel it, the fierce its attacks became.

My lack of success in getting rid of the bird made me question my approach; so I went back to the philosophy of my earlier years. I asked: "Why do I defend myself so strenuously? After all, I am not so important. Other people are much more important, and there are many more of them!" so I tried to be friendly to the fierce bird. I said to him: "Come on. I am at your service." This cordial invitation had a dramatic effect. It seemed that the one thing against which it was helpless, the one thing it could not stand, was being treated in a familiar way and without respect. The ferocious bird became disgusted and suddenly flew away. When I tried to fill my thinking with the idea "I am not so important" and when I told myself that it did not matter whether or not all those unripe thoughts that I felt growing ever came to fruition, I would feel a sudden relaxation in the region of my heart. My attacks of anxiety stopped. These experiences made me believe very much in a relation between egocentricity, tension, and anxiety, something that is doubtless familiar to people who deal with such problems, recently to people who work with biofeedback.

This was the first time that I had become aware of changes in tension. Since then I have learned more about how to recognize them and how to influence them. I know the pleasant feeling when the blood is flowing out into my limbs and when relaxation is spreading over my body. I try to get this feeling every day as I am going to sleep. The motif "I am not important" still has a place in my mental equipment. I would guess that it has saved me some heartache and frustration, and it is also a balance to counteract the opposed force of my own importance that I have in common with most people.

I should like to add to these remarks about the anxiety attacks that there was the possibility of a mere physiological contributing factor, and that was my smoking. I was never what one would call a heavy smoker. At the time about which I am writing I usually smoked half a pack of cigarettes a day and one or two small cigars with my afternoon tea. However, it was difficult to ventilate my large third-floor study thoroughly. The windows were small and not easy to open, and the air in the room was rather heavy with smoke and with the dust that inevitably comes from accumulations of books. Eventually, I cut down on my smoking and aired the room more often. These measures may also have contributed to the abatement of my troubles.

To a person familiar with the concepts of Jungian analytical psychology, Heider's dream about his Promethean situation would be taken as an event from the collective—as opposed to the personal—unconscious. According to ancient Greek mythology, Prometheus, himself a god, had angered Zeus, the chief of gods, by giving fire to men and thereby elevating humans to a position too close to the gods. Zeus punished Prometheus by chaining him to a rock and prohibiting either sleep or rest. Zeus also threatened even greater torture if Prometheus did not reveal a great secret. Fate had informed Zeus that one of his sons would dethrone him but had not told him who the mother of this son would be. Prometheus, however, knew who this was and refused to tell. Hermes warned Prometheus that if he did not tell, "An eagle red with blood . . . will tear to rags your body, feasting in fury on the blackened liver" (Hamilton, 1940, p. 72).

Eventually, Heider responds to his dream by talking to the ferocious bird "in a familiar way." From the perspective of analytical psychology, Heider's decision to deal with the bird means that he addresses his unconscious (Jung, 1963, p. 173 ff.). The Promethean drama is archetypal. To reach this point he had to put aside his own ego: "Why do I defend myself . . . I am not so important." Kelley's reflection on Heider's dramatic moment gives a different interpretation. He wrote, "There is a *morality tale* [emphasis mine] for all of us who are inclined to place far great importance on ourselves and our work (Kelley, 1984, p. 456)." Kelley makes no mention of the archetypal contents of Heider's dream. He seems to see putting aside of the egoism as the desirable end state, the "morality tale." My own view, influenced by Jungian psychology, is that the deemphasis on ego was a necessary but not sufficient condition for Heider's development. The remaining step was for him to address the bird—that is, to deal with collective contents from his own unconscious. One could suggest that Heider himself might have been of a similar view; otherwise, why would he have described the dream contents and made the connection to the mythological pattern?

Heider's acceptance of the archetypal material as an explanation for his reduced anxiety, however, remained uncertain. In the subsequent paragraph, he raises the possibility that his change came about from a "mere physiological factor . . . [the reduction of] my smoking." Thus both Kelley as reviewer and Heider as reporter show their struggles between Scientist and Self. Kelley shows his alertness to the importance of this moment as a crucial turning point in Heider's personal and professional development. Yet he seems to ignore the archetypal material and to prefer an externally based explanation. Heider reports his confrontation with the unconscious and adds a contributing factor in the form of reduced smoking as if he cannot fully state that his own psychic change was as important as it seemed to be.

Ultimately, Kelley sees Heider's change as cognitive restructuring, getting a research grant, and moving to Kansas. He omits the intrapsychic activity that Heider describes and I emphasize, and he draws a different moral injunction than I would. I would argue that Heider makes his self more complete by attending to both ego and unconscious functions. The grant, the move, and the book that were to follow after this dramatic period *reflect* the change in Heider's intrapsychic condition at least as much as they caused it. I suggest that the "friendly spirit" to which Heider refers in the final sentence of his book and to which Kelley attends in the opening sentence of his review is not superstitious at all (at least as the term is usually used) but rather a symbol for the extent to which Heider's self consisted of a favorable integration of unconscious and ego.

FREUD

Discussion of Freud's work pertains to a specific empirical-conceptual element in psychoanalytic theory. Careful scholars of psychoanalytic history know that the issue has been a subject of energetic attention since Freud developed his theory and method. For the most part, debate has been confined to the inner circles of psychoanalytic journals and associations. However, in August 1981, the topic qualified for two major articles in the *New York Times,* and, in 1984, Jeffrey Masson's book *The Assault on Truth: Freud's Suppression of the Seduction Theory* was published by Farrar, Straus & Giroux.

The crucial question pertains to whether reports of early childhood incest from patients who are in psychoanalytic treatment should be viewed as empirically reliable or mainly fantasy. Freud himself stated opinions on both sides of the question. His strongest statement supporting the veracity of patient reports about incestuous experiences came in a paper entitled, "The Aetiology of Hysteria," read before the Vienna Society for Psychiatry and Neurology in April 1896 (Masson, 1984, p. 251). Freud then repudiated his earlier opinion in the well-known book, *Three Essays on the Theory of Sexuality,* first published in 1905.

Masson (1984, 119 ff.) found evidence of correspondence between Freud and Leopold Lowenfeld that suggests that the founder of psychoanalysis gave public evidence of changing his opinion between 1900 and 1902. In personal letters to Wilhelm Fleiss, Freud claimed to abandon the seduction theory in September 1897. Yet Masson (1984, p. 114 ff.) reports a letter to Fleiss from December 1897 in which Freud appears to retain his faith in the original theory. The published version of this later letter to Fleiss, however, was edited by Ernst Kris and Anna Freud to remove evidence of Freud's internal questioning about which theoretical position was preferable.

A reader unfamiliar with the inner realms of psychoanalysis may wonder about the significance—practical and theoretical—of whether Freud and successive analysts held or abandoned the original seduction theory. The crucial issue is the proportion of times when patients' fantasies of seduction are associated with facts of seduction. Few would argue that Freud thought such reports were *always* fantasy. Masson (1984), for example, shows that Freud was familiar with the medical legal literature on child abuse of the 1880s and 1890s. But there is a matter of degree. Freud's later views, which have become a central tenet of orthodox psychoanalysis, take the position that the fantasy of seduction is far more frequent than the fact and that the fantasies are more important for treatment than the (apparently) relatively few instances of actual seduction.

The implications of the later view are wide ranging. Analysts taught to believe that reports of seduction are more likely to be fantasy than reality are less likely to be empathic toward patient reports to the contrary. Existing statistics about incest indicate that the phenomenon is far more likely to occur to women than to men (Herman, 1981; Gelinas, 1983). Thus Freud's later views function not only to dissuade analysts from keeping an open mind to their patients' experiences but also to do so in a manner that is more likely, on average, to be damaging to women than to men.

The effects of gender on the verification of incestuous behavior were in evidence during Freud's period of discovery. Masson (1984, p. 114) provides evidence that Freud's original seduction theory was independently confirmed by Emma Eckstein, a former patient and subsequent supervisee of Freud. Prior to Masson's (1984) work based upon his access to the Freud archives, Marie Balmary (1979) developed a carefully reasoned argument in favor of the original seduction theory by using only published material. Masson (1984, p. 189) identified a number of "recent authors, Florence Rush, Alice Miller, Judith Herman, and Louise Armstrong," who believe that the incidence of sexual violence among children is much higher than is generally acknowledged.

Patients are not the only persons likely to be affected by strictly held beliefs about incest that may be inaccurate. The entire psychoanalytic system of organization and training is also potentially subject to the theory's consequences. Reflecting on the consequences of her reanalysis of Freud's material, Marie Balmary (1979, p. 155 ff.) wrote,

> We have stated that a number of analysts, whose purpose is above all to help their patients . . . have put the theory back in the place from which it should never have left: that of a formulation that can always be revised. . . . The analysts' clinical practice is perhaps more closely allied to Freud's first discovery. . . . It nonetheless remains difficult for an analyst to share with his colleagues those things in this experience that disagree with the reigning theory. . . . It seems to us that their attitude oscillates between two poles: either they accept the theory, reject what they experience, and become embittered workers who haunt psychoanalytic societies seeking from a master or a group something that they would be certain not to understand; or they accept what they experience, reject the theory, grow distant from professional groups, and bear in difficult solitude the burden of their calling.

More recently, Janet Malcolm (1981) has provided a detailed case study of the difficulties and dilemmas of classical psychoanalysis, practiced orthodoxly. Her account, derived from a thorough reading of Freud's work and extensive interviewing of a practicing analyst, portrays a character deeply caught up in the New York Psychoanalytic Society. Her picture of "The Impossible Profession" provides a concrete account of Balmary's first alternative. An example of the second mode of adaptation can be found in Heinz Kohut's writings (e.g., Kohut, 1977, 1984)—especially in his efforts to persuade members of the psychoanalytic establishment to open their minds to his innovations.

> I am fully aware of the strength of the hold that the classical psychoanalytic conception of man has come to exert on our imagination; I know how powerful a tool it has become. . . . And I know, therefore that the suggestion that it is inadequate, or even that in certain respects it leads to an erroneous outlook on man, is bound to arouse opposition. . . . And is it not, to anticipate an argument on the moral side, an escapist move, a cowardly attempt to clean up analysis, to deny man's drive-nature, to deny that man is a badly and incompletely civilized animal? (Kohut, 1977, p. xviii)

Kohut speaks as a respected and accepted member of the psychoanalytic establishment; he was president of the American Psychoanalytic Association, Vice President of the International Psychoanalytic Association, and Vice President of the Sigmund Freud archives. When he anticipates broad-scale resistance to his efforts at innovation, he knows well the group about which he speaks. The questions are why the conceptual system is so closed, and why it has so successfully resisted change. Answers to these questions turn both on the personality of Freud and on the psychoanalytic organization that was a part of his legacy.

Freud's struggle with formulating the theory brought him to difficult questions about his own family—especially his father. Balmary (1979) reports documentation showing that Freud's father married three times in contrast to the two times of public record. One of Freud's letters to Fleiss during the crucial period when he was changing his mind about the original seduction theory includes the passage, "Then the surprise that in all cases the *father* [emphasis in original] *not excluding my own* [emphasis mine] had to be accused of being perverse—the realization of the unexpected frequency of hysteria, with precisely the same conditions prevailing in each, whereas surely such widespread perversions against children are not very probable" (Masson, 1984, p. 108). At the time he was considering the theoretical revisions, Freud was confronting his own grief about his father's death (Balmary, 1979) and was troubled by incestuous desires about his own daughter (Herman, 1981). Freud himself was not analyzed through a relationship with another person; thus the discoverer of the transference did not take the optimal opportunity to continue his own self-analysis. The inevitable result, if Freud was correct in his own theory, was that he continued throughout life with certain blindspots that might otherwise have been diminished (Neumann, 1979).

Moreover, the Oedipus myth became a key element in psychoanalytic theory, based in part on the invalidity of the seduction theory. As employed by Freud, the myth omits the crime of Laius, who was Oedipus' father. Prior to the birth of Oedipus, Laius had had a homosexual relationship with the son of a friend. This boy subsequently committed suicide due to remorse about his relationship with Laius. In turn Laius was cursed by the gods, and the stage was set for Oedipus to kill his father and marry his mother. Freud's use of the myth in his theory omits the role of Oedipus' father, and the psychoanalytic theory thereby also protects Freud's memory of his own father (Balmary, 1979; Alderfer, Charleen J., 1982). Freud's theory of ego development was tied to a partially misunderstood version of an archetypal myth.

To report these facts about the founder of psychoanalysis and to trace out their implications is also to enhance my respect for Freud's courage and genius. For some people, saying aloud that an acknowledged great person had limitations, retained certain blind spots, and demonstrated natural human frailties is an anathema. I believe otherwise. Freud's deepest commitment was to the relentless pursuit of truth about human psychology. He made many of his major discoveries through self-analysis. It seems only natural, and quite in keeping with both the spirit and the content of his work, that succeeding workers would employ the essential tenets of his own method to improve upon his contribution.

Masson's (1984) efforts to explain Freud's change of mind about seduction theory suggest additional forces that may have influenced the founder of psychoanalysis. When Freud presented the original seduction theory he was met by stony silence from the psychiatric community of his era. Initially Freud stood firm in the face of this resistance, but eventually, if Masson's report is sound, he did change his mind in response to peer pressure. Beyond the generic social forces, Freud may also have been subject to a much more personal kind of influence. Masson (1984) strongly suggests that Wilhelm Fleiss, Freud's trusted confidant of this era, was himself abusing his son, Robert Fleiss. Masson's (1984) evidence is based on very careful reading of several books by Robert Fleiss, who turned out to become a prominent analyst himself. Robert Fleiss wrote, "I have clarified the picture of my father in the two expert and thorough analyses, the last in middle age with Ruth Mack Brunswick," who was a member of Freud's innermost circle (Dyer, 1983). Again, it appears that a woman plays an important part in the clarification of conditions surrounding the development of the seduction theory.

Finally, there is the role of Freud's daughter Anna in managing the historical data surrounding the theory. From her father's death until her own demise, Anna Freud's role as symbolic leader of the psychoanalytic movement and inheritor of her father's authority was widely recognized. In her adult years, Anna Freud's relationship to her father was close. Dyer's (1983, p. 44) biography states, "In later years the psychoanalytic Zeus had no intention and no reason for relinquishing his daughter to lesser mortals." Anna Freud received her training analysis from her father (Dyer, 1983, p. 26) and throughout Sigmund Freud's mature adulthood and declining years, Anna served "as colleague, companion, secretary, nurse, and business and personal courier" for her father (Dyer, 1983, p. 56). In preparation of his study about the seduction theory, Masson (1984, pp. 112-114) uncovered several instances where Anna, sometimes working with prominent male colleagues in the psychoanalytic establishment, had omitted key elements of Sigmund Freud's correspondence that bore directly on the older Freud's internal debate about the soundness of the revised theory. Anna's special place as keeper of her father's historical legacy and as key figure in the careers of many prominent male psychoanalysts may have further served to keep data relevant to the seduction hypothesis from being adequately examined.

The drama surrounding Freud's seduction theory shows signs of both ego-identity and intergroup forces shaping the theorist's product. Within his own psychology, Freud showed evidence of being deterred from greater accuracy by unresolved feelings about his father, a close friend, and his colleagues of the day. Eventually he took a theoretical position that not only was probably in error but also in such a manner that it was more detrimental to women than to men. Furthermore, it is possible that this theoretical problem was preserved from scrutiny by Freud's own daughter acting in cooperation with some of her most distinguished male colleagues in psychoanalysis.

With the cases of Heider and Freud we have different ways in which the selves of the psychologists apparently influenced their work. For Heider, the focus of attention was the effect of his self analysis on releasing his own productivity, which led ultimately to the production of his masterwork. The actual content of Heider's self awareness was not of major concern, although Heider himself throughout his autobiography made numerous connections between his own life experiences and his theoretical formulations. The chief theory for explaining Heider's change was Jung's analytical psychology. For Freud, on the other hand, the main issue pertained to the content of a major element in his theoretical concepts. There is evidence of both ego-identity forces and intergroup dynamics shaping Freud's thinking. Beyond Sigmund Freud's individual decision about his theoretical position, there were also the enormous forces of the psychoanalytic movement, which served to reduce the likelihood of detecting Freud's apparent error and correcting it.

The Heider and Freud cases were similar in that both men themselves seemed to avoid full confrontation with the self forces influencing their work. Both were also assisted by colleagues in their denial. Heider spoke to diminish the importance of his dream work directly after reporting it, and Harold Kelley, an ardent admirer of Heider, wrote as if the archetypal material played no part in Heider's change. Freud's struggle with the seduction theory was covered over by his own hand, by his favored daughter's management of his literary estate, and by orthodox analysts who followed after the father and his daughter. The dialogue between Self and Scientist was alive and well for Heider and Freud and for their respectful followers.

THE ORGANIZATIONAL PSYCHOLOGY
OF THE SOCIAL PSYCHOLOGY LABORATORY

Beginning with papers by Martin Orne (1962) and Henry Reicken (1962) and continuing to the present, social psychologists have been concerned with the social complexities of their laboratories. By now there is an extensive empirical literature on the "social psychology" of the social psychology laboratory (Rosenthal, 1966; Rosenthal & Rosnow, 1969, Wuebben, Straits, & Shulman, 1974). The effect of this research has been to stimulate a notable degree of self criticism and reflection on the part of social psychologists (Festinger, 1980). Three conceptual positions have emerged for dealing with the empirical findings about the social psychology laboratory. These approaches differ in the degree to which they attempt to achieve a holistic sense of the laboratory as a social system. Labels for the respective orientations reflect varying degrees of conceptual integration between laws applicable to the laboratory and to its "subjects."

(1) *Laboratory as technology.* The contemporary emphasis in this orientation is on the laboratory design as derived from the assumptions of analysis of variance. Writers of this school emphasize the rational justification for laboratory procedures. Usually there are three:

(1) random assignment of respondents to conditions;
(2) independent observation of each respondent's data; and
(3) control over extraneous sources of variation through experimental procedures.

If all three assumptions are satisfied, investigators believe that they can draw valid causal inferences about the relationship between independent and dependent variables. From the perspective of laboratory as technology the subtle forms of communication and behavior that have been identified in empirical studies are error. The aim is either to control their appearance through tightly and precisely executed procedures or to cancel out their effects through strictly randomized assignments of people to experimental conditions. In the laboratory as technology, there is minimal conscious incorporation of what is known about human behavior into the conduct of laboratory activities, except in the form of independent variables.

(2) *Laboratory as carefully managed interpersonal relationships.* The focus in this orientation to laboratory behavior is on the experimenter-respondent relationship. There is acceptance of the subtle authority

dynamics in this relationship, and efforts are made to take account of these dynamics in a manner that presumably more adequately permits investigators to make valid inferences about the relationships between independent and dependent variables. Included in these efforts are controls that vary experimenter expectancies about research outcomes and that replace live experimenters with video- or audiotape recordings. These approaches accept as valid that complex social processes occur in social psychology laboratories. They tend to respond to these phenomena either by making key authority figures in the laboratory (i.e., the experimenter) more psychologically distant from respondents or by increasing the degree of deception utilized during experimental procedures. Rosenthal (1966), for example, suggests doing more than double-blind procedures according to which two levels of experimenters do not know what is expected from the experimental treatments. He suggests actively misleading experimenters so they believe the opposite of the expected results. If such experiments also involve deceiving respondents, which they often do, this mode of coping with the authority dynamics of the laboratory results in deception now in two directions— among those in authority (namely, the experimenters) and between those in authority and those in submission (namely, the experimenters and the respondents). Thoughtful researchers (e.g., Rosenthal, 1966, p. 288 ff.; Carlsmith, Ellsworth, & Aronson, 1976, p. 93 ff.) now discuss the "ethics" of being dishonest with respondents and usually conclude that they find no evidence of harm being done or that the advances in knowledge outweigh any potential harm. Committed experimenters generally do not question what happens in the social system of the laboratory as a whole when there is widespread and officially supported deception going on among several key groups. In order to do this, it would be necessary to have a theory about the laboratory as a social system.

(3) Laboratory as social organization. This orientation views the laboratory as a human organization.

A *human organization* is a set of interdependent human groups who consciously accept a collective mission and therefore subordinate group interests when necessary and who publicly receive support from the larger social order for the legitimate pursuit of their collective mission.

A *human group* is a collection of individuals who have interdependent relations with each other; who perceive themselves as a group by reliably distinguishing members from nonmembers; whose group identity is recognized by nonmembers; who acting alone or in concert have interdependent relations with other groups; and whose roles for the group are a function of expectations from themselves as individuals, from other group members, and from nongroup members (Alderfer, 1984).

Figure 2.1 provides a schematic diagram that portrays the significant groups that shape the human system of the social psychology laboratory. Like any other organization, the laboratory can be analyzed in terms of organization groups that are determined by the organizational position of members and by identity groups based upon the biological origin of people. Both classes of groups and their interaction importantly influence what happens in organizations (Alderfer, 1977, 1984).

In terms of organization groups, there are bodies both outside and inside the system. Within the system there are at least three and as many as five hierarchical levels. Each lower level is somewhat dependent on the immediately higher level; the middle levels (confederates and experimenters) also often have aspirations to move upward in the laboratory hierarchy. This view of the internal dynamics of the laboratory includes a place for all of the findings about demand characteristics, experimenter bias, and the like, and it puts these phenomena into a larger context of the intergroup dynamics inside the system. It raises questions about whether the primarily interpersonal orientation of researchers such as Rosenthal (1966), Orne (1962), and others is adequate to explain or to manage laboratory events. It suggests that intergroup dynamics of hierarchy, for example, are likely to affect how subjects relate to confederates, how confederates relate to experimenters, and how experimenters relate to senior investigators (Smith, 1982a).

Outside the laboratory organizations there are at least three organization groups that potentially influence what happens inside the system. The ultimate aim of research is publication, which is controlled by journal editorial boards. These groups are carefully selected to include individuals who have demonstrated their capacity to meet existing standards of social research—either as senior statespersons or as very promising younger members. Human subjects committees represent the public interest, ideally, and their objective is to be sure that respondents are appropriately warned and protected from potentially harmful behavior by investigators. These committees are frequently populated by the same kinds of people who belong to editorial boards. Informally, members of the field acknowledge that investigators tell review committees only as much as is necessary to gain their approval, and the committees do only what they must in order to maintain credibility with the governmental bodies that require their operation in order to provide funding. Finally there are the funding bodies, private and public. Laboratories receive support within universities by means of space, equipment, and supplies. They receive external support through funding. Members of these review bodies are characteristically senior established members of the field whose own investigations have laid the groundwork for contemporary directions. In sum, the laboratory is a complex social organization of groups, the natural dynamics of which one would expect to produce carefully controlled, systematically biased information (like any other human organization) unless conscious efforts where taken to reverse such normal tendencies.

There has been some conceptual analysis identifying properties of the internal hierarchy of the laboratory (Argyris, 1968). The fact that laboratories as organizations produce different empirical results while replicating the same experiment was shown by Vidmar and Hackman (1971). Wuebben, Straits, and Shulman (1974) have summarized a variety of studies showing that subjects, who are treated statistically as independent observations because they are asked to remain silent about experimental procedures, in fact show a marked propensity to tell others (potentially in their group) about laboratory events. These sorts of findings do not fit with the concept of laboratory as impersonal technology or with the idea that effective control can be maintained by dealing only with experimenter-respondent relationships. The findings are consistent with the model of laboratory as social organization.

Identity group effects of laboratory organizations have also been shown empirically. Among experimenters, people have long accepted as an element of laboratory lore that certain studies were more likely to show results if female subjects were employed. When carefully reviewed, a vast array of social influence experiments were shown to have results dependent in part on gender differences between investigators and respondents (Eagly & Carli, 1981). Roberts (1981) has also brought together a series of papers describing gender effects in the groups external to the laboratory organization, while Boykin, Anderson, and Yates (1979) have done similar work with regard to race.

An example of the interaction of identity group and organization group dynamics follows.

Sixty-three college women were recruited as volunteers to participate in a series of group discussions on the psychology of sex. This format was a ruse, created in order to provide a setting in which subjects could be made to go through mild or severe initiations in order to gain membership in a group.

Each subject was tested individually. When a subject arrived at the laboratory, ostensibly to meet with her group, the experimenter explained to her that he was interested in studying the "dynamics of the group

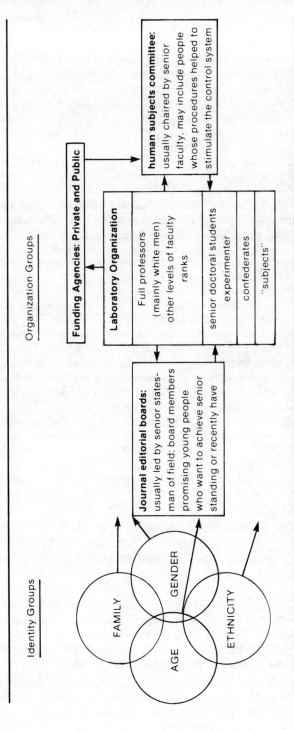

Identity Groups

FAMILY

GENDER

AGE

ETHNICITY

Journal editorial boards: usually led by senior states- man of field; board members promising young people who want to achieve senior standing or recently have

Organization Groups

Funding Agencies: Private and Public

Laboratory Organization

Full professors (mainly white men) other levels of faculty ranks

senior doctoral students experimenter confederates "subjects"

human subjects committee: usually chaired by senior faculty; may include people whose procedures helped to stimulate the control system

Figure 2.1 The Social Psychology Laboratory as Human Organization

discussion process" and that, accordingly, he arranged these discussion groups for the purpose of investigating these dynamics, which included such phenomena as the flow of communications, who speaks to whom, and so forth. He explained that he had chosen as a topic "The Psychology of Sex" in order to attract a large number of volunteers and that this had proved to be a successful device, since many college students were interested in this topic. He then went on to say that this topic presented one major drawback, namely, many of the volunteers were embarrassed and found it more difficult to participate in such a discussion than they might have if the topic had been a more neutral one. He explained that this study would be impaired if any member failed to participate freely. He then asked the subject if she felt she could discuss this topic without difficulty. The subjects invariably replied in the affirmative.

The instructions were used to set the stage for the initiation. The subjects were randomly assigned to one of three experimental conditions: a severe-initiation condition, a mild-initiation condition, or a no-initiation condition. The no-initiation and mild-initiation conditions constituted the control groups. . . . The experimenter told these subjects [in the mild and severe conditions] that he had to be absolutely certain that they could discuss sex frankly before he could admit them to a group. Accordingly, he said that he had recently developed a special test which he was now using as a "screening device" to eliminate those girls who would be unable to engage in such a discussion without undue embarrassment. In the severe-initiation condition, this embarrassment test consisted of having each subject read aloud (to the male experimenter) a list of twelve obscene words and two vivid descriptions of sexual activity from contemporary novels. In the mild-initiation condition, the girls were merely required to read aloud a list of relatively inoffensive words related to sex. This elaborate procedure constituted the empirical realization of the independent variable.[4]

Suppose the material presented above was reframed into the language of intergroup theory to make the self dynamics of the laboratory more explicit; what would the account look like? Here is one possibility.

Two male Stanford University advanced graduate students in their late twenties[5] invited female undergraduate women to participate in a study about the psychology of sex. After attracting the women to the laboratory on the ruse that the study was about sex, the men explained that their interest was really about the dynamics of the group discussion process.

To establish three levels of severity of initiation the senior older men told the junior younger women that they would have to take a test to determine whether they would become too embarrassed to participate freely in the experiment and thereby impair the results. Women in the no-initiation condition simply were asked to say that they had no qualms about discussing sex. Women in the mild-initiation condition were required to read aloud a list of relatively inoffensive words related to sex. Women in the severe-initiation condition were required to read aloud to a senior older male experimenter a list of twelve obscene words and two vivid descriptions of sexual activity from contemporary novels.

When the initiation activities were finished the women were asked to "sit in" on a group discussion by means of listening through earphones. In fact, there was no live discussion, and the women were told not to speak, lest they discover that no one would respond. To be sure the junior younger women would not inadvertently uncover this deception, the senior older male publicly disconnected the microphone that the women might otherwise have used to speak to the fictitious group.

Carlsmith, Ellsworth, and Aronson (1976) explicitly discuss the use of deception in this and in other experiments at several points in their text. They devote an entire chapter to ethical issues, including a section on deception, and they provide another chapter on methodological concerns about deception. Thus, they show an awareness of ethical problems with deception, and they report data that questions empirically whether deception has the intended effects. They also discuss problems as well as advantages of the Aronson and Mills (1959) study. In a 1984 interview with *Psychology Today*, Aronson stated, "I've found it increasingly difficult to do the kinds of experiments we were doing 15 or 20 years ago. For one thing, we've gotten much more concerned ethically about lying to people while conducting an experiment. This limits the kinds of questions we can ask and the realness of the experience we can create in the laboratory" (Aronson, 1984, p. 45).

As I understand their analysis, however, a split occurs between experimenter behavior that serves laboratory realism and experimenter actions that satisfy truthfulness. The quotation in the preceding paragraph, for example, takes the position that a reduction in lying limits investigations of certain questions. Another place where the split occurs is in debriefing after the experiment. Here again, the writers raise a variety of important questions about the debriefing process and caution against experimenters being callous, cavalier, arrogant, or insensitive. They recognize the unequal status of experimenter and subject, and they acknowledge that the authority difference may influence how the subject responds to debriefing. My sense is that they want experimenters to behave as sensitive and caring authority figures, and they want subjects to act cooperatively. A more difficult question, which they do not address, is how benevolent authority figures act when their scientific interests conflict with their subjects' human interests. Several statements from the book do bear on the question:

No amount of post experimental gentleness is as effective in relieving a subject's discomfort as an honest account of the experimenter's *own* [emphasis in original] discomfort. Although no one enjoys being deceived, much of the displeasure may stem from a feeling that one's deceiver is feeling smug about it. (p. 102)

It is important to allow the *subject* [emphasis in original] to decide whether or not it was valuable. . . . The experimenter has no right to assume that this commitment to science is shared by the subject. (p. 103)

It is conceivable that some subjects might feel that they must act like "good sports" or help the experimenter save face and so may pretend to be in good spirits while remaining in inner turmoil. . . . A good way of getting a subject to reveal any lingering disturbances or uncertainty about the experiment is to solicit suggestions for improving the experiment. (p. 104)

In addition, this procedure [of encouraging criticims of the experiment] often allows the subjects to admit that they were (or still are) upset . . . by the deception; if this should occur, further efforts must be made to bring the subjects to a full understanding of the reasons for the procedure and an acceptance of their own response to it. (p. 306)

Viewed in interpersonal terms, these assertions could be conceptualized as advising experimenters to be warm, supportive, self-revealing, and empathic to subjects in the debriefing so that the people leave the experiment feeling good about themselves and about the experimenter. The experimenter has a further interest in the subjects' feeling good and closely identified with the experimenter, as Carlsmith et al. recognize when they write, "The experimenter who has been open and honest in dealing with the subject during the post-experimental debriefing period can be reasonably confident that few subjects will break faith" (1976, p. 307). Viewed through the concepts of intergroup theory, the experimenters are using their authority and interpersonal skills to bring the deceived subjects into their own group after the experiment is over. Instead of the subjects feeling angered at social scientists who have deceived them, they will feel like cherished members of the higher status group and "keep faith" as an act of loyalty to their new group. Intergroup analysis would focus more on creating conditions through which subjects can express their anger at the people who deceived them, assuming that the aims of debriefing are to deal with the consequences of the deception and to assist subjects with unburdening themselves of the anger that usually arises in people who learn that they have been consciously and willfully deceived. Intergroup theory applied to the problem of respecting the dignity of individuals brought into the laboratory for scientific purposes argues for strengthening the boundaries of the subject group so they can stand autonomously in relation to the experimenters, not weakening those boundaries by drawing the subjects closer and more subordinate to their deceivers.

A related question that Carlsmith et al. (1976) do not address is whether an "open and honest" postexperimental debriefing is realistically possible after an experiment that has actively and consistently misled subjects. In the Aronson and Mills (1959) study, the senior men lied twice to the junior women about the purpose of the experiment. First they said it was about the psychology of sex, and then they said it was about the process of group discussion. They also lied twice about what the women were doing. First they said the women had to take a test, and then they said they were to sit in on a group discussion. Thus, there were at least four substantial lies in that study. The textbook authors come close to seeing the problem when they acknowledge that some experimenters use the debriefing period for additional deception. They state, "If experimenters continue to violate this aspect of the contract, subjects will have no way of knowing for sure when the experimenter is telling the truth and when expressed sincerity might be a further ploy" (p. 109). I accept that Carlsmith et al. (1976) want consciously to keep deception out of the debriefing period. But behavioral reality may exceed their wishes. How does one tell the truth about the experiment—which means uncovering all the lies—and then convince the people who were subjects that "now" one is telling the truth? This is especially difficult when the experimenters—for a variety of reasons— act in a manner that keeps subjects' anger and resentment largely suppressed. Carlsmith, Ellsworth, and Aronson (1976) represent the more self-reflective end of the scale among dissonance researchers. Although I believe they miss important aspects of how organizational groups within the laboratory create a self-maintaining culture of deception, they do not deny that serious problems exist in the realm of interpersonal relationships. Leon Festinger (1980, pp. 249-250), the founder and original leader of the dissonance tradition, however, concludes a book devoted to examining fifty years of social psychology research with statements such as the following:

No one would want to minimize the importance of ethical considerations.

I don't want to dwell too long on such difficult [ethical] problems.

These ethical issues never seemed extraordinarily difficult to me.

In none of these issues do questions of harm to the subject arise in any real form. . . . There is also no real issue of invasion of privacy or maintaining confidentiality that cannot be adequately dealt with.

Scientist speaks loudly and clearly through Festinger's words.

In the concepts of intergroup theory, the understanding, the use, and the explanation of deception in the laboratory is a function of group relations inside the laboratory and outside. Inside are usually at least three hierarchical levels—principal investigator, experimenter, and subject. Outside is often a national network. In the case of dissonance work, Leon Festinger is still at the top even though he "left the field" nearly twenty years ago (Festinger, 1980). The Carlsmith et al. (1976) textbook is a product of a national network. Aronson's (1984, p. 43) *Psychology Today* interview shows that Festinger remains an important authority figure for him, and Festinger's 1980 book on *Restrospectives on Social Psychology* indicates that Festinger and the national network remain important for each other.

The Aronson and Mills (1959) experiment also provides important illustrative data about the effects of gender groups in the laboratory organization. Unlike the phenomena of deception, the dynamics of gender in the laboratory do not receive significant self-reflective attention by the textbook authors because their implicit theory of interpersonal dynamics in the laboratory does not recognize gender differences. The kinds of questions intergroup theory would raise about the Aronson and Mills (1959) study include these:

(1) What does it mean when an all male research team uses their university based authority to persuade an all female group of respondents to engage in sexually explicit talk in one-to-one encounters with higher status men?

(2) What does it mean when the study is selected seventeen years later by a two-male/one-female team of textbook authors to illustrate "the advantages of laboratory experimentation"?

(3) What does it mean when a mixed gender team does not examine the effects of gender dynamics when they review the Aronson and Mills (1959) experiment?

These are among the kinds of answers that intergroup theory provides:

Question 1. The strong tendency for only men to occupy senior positions in organizations and for women to have access only to junior roles was characteristic of many organizations during the era when the study was done (Alderfer, 1977). When Aronson and Mills (1959) designed their study, probably they were simply participating in the cultural norms of those times. As male graduate students aspiring to advance in the then male-dominated field of social psychology, they would be unlikely to perceive the problematic features of the gender relations in their study, or, if vaguely uneasy, they would be unlikely to raise such a question among themselves or with their supervisors.

Question 2. At the time of the textbook writing, the authors show some awareness of gender dynamics. In a footnote at the conclusion of the experiment's description, they write, "It is important to remember that this experiment was carried out in 1959, a time when female undergraduates were unaccustomed to seeing (much less verbalizing) explicit obscene words and descriptions of sexual activity. As in most social psychological research, the independent variable must be understood in the cultural context of time and place" (1976, p. 30). The point of this footnote is to caution readers in 1976 that the 1959 experimental treatment might not work in contemporary times because of the changed societal relations between men and women. I believe the authors are unaware that they give an unconscious message about gender dynamics by selecting this study as the first illustration in a section of their book entitled "The Advantages of Experimentation." If their way of working included reflecting on how their own identity group memberships affected their work as some versions of intergroup theory propose, then they would have been much more likely to question themselves thoroughly about how gender dynamics were portrayed in the book (Alderfer, 1984). A situation of two more senior men (Carlsmith and Aronson) working with a less senior woman (Ellsworth) would be accepted as a legitimate subject for inquiry whenever gender dynamics were relevant to the work.

Question 3. The Aronson and Mills (1959) experimental procedure employs one of several possible relationships between men and women in the experimental treatments. The full set of possibilities is (a) male experimenters and female subjects; (b) male experimenters and male subjects; (c) female experimenters and male subjects; and (d) female experimenters and female subjects. The study used only case a. On the surface, I do not see anything in dissonance theory that explains why this particular option was appropriate for testing the theory and the others were not. If that is correct, then the experiment would be stronger if more than one of the conditions were employed; it would be strongest if all four were used. My hypothesis is that neither b, c, nor d would have produced results similar to a. However, if only one of the additional conditions had failed to reproduce the original findings, then the study would have an important source of invalidity—termed a subjects X treatment interaction by Campbell and Stanley (1963). In this regard, it is interesting to note that the textbook authors (1976, p. 221) consider a study by Gerard and Matthewson (1966), which used electric shocks instead of sexually explicit talk and kept condition a the same, as a valid replication of Aronson and Mills (1959). In several senses this study does replicate the earlier one. Men are in the dominant position in the laboratory again. Women are subject to stressful experimental treatments by men again. The results are consistent with dissonance theory predictions again. And, once more, the textbook authors do not question whether there was a possibility of a subjects X treatment source of invalidity. Intergroup theory suggests that on this issue, if the writers had been able to discuss their own gender dynamics, they would have been more likely to identify a subjects X treatment as a potential source of invalidity in both experiments.

As stated at the outset of this chapter, the aim of the section on the social psychology laboratory was mainly to illustrate the operation of group-level self effects. Individuals are nevertheless involved, and, as a matter of custom, we do mention names such as Aronson, Mills, Festinger, Carlsmith, Ellsworth, and others. But the main point of the analysis was to view these individual people as group representatives. Chief organization groups were dissonance researchers as a functional group and roles in the laboratory as hierarchical groups. The primary identity groups were men and women. I recognize that readers unfamiliar with intergroup theory may have difficulty focusing on the people as group representatives. That nevertheless is what examining the laboratory with the concepts of intergroup theory leads one to do.[6]

CONCLUSIONS AND IMPLICATIONS

In the preceding sections I have presented a variety of data to illustrate the operation of self effects in the conduct of professional meetings, in the construction and modification of theories, in the execution of laboratory experiments, and in the teaching of research methods. The data for these illustrations typically did not come from published research reports. Rather they usually came from more personal reports by the authors themselves or their biographers. As the standards for social research stand today, much of what I have written would not be considered scientific. Needless to say, I wish to question those standards. An essential quality of the scientific method is a process of continuing correction. Concretely, this means a persistent quest for better methods, improved theories, and less misleading data. Should we put investigators and their organizations consciously into the theory-method-data dialogue rather than mislead ourselves by acting as if investigators are not people when they do research and professional organizations have no effects on the behavior and attitudes of their members except those intended by research hypotheses?

The three quotations that began this chapter represent a continuum of acceptance for self dynamics in social research. Stevens, the committed positivist, argues that the independent observer *must be* assumed. Heider, the self-reflective theorist, notices the self-inflation of psychologists who place themselves outside the phenomena they observe, and Jung, the depth psychologist, observes that our really serious problems in living are never fully solved and warns us about the potential loss of vitality if they should appear to be. The person familiar with the dynamics of projection may notice that the conditions desired by Stevens are closest to the circumstances that are most likely to induce observers to dissociate and deny their own experience and to project it upon "the others" they study. Heider appears to be at least subliminally aware of this tendency toward splitting, which pursuit of a distantly objective social science seems to promote. Jung, on the other hand, argues that we escape our psychological problems only with the achievement of stultification—an assertion that seems remarkably in accord with Heider's sense that when he spoke to psychologists, he had a sense of not living in quite the same manner as he did when relating to others.

I believe the quest for objectivity in the sense demanded by Stevens and enacted by Scientist in our dialogues is founded on a complex of fears, which are extraordinarily difficult for individual social scientists to acknowledge to themselves—let alone to critical colleagues. The cornerstone of this complex is that allowing for greater consciousness of their own experience would unleash powerful emotions—in others, to be sure, but also in themselves. The next step is the belief that these emotions will get out of control and disrupt any realistic possibility of rational understanding. As a result there is a decided—one could almost say compulsive—desire to control. The acceptable language is experimental control or statistical control, but the focal tension beneath the language of rationality is a fear of disorder or chaos. In order to cope with these fears, the regime in authority adopts repressive measures and resists mightily efforts to examine the fundamental bases of their assumptions.

The choice, however, is not between chaos and repressive control. One need not decide between the apparently cool, detached, robotlike investigator dressed in a white coat, perhaps shown on a video tape, and the unrestrained, enmeshed, overpersonal "human being" who "goes native" and loses all sense of a professional role and behavior. The alternative orientation—and it is a way of being, not a commitment to a particular methodology—is a theory-based and disciplined approach to self examination. Difficult and emotionally problematic features of methods are brought forward and examined; they are not denied, suppressed, or in other ways covered over. Problems of different self-perspectives are "controlled in" rather than "controlled out" so that conscious dialogue and dialectic is possible. In fact, the idea that these phenomena can be controlled out simply does not stand up under scrutiny from self analysis. Philosophically, the basic orientation partially is present in the idea of a crucial experiment which consciously pits alternative theories against one another in order to choose the better. It is also partially present in the clinical concept of "working on" (and sometimes "working through") key conflicts. Effective dialogue and dialectic, however, does not assume that one or more contending viewpoints must be eliminated. New syntheses that incorporate valid elements of several apparently conflicting perspectives may emerge.[7]

The conscious incorporation of self dynamics into research procedures of all kinds—field and laboratory, individual and collective—is not a straightforward, easily achieved change. It is not, for example, simply adding another independent variable to the design of laboratory studies, as is the habitual response of investigators steeped in this tradition. It involves fundamental reconceptualization of what investigators do when they do research, and it implies significant behavioral change by researchers.

Few may think this sort of change is desirable. None may find it is possible. In light of the broad-scale resistance that is already well documented, I shall not suggest that such changes *should* occur. Instead, I outline the kinds of changes that would permit a serious engagement of self dynamics in social research only to show the concrete meaning of acting in accord with the analyses presented above. As Scientist might say, "I shall attempt to change no one's behavior, no one do you hear me, NO ONE! And furthermore, I shall make no recommendations about organizations, NONE, do you understand that?" To which Self might respond, "I shall not insist that you do anything that is contrary to your basic nature." The implications of this follow:

(1) Accept the autobiographical self expressive nature of social and psychological research.
   (a) Select individuals for the profession based on their interest in and capacity for self-reflection. Include both issues of individual development (needs, values, modes of coping) and group membership (gender, ethnicity, hierarchical position).
   (b) Provide education and training (and reeducation and retraining) to encourage a continuing sense of self-reflection and self development for researchers throughout their careers.
   (c) Ask people to file autobiographical statements every 7-10 years, in accord with adult development theory, to encourage self-reflection

and to provide data for literature reviewers who wish to include information about investigators in their analyses.

(2) Increase consciousness of the problematic features of social science organizations as both investigatory and professional bodies. Decide to address actively the features of the system that are likely to shape research results covertly if they are not explicitly examined.

   (a) Enlarge the methods sections of research reports to include much more detailed and thorough accounts of the relations among investigators in their different roles and between investigators and respondents.

   (b) Provide education and training (and reeducation and retraining) on the diagnosis and design of social organizations for investigators (Alderfer, 1980a).

   (c) Establish a shared understanding that progressive social science organizations have periodic "audits" by visiting professionals who examine and report on how the human system is understanding and managing the problematic features of its own social organization. Make these studies available to members of the system so they can learn from them and to other scholars who wish to investigate how properties of the human system may influence research findings produced or interpreted by its members.

Each proposal provides for a long-term view of how the individuals and the institutions of social research might change to incorporate self dynamics creatively in social research. Individual changes lead to a greater sense of personal vitality with self reflection among particular people. Institutional changes create conditions that permit utilization of self dynamics in particular studies. To the degree that we can examine in our various selves the phenomena we investigate in others, we shall move toward a more conscious understanding of social science, withdraw many of our unconscious projections, reduce repressions that have long supported an illusory concept of objectivity, and move toward a profession that engages its members and its public in self enhancing inquiry.

NOTES

1. This chapter is a sequel to an invited speech I gave at the American Psychological Association convention in September, 1979 entitled, "Why Organizational Psychologists Act Like Fruitcakes." It has not been easy to get that speech published. People who wish to receive the first paper may write to me, and I will respond gratefully. Portions of this chapter were presented as a colloquium for the Social Psychology Program at Yale University on February 20, 1984, and as a keynote address at the Fifth Annual I/O and OB Graduate Student Convention at Old Dominion University on April 28, 1984.

I, of course, did not participate in this talk about sexual behavior. When it was over, I pulled out two copies of the Job Description Index that I carry for such moments and asked my friends to complete them. Both refused and asserted that the questionnaire items were not relevant to their recent experience. I add this footnote to indicate that, unlike others, I retain scholarly attitudes and inappropriate objectivity even during the most trying moments at professional meetings.

2. I choose to undertake this exploration by leading with theory rather than with the vast array of confusing and inconsistent empirical findings on the self as they have been accumulated by a variety of authors such as Wylie (1961, 1968) and Gergen (1971). This choice reflects both an intellectual prejudice and an enactment of the major theme of this chapter. The intellectual bias is nicely stated by Northrup (1947, p. 22):

> Galilei would have thrown and shot off all kinds of projectiles, carefully observing and describing what happened, gathering more and more detailed empirical information until this information added up to a generalization which was the answer. It is likely that had Galilei done this, he or his successors would still be observing, with the problem unsolved.

This is to place one's energy on the side of theoretical development when a choice is necessary between conceptual statements and empirical findings. Philosophically this chapter belongs to the critical as opposed to scientific orientation to theory (Geuss, 1981). Critical theories aim at emancipation rather than domination of the external world; reflect upon themselves rather than "objectify" the phenomena they attend to; and are accepted or rejected both by normal positivist empirical standards and by judgments from those the theory aims to serve. The aim of this chapter is to free social research from a variety of dysfunctional limiting conditions that arise because methods of self-reflection are largely avoided by the vast majority of U.S. social scientists. The approach here will provide linear statements that describe and explain self-reflective processes; report data from several empirical traditions that illustrate failure and success at self-reflection; and offer material to evoke self-reflective behavior by readers. I am indebted to David Morgan for calling my attention to critical philosophy.

3. Samples of biographical works include Jones (1953) on Freud, Hannah (1976) on Jung, Marianne Weber on Max Weber (1926), Marrow on Lewin (1969), and Perry (1982) on Sullivan. Autobiographical examples include those of Jung (1963), Roethlisberger (1977), Heider (1983) and the edited series by Krawiec (1972) on contemporary psychologists.

4. This excerpt was taken from *Methods of Research in Social Psychology,* a textbook on the conduct of laboratory experiments by J. Merrill Carlsmith, Phoebe C. Ellsworth, and Elliott Aronson (1976, pp. 29-30). The experiment described by the authors was published by Aronson and Mills (1959). The description of the experiment was given in a section entitled "The Advantages of Experimentation" in Carlsmith et al.'s book.

5. The material on the ages and university location of Elliot Aronson and Judson Mills at the time of the study was taken from the Biographical Directory of the American Psychological Association (1975).

6. On a personal note, I do want to acknowledge the valuable assistance I received from Elliot Aronson on an earlier version of this paper. This in no way implies that he agrees with what I say—only that he gave me extensive comments that I found very helpful.

7. A good example of a dialectic made of incorporating self dynamics into research may be found in Robert Tucker's (1984) recent paper, "Towards a Philosophy of Social Science for Black-White Studies."

THE HERMENEUTIC TURN AND THE SINGLE CASE STUDY IN PSYCHOANALYSIS

Marshall Edelson

FACING THE CHALLENGE
OF THE "CLINICAL" DEMANDS
OF SOCIAL SCIENCE RESEARCH

Science, above all, teaches us to doubt—to question our conceptions of the world. It is an institutional embodiment of Freud's reality principle. It requires us to justify our beliefs about the world on empirical grounds. To provide such grounds, we pit our own hypothesis against a rival hypothesis and, when the data we obtain favor our own hypothesis over its rival, we consider what alternative explanations would account for our having obtained these data even if our own hypothesis were false.

Two kinds of deviation from the values and norms of science must especially concern social scientists. The scientistic deviation refuses to accept the demands of a thoroughgoing skepticism. Although this rebellion is disguised by an apparently zealous conformity to "science," it is revealed when an investigator neglects the "clinical" or human demands of social science research. He ignores, in other words, personal and social forces operating in such research, which influence what data are and can be obtained.[1]

The hermeneutic deviation also refuses to accept the demands of a thoroughgoing skepticism, but rebellion here is expressed by "dropping out"—abandoning the quest for scientific knowledge altogether. Under some circumstances, perhaps, this deviation has its beginnings when meeting the clinical demands of social science research becomes an end in itself.

The scientistic deviation expresses itself in the overinfatuation of some scientists with the form of conventional research designs. A research design, however, is merely a means to enable an investigator to argue that provisional acceptance of a test hypothesis over rival and alternative hypotheses is justified; the argument is the substance. A particular research design is rationally valued only if it does its job in the study of persons or social systems, no matter how successful it has been in other kinds of studies. In the social sciences, the intrapersonal processes of the investigator, his values and biases, his conscious and unconscious wishes, fears, anxieties, and defenses against impulses and dysphoric affects, influence what information he is able to obtain from the human subjects with whom he interacts and how he interprets the information he does obtain. Unavoidably, he affects his subjects and they affect him. The intrusion of the personal and the social in social science research is a major source of alternative hypotheses, which would account for his having obtained the data favoring his own hypothesis, even if this hypothesis of his were false. The possible influence of such factors casts doubt on the conclusion that his data necessarily support his hypothesis. Ignorance or willful neglect of the clinical aspects of social science research will lead the investigator to overestimate his own hypotheses and to interpret the data he obtains uncritically.

Many papers in this volume are concerned with the scientistic deviation in social science research; this chapter shall have very little more to say about it. The concern here is rather with the second deviation, which strongly asserts itself currently in the psychoanalytic community. Some psychoanalysts at least, and their allies in the humanities and social sciences, regard the emphasis in science on testing hypotheses not as an expression of the reality principle but rather as some eccentric offshoot of an aberrant logico-philosophical movement (*logical positivism* is the usual epithet) that is out of touch with what most scientists do. This attitude leads quickly to the conclusion that testing hypotheses is not what "we" are up to—because psychoanalysis is a special science, with its own rules of inference and evidence (whatever these might be) and its own mode of understanding ("Verstehen"), or because it is not science at all but a hermeneutic endeavor, which in its objectives more resembles "reading" (i.e., interpreting) a text than explaining a state of affairs. In the context of a discussion of responses, evasive or otherwise, to the clinical demands of social science research, it should be noted that likening the psychoanalyst's activity in making clinical interpretations to the humanist's activity in interpreting a text quite plays down the reciprocal interactions of psychoanalyst and analysand as well as the crucial contribution to clinical interpretation made by the analysand's own activity.

The recoil from the discipline of hypothesis testing may take a less extreme form, apparent, for example, in a tendency to deprecate work in the context of justification and to emphasize disproportionately discovery and the invention of explanations as quintessential scientific activities. Those who are enthusiastic about the psychoanalytic case study join its detractors in relegating such case studies to the context of discovery, since both groups believe that, however richly suggestive the ideas generated and however satisfyingly complex the explanations proposed, case studies lack design controls, and cannot, therefore, provide scientific support for the credibility of psychoanalytic hypotheses.

In this chapter, questions are raised about all these versions of the hermeneutic turn in psychoanalysis—and by extension in any of the social sciences.

SOME PERNICIOUS EPISTEMOLOGICAL JUSTIFICATIONS OF THE CASE STUDY

Recently, in *Hypothesis and Evidence in Psychoanalysis* (1984), I took the position that psychoanalysts can and should conform to the canons of procedure and reasoning that characterize science and distinguish it from other human endeavors, especially so when they use clinical data from the psychoanalytic situation to provide support for psychoanalytic hypotheses. It will certainly be held by some colleagues that, as a psychoanalyst, I have given away too much when I accept the view of science held by those who question the scientific status of psychoanalysis, and especially those (e.g., Grunbaum, 1984) who believe that data obtained in the psychoanalytic situation cannot be used to *test* psychoanalytic propositions.

In my experience, this kind of response from colleagues comes eventually to rest on an appeal to epistemological justifications for the proposal that psychoanalysis is and should be exempt from scientific canons. The methods of study and manner of reasoning in psychoanalysis are—and must be—different, so the argument goes, because the way in which psychoanalysts acquire knowledge, as well as the kind of knowledge they acquire, differ qualitatively from the way in which natural scientists acquire knowledge and the kind of knowledge they acquire. First, the phenomena, and our ways of knowing them, are subjective rather than objective. Second, our interest is in knowing or understanding the meaning or meanings of phenomena and not in determining their status as cause or effect. Third, we seek to understand (rather than explain or predict) phenomena—and in all their complexity, wholeness, and uniqueness, not merely as exemplars or instances of generalizations about relations between or among a set of relatively few variables that are themselves the colorless result of a process of conceptual analysis or abstraction from multifaceted phenomena.

These differences, the argument concludes, justify a preference for the case study and all its relatives over the experiment and all its relatives. Just contrast the former's richness, narrative complexity, presentation of a unique individual who is to be understood as a whole, and emphasis on the subjective and the qualitative, with the latter's preoccupation with deductive and inductive schemata, reliance on quantification and prediction in testing hypotheses, concern with empirical generalizations involving simple relations among a few variables, and efforts to control (e.g., hold constant or eliminate) the influence of many factors in order to demonstrate the influence of an isolated few.

In this chapter, I shall examine what is meant by references to subjectivity, meaning, and complexity and uniqueness (which are contrasted with objectivity, causality, and abstraction and generalization), and I shall reject these epistemological justifications of the case study, and the view based on them of psychoanalysis as a hermeneutic enterprise, a special "science," exempt from ordinary canons of scientific method and reasoning. I shall conclude, perhaps unexpectedly in light of what has gone before, that the case study is indeed a valuable method in psychoanalysis and, specifically, is capable of providing data that will test psychoanalytic hypotheses—just as clinical methods, in general, are valuable in the same way in social science. The use of such a method, however, not only does not imply rejection of, but can and indeed should conform to, the canons of method and reasoning that are characteristic of science no matter what its subject matter is. The psychoanalytic case study in particular, and case studies in general, should not only *not* be relegated to the context of discovery but can and should be used to make various kinds of arguments that justify on empirical grounds provisional acceptance of some hypotheses as more credible than others.

SCIENCE

Certain presuppositions, stated below in italic, underlie ordinary canons of scientific method and reasoning. It is difficult to conceive that those who want exemption from the canons are indeed prepared to discard the presuppositions.

(1) *The actual world is as it is independent of our descriptions or knowledge of it; our values, preferences, and emotional responses to it; and our attempts to understand or explain it.* To deny that there are

brute facts indifferent to our wishes and feelings, to talk as if there is no actual world, only symbolic forms constructed by symbol-making organisms, is to show oneself somewhat deficient in a sense of reality. Of course, our values, wishes, and emotions influence what questions we ask, what problems we address, and how we interpret states of affairs—specifically, how we classify them and what significance we attribute to them; but that this is so does not constitute an insurmountable obstacle to testing and revising our beliefs about the actual world. Here, for one, we are able to depend on our senses, our instruments for obtaining information, which accommodate to brute reality and do not merely assimilate what is observed to already existing schemata, as well as on canons of scientific method and reasoning.

(2) *The scientist, therefore, adheres to a correspondence theory of truth.* A scientist asserts that a certain state of affairs obtains in the actual world. If the state of affairs does obtain, the assertion corresponds to reality: It is true. If it is not true, then it is false. The truth-status of a sentence expressing such an assertion is independent of our state of knowledge or our capacities for acquiring knowledge. If a sentence is true, it is true whether or not we know it is true or are able to construct an argument concluding that, given the empirical data and the way these data were obtained, this sentence is more credible than its rivals and, therefore, should be provisionally accepted as true.

(3) *All hypotheses are underdetermined by data, facts, or evidence. There is no criterion for deciding that some hypothesis is the best (the one, the certainly true) hypothesis. There are only criteria for deciding that some hypothesis, which is a member of a set of hypotheses, is a better (more credible) hypothesis, given the available evidence, than the other members of that set of hypotheses. In general, a hypothesis will not be accepted provisionally as credible just because positive instances of it are observed; it will be so accepted only if evidence favors it over rival hypotheses.*

Any data obtained are entailed by, and therefore in that sense explained by, any one of an indefinite number of rival hypotheses about the actual world. It is always the case that any one or any combination of a number of causally relevant factors may have been responsible in the research situation for generating particular data. A scientist is always faced with the problem, then, of obtaining data that favor his hypothesis over another, and of eliminating from consideration possible plausible alternative explanations other than the truth of his hypothesis of how he came to obtain these data.

It follows that scientific knowledge is never certain. Scientific belief in the truth of a hypothesis is always provisional, relative to the rival hypotheses that have been challenged by the hypothesis; the available data that have been brought to bear to support the hypothesis over its rivals; and the alternative hypotheses also capable of accounting for these data that have been eliminated. Scientific belief is inevitably relative, therefore, to the conceptual tools and methods for acquiring knowledge we have and the background knowledge we presume to be true when a hypothesis is tested.

Data do not support a test hypothesis unless those data can be argued to favor a test hypothesis over some rival hypothesis about a domain. Further, these data must have been obtained in a way and under circumstances justifying the conclusion that the truth of the test hypothesis is a more credible explanation for the fact that these data have been obtained than plausible alternative hypotheses. Contrary to what is assumed by many clinicians, observations, no matter how great their number, cannot be said to support a hypothesis just because they are consistent with or entailed by it.

(4) *The canons of scientific method and reasoning are independent of subject matter. These canons do not depend in any way upon and are not altered by what domain an investigator chooses for study; they are not affected, in other words, by what kinds of observable or hypothetical entities, and what kinds of properties attributed to these entities, constitute the subject matter of any particular science.*

Scientific activity may be said to occur in either the context of discovery or context of justification, depending on what objectives, and therefore what skills and attitudes, are given priority.

Scientific activity occurs in two analytically distinguishable phases, discovery and justification. These are embedded in the work undertaken, for example, when a scientist devises a model, evaluates it, revises it, evaluates it again, revises it again, always with the objective of coming closer to what is true of the actual world. Science cannot do without either discovery or justification.

In the context of discovery, establishing a frame of reference for investigation (selecting a domain, identifying the kind of entities constituting the domain, deciding what kind of properties are of interest that may be attributed to such entities), and inventing powerful iconic and/or discursive causal explanations of facts of interest, have priority. Decisions in the context of discovery are not constrained in any simple way by what is true of the world. These decisions are matters of conceptual invention. While there are many circumstances and heuristics that appear to facilitate acquisition of insights leading to the formulation of new hypotheses, it is quite difficult to state precisely what these are. A hypothesis may come to a scientist as the result of a dream, or following immersion in—or painstaking examination of—a body of data. Neither route automatically decides that the hypothesis will survive, or fail to survive, tests of its scientific credibility.

In the context of justification, taking a skeptical or critical attitude toward causal explanations and subjecting them to rigorous empirical tests have priority. Here, the question is not how powerful or otherwise satisfying an explanation is, but how accurate it is. Accuracy is evaluated by addressing two questions: How warranted is the conclusion that a causal explanation is better (i.e., more credible) than some rival? How warranted is the conclusion that the truth of this causal explanation accounts better for the fact that certain favorable data have been obtained by an investigator than do alternative explanations?

SUBJECTIVITY

In criticizing subjectivity, meaning, and complexity and uniqueness as epistemological justifications for exempting the case study from canons of scientific reasoning and method, I do not of course intend to deny that, for example, insight into one's own motives as well as special interpersonal skills may be required to obtain data in case studies (whether of persons, groups, or organizations). Nor do I intend to devalue the use of case studies to achieve objectives other than acquiring and evaluating scientific knowledge. (See Edelson, 1984, pp. 70-73, for a discussion of various objectives a case study may have.)

What I am arguing is rather that such epistemological justifications as these do not work to exempt the case study that purports to make a contribution to scientific knowledge from canons of scientific reasoning and method. These canons apply in acquiring and evaluating scientific knowledge of any kind and therefore apply also in case studies in psychoanalysis in particular—and clinical studies in social science in general—if these are to be used as a means of justifying claims about the actual world.

What is meant by references to subjectivity when warrant for exemption from scientific canons is sought? Here are some possibilities.

(1) *There is no actual world that is as it is independent of any particular observer's descriptions or experience of it. What we have are sets of unique symbolic representations of "reality" and these constitute the only reality we shall ever know.*

Currently, in psychoanalysis, this assertion takes the form of emphasizing an analysand's language and his rules for using it in different ways in thought and communication (a hermeneutics) rather than to what in the actual world the analysand refers or what in the actual world is responsible for his capacity to use language at all or his various uses of language on particular occasions. If any "explanation" occurs here, in answering, for example, such questions as "Why does the patient say that?", it consists of references to syntactic (form-determining and form-transforming) and semantic (content-determining and content-trans-forming) rules, which are then applied to decode or translate one verbal production (what is to be explained) into another verbal production (the explanation). When there is no concern, as here apparently there is not, with what constraints or conditions actually determine what syntactic and semantic rules have been in fact used on a particular occasion by an analysand, then an infinite number of translations are possible and there is no way to assess the truth of a claim that such and such *is* (not just *may be*) in this instance the translation of such and such. If this description captures at all what is meant in some references to subjectivity, then out of considerations of consistency it makes little sense to talk of science or scientific knowledge at all. This is not to say that the attitudes, beliefs, and activities just described might not have considerable value of another kind.

It is possible that what is at issue behind this kind of reference to subjectivity are simply an investigator's preferences

(a) for a particular kind of data—the verbal reports of a subject over classifications or ratings of the subject's behavior by others;
(b) for assessing and attributing causal status to how objects or states of affairs in reality are represented by, look to, or are interpreted by, different subjects (or the same subject at different times), over assessing and attributing causal status primarily or solely to intrinsic features of a subject's situation.

These preferences do not constitute grounds for abandoning canons of scientific method and reasoning, or make it impossible on logical grounds ("in principle") to conform to such canons.

(2) *In psychoanalysis and the social sciences the investigator's stance must be subjective rather than objective if he is to acquire knowledge of his subject rather than about his subject.*

(a) *The investigator must be involved with, rather than a detached observer of, the subject. He acquires knowledge of, rather than about, the subject through empathic identifications with him, or by noticing the various internal states stirred in himself, as a participant who interacts with, is influenced by, and reciprocally responds to the subject he studies.*

(b) *The investigator inevitably brings to bear all his own biases, preferences, and values, and he responds with his own largely unconscious anxieties and his largely unconscious defenses against the impulses and anxieties aroused in him, as he interacts with the subject. These aspects of his own mental life determine how he influences the subject and, therefore, what the subject says to him and shows him; what he selects or is able to receive of what the subject says to him and shows him; and how he interprets what is said or shown, when it is ambiguous (as it usually is).*

My response, when the above statements capture what is meant by subjectivity, is as follows.

(a) We may suppose that the investigator who uses empathic identifications or reciprocal responses as a means of knowing is in the context of discovery. What he concludes from observation of his own internal states, what hypothesis about the subject he forms as he makes such observations, remains to be tested against plausible rival and alternative hypotheses.

However, we may also regard the investigator's reports of his internal states as the same kind of data as the subject's reports of his internal states. For example, if a kind of investigator-state, or report of such a state, is associated or correlated with a kind of subject-state, or report of such a state, that itself becomes a fact to be explained or a fact that might provide support for one hypothesis over another.

(b) The way in which aspects of the mental life and propensities of the investigator determine what data are accessible to him, what data he selects or notices, and how he interprets such data, is a strong argument for the implementation of the canons of scientific method and reasoning. For here we describe, in fact, a plausible alternative account of how the investigator might come to obtain observations that seem to support his conjectures about the subject, even if these conjectures are false.

To be a skilled observer requires the ability to acquire the kind of insight into one's own mental life and propensities that will expand one's observing capacities. The canons encourage the investigator to become aware of his characteristics as an instrument for making observations, and to discover what systematic and random influences upon his observations arise from his own nature.

In addition, these canons check the investigator's overinvestment in his own conjectures, counter his credulity where these are concerned, and provide him with the means to give primacy to the reality principle rather than to the pleasure principle. Such canons, above all, impose a conceptual discipline upon the investigator to seek out, to imagine, and explicitly to formulate rivals to the belief he seeks data to support, and alternatives to the explanation he favors in accounting for the data he obtains; he must wrestle with these. The value of a case study, with respect to its contribution to scientific knowledge, is diminished when it makes no mention of rival or alternative hypotheses and how these are assessed in relation to the hypothesis the data of the case study supposedly support. It is clear, for example, that Freud's extended consideration of rival and alternative hypotheses in *The Interpretation of Dreams* enhances the value of that work.

Is it really true that, because of biases, values, and unconscious meanings, there can be no agreement about what the facts are? Judges can be used to classify or rank order the contents of protocols of psychoanalytic sessions (Luborsky, 1967, 1973; Luborsky & Mintz, 1974), judges who are blind to the purposes of the investigator and who do not necessarily share his biases. Such judges, no matter the differences in their intrapsychic processes, can be shown to be capable of agreement among themselves in carrying out such tasks.

If an investigator is smuggling in evaluative assessments, preferences, or proposals as matters of fact, then it is possible to make use of conceptual analysis to expose this deception.

(3) *We work within a subjective frame of reference, not in the objective frame of reference of the natural scientist. What we study is "inside" the subjective life of the subject. There is nothing objective "out there" to measure; and objective methods, in general, are unavailing applied to subjective phenomena.*

(a) *We do not study the subject as a physical object, as a natural scientist would. We study wishes and beliefs, the whole range of kinds of psychological entities or intentional states. These are individuated by subject; by content (object, state of affairs); and by psychological mode (a subject's psychological state, or attitude or relation to the content)— and not, for example, by spatiotemporal location. These psychological entities or intentional states are not physical objects.*

(b) *We do not study the intrinsic properties of states of affairs, events, or objects as the natural scientist does, but rather how they seem to, how they are interpreted by, and what they signify or mean to the subject. Inevitably, therefore, we study irrational as well as rational phenomena, and the rationality and logical arguments of the natural scientist have no relevance in any effort to understand such subject matter.*

If this is what is meant by subjectivity, my response is as follows.

(a) Neither the canons of scientific method and reasoning nor the character of scientific explanation are dependent on the subject matter of science, the choice of a domain for study, what kind of entities are selected for study, or what kinds of properties are attributed to such entities. Edelson (1984, especially pp. 86-101) and Searle (1983), for example, have shown, in somewhat different formulations, how psychological entities or intentional states can be individuated, and that the choice of a domain of such entities for study, or of the kinds of properties to be attributed to them, does not need to affect in and of itself the scientific status of that study. There is no reason to suppose a priori that there are no regular relations between and among kinds of wishes and beliefs (or other such entities). There is no a priori logical basis for concluding that the causes of the properties of, or the causal relations between and among wishes and beliefs (or other such entities), or the causal efficacy of such properties or relations with respect to other phenomena, cannot be studied according to the canons of scientific method and reasoning, however difficult such study might prove to be.

Measurement in this subjective realm is possible. If an investigator is able to classify kinds of psychological entities or intentional states, for example, according to the kinds of contents characteristic of each, or is able to order them, for example, according to their relative strength or intensity, as in everyday life we certainly in a rough and ready way already do, and as every psychoanalyst certainly does, he is making use of a kind of measurement. Such nominal and ordinal measurements are not to be despised. Even if in this realm we never achieve the level of equal-interval measurement (i.e., each entity has so-and-so many equal units of some property), nominal and ordinal measurements are sufficient to carry out much scientific work.

(b) Suppose that the relations of interest, those that lead to fruitful explanation, are just those that depend on the way in which the subject himself classifies the states of affairs, events, or objects that are the contents of his psychological or intentional states; or that assignment of a particular psychological entity or intentional state of a subject to a class depends critically on whether or not the investigator believes that that entity or state is for that subject a member of that class. This sort of subjectivity does not constitute an intrinsic obstacle to work according to scientific canons. What is important here is that the investigator be able to specify in what way his hypothesis that the subject classifies a particular entity or state in a particular way is supported by evidence.

To do this, the investigator must keep very clear the difference between his data and his inferences or hypotheses about the subject. That such and such is a content of a psychological or intentional state of the subject, according to the subject's own statement, may be accepted as data. If an investigator wishes to be very cautious, he may accept as data only that the subject reports that such and such is a content of a psychological or intentional state of the subject's own.

The psychoanalyst's assignment of the content of an analysand's verbalizations to a class of contents characterized by a state of affairs in which one object *takes in or merges* with another object, or a state of affairs in which one object *hides away or keeps in* another object, or a state of affairs in which one object *penetrates* another object with a third object—or the psychoanalyst's inference that for the analysand the content is so classified—may be based upon such evidence as the particular choice of words used by the analysand in describing his psychological or intentional states. The evidential status of the analysand's choice of words constitutes one reason for the psychoanalyst's careful attention to the nuances associated with the exact words used by the analysand; he would and should not be satisfied by some rough approximation to or translation of these words by someone other than the analysand.

These considerations about classification apply also to assigning relative strengths or intensities to psychological or intentional states.

What also seems to be at issue behind both these kinds of references to subjectivity (3a and b above), besides the two preferences previously mentioned, is an investigator's unproblematic (with respect to scientific canons) preference for regarding performances or behaviors as effects of internal states, or as manifestations or realizations of dispositions or propensities, over regarding performances or behaviors in and of themselves as both the causes and effects of interest.

(4) *Objectivity as a characteristic of scientific method depends on the possibility of intersubjective agreement, at least in principle, among observers. In psychoanalysis, however, such intersubjective agreement is impossible. The psychoanalyst can read anything he wants into what the analysand says. One psychoanalyst will hear as "anal efforts to control" what another psychoanalyst hears as "compensatory strivings to overcome a sense of inferiority." So, Freudian, Adlerian, and Jungian psychoanalysts all claim that the data support their hypotheses. Surely, what we have here are different stories, each with its own value, and no way to choose between them on grounds of veridicality.*

Meehl (1983) gives this particular problem of subjectivity extended consideration in one of his characteristically brilliant papers. He argues convincingly that there are ways to achieve intersubjective agreement about the inferences made from the analysand's reports.

The general problem is just what degree of intersubjective agreement can be achieved about what the data are. When Meehl refers to the subjectivity of inference in psychoanalysis, however, he means in part by "inference" how data are classified; the problem becomes the possibility of intersubjective agreement about such classifications. In his example, he argues there is a way of achieving intersubjective agreement about how a set of utterances by an analysand in a particular psychoanalytic session should be classified according to type of theme. However, the classification of themes Meehl presents (i.e., the kind of facts he picks out to be explained) seems to me to be dependent on psychoanalytic theory in just the way I argue in what follows that it must not be.

My own response to the problem of achieving intersubjective agreement is as follows.

(a) The difficulty in achieving intersubjective agreement in psychoanalysis follows from the preoccupation with seeking confirming instances, without regard to the problem of excluding plausible alternative explanations of the occurrence of such instances.

(b) More attention must be paid to keeping clear the difference between data and inferences based on data. Data include, for example, that such and such is the content of an analysand's psychological or intentional state, according to his own statement; or that such and such a content is assigned to one or another class or rank—where the classifications or bases for ranking involve reference to nontheoretical properties of such contents; or even that one kind of content, so classified, co-occurs regularly with another kind of content, or that the strength of one kind of psychological or intentional state covaries with the strength of another kind. Inferences from data include interpretations or hypotheses about the analysand entailed by a conjunction of particular psychoanalytic hypotheses (making use of theoretical concepts) and particular data. The interpretations of psychoanalysts clearly are not first-order facts, and should not be, as they often are, presented as such.

If incompatible inferences about an analysand, based on different theories, are made by different psychoanalysts, then the same kinds of scientific arguments about the relation between rival or alternative hypotheses and evidence I shall describe in the penultimate section of this chapter must be used to decide which inference or hypothesis is to be provisionally accepted over another.

In connection with the need to keep clear the difference between data and inferences or interpretations, note that the classification "taking in or merging," "hiding away or keeping in," and "penetrating" is not the same as the classification "oral," "anal," and "phallic." The former classification is based on rather commonsense notions—knowledge, for example, of metaphors and figures of speech; it is not knowledge of the psychoanalytic theory of psychosexual development. Therefore, this classification may be considered nontheoretical, not because no theory is required to use it, but because carrying out a classification of psychological or intentional states according to these notions does not require knowledge of psychoanalytic theory, which the investigator wants to use these data to test. (Here, we have some way of understanding the emphasis on metaphors and figures of speech in Freud's writing and in psychoanalytic practice.)

That this classification is nontheoretical, in the sense described, is so, even if considerations based on psychoanalytic theory have led to a decision to use such a classification. In the same way, the usefulness of characterizing physical objects in terms of location in space and time is certainly suggested by Newtonian theory, but knowledge of that theory is not required, although knowledge of some theory is required, to assign a physical object to a particular spatiotemporal location.

It is quite otherwise with a classification such as "oral," "anal," and "phallic." In my opinion it is a mistake to consider a statement such as "the analysand's utterance or state is anal" as a typical data statement in psychoanalysis. For, if the distinction nontheoretical-theoretical is not kept in mind, an investigator is in peril of guaranteeing acceptance of a theory by assuming it to be true prior to any empirical justification for accepting it as true, and smuggling it into the very constitution of the facts that are held to test it. Including as a premise in an argument the very conclusion that is supposed to follow from a set of premises results in tautology.

Clearly none of this denies that all data are both theory laden and corrigible. What is asserted here is that data must not be laden with the very theory one is using them to support, and that what are regarded as facts at any time are those nontheoretical assertions about the actual world about which it is easiest, at that time, to achieve intersubjective agreement.

MEANING

Psychoanalysis is not natural science. It is a hermeneutics, an explication of the meaning of what the analysand reports, which is regarded as a text to be interpreted (in the sense "decoded" or "translated"). The relations to be explored are between signifiers and what they signify, symbols and what they represent, signs and what they refer to, allude to, or stand for—not between causes and effects.

Psychoanalysis is the study of a signifying or symbolizing function. If that study involves explanation at all, it is closer to the kind of "explanation" exemplified by answers to questions about the meaning of words, phrases, concepts, or proverbs than it is to causal or functional explanations exemplified by answers to questions about the origin or source of some state or condition, how some change or difference in state or condition has come about, or how something works. What is at issue are logical connections (in a broad sense), denoted by such terms as "means," "symbolizes," "is a paraphrase of," "implies," or "is by analogy like"—primarily conceptual connections between linguistic entities (including descriptions of nonlinguistic entities), or their counterparts, rather than intrinsic connections obtaining in the actual world between or among nonlinguistic entities themselves. (See Sherwood, 1969, for a discussion of explanation in terms of significance, as distinct from explanation in terms of origin, genesis, or function.)

The case study is not a scientific argument. It is not an account of causal connections. It is a story, which reveals the complex, coherent network of signifiers and signifieds that makes sense of the analysand's symptoms, dreams and parapraxes. It translates and decodes, rather than causally explains, these.

My response to this characterization of psychoanalysis and the case study follows.

A careful reading of Freud's work reveals that he persistently sought causal and functional explanations of mental phenomena. See Shope (1973), in his excellent paper on Freud's uses of the term "meaning," and my comparison of Freud's theory of dreams and Chomsky's theory of language (Edelson, 1972, 1975) for citation of relevant passages. Certain passages of Freud's (occasional rather than preponderant) do allude, often metaphorically, to symbolizing activities in human life. I think these could be argued to indicate an effort on Freud's part to clarify by analogy aspects of the subject matter he is studying, including in some instances aspects of the clinical activity of the psychoanalyst—while at the same time perhaps he paid too little attention to disanalogies—rather than to indicate any abandonment on his part of the explanatory objectives he so clearly pursues. There is no more reason to suppose that just because Freud refers to language, symbols, representations, and symbolic activity (part of his subject matter), he has rejected, or should have rejected, canons of scientific method and reasoning than to suppose that just because Chomsky studies language (his subject matter) his theory of linguistics cannot be a theory belonging to natural science and that he cannot be seeking causal explanations in formulating it.

Of course, that Freud sought causal and functional explanations is no reason to suppose psychoanalysis continues to do so, but I would argue that clinical psychoanalytic theory as we know it, which is what is applied as far as I know in most current instances of psychoanalytic treatment, exemplifies causal and functional explanation; any other characterization of the clinical theory of psychoanalysis involves a rather bizarre misreading of it or is in the service of a radical revision of it. In the latter case, there is no particularly good reason to call the revision a version of psychoanalytic theory.

For psychoanalysis, the *meaning* of a mental phenomenon is a set of unconscious psychological or intentional states (specific wishes or impulses, specific fears aroused by these wishes, and thoughts or images that might remind the subject of these wishes and fears). The mental phenomenon substitutes for this set of states. That is, these states would have been present in consciousness instead of the mental phenomenon requiring interpretation had they not encountered, at the time of origin of the mental phenomenon or repeatedly since then, obstacles to their access to consciousness. If the mental phenomenon has been a relatively enduring structure and these obstacles to consciousness are removed, the mental phenomenon disappears as these previously unconscious states achieve access to consciousness.

That the mental phenomenon substitutes for these states is a manifestation of a causal sequence. An example of one such causal sequence: A wish leads to an image of a dreaded state of affairs, which the subject believes will follow upon the gratification of the wish. Therefore, imagining the gratification of the wish, and believing that gratification to be possible and imminent, produces anxiety. Anxiety may lead to changes in states of consciousness and to various operations (e.g., the dreamwork, primary process, defense mechanisms) upon these psychological or intentional states, which determine the form and content of the mental phenomenon that comes to substitute for them. The psychological or intentional states, in conjunction with or by means of the various operations upon them, cause the mental phenomenon to come into being (i.e., make it happen).

For psychoanalysis, the *meaning* of a mental phenomenon is also the purpose (e.g., the wish fulfillment) the mental phenomenon serves, and here we may have reference to the functions it serves both in keeping rejected contents out of consciousness in order to avoid dysphoric affects such as anxiety, and in providing unconscious motives, drives, or impulses a means of expression (i.e., a path to satisfaction).

Meaning, in the first sense, requires causal explanation of a mental phenomenon (i.e., an answer to the question, What makes it happen?). Meaning, in the second sense, requires functional explanation of a mental phenomenon (i.e., an answer to the question, To what end does it serve as a means?). With reference to meaning (in the first sense, especially) Freud writes of that which fills a gap, repairs a discontinuity, or finds its place in psychic continuity (i.e., fits in with other psychological or intentional states in conscious mental life or belongs to a sequence of such states that has been interrupted). With reference to meaning in either sense, Freud writes of that which, by virtue of psychoanalytic explanation, gives intelligibility or significance to a mental phenomenon that does not make sense. (For a similar account of meaning in psychoanalysis, see Shope, 1973.)

The following points are especially important.

(a) Semantic explanation, which refers to meaning or significance (see, e.g., Sherwood, 1969), is not, in psychoanalysis at least, a noncausal kind of explanation. Suppose the question is, Why does the analysand fear the snake so? Suppose the answer to that question is, A snake stands for or symbolizes a penis. It is easy to see that by itself this is no answer at all; for one thing, it leads immediately to the question, Why does the analysand fear a penis so? The question is about an inexplicable mental phenomenon (i.e., "fearing the snake so") and its answer depends on an entire causal explanation of the kind described above. "A snake stands for or symbolizes a penis" makes sense as an answer only if it is understood as shorthand for a causal explanation of that kind. Similarly, to say that the child stands for or symbolizes the boss is not a satisfactory answer (it does not even sound right) to the question, Why does this father beat his child?

(b) Causal and functional explanations are, given the above account, two different perspectives on, or two different ways of talking about, the same relations between or among events or states of affairs. Explanation in terms of purpose or function (reference is to a means-end schema) should not be contrasted as teleological (i.e., determination by ends) to causal explanation (i.e., determination by antecedents). No *future* state of affairs is required by functional explanation to explain what obtains or occurs in the present. Causal efficacy resides in the representation in the present of possible future states of affairs; in a present image of, orientation to, or anticipation of a possible future state of affairs; in a present desire or wish that an imagined state of affairs obtain in the actual world; in a present intention to make that imagined state of affairs happen; in a present plan for bringing that imagined state of affairs into being, a plan that is based on beliefs about means-ends relations.

An unconscious image of an end state of affairs modeled on past memories of the gratification associated with that kind of state of affairs can dominate psychological life, even in the absence of conscious intentions to make such a state of affairs happen. The subject repeatedly imagines that kind of state of affairs, acts to bring it about, interprets whatever he perceives as that kind of state of affairs, and then acts and responds in terms of this interpretation. The image is endowed with the power to compel the subject to repeat over and over again his attempt to resurrect that kind of state of affairs.

(c) Empirical generalizations describing statistical associations or correlations entail and therefore may be used to "explain" or predict singular facts. They are also themselves facts the scientist wishes to explain. To do so, he has recourse to causal mechanisms. In the absence of an explanation that spells out a causal mechanism, an empirical generalization remains a description of an accidental relation, rather than, for example, a scientific law.

Causal explanation (e.g., as explicated by Harre, 1970) traces how one event or state of affairs leads to, produces, or generates another. To elaborate such explanations, a scientist may call on a regress of causes and effects—for example, may identify an antecedent event or state of affairs as an even more remote cause, or interpolate between any cause and effect of interest other cause-and-effect links that constitute steps from the one to the other.

Causal explanation may also make use of a move from whole to part or from part to whole. How the parts or constituents of a kind of enduring structure are organized or relate to each other, and what properties such constituents have (usually different from properties the structure itself has), may be shown to produce or generate facts about such structures. Conversely, facts about a structure may be shown to result from, or involve, responses by the structure to causally relevant events or states of affairs in its situation; situation and structure, then, form the larger whole of which the structure itself is a part.

So, physicists explain macro-characteristics of physical objects (e.g., temperature, the change from water to ice) in terms of the properties of and relations among micro-constituents of such objects. Freud explains psychological phenomena as the result of both the properties of and relations among intrapsychic constituents (e.g., wishes and beliefs) of a psychological system and the impact of that system's relations with situational objects (including its own body). Talcott Parsons explains sociological phenomena as the result of the interaction between internal relations (inputs and outputs) among the subsystems of a social system and that system's external relations to conditions, resources, and obstacles, in its situation.

Freud wishes to account for the properties of mental phenomena, including why they should have such and such contents, by causes that are also mental. The mental phenomenon that does not make sense is both caused by and is the realization of a set of relations among hypothetical (i.e., unconscious) psychological entities or intentional states, which do make sense, somewhat as the properties of water or ice both are caused by and are the realization of the movement of molecules under different conditions of volume and pressure—molecules that have properties unlike those of water or ice.

A major contribution of psychoanalytic theory is not to rest content with empirically observable properties or regularities (co-occurrence or covariation) but to spell out the mechanisms by which the properties of and relations among a set of psychological entities or intentional states cause (make happen, produce, generate) and are realized by a phenomenon with somewhat different properties than they have. A single case study is often used to spell out causal mechanisms; this is a particularly important feature of Freud's case studies. What is called a psychoanalytic narrative by some is in part at least an effort to explicate causal mechanisms, to show how one kind of state of affairs or event can lead to, produce, or generate another, or how relations among constituent entities can cause or be realized by the properties of a certain kind of structure.

COMPLEXITY AND UNIQUENESS

The case study captures the subject completely, presents the subject vividly, matches with fidelity the complexity of the subject, and preserves what is unique about the subject—in a way that no objective-quantitative study can.

But scientists do not presume to capture "all the phenomena." They seek to study a specified domain or domains, constituted by certain kinds of elements, which are characterized in certain ways. An interest in vivid presentations more often than not disguises a reliance on rhetorical persuasion as a strategy for compelling belief in place of logical argument about the relation of hypothesis and evidence. An emphasis on complexity more often than not disguises a shrinking from the necessary work of abstracting out aspects of reality—properties of interest (ultimately variables)—in order to investigate just the relations between or among these. Discouraging talk of countless variables (and the different kinds of relations, and the possibly very complicated network of relations, between or among them) is no substitute for beginning to specify what these variables are and to map their interrelations.

Those who emphasize the *complexity of psychological phenomena* perhaps appreciate too little the complexities of physical phenomena. We may say, for example, that such an event as striking a match causes such an event as fire. A moment's reflection reveals the complexities here. Such necessary conditions as the presence of oxygen, and the dryness of the match and of the surface against which it is struck, must be distinguished from causes. A cause makes the difference; it makes something happen. The necessary conditions contribute to the production or generation of the effect, but they cannot by themselves cause it.

The concept *cause* implies a capacity or power to produce, bring about, make happen, or generate, and also implies a causal mechanism, which explicates the nature of this capacity or power. But a great many things are, if not causes, *causally relevant*. Anything is causally relevant if it makes a difference. A kind of event or state of affairs is causally relevant—even if it cannot be shown to or does not determine an effect (i.e., bring it about without exception)—if it increases the probability of that effect from what the probability of it would be in the absence of that kind of event or state of affairs. (A kind of event or state of affairs can also be causally relevant, but in a negative sense, if it decreases its probability.) Causally relevant events or states or affairs may not have the power or capacity to produce or generate an effect, even if they are necessary conditions without which the effect will not occur. These necessary conditions are often part of, or used by, a postulated causal mechanism; without them, therefore, a cause cannot produce its other-wise expectable effect.

In psychoanalysis, Freud distinguishes not only between dispositions or propensities (e.g., fixations), favoring circumstances (e.g., fatigue or debility), instigating causes (frustration and regression), and essential causes (unconscious conflict), but also between the mental cause of a mental phenomenon such as a dream (e.g., its motive force) and the sources of the manifest contents of that dream (recent indifferent impressions, somatic stimuli, symbols), those materials that are made use of in generating the dream but that themselves do not have the power to cause it.

Concentration and abstraction, and in this sense a simplification of the phenomenal world, are essential to science. No scientific theory ever seeks to explain everything there is to be explained. That would be impossible. No set of hypotheses can encompass all properties, for some of these belong to different kinds of elements and are at different levels of analysis. Unfocused indiscriminate impressionability, passive pro-miscuous immersion in phenomena, in and by themselves cannot bring forth scientific thought. No one can advance scientific knowledge who bemoans that dissecting out certain features of a person (or a cell, for that matter) is destructive to its complexity, or that no person (or cell), event, state of affairs, or structure is exactly like any other (which, of course, is always true). Striving to get it all, to get more and more of it, not to miss anything, as if the more phenomena, the more truth, to capture the look as well as the physics of the rainbow, are not so much anti-scientific as in many ways just beside the point for scientific work.

Discussions of the *uniqueness of the individual* more often than not miss the point that scientists are interested in relations—ultimately, relations between or among variables. Every statement about relations between or among kinds of states of affairs, properties, or amounts of properties is a generalization over a set of instances in each one of which values of different variables coincide. The set of instances may be generated by a group of persons, each instance by a different person. In the case study of a person, the set of instances are generated by that one person; each instance, for example, is a different exemplar of a kind of mental phenomenon or performance produced by that person, or is a different time-slice of that person. The phrase "individualizing or idiographic versus generalizing or nomothetic science" marks a pseudo-issue, as Holt (1962) has decisively and devastatingly argued. I add only the following to his discussion.

The same kind of reasoning about hypothesis and evidence may be used in studying a domain whose elements are collectives (societies, organizations, groups, or families); a domain whose elements are persons; a domain whose elements are cultural objects (books, movies, games or athletic contests); or a domain whose elements are physical objects. A single person, a single cultural object, or a single society, organization, group, or family, each with its distinctive elements and their properties, may each constitute a domain that is the subject of a single case study. We may study the interpersonal transactions or interactions bounded by a particular single collective; or the intrapersonal events or entities bounded by a particular single person—the perceptions, beliefs, memories, feelings, wishes, dreams, symptoms, dysfunctional performances, or achievements of, or objects produced or occasions occupied by that person.

In each kind of domain, a limited set of properties of the elements of the domain and the relations between or among these properties is what is of interest. Each element, generated by the single case regarded as a domain of such elements, together with the property or properties the element exemplifies, is the focus of a potential act of observation. The methods of making and recording observations, and the mode of reasoning about the relation between hypotheses and the evidence provided by such observations, are not fundamentally different in the study of an intrapersonal domain from those used in the study of a population of persons. In both, for example, groups of elements allocated to different conditions, or samples of different kinds of elements, may be compared. In both, each element observed instantiates a particular value of every variable of interest.

A hypothesis is always a hypothesis about a particular domain. The question raised when a hypothesis is tested is whether it, rather than some rival hypothesis, can be provisionally accepted as true about that domain. One may also raise a question about the scope of a hypothesis. Different arguments about the relation of hypothesis and evidence are required, depending on whether the question is about the truth of a hypothesis about a particular case (e.g., Does a postulated relation hold for a particular subject?) or the question is about generalizability (e.g., Under how many conditions to which the subject is exposed or for how many such subjects does the postulated relation hold?).

Statements asserting that certain relations between particular concepts or variables hold for a single case, that in a single case one kind of state of affairs is causally relevant in bringing about another kind of state of affairs, or merely that a single case has a certain kind of property, are just as much hypotheses as statements making similar claims about populations of such cases. Indeed, contrary to an attitude sometimes apparent in critics of case studies, it is not necessarily a trivial achievement to provide evidence making a causal hypothesis about a single case scientifically credible, even if it is not also possible to provide evidence from a study of the case that would justify generalizing the same hypothesis to other cases. (A series of cases, however, might provide evidence justifying such generalization.)

THE CASE STUDY AS A SCIENTIFIC ARGUMENT

It is pernicious to relegate case studies to the context of discovery, for it discourages rigorous argument about the relation of hypothesis and evidence in such studies. My impression is that, in fact, in most case studies that have had an impact on the scientific community, there is a challenge, even if it is latent, to at least one rival set of concepts and hypotheses—a challenge that indeed motivates the case study. There is also an argument, however informal, that the data of the case study give greater support to the challenging than to the challenged set of hypotheses. The scientific value of such a case study ultimately depends upon the adequacy of that argument.

Such an argument usually presupposes that the author of a case study is able convincingly to provide warrant for the following assertions.

(a) He can reliably identify instances of nontheoretical states of affairs. Consider Luborsky's painstaking explication of criteria (1967) for deciding whether what is reported is to count as an instance of momentary forgetting, or Freud's discussion (1900) of what shall count as a dream.

(b) He can make such an identification without using—or depending upon procedures, instruments, or tests which presuppose the truth of—the test hypothesis he is proposing, or any other hypothesis that entails or follows from that test hypothesis. Consider the background theoretical knowledge, which is not being tested, that is presupposed by the use of a thermometer, a microscope, or free association in obtaining the facts that are to serve as evidence for hypotheses that themselves do not depend in any way on this background theoretical knowledge. (For a discussion of what is presupposed by the method of free association, see Edelson, 1984.)

The contribution of the case study to scientific work is increasingly held to be both limited and minimal (e.g., Kazdin, 1980, especially pp. 9-32). The prevalence of two arguments especially about the relation of hypothesis and evidence in such studies has done much to discredit them. These two arguments should not be used. One argument is that an empirical instance of a hypothesis, which follows logically from it, confirms the hypothesis, and that is sufficient to enhance its scientific credibility. Indeed, the argument, implicit if not explicit, is that the greater the number of positive instances of a hypothesis obtained, the more credible the hypothesis. Another equally dubitable argument concludes from the mere concomitancy of two states of affairs, events, or processes reported in a case study that one is the cause of, or causally relevant in the production of, the other.

What arguments, then, can and should an author of a case study use? In general, a case study shall be considered to provide some support for a test hypothesis—to make it to some extent scientifically credible—only if the author of the case study argues and is justified in arguing that all three of these assertions about it are true.

(1) The test hypothesis has the power to explain the kind of observations made and reported in this case study, and some rival hypothesis does not. The observations are predictable or expectable if the test hypothesis is true, but are not predictable or expectable if the rival hypothesis be true instead.
(2) In this case study, the test hypothesis ran a real risk of being rejected in favor of that rival hypothesis.
(3) The test hypothesis accounts better than some alternative hypotheses for the fact that the observations apparently favoring it were obtained by the author of the case study.

It is my thesis that arguments such as the following about the relation between hypothesis and evidence can and should be used when the data are obtained by case study (or, generally, by clinical methods in social science) just as much as when they are obtained by experimental or objective-quantitative methods. (For a discussion of the contributions of Platt, Hacking, Popper, Campbell and Stanley, and Glymour to the formulation of one or another of these arguments, see Edelson, 1984.)

Indeed, if it were not possible to make these arguments when the data are obtained by case study, much of my objection to what I have called pernicious epistemological justifications of the case study would lose its cogency.

EXPLANATORY POWER AND THE VANQUISHED-RIVAL ARGUMENT

Authors of case studies should not, as they often do, confuse explanatory power and scientific credibility. Explanatory power is necessary, but it is not sufficient, to establish credibility. Von Eckhardt (1982) makes the distinction clear and claims (incorrectly, I believe) that Freud in his case studies ignored it to the detriment of the scientific value of these studies. The argument "because data statements confirm a hypothesis (i.e., follow logically from it), the hypothesis is scientifically credible" is, as has been previously pointed out, an unacceptable argument.

Even if an author of a case study should succeed in arguing conclusively that his hypothesis "explains" (i.e., entails) his data, it does not, if he wishes also to argue for its scientific credibility, absolve him from the responsibility to test it in his case study. He tests it both by exposing it to at least some risk of rejection and by pitting it against rival and alternative hypotheses. Any attempt of this kind on his part, limited though it may be, will do much more than mere submission of a record of confirming instances of the hypothesis to convince a reader that the hypothesis is to some degree worthy of provisional belief and to inspire a reader to want, and perhaps even to carry out, additional tests.

What is especially important is presentation of some version of the vanquished-rival argument. The author of the case study shows that given the evidence, his hypothesis is more credible than one or more of its rivals. The rival hypothesis, which is held or entertained prior to the attempt to obtain evidence to support the test hypothesis, expresses a belief about the domain of interest different from that expressed by the test hypothesis. The author of a case study may argue that

(a) the rival hypothesis entails that a particular event or outcome, the occurrence of which is consistent with or deducible from the test hypothesis, will not occur, and so that it did occur favors the test hypothesis over the rival hypothesis;

(b) the rival hypothesis entails that a particular event or outcome, the occurrence of which is either likely, probable, or expectable given the truth of the hypothesis, is rare, improbable, or unexpected given the the truth of the rival hypothesis, and so its occurrence favors the test hypothesis over the rival hypothesis; or

(c) the rival hypothesis does not entail that a particular event or outcome will occur or will not occur (it has nothing to say about such an event or outcome), while the test hypothesis entails that the event or outcome will occur and so that it did occur favors the test hypothesis over the rival hypothesis.

An important subspecies of the vanquished-rival argument is the Bayesian probabilistic impact-of-new-information argument. The author of a case study may argue that the way in which new information, obtained in a study, changes both the prior probability attached to the proposition that a test hypothesis is true, and the prior probability attached to the proposition that a rival hypothesis is true, favors the test over the rival hypothesis. (Prior probabilities are based on information available before the study.) In other words, given new information, posterior probabilities are now attached to the two propositions and these posterior probabilities favor the test over the rival hypothesis. This argument is implicit in much clinical reasoning, including that which goes into working out a differential diagnosis, or deciding upon, or changing, a patient's diagnosis, given new information about the patient. (Note that this argument does not involve simply the different probabilities some event or outcome has under different hypotheses, as in the vanquished-rival argument [b above] but rather the probabilities attached to hypotheses themselves.)

THE RISKY-PREDICTION ARGUMENT

Suppose that the failure of a particular event or outcome to occur under conditions of investigation would be held to favor a rival hypothesis over a test hypothesis. Suppose that, given prior background knowledge, the probability that the particular event or outcome under conditions of investigation will indeed fail to occur is very high. To predict, then, nevertheless, that under conditions of investigation the particular event or outcome will in fact occur because the test hypothesis is true is to subject the test hypothesis to a correspondingly very great risk of rejection. If, therefore, the particular event or outcome subsequently under conditions of investigation does indeed occur, its occurrence provides correspondingly very strong support for the test hypothesis.

It is important, if an author of a case study is to be able to make this argument, for him to anticipate and identify with the critical skepticism his hypothesis will inevitably encounter by subjecting it to a real risk of rejection. If the cards are not to be stacked in favor of his hypothesis, he must choose a particular case or obtain observations in studying that case in a way that makes rejection of the hypothesis not only possible but indeed more probable than acceptance of it.

Any wish to accept a hypothesis must be checked by making it difficult to accept it, by setting it up to be rejected. The author of a case study will, therefore, specify which observations, if he had obtained them, would have led him to reject his hypothesis—and how he proceeded in such a way that just these observations not only might have occurred but (though they did not occur) were very likely to have occurred. He will show that he avoided particular steps that might have prevented their occurrence and in fact took particular steps to increase the likelihood that, if they could be obtained, they would be obtained.

Any one of the following arguments may be used to justify a claim that the hypothesis in a particular case study survived a real risk of rejection: (1) the least likely case argument; (2) the rare cause argument; (3) the improbable outcome argument; (4) the convergence argument; and (5) the bootstrap argument.

The least likely case argument. If a hypothesis is a generalization of the kind "all dreams are wish fulfillments," then a counterexample falsifying the hypothesis is "this dream is not a wish fulfillment." A case that might be chosen for study, then, is one involving a dream which appears not to be a wish fulfillment, given existing knowledge (which does not include the test hypothesis).

For example, the dream in the case study is made up of images of misery and pain. On the commonsense background assumption, which at the time of testing the hypothesis is widely accepted, that human beings do not wish for misery and pain, the expectation is that evidence obtained in a study of such a dream will show that the dream is not a wish fulfillment. The choice of this kind of dream for study increases the probability that the test hypothesis will be rejected. If, even so, the evidence obtained does show that the dream is a wish fulfillment, that improbable outcome counts more toward establishing the credibility of the test hypothesis than such an outcome would have counted if the dream chosen for study had been made up of images of joy and pleasure.

Similarly, in testing a hypothesis that all societies are rule governed, a society whose members are apparently all wild and lawless, or a primitive society whose members as children of nature are thought to behave spontaneously, might be chosen for study. Or, in testing a hypothesis that an unconscious conflict involving homosexual impulses is causally necessary to produce a certain kind of psychopathology (e.g., paranoia), a patient who is apparently unconflicted about his homosexual behavior but who is also paranoid might be chosen for study.

The rare cause argument. In testing a causal hypothesis, if the supposed cause of an effect is known to occur relatively rarely in a population, a case study in which these two events co-occur is a more convincing instance of the hypothesis than a case study in which the supposed cause is known to occur relatively frequently in the population.

A hypothesis describes a relationship, for example, between a childhood event, such as the one postulated by Freud in the Rat Man Case (a child is punished by his father for masturbating) and a mental phenomenon in adulthood (e.g., a neurotic symptom). In what follows, assume the frequency of the mental phenomenon in the population remains constant. If the childhood event occurs relatively frequently in the population, then a case that manifests the mental phenomenon is, quite probably, a case in which the childhood event also occurred, even if there is no causal relation between the two. In other words, the probability of obtaining a confirming instance of the hypothesis is relatively high, even if no causal relation between the childhood event and mental phenomenon actually exists.

However, if the childhood event occurs relatively rarely in the population, then a case that manifests the mental phenomenon is, quite probably, a case in which the supposed childhood event did not occur unless the two are causally related. Here the probability of obtaining a negative instance of the hypothesis is relatively high, if the two are not related. When an author of a case study postulates a cause that he knows occurs relatively rarely in a population, he can argue with some justification that he has thereby increased the probability of rejecting his hypothesis and that, therefore, obtaining a positive instance of his hypothesis in his case study counts more toward establishing the credibility of that hypothesis than if he had postulated a relatively frequently occurring cause.

In passing, note here that the report of a rare case of something is to be distinguished from a report in which a rare cause is postulated to explain something. A rare case is one that is known to occur—or that a review of the literature shows to have occurred—very infrequently. Since there is so little opportunity to observe such a case, it may be thought worthwhile just to describe "the facts" in detail, even if the state of knowledge is such that no hypothesis presents itself to account for these facts and no hypothesis's credibility seems undercut by them. Facts, however, are always relative to a choice of elements and ways of characterizing elements and, therefore, presuppose some sort of assumptions about what in the phenomena is worth noting. The scientific value of such a report tends to be overrated, therefore, since it is unlikely that the author will include just those facts that will turn out to be relevant to a consideration of hypotheses that are at some later time of interest.

The improbable outcome argument. The improbable outcome argument may take the form of (a) the unexpected prediction argument; or (b) the precise deduction argument.

The unexpected prediction argument. When an author of a case study makes a prediction, he asserts that a state of affairs has obtained, does obtain, or will obtain, or that an event has occurred, is occurring, or will occur, when in fact he cannot know that the assertion is true. It is not based on direct experience. It does not follow logically from any background knowledge available to him. It does follow logically from the hypothesis he tests by making the prediction. If this hypothesis is true, then his prediction must be or is likely to be successful; if the prediction should turn out to be unsuccessful, then the hypothesis must be or is likely to be false.

The probability that his prediction will turn out to be successful is, given his background knowledge, low indeed. Essentially, then, the author of the case study tests his hypothesis by deducing from it what is, based on established knowledge and excluding the hypothesis in question, an improbable state of affairs or event.

The predicted state of affairs or event will probably not occur. Its failure to occur, which is expected, would suggest rejection of the test hypothesis. Therefore, if this improbable state of affairs or event does occur, the hypothesis has survived a real risk of rejection. This unexpected occurrence, then, counts more toward establishing its credibility than the occurrence of a state of affairs or event observed in the course of studying a case, which also follows from and is therefore explained by the hypothesis but which was not predicted.

That a state of affairs obtains or an event occurs when the author of a case study knows it obtains or occurs is completely probable. He cannot claim that the hypothesis has run any risk of rejection unless he has predicted the state of affairs or event before knowledge of it. What has already been observed in a case study may be regarded, if no existing knowledge accounts for it, as in that sense "unexpected," but it is certainly not improbable in the sense of unlikely to occur. (It has in fact already occurred.) The author of the case study, in referring to such an "unexpected" observation and its relation to his hypothesis, has only demonstrated that this hypothesis has more explanatory power than other hypotheses in the body of knowledge previously available to him. He has not, however, exposed that hypothesis to any risk of rejection.

To do that, he, not knowing an event has occurred or will occur, must predict that given his hypothesis it will occur or has occurred, when existing knowledge leads to the prediction that it is impossible for it to occur (or that it should occur only very, very infrequently).

An "unexpected" observation may simply be one that a case study documents has not been reported before. A case study may be written to record such an unusual observation and to announce what hypothesis the observation has instigated the author to formulate in order to explain it or what hypothesis is called into question by it. The unexpectedness (in the sense just described) of this kind of observation contributes nothing at all to making the intended-to-be-explanatory hypothesis credible, although it may cast real doubt on the credibility of a hypothesis with which such an observation is incompatible.

There is no way to guarantee that an author of a case study will take a critical attitude toward his own hypothesis and will do everything he can to subject it to some risk of rejection. That is one reason that both the possibility of replication and the fact of replication are so important in scientific work. Even when an observation in a case study is described as unexpected because its occurrence when predicted was improbable, a reader cannot be certain that it was actually predicted. An author of such a study may write his story as if he predicted first and observed later, although in fact he observed first and "predicted" later.

Similarly—when multiple independent predictions are made from a hypothesis or a set of hypotheses and no existing knowledge entails that they should be jointly successful, or when a predicted outcome is measured in a variety of ways—an author of a case study may not reveal, or may report but ignore, how many of his predictions in fact did fail; he may report only positive findings. Indeed, any researcher may not calculate, or may calculate but ignore, what proportion of his positive findings would in fact have been expected to have occurred by chance even if his hypothesis were false. Achieving some successful predictions among many unsuccessful ones does not justify rejecting a plausible alternative hypothesis—that the proportion of successful predictions was itself a matter of chance.

Taking a pessimistic view of the capacity of people to be skeptical of their own ideas, one may say that how determined an author of a case study or any research is to be critical of his own hypothesis can be decided ultimately only from the fate of tests of his hypotheses carried out by others. However, since whether an assertion is actually a prediction (in the sense given to that term here) determines in part at least whether a hypothesis has run a risk of rejection, it is important for an author of a case study at a minimum to document that he has in fact made a prediction when that is how he justifies his claim that his hypothesis has run such a risk. He should specify, for example, what he knew and didn't know when he made the prediction, what procedures he followed in making the prediction, and just exactly what prediction he made. Did he predict from one *part* of a session, interview, or psychological test to another; from one *entire* session, interview, or psychological test to another; or from one kind of information to another kind of information? How precise was his prediction? His documentation should show, if true, that he took particular steps to elicit, discover, or search out observations damaging to his hopes, and that the observation he did make was not one that just anyone, without the aid of his hypothesis, could easily have stumbled over.

The precise deduction argument. A hypothesis does not, of course, run much risk of rejection if a prediction from a hypothesis or an observation deducible from and therefore explained by a hypothesis is one of a set of a few grossly discriminated states of affairs or events. Not much of what is possible can be excluded by a prediction or deduction when the possible outcomes an author of a case study specifies are few in number or vaguely discriminated, or both, or if—as frequently happens—he does not even specify the states of affairs or events excluded by his hypothesis, while emphasizing what state of affairs or event follows from it. The freedom from risk of rejection is even more enhanced when the occurrence of any one of a relatively large subset of possible states of affairs or events is considered to be compatible with the truth of the hypothesis.

The degree of risk of rejection a hypothesis runs increases as the degree of precision of a prediction or deduction from that hypothesis increases. The degree of precision of a prediction or deduction increases as the degree of fineness of discrimination of possible outcomes increases. The degree of fineness of discrimination is measured by how many possibilities are discriminated and how free the discrimination is from vagueness. Precision in a case study may depend, for example, upon how detailed the description of conditions is that must be satisfied for a state of affairs or event to be counted—or to fail to be counted—as a positive instance of a hypothesis. Degree of precision also increases with every increase in the size of the subset of possible outcomes that are negative instances of a hypothesis (those inconsistent with it) relative to the size of the subset of possible outcomes that are positive instances of the hypothesis.

The degree of precision of a prediction or deduction from a hypothesis may be used to argue that the hypothesis has indeed run a risk of rejection. The more precision, the greater the risk. The greater the risk, the more severe the test. A hypothesis surviving a more severe test than a comparable rival hypothesis has, other things being equal, more credibility than its rival.

Mathematicization and quantification acquire their value in scientific work both from the lack of vagueness or ambiguity in what is deduced or predicted from a hypothesis and from the enormous range of possible outcomes excluded by a prediction or deduction, both of which ensure that the tested hypothesis runs a high risk of rejection. There is no reason not to try to approximate in a case study achievement of such desiderata: (a) specifying an exhaustive set of mutually exclusive possible outcomes (states of affairs or events), which are discriminated from each other as sharply, with as little vagueness and ambiguity, as possible; (b) making this set of well-discriminated possible outcomes as large as possible; (c) specifying which of these outcomes follow from a hypothesis and which at the least cast doubt upon it; and (d) attempting always as much as possible to make the size of the subset of negative possible outcomes much greater than the size of the subset of positive possible outcomes.

The convergence argument. An author of a case study shows that he can make multiple independent deductions from the same hypothesis. The deductions are independent if and only if (a) the different observations, which are used to arrive at the same conclusion, are obtained from different sources, by different methods, or in different settings or life epochs, or involve different kinds of subject-performances, and when possible are obtained by different unrelated observers; and (b) no available knowledge entails that these different kinds of observations are actually of the same sort (have the same cause) and should coexist. The author may then argue that since each deduction independently has exposed his hypothesis to the possibility of being rejected, he has, by making multiple independent deductions, increased the opportunities for such rejection and therefore the risk the hypothesis has run in the case study.

The improbability of the assumption that the hypothesis is false, given a set of such observations, makes the argument more than merely an argument for the explanatory power of the hypothesis. In arguing about explanatory power, that a vast number of observations follow deductively from a hypothesis is what is emphasized. Here, the emphasis is on different kinds of observations obtained by different and independent routes. In each study or with each different method, different alternative hypotheses, which might have accounted for the data, will be regarded as plausible and may be eliminated. If so, it is more probable that the test hypothesis is true than that (1) the test hypothesis is false, and (2) in each study some different alternative hypothesis, which was not eliminated from consideration, accounts for the occurrence of the event or outcome.

The bootstrap argument. A subset of independent but interrelated hypotheses are jointly supported if they converge upon the same outcome. For example, one hypothesis in conjunction with some data entails the occurrence of an event or outcome (that a variable has a particular value) and another hypothesis in conjunction with some other data entails the occurrence of the same event or outcome (that the variable has that value), and the event or outcome occurs (the variable is observed to have that value). Or, if a variable is theoretical, one hypothesis in conjunction with some data entails that it has a particular value, and another hypothesis in conjunction with this computed value entails the occurrence of an event or outcome (that another variable has a particular value), and the event or outcome occurs (this other variable is observed to have that value). In each instance, it is possible that the expected event or outcome may not occur; then, one hypothesis at least among the subset of hypotheses must be false. The subset of hypotheses runs this risk repeatedly, as each prediction is checked. Glymour (1980) has shown how the author of a case study (Freud, in the Rat Man Case) can carry out such a test of a subset of his hypotheses.

ALTERNATIVE EXPLANATIONS OF THE EVIDENCE

An alternative hypothesis expresses some belief about which factors operating during the process of obtaining data, or operating in the situation in which data are obtained, might have led to the occurrence of an event or outcome held to support a test hypothesis (i.e., what factors might account for the data obtained) even if the test hypothesis were false. Similarly, an alternative hypothesis could express some belief about what factors of this kind might have been responsible for the failure of an event or outcome to occur (when its occurrence would have been held to support a test hypothesis) even if the test hypothesis were true.

If different observations favoring a test hypothesis are obtained in very different ways, in the same case study, in different case studies, or in different kinds of studies, it can be argued that it is improbable that these independent observations should all, or in so vast a proportion of instances, be obtained if the test hypothesis were in fact false. Since the favorable observations were reached by such different routes, in each one of which different alternative explanations were relatively implausible or eliminated, it is not parsimonious to assume that different alternative hypotheses each time—rather than the test hypothesis all through—account for obtaining the observations.

This line of thought leads to the suggestion that the same hypothesis should be tested by carrying out different kinds of studies, including the case study, in each one of which a different alternative explanation for the data cannot be considered to be really plausible or, if plausible, is controlled or eliminated. Replication of a case study with similar subjects—preferably, for example, by different investigators, working in different settings, and perhaps following somewhat different methods, but testing the same hypothesis—can also be convincing on much the same kind of reasoning. The case series for this reason continues to influence clinical practice, despite the disrepute in which the case study is held.

The use of various designs in single case study, which make use, for example, of carefully documented comparisons of phenomena of interest under different conditions over time (including a baseline period of observation), or which enable the investigator to show that the level of some symptom or performance of a subject's is over time consistently higher under one condition than under another, and which eliminate various alternative hypotheses as less plausible than a test hypothesis, are well described in such works about developments in the methodology of single subject research as Barlow, Hayes, and Nelson, 1984; Campbell and Stanley, 1963; Chassan, 1979; Edelson, 1984, especially Chapters 4 and 11; Kazdin, 1982; and Shapiro, 1963. (For additional citations, see Edelson, 1984.) As these works also make clear, it is possible to perform statistical tests in some single case studies in an attempt to reject a particular kind of alternative hypothesis—the null hypothesis that the apparently favorable outcome probably came about as the result of chance or extraneous factors.

Finally, the appropriate, effective use of "historical controls" (e.g., previous clinical experience) or "external controls" (in general, the use of data from other sources to make relevant comparisons in a case study) in order to eliminate alternative hypotheses from consideration are described by Bailar, Louis, Lavori, and Polansky, 1984; Campbell and Stanley, 1963; and Lasagna, 1982.

CONCLUSION

The case study does not necessarily imply deviation from canons of scientific method and reasoning. It should not be relegated to the context of discovery. The case study can be an argument about the relation between hypothesis and evidence. The probative value of a case study (i.e., its ability to test a hypothesis) depends on the validity of the author's use of it to claim that his hypothesis or set of hypotheses has explanatory power, has run some risk of rejection, and is more credible than rival or alternative hypotheses.

The author of a case study should carefully separate facts from hypotheses (inferences, interpretations). He should specify his hypothesis and which outcomes of his study he would consider to be warrant for rejecting that hypothesis. He should present not only evidence supporting a hypothetical causal link, but evidence for the hypothetical mechanism by virtue of which the cause has the power to produce or generate the effect. He should describe one or more rival hypotheses about his subject matter and present an argument for favoring his hypothesis over its rival or rivals. He should describe one or more alternative hypotheses, which would account for his having obtained the evidence he regards as supporting his hypothesis even if his hypothesis were false, and present an argument (even if it is a nondesign argument) for favoring his hypothesis over such alternative hypotheses. He should indicate specifically the way in which the scope of his hypothesis is limited by counterinstances, if he is not prepared to reject his hypothesis because of these counterinstances.

Such a case study would not have to be justified by the claim that considerations of subjectivity, meaning, and complexity and uniqueness required the author to abandon ordinary canons of scientific method and reasoning.

NOTE

1. Throughout this chapter *he* and *his* are used in their generic form unless otherwise specified.

Commentary

A common thread binding the three chapters in this first section is the theme of doubt. The authors encourage us to keep a healthy skepticism in the forefront of our research lives: When we think we have *the* explanation we should entertain the possibility that the conclusions we find compelling may be a consequence of our reactions to the nature of the research topic or the research relationship and might lead us to believe flawed or myopic explanations of the world.

The exhortation to preserve doubt is not an invitation to negativism; it is not a claim that nothing can be known, that reality does not exist, that nihilism is the only logical conclusion to our endeavors. Rather it is a statement of the contention that doubt forms the foundation of good research. Doubt is the precondition to the questioning nature of our work. At the intellectual level it keeps us open to the possibility of alternative explanations. At the emotional level it makes us open to learning about that which runs counter to our instincts or biases. Doubt in research is an affirmation that scrutinizing our selves, the process by which we draw our inferences, and the unconscious dynamics operative beneath our manifest actions are the hallmarks of a complete research method.

In all three chapters there is a recognition that research is a process that is deeply involving. It cannot be undertaken in any mechanistic way. It puts methodological and personal demands on the researcher. The theme of involvement is the cornerstone of Section III of this book but it is evident that even as the introductory ground is covered, involvement surfaces as a powerful issue.

We are all aware that the research process is demanding. Our methods courses teach us a great deal about these demands. None of us, however, is really prepared for the overwhelming demands that result from the unconscious material Alderfer's chapter addresses. It is easy to think of the unconscious as a source of bias, a contaminating force that interferes with the purity of our rational processes. Most research perspectives take the view that unconscious dynamics are error to be minimized. Alderfer argues that unconscious dynamics are always present and play a powerful role in the creation of data and theory. The quality of this creative force will depend on how we are able to treat the unconscious material. Nurture it, explore it, give it legitimacy, and it may become one of the researcher's greatest allies. Invalidate it, ignore it, or legislate it out of our work and it may well become a serious detractor.

Alderfer suggests that the unconscious material with which we all must struggle may derive from a variety of sources. Our upbringing, the roles we played (or are playing) in our families, the historical context in which we live, our professional training, our locations in social hierarchies, the culture (or cultures) to which we belong, and the symbols out of which our realities are constructed all mix to give us unconscious lives that contain individual, institutional, and collective dimensions. By granting legitimacy to these "invisible" sides, the split between the self and scientist lessens and we are able to draw on a much broader array of data to inform our understanding. The manifest becomes understood in relation to the latent just as the lines of tension beneath the surface are understood in relation to the deep structure of Picasso's *Bull*.

Edelson's chapter begins where the Alderfer argument leaves off. Once this additional information is made clearer, he asks, What do we do with it? Edelson argues that it should be treated like all other evidence. Simply that it is unconscious, emotional, or relational information does not excuse if from rigorous rules of inference. He does not subscribe to the often held view that traditional science is irrelevant to data not represented in physical forms. He affirms that the investigator who would draw lines of any kind, even in single case research, must be able to specify the rules of operation by which the categories are created and the links made. These must be contrasted with other categories and links created by similar rules or with explanations that might result from alternative rules of operation. Edelson is strong in his claim that what we view as knowledge should be built upon hypotheses and evidence that have been subjected to the canons of science.

The clinical side of research methods is often labeled "soft" in contrast to the tight experimental and statistical procedures regularly characterized as "hard." In the opening section of this book the authors make clear that the clinical side requires hard and disciplined work. The nature of the work cannot be routinized quite like experimental methods, making it difficult, not soft. This section puts the issue of rigor in clinical research squarely in front of us. In some ways it is a "call to arms." For those who lay claim to the term "clinical" but ignore the hard work, this is a reminder that there are standards in clinical work and that clinical research skills bring with them obligations that should not be compromised. For those who would grossly misrepresent the clinical as idiosyncratic whim, this section seeks to educate and to warn: This level of dismissal is destructive and runs the risk of creating divisions that endanger our science and our profession. For those dedicated to serious clinical scrutiny, this section is a statement of what guides the clinical dimensions of our work.

Clinical Understanding

The question in this section is not primarily *what* we know but *how* we know about the social world. Each of the five chapters that follow examines some of the factors that influence how we understand human behavior. These factors are always present, always shaping what we notice, what we choose to ignore, our criteria, and our concepts. A clinical method seeks to understand these influences in pursuit of an epistemology, a theory of knowing, that describes the many different ways by which the social world is known.

Using the concept of "action usable knowledge," Cammann explores the implications for research of adopting "usefulness" as a criterion for social science knowledge. He makes clear that the way we learn about social systems and, consequently, what we are likely to understand about them are very dependent on why we want to know. Smith's chapter complements Cammann's with its analysis of the influence of context on meaning. Smith urges us to consider the contextual issues we often overlook as we attribute meaning to events and he offers suggestions on how to broaden our field of vision to include both figure and ground. Together these two chapters send us off into a sea of alternative ways of understanding social reality.

The third and fourth chapters, by Perry and Reinharz, respectively, examine the cultural, political, and sexual influences on how we think about human behavior and social institutions. Perry's chapter views ideas as cultural products and shows, for example, how the meaning and complexity of a concept such as color are powerfully influenced by cultural socialization. He takes the issue further by illustrating how all knowledge carries with it the cultural and political values of the society that spawns it. Reinharz, in a feminist critique of sociological theory, painstakingly examines the ways in which sexist and racist nonconscious ideologies are manifest in the sociological literature. In her analysis of a number of prominent sociological texts, Reinharz points out that the sociological establishment's unwillingness to systematically mistrust *how* it came to know the social world created serious and destructive distortions. Her chapter urges social scientists to scrutinize cultural and political influences on their methods of knowing.

Finally, Lowman's chapter offers some thoughts on a clinical way of knowing, differentiating it from nonclinical approaches. His chapter includes a description of the skills, knowledge, and attributes of the clinical researcher—

the prerequisites for clinical understanding. Lowman examines the person and the training behind clinical knowledge.

How do we understand the core issues in people's lives? There appear to be many ways, just as there are many ways to know a sunset. Any epistemology must come to understand the many ways of knowing and the many influences on knowing if it hopes to aid researchers in learning about the social world. Each of the chapters in this section takes us a step toward developing such an epistemology.

CHAPTER
4

ACTION USABLE KNOWLEDGE

Cortlandt Cammann

For more than ten years now, I have been working as an agent of change in organizations. During that period, I have done a lot of learning, often painfully, about what it takes to be successful in helping organizations to change. There is still much that I do not know, but one conclusion that I have drawn is that there are a number of forms of knowledge that are helpful to people who are trying to create organizational change that are not of central focus in many graduate programs in organizational behavior or organizational development. My purpose in writing this chapter is to describe the areas of knowledge that I believe can help people who want to conduct change, in hopes that these areas will become legitimate domains for teaching and research in the future. I do not intend to argue against traditional theory and research. These are very useful for people who want to understand organizations. They are not, however, complete. Conducting change work requires knowledge that has less academic acceptance, and approaches to using knowledge that vary somewhat from the orientations that are often taught in graduate schools. Collecting information that is scientifically acceptable, for example, requires following a variety of procedures that are often not feasible within organizational settings. Change agents have no less requirement for valid information about organizations they are working in than do scientists, but they need to be able to collect the

AUTHOR'S NOTE: I cannot acknowledge all of the people whose ideas have influenced the ideas presented in this chapter. A broad range of literature has influenced my thought, although the works of Clay Alderfer, Chris Argyris, and Ed Lawler have been particularly important. Colleagues like David Berg, Lee Ozley, Stanley Seashore, and Debbie Tracey have done much to shape my thinking, and clients have continually been a source of ideas. The editors of this volume provided much valued help in sorting through my ideas. While the ideas here are my responsibility alone, I appreciate the many ideas and critiques that have shaped my thoughts.

109

information whether they can use scientific data collection procedures or not. Consequently, change agents need to develop less scientific—but still valid—ways of understanding the way an organization works.

In the sections that follow, I will describe some of the key elements of knowledge that are useful to people who are trying to act in actual time settings to create change.

KNOWLEDGE OF NORMATIVE MODELS AND VISIONS

Throughout my student career, I learned that the scientific approach is based on impartiality. As a scientist, one is supposed to look at problems dispassionately, consider all options, and design empirical ways to test one option for explaining a phenomenon against another. Of course, there was always the reality of science, which did not match this ideal too closely, but the logical, empirical approach was clearly the ideal. As I began to work with organizations in creating change, I came to realize that this value helps little in the world of change.

The scientific problem of accurately describing a phenomenon and the way it works can be idealized as a rational process. Organizational change, however, is not a rational process and rational models do not seem to be the most useful ones for guiding its creation. It is rare to find people in organizational settings who are willing to "rationally" experiment with options to find out which one is "best" so that a change can be made in the "most favorable" direction. Power, politics, personal viewpoints, distrust of rational arguments, and individual interests all make such approaches untenable. Imagine, for example, the likelihood that the scientists in a university community would do an experiment to test the true value of the tenure system by randomly assigning a group of full professors at a selected set of universities to the tenured and nontenured conditions to test the results.

I also found that I could not comfortably take the role of disinterested scientist in doing change work. I could not easily help an organization do something that I personally did not believe would be successful or that would hurt the quality of work life of the people who worked in the organization. While not a dispassionate view, I hoped that my work would make a difference in the way people would experience their organizational lives. I knew that I would make mistakes and that all change runs the risk of leaving some people feeling worse off, but I could only work comfortably if I felt that the directions were, as best I could tell, positive ones according to the belief system that I hold.

Consequently, I concluded that I could not view my work as an agent of change as being purely experimental. I was engaged in a process of trying to create worlds that I felt were valuable both in order to learn how to do it and to see if they were viable improvements as I believed. As I came to these conclusions, I discovered two interesting things. The first, ironically, was that "scientific" findings did in fact facilitate organizational change. There were times when I or people that I was working with would present a theory in some area such as job design, and the people in the organization would say, "Let's do it." They were not doing it for rational reasons, however. They rarely inquired about the nature of the evidence for the theory, and never asked what competing theories there were. They wanted to act because they saw the theory as a clear direction that had been proven by science and proposed by experts. In many cases changes made in this way were viewed as successful since the people who were involved became convinced that the change represented a better way to do their work. When they made the change they found that their prophecy was right. Whether an independent evaluator would agree was often a mute point.

The second thing I learned was that the clearer I was about my own values and the type of world I wanted to create, the more effective I could be as an agent of change. It made it easier for me to figure out how I wanted to act as I moved from situation to situation and dealt with the inevitable, unexpected problems that develop when a change is underway. It made it easier to communicate effectively my own vision of a better future so that organizations could decide whether they wanted to work with me. And it made it easier for me to help organization members develop their own vision of the future so that they could figure out how to design changes that would help them get there.

Together these learnings led me to the conclusion that normative models are an essential ingredient in the process of change. Organizational change is an uncertain activity in which neither the change agent nor the people in the organization can control all the forces that will influence the change that occurs. A downturn in the organization's marketplace, a change in key leadership positions, a new technology developed by a competitor, a tornado, and other unforeseen events can disturb efforts at planned change. Further, organizations are maintained by a complex set of interdependent forces, and any set of changes will create secondary reactions that will disturb the change process and alter the intended results. Consequently, change is unlikely to be created successfully by any planned sequence of activities. Rather, it requires an image of the result that is desired, and people who can invent activities as necessary to bring the result about. Normative models of organizational functioning play an essential role in helping people develop and share the image of the organization that they wish to create.

INFLUENCE

A second problem that I rapidly discovered was that theories of organizational dynamics described what I would see in organizations, but did not help me figure out what I should do to change them. To create change it was not enough to know what had to change; I also needed to know how to influence people to make the change.

INFLUENCING INDIVIDUALS

One of the first areas I needed to understand was how to influence individuals. All stages in a change process, from the creation of a vision to the alteration of specific behaviors and systems, require people to change, and one of the essential jobs of a change agent is to help them change in constructive ways.

In many cases, influencing the people I worked with was not too difficult. They often shared my basic values and beliefs: Individual development is good; people should have as positive a work experience as possible; things can be accomplished more effectively by having people cooperate together; and doing things well is preferable to doing them poorly. In these cases, exercising influence inolved helping people see that there were ways to accomplish these objectives that were more effective than the ones that they were using. Generally speaking, if it were possible to create the conditions where these individuals were not being punished for changing, the process of influence involved getting them to focus on the values they held and to find ways of realizing their goals. At this point, I think our field is developing better and better theories for explaining and guiding this type of influence process. This type of knowledge is very important for people who are trying to help others change.

There were other situations that I found much more difficult. There were people who resisted changes because they did not understand them, because they felt it would be harmful rather than helpful to the organization, because they expected to be disadvantaged by it, or because they preferred stability to uncertainty. Often these individuals could be left alone and allowed to watch the change to see if they could become more comfortable with it. Equally often, however, resistant individuals occupied critical positions; if they did not support the change, it would have been hampered.

Over time, I have helped organizations use a variety of strategies to influence individuals in these situations. These have included the use of organizational rewards and punishments ("you will be fired if you don't change"), the use of authority ("changing is one of your key job objectives"), personnel movement (put the person in a job that isn't critical so that they won't block the change), education (send them to a T-group), exposure to other situations where the change has worked (send key managers to other similar organizations to talk to people who made the changes successfully), and so forth. Each time the decision of what to do has involved struggling with the dilemma of trying to influence the people without using an influence process that is contrary to the values and directions of the change being made. Sometimes the attempts have been successful, other times they have failed. I know of change situations where people who were not able to manage in participative ways were moved out of key positions autocratically, which then undermined the credibility of the change effort. In other cases, the same actions have been seen as an indication that the management of the organization was serious about participation.

Understanding how to influence people who resist change is one of the most difficult tasks facing someone trying to help organizations develop. It is not an area that our current theory explores in much detail, and represents a domain where we need to understand better both the knowledge and the skill that is involved if we are going to help people learn to act more effectively as agents of change.

INFLUENCING PROCESSES

In addition to learning how to influence individuals, I found that acting as an agent of change involved being able to influence the process by which things got done in the organizations I was working with. I often found myself in situations where I knew what should be done, but the flow of action and interaction made it impossible for me to get it done. I found myself in meetings where people would not listen to each other and critical information was not being shared. I watched groups fighting without ever identifying the problems they were fighting about. I watched individuals carefully manipulate the flow of conversation so that decisions they opposed would never be made. I watched people make decisions without considering what appeared to be obvious and better alternatives, and groups founder in ways that led them to conclude that working together was inefficient and impossible. In all of these situations I found that the flow of events was overwhelming my ability to create change, and that I needed to learn how to influence the process if I were going to produce a useful result.

For example, in dealing with Union-Management Quality of Work-life projects, the leaders on both sides often have opinions, feelings, and assumptions about the other side that need to be expressed or they will continue to influence the perception of events and the nature of reactions. Yet, if this does not happen at an appropriate time and in an appropriate context, the sharing of information can create anger and reinforce the adversarial nature of the relationship. I needed to find ways of identifying the right time for this type of sharing, and to learn ways to help the people involved do it successfully.

Similarly, reward, budget, and management systems often put managers in a position that makes it difficult for them to allow change. Unless these issues are addressed relatively early, it can be fruitless to attempt too much floor-level change. I needed to understand the appropriate sequencing of change attempts to enable people to make the necessary changes. Then, I needed to learn how to develop contracts and planning mechanisms so that appropriate sequences could be developed.

Finally, managers in organizations develop their own style of exercising influence. Once they develop an image of a change they would like to create, they are likely to use their previously developed skills of influencing others to make the change happen. This can create a problem if their previous style is autocratic and manipulative and the change objective is to create increased participation and openness. I found that I was often frustrated because key managers who were working to create a change would frustrate themselves by the way they tried to influence others to make the changes come about. Ordering subordinates to be participative was generally not the most effective way to get participation implemented, particularly when the subordinates had no more idea about what being participative was than did the manager. I needed to learn how to help other people exercise influence in a different way than they had in the past. This involved helping them find different mechanisms (e.g., groups), different approaches (e.g., problem solving), and different personal styles (e.g., listening) so that they could exercise influence in a manner that was congruent with the type of organization that they were trying to develop.

The ability to influence the processes by which things are done in an organization is an important skill for people who work as agents of change. People in our field know a great deal about the different types of processes that exist and the effects of using them, but this knowledge needs to be better integrated into our teaching programs and needs to be taught as skills to be learned, not just as knowledge to be acquired.

INFLUENCING SYMBOLS AND PRINCIPLES

Finally, I learned that I needed to understand how to influence the symbols and principles that guide the activities of organizations if I wanted to have a significant effect. I found that creating change in a large organization could be a lot like trying to shape a balloon. I could help a group learn to solve problems effectively, only to have the membership change. I could help set up a cooperative union-management group, only to have union-management tensions from other areas erode the cooperation in the group. I could help one group of managers learn to work in a participative manner, only to find that none of the people they worked with were changing and that eventually they went back to their old approaches because it was easier. The basic problem was that each change activity had the potential of becoming an isolated event that was disconnected from the mainstream of the organization. Unless there was a way to integrate different change activities and give them a coherent thrust, they ran the risk of becoming isolated ineffectual activities.

In part the solution to this problem was to influence key individuals and key organizational processes so that the change activities were central to the functioning of the organization. I have found, however, that this is not enough. The changes need to be reinforced by symbols and principles that are communicated and meaningful for all of the people in the organization. These symbols and principles become a map that people in the organization can use to make sense out of change activities and to see their centrality for the organization. They are the vehicle for helping people to realize that isolated change activities are part of a pattern of change that will not go away; they give shape to the balloon.

While I am convinced that influencing symbols and principles is a critical task for people conducting organizational change, I do not think we know enough about how this can be done. Symbols can be powerful, but we need to learn a lot more about their use and effects so that they can be used more effectively as tools in creating change.

KNOWLEDGE THAT LINKS THEORY AND ACTION

Another discovery that I made early in my consulting work was that having a theory that helped me to understand was not necessarily the same as having knowledge that could guide my action. I can vividly remember sitting in meetings where I was trying to understand the group dynamics so that I could help the group develop. There was a period of time where I would have to sit down after the meeting to figure out what was going on and what I could do about it. Then there was a period of time when I could figure out what was going on while I was watching the group, but still needed to sit down and think about it before I could figure out what to do. The most frustrating period came next. I could see what was going on, and I could figure out what I should do to influence it, but the lag time was a few minutes and by the time I figured it out it was too late. Finally, I reached the point where I could understand what was happening and be able to act appropriately almost without thought.

From the perspective of an agent of change, knowledge is not helpful unless it can be turned into action. This action can take many forms, but for people who are trying to develop organizations, it means that the knowledge must help them move from the perception of events to a plan of action to the execution of the plan within very short time frames (often minutes or seconds), and under circumstances that are not conducive to reflection. It is one thing to be able to plan a change strategy in the quiet of your office, and another to try to figure out how to move it forward in the middle of a meeting where representatives from sales and manufacturing are yelling angrily at each other about who is at fault for the fact that there will not be enough business in the next six months for the plant to survive.

There are two characteristics of knowledge that seem to make it useful as a basis for action. First, knowledge is more useful when it encompasses a whole action sequence. Frequently, knowledge is passed on in a symbolic form through writing or discussion. Consequently, it results in understanding that fits a pattern, but is not linked closely to reality or action. For example, we read an article that says participation in planning changes can be helpful in creating effective implementation and includes research to justify the claim. This article is convincing, so the next time we are involved in creating change we try to do it in a participative way. As a result, we learn that there are a few things that the article did not cover. It did not provide enough description of the context so that you could recognize the organizational conditions under which participation will work; it didn't give guidelines for figuring out who should participate when dealing with anything more complex than a few work groups; it didn't help identify the characteristics of people who will resist the participation or for whom a participative approach might not be appropriate; it did not provide guidelines on how to hold a successful participative meeting (or even suggest that this might be an issue); it didn't describe how you would feel when a meeting you were leading began to deteriorate, or how to react constructively; and it did not indicate that acting participatively requires certain skills on the part of the change agent.

Useful knowledge helps the change agent predict how events are likely to unfold following specific actions; what roles and activities are going to be required; how being in the flow of action will feel; what emotional, political, developmental, and rational dynamics are likely to be triggered and how they can be managed; and how each sequence of intervention activities will fit into the broader pattern of organizational transformation that is under way. Personally, I find theories and models to be the most useful when they are linked to cases that illustrate their application, when they include descriptions from the view of people trying to use them to create change, and when I can use my own direct experience to test them and find out how they can help me in my work. Abstract ideas that are minimally specified and illustrated are interesting for stimulating my thoughts but are not directly helpful in guiding my actions.

Second, knowledge will be more useful in guiding change if it is composed of complementary simple models that together create a holistic view. This particular form of organizing knowledge has a number of advantages for the change agent. First, models can help a change agent develop an understanding of the situation that can serve as a basis for action. A change situation is usually full of information, and the change agent's problem is to organize the information into a picture that can be used to guide change activity. Models, analogies, metaphors, and other forms of symbolic representation are crucial in helping change agents get the most out of the information available to them. They provide schema that can help the change agent notice information that is available, and they provide a tool for generating hypotheses and predictions. By helping the change agents focus on critical information and by helping them predict the consequences of events, the models can help change agents work more effectively.

For example, I find that a systems model can be a useful way to organize my understanding of an organization. It highlights the fact that an organization and each subunit within it represent entities that need to be understood. It gets me to focus on the relationship between the system and its environment, on the way it is organized to transform its inputs into outputs, and on the nature of the boundaries that exist within and outside of the organization. It makes it easy for me to ask what the ideal state of the organization would be like, and to contrast it with the way the organization is at the moment. The form of the systems model is very simple and I can carry it around in my head as a picture, yet it allows me to organize a great deal of information and keep my understanding of the organization integrated. I can easily use the systems model to generate analogies to other organizational systems with similar characteristics to the organization I am working with, which helps me develop a richer understanding of the organization and link what I am doing to elements of my past experience.

To be helpful in change situations, the models need to be quite simple. Complex models are fine for trying in retrospect to sort out what happened, but they are of little help when you are in the middle of a situation that demands action. A model that says behavior is an interactive function of complex personality variables, situational factors, and interaction dynamics is not very helpful when the problem is to decide what to say next to the vice-president of manufacturing to get permission for an experimental project. A model that gives action guidelines (e.g., present all the available information in a way that gives the vice-president valid information, free informed choice, and will create internal commitment to the results) is much more helpful when there is little time to plan. Of course, simple models must be consistent with reality and with the objectives of the intervention in order to be helpful.

Just as simplicity makes models easier to use under real time circumstances, concreteness makes them easier to link to the situation in which one is acting. In spite of my training, which has taught me the value of abstract theory, I find that much of my change work relies on using metaphors and examples to understand what is happening and to explain ideas to others. If a picture is worth a thousand words, a metaphor is worth a dozen correlations. The most helpful theories are those that are able to combine simple, abstract theory with metaphors and examples in a way that makes them usable in concrete situations.

Finally, the models will be more useful if they easily fit together to create a holistic picture of what is happening in the organization. Our models tend to describe organizational patterns at different levels of analysis. We use these constructions to help us understand the complexity of organizational events, but the stream of activities is always a totality that we break apart conceptually. The activity of a change agent becomes a part of that stream; so even though our action may be based on a theory that exists at one level of analysis for purposes of simplicity, the consequences of the action occur at all levels simultaneously. For example, many Quality of Worklife interventions use the tool of a joint Union-Management Steering Committee to coordinate and oversee project activities. Often, the membership is developed to give the committee good representation of the different groups in the organization that need to be included in the intervention. Such designs are based on organizational and intergroup theories, and generally will produce the expected consequences if they are appropriately developed. The consequences of these committees at the individual level can be quite severe. As the members of the Quality of Worklife committee begin to learn more about the members of other groups, they begin to change their views and become different from the people they are on the committee to represent. This can cause personal stress, alienate them from their support group, and make it more difficult for the committee members to maintain their places in the organization. This is a necessary part of the change process, and if the individuals are able to maintain their credibility they can begin to change the groups that they represent. If the individual consequences of the intervention design are not recognized and dealt with, the organizational consequences that are expected may not develop.

To summarize, my experience as a change agent has led me to believe that action usable knowledge has some important characteristics. The conceptual elements of knowledge need to be connected with appropriate behavioral skills so that understanding can be linked to action in an effective way. The knowledge needs to include simple, concrete models that can be used to interpret events and guide actions in real time settings, and the models need to be congruent enough to be used simultaneously. Finally, the models need to be framed in very concrete terms so that conclusions from the models can easily be translated into sequences of actions.

CREATING CHANGE REQUIRES KNOWING YOURSELF

The final type of knowledge that is critical for people who are creating change is self-knowledge. In helping people to develop visions, or influencing people to help make visions a reality, the change agent is the primary tool in creating change. Consequently, it becomes very important for change agents to understand themselves and the consequences of their behavior. The extent to which change agents understand themselves will determine their effectiveness in a variety of ways.

First, much of a consultant's effectiveness depends on the adequacy of the consultant's organizational diagnosis. It is easy for the diagnosis to be distorted by individual preferences and biases, but this can be easily counteracted if the consultants know their biases and systematically look for alternative explanations for events. Similarly, the diagnosis will be influenced by the information that the consultant collects. If the consultant tends to collect information in some areas and not others or to interact with some people and not others, he or she can get a distorted picture of what is happening. This can be prevented by actively balancing the information sources used. My personal experience is that it is bothersome to keep checking my understanding of the organizations that I am working with and I do not like systematically talking with people that I don't find pleasant, but I also find that when I do these things, I develop a much better and more complete understanding of the organization I am working with.

Second, one of the best, most direct sources of information for change agents is their own direct experience. When consultants feel that the organizations they are working with are discounting their needs, manipulating them to do things that they do not want to do, or channeling their efforts so that they cannot work on problems in a holistic way, they are getting direct information about the way in which the organization affects people who deal with it. The problem in using this type of information is that the change agents must know themselves well enough to be able to distinguish between their reactions and the organizational causes that may affect others in different ways. My experience has been that when I can do this task well, it gives me a quality of understanding of the organization that I cannot get in any other way because it is the only time when I am learning about the organization directly instead of by inference or report.

Third, change agents are more effective if they are able to identify and accept the consequences of their actions as well as the limits on what they can do. It can be difficult to accept that helping a manager figure out how to ethically and humanely remove a subordinate from a key job may be increasing the pain for the subordinate because it delays the decision, or that strategies for influencing key managers are not being successful in helping them to change. Recognition of failure is an important ingredient in changing approaches when necessary, and looking carefully at the consequences of actions is critical for reducing the chances of failure in creating change.

Fourth, change agents are more effective if they can use their intuition to design action. Many situations are complex enough and emotional enough that rational planning and designing will not work. The change agent cannot consciously integrate all of the necessary information, and the appropriate actions may not be anything that the change agent has done before. In such circumstances, all the effective change agents that I know work from their intuition and frequently are able to invent effective interventions. Working intuitively in this way requires a lot of self-confidence: It requires acting in ways that feel right but are not easily rationally defensible. I do not believe that this self-confidence can be built without both understanding oneself and experimenting with using intuition and evaluating the results.

Finally, change agents need to be able to deal with interpersonally stressful situations. Creating organizational change involves the creation of pain. People feel pain as they change and as they see change in the organizational world that they are used to living in, and often the change agent is seen as the cause of the pain. Change agents need to understand why they are disliked, sabotaged, and resisted so that they keep up their activity when the activity is appropriate and stop when it is not. In this context, it is also important that change agents be able to keep a clear vision of the objectives of the change project and a clear understanding of progress that is being made. There are times when everyone involved in a change project will doubt whether it can succeed (including the change agent), and it is only by keeping grounded in the vision and the progress that it is possible to keep moving forward.

CONCLUSION

In this chapter I have described types of knowledge that can help people conduct organizational change and that are not typically provided in our current graduate programs. I have argued that change agents need knowledge that is useful in facilitating action and that action usable knowledge has a number of characteristics:

(1) It includes normative theories that change agents and their clients can use to develop pictures of the futures that they want to create.
(2) It includes knowledge about the use of influence, the consequences of its use, and the ethics of being influential.
(3) It includes models, metaphors, and maps that can be used to create an understanding of organizational events and patterns in real time frames and normal conditions. These models must be simple and holistic but, more important, the change agent must be able to use the models that work best at the time and switch or create new models when the old ones lose their predictive power.
(4) The knowledge and skill must facilitate intervention activity. It must help a change agent produce the right action at the right time to produce intended consequences.
(5) It must include knowledge of oneself. In the end, it is the change agent who is the tool for change; and the better change agents understand themselves, the more effective they are going to be in accomplishing their objectives.

Taken together, these knowledge requirements suggest that to train change agents effectively we may need new theories and different approaches to training than current graduate programs generally provide. It suggests that there is a positive value to normative theories of organizations that has often been overlooked, that theories that are concrete, simple, and not broadly generalizable may have as much value as more abstract and general ones, and that theories and practices that help develop the skills of change agents may be as valuable as theories and practices that allow us to describe and evaluate what they do. We need to examine the types of knowledge we are building in our field, and change our theories and methods so that we can effectively prepare people to fill the role of agents of change.

EPISTEMOLOGICAL PROBLEMS IN RESEARCHING HUMAN RELATIONSHIPS

Kenwyn K. Smith

One special epistemological bind plagues our attempts to research human relationships. The dilemma? That the research process is itself a relationship. Hence, whatever we observe about the relationships of the groups and people we research may be just as relevant to our relationship with them. There is probably no endeavor for which the truism *what one knows depends upon how one knows* is more applicable.

Consider the topic of ethnocentrism (Sumner, 1906; Levine & Campbell, 1972)—the tendency for groups in conflict to see their own actions in a positive light while viewing the behavior of others negatively. Typically, when we are embroiled in the dynamics of ethnocentrism we posture our social distance from others so that we can see in their actions whatever we wish. If we stay far enough away we can overlook the differences among their members and make the attribution that their actions are an expression of their character as a whole. Meanwhile we can maintain that our actions are a consequence of the forces to which we are being subjected. Only as each group transcends the boundaries separating them is it possible to recognize that others appear as they do less because of what they're like than as a result of the filters through which they're being examined.

AUTHOR'S NOTE: The ideas in this chapter were formulated in my collaborative work with Valerie M. Simmons. We are grateful to H. Peter Dachler for his exhaustive and exhausting commentaries on our earlier writings, which led to the recognition it was not possible to elaborate our arguments in a single paper. This stimulated the decision to abandon the original paper in favor of working on this book. The price was that the passage of time, distance and our respective personal developments made the ongoing coevolution of our thoughts on this topic no longer possible.

Could it be that decades of research on human interactions have been, in part, a consequence of the ethnocentrism of social science? Certainly, many methodological standard-bearers have exhorted us to remain distant and detached from the object of our research, to eliminate any subjective encounter that might contaminate our findings. And certainly for a long time our field pursued questions posed by white male researchers in forms such as "Do black students perform more poorly than whites because of lower intelligence?" or "Will women be able to handle the emotional strains of managerial responsibility?" or "What personality characteristics cause bizarre behavior in developing children?" It took a Herculean civil rights effort to have these issues reframed in interactive terms—so that school performance of all children could be seen as a consequence of a wide range of social processes; so that demonstrative releases of emotion, which women seem to be more capable of, could be viewed as adaptation superior to the ulcers and coronary attacks so often experienced by men in powerful positions; so that the "acting out" behavior of a child in a family could be seen as giving expression to feelings on behalf of the family as a whole.

With the benefit of hindsight it is possible for us, as white males, to admit that racial and gender-based ethnocentrism was at play in our research endeavors. But the more troubling question is whether our current social theory is still being driven by a subtler but just as powerful form of the same process. If so, how might we recognize it? And if it is unavoidable, how can we at least learn from it?

In this chapter, I want to raise some of the dilemmas involved in researching relationships in organizations. I wish it were possible to formulate a methodology that might lead to the development of a general theory of relationships, but that task is clearly beyond my reach. There are, however, some interim steps that I feel we can take. Some of these are central to this chapter. These concerns are formulated both as minefields to be sidestepped and as a crossroads that requires the researcher to make critical epistemological decisions.

An example of a theoretical choice point faced by psychological researchers in the past was the tendency to look at the characteristics of the actors in interaction as opposed to the characteristics of the *interaction patterns* themselves (Goffman, 1959). This has led to enormous energy being poured into measuring, in microscopic detail, the characteristics, dimensions, properties, and so on of the entities engaged in the interaction while transforming the interaction itself into exclusively statistical terms. This mind-set has encouraged researchers to take what might be described as characteristics of the relationship, objectifying them (calling them "things"), and then putting them into one of the entities enacting the relationship. This, I believe, is a misattribution; it is analogous to noticing a figure emerging from a ground in gestalt psychology and treating the boundary that distinguishes figure from ground as a characteristic of either the figure or the ground (Sherif & Sherif, 1969). As Wilden (1980) points out, the boundary is neither an attribute of figure nor of ground. It is best understood as a statement about the relationship between figure and ground.

As a precursor to the development of a general theory of relationships, we need to formulate ways to translate into a relational form that which appears on the surface to be an attribute of an entity. When we hear complaints about poor leadership, can we recast this as a statement about the relationship of a group with its idealizations (goals)? When a group member is being discussed in derogatory terms, can we think of this as being an expression of within-group dynamics rather than a statement of reality about the individual's character? When we hear of workers being described as uncooperative, or management as uncaring, can we pose this in terms of intergroup relations between management and labor?

I am not proposing that a relational frame is the *only* right one for understanding organizational phenomena. It does seem important, however, for us to develop an adequate theory of social *relations* so that we can meaningfully debate the relative merits of relational perspectives with the more traditional views. Otherwise we live with the danger of being driven by our shared epistemological blindspots.

SETTING THE FRAME

The terrain still to be mapped in this field is enormous. Hence, in this chapter I want to take on a modest task that consists of two phases. First I want to discuss four of the key minefields that I think researchers of human relationships must deal with. These are (1) the problems of dialectical thinking in organizational action; (2) the trade-offs between stability and resilience; (3) the existence of invisible texts—the role of rules and the difficulty of gaining access to latent content; and (4) the close link between process and structure in organizations. In the second part of this chapter I wish to point out three types of clinical research skills I consider necessary for a theory of relationships to have a reasonable chance of evolving. These are the art of double description, the art of contextualization, and the art of reframing.

CRITICAL MINEFIELDS

THE PROBLEM OF DIALECTICAL THINKING

A great deal of organizational research is done as a response to pleas for external help from organizations that are having problems. Invariably, implicit in an organization's thinking about the nature, cause, and solution to its problem may be found faulty logic such as "Since A is the problem, not-A must be the solution" (Watzlawick, Weakland, & Fisch, 1974). Hence the request for assistance often comes in the form of "please help us implement not-A." It is commonplace to be presented with requests such as "We're having problems with our present workers, so we want you to help us design a new selection system," or "The workers are complaining about pay, so we'd like you to build a new incentive system," or "We're obviously not going in the right direction, so we want your help in selecting a new chief executive officer." Such thinking is fraught with A/not-A dilemmas.

For the action researcher who needs to understand what's going on before any attempts to produce change are made, it is necessary to confront this type of thinking head on. While problems may become manifest in the form of A, it is rare that not-A provides any type of solution.

Bateson (1972), in one of his delightful metalogues with his daughter, makes clear the A/not-A problem as he addresses her question "Why do things get in a muddle?" He points out that while there may be just one way for things to be properly organized there are a large number of ways in which they can become disorganized. Certainly, by negating organization, you get disorganization. However, negating disorganization in no way leads to organization. Organization and disorganization are two conditions of a logically different kind (Russell, 1960) and the pathways from one to the other are not mirror images of each other.

As researchers, all of us need to be very careful not to buy the logic that the solution to a problem consists of doing the opposite of what created the problem in the first place. While in mathematics a negative multiplied by a negative produces a positive, this is not the case in the day-to-day human condition. This is most evident if I'm unhappy (a condition defined in negative terms). Negate nonhappiness and it does not automatically follow that I will be happy. I'm just as likely to become depressed, or something worse than the original unhappiness. This means that every organizational problem formulation must be undergirded by a good diagnosis before actions designed to create solutions are taken.

Another type of faulty logic that comes from dialectical thinking can be found among those organizational actors that view themselves as problem-solvers. While their solutions may be effective after a problem has surfaced, the solution mentality tells us *nothing* about what to do to avoid the problem in the first place. This key dilemma can be seen in the following analogy. If your house is burning down, the solution is to have firefighters douse it with water. Who of us, however, to avoid having our house burn down would argue that daily we should spray it with water! Understanding an organizational problem requires a different logic when our goal is to avoid the problem in the first place as opposed to solving it after it has occurred.

One way in which the action-researcher is regularly confronted with a dialectical dilemma is when he or she is called in and asked for help—a typical beginning point for a great deal of our organizational research. It is usual that an organization seeks the assistance of outsiders when it can no longer work out what to do to help itself. Hence it approaches the outsider as the expert and in the process puts itself into the functional equivalent of the dependent, inept child at the feet of the all wise parent. Now, as every parent knows, the best help is often to support the child in the stumbling process. Telling him or her how to walk is often less useful than encouraging the faltering steps. When an outsider enters into a helping role, taking on the mantel of the expert, it is just as likely that he or she will become trapped in a relationship in which the actions seen as helpful are the opposite of what is needed. Anyone invited in as an expert would be well advised to treat the invitation for help as diagnostic data about the patterns of dialectical thinking operative in the organization's self-reflections. To accept the request for help without appropriate diagnosis is to rob the research process of many options that may prove valuable.

STABILITY VERSUS RESILIENCE

One set of cybernetics concepts that is helpful in thinking about relationships is the contrast between stability and resilience. Traditional systems theory has argued that living systems operate on the principle of homeostasis. This means that if there is a disturbance, either internally or externally produced, that leads to some type of disequilibrium, energy from the system will be poured into restoring equilibrium as quickly as possible because instability threatens the system's basic order.

Recent theory (Jantsch & Waddington, 1976; Jantsch, 1980) has proposed a rival thesis that operates on the principle of order through fluctuation. Instead of viewing fluctuation as equilibrium disturbing, it is seen as a major vehicle for creating order. The converse of homeostasis is argued. The key point is that around equilibrium order is threatened. However, far from equilibrium, order is maintained. Within this frame of thinking, the viability of relationships depends more on resilience than upon stability.

Drawing the distinction between stability and resilience is important for our attempts to understand relationships in organizations. Holling (1976) defines *stability* as the capacity of a system to "return to an equilibrium state after a temporary disturbance; the more rapidly it returns and the less it fluctuates, the more stable it is." On the other hand, *resilience* may be viewed as a measure of the persistence of a system and its ability to absorb change and disturbance while still maintaining the same relationships with other entities in its ecosystem. These two concepts, when taken together, make it possible to think of an entity becoming more unstable as a result of large fluctuations; but learning how to survive with these fluctuations makes for greater resilience in that a lot of changes can be absorbed.

The contrast between stability and resilience may be seen in comparing *fail-safe* with *safe-fail* strategies. Since the stability view emphasizes equilibrium, this makes the maintenance of a predictable world all-important. On the other hand, a resilience view focuses on persistence, with the emphasis being upon keeping options open and examining events from a regional rather than a local perspective. Here the assumption is that the future will be unexpected rather than predictable; thus whatever stability there is will be less a result of general stasis and more an equilibrium created out of a dynamic network of the complex intersection of internal and external forces (Smith, 1984a).

There is a marked difference between the stability and resilience approaches as to the focus of interest in the generation and maintenance of order. Within the stability frame, the focus is on keeping the relationships among the inner parts ordered so that the whole remains basically the same. Within the resilience frame, the order is "located" more external to the entity. The key patterns are the relationship between the entity and others in its ecosystem. So long as these external patterns can be survived, with the various fluctuations generated by many entities banging into each other as part of the dynamic of the ecosystem, then the long-term order of the entity will be preserved. This may be, however, at the price of significant internal disorder. That is, the trade-offs may often be resilience at the cost of instability and stability at the cost of loss of resilience.

With the interpersonal, intragroup, and intergroup interactions that constitute a large proportion of the key relationships in organizations, conflict often emerges. Then choices have to be made as to how they are to be handled (Simmel, 1955). There are several potential paths.

(1) Conflict may be viewed as relationship disturbing and therefore to be eliminated or minimized. This translates into either barring the troublesome themes from surfacing or trivializing them when they do, producing an overall cordiality that, at best, is superficial. The relationship appears stable so long as it remains contextually bound, but it could not be described as resilient.

(2) Conflict may be viewed as relationship disturbing but legitimate since turbulence is an integral part of closeness. This perspective places resilience above stability, with the turbulence being viewed as a part of growth and creativity—painful, but in the nature of things.

(3) Conflict may be denied, displaced, and then enacted elsewhere in the system. When conflict is avoided, often it simply gets moved to some other part of the system, creating disorder elsewhere while allowing stability to be maintained in the location from whence the conflict originated.

The particular implications of stability versus resilience approaches in research relations are rather profound. These concepts can help us map some of the delicate territory around one critical minefield. It has always been my experience that as I approach a new organization I want the entry process to go smoothly—for there to be a clear and logical way to negotiate a research contract. This rarely happens. However, when entry has gone easily for me the project has turned out to be more difficult than when entry was hard. Without a doubt my best research relationships have evolved when entry was so turbulent and difficult that I thought it would be almost impossible. When in the midst of such turbulence, the expectation of a favorable outcome has given me little comfort. But from a distance I can see that easy entry seems to set the relationship in stability terms; then, when subsequent conflict between them and me surfaces, the potential disequilibrium stresses our relationship, making the brittleness painfully visible. A difficult, turbulent entry, on the other hand, means that from the outset both researcher and the researched have to confront differences, learn how to manage their conflicts, and decide to proceed in the light of the knowledge that the relationship may be rather disturbing. Such struggles seem to create resilience. And the exasperating thing I've learned is that when entry takes a long time, when it seems protracted and involves moving gradually into the complexity of the system, the overall project is richer.

The stability-resilience trade-off becomes most visible on occasions when feedback is being given. Since valuable feedback involves learning to discuss that which normally is not talked about, many sensitivities must be approached. As internal members struggle with these difficult themes, there is always the likelihood that rather than confront the message they will turn and kill off the messenger. A resilient relationship between researcher and the system, built out of turbulent struggles earlier, makes this phase both more survivable and more rich than a relationship built on the principles of stability.

INVISIBLE TEXTS, LATENT CONTENT, AND RULES

Whenever we observe interactions among people or between groups, our task as researchers is to look for some kind of order. We may do this by trying to identify the patterns latent in what we see, or by mapping onto our observations category systems already established in our awareness from other social situations. In the former case we are struggling with an *emergent* order, whereas in the latter case we're involved with *imposed* order. In our field we already know a lot about the epistemologies relevant to imposed order. The standard scientific approach of deriving hypotheses from established theory and then seeking empirical evidence to confirm or disconfirm our propositions is predominantly driven by an ordering principle of an imposed kind.

The task of mapping the emergent order is a very different type of process. It requires that we look, as it were, to an invisible text latent within what is seen and derive the unwritten text that ties the surface behavior into a coherent whole. This type of ordering requires a derivative approach and is full of speculation.

Perhaps the most simple, though very powerful, concept of invisible text is that of rules. At some level, all behavior is driven or rather contoured by rules, usually known to those who enact them but mysterious to outside observers.

An example of what is meant by latent rules may be seen in the following event. In Australia there is a football game unlike anything know to Americans. It is played with a ball about 1½ times the size, but the same shape, as an American football, on an oval field approximately 200 yards by 120 yards at the longest and widest points, respectively. Each team has 18 players with opponents guarding each other across the whole field, as in basketball. The game involves kicking, jumping, catching, punching, bouncing, and running with the ball. At the end, the score may be Team A 15-18-108 defeated Team B 14-22-106. For me, a fun thing to do is to sit a group of American sports buffs in front of a video, without sound or commentary, and ask them to derive, merely from their observations, the rules by which the two teams play. The processes they go through and the conclusions they draw are fascinating. Of course, in the sports example above there are such things as explicit rules known by the players, whereas in regular social discourse the rules are implicit. For the observer not knowing the rules, the sports game is but a jumble of what appears to be pointless acts. However, once the rules are understood there is a template that binds together, into a coherent whole, behaviors that would otherwise appear unlinked.

In the case of the game, there is an easy path to knowing the rules. We can ask the players. However let's imagine we were watching some young children playing a pick-up game of Australian football in the parking lot. Chances are they would have been playing according to the rules they had absorbed through normal socialization but which they could not actually describe. To ask them why they do X or Y would probably bring the unenlightening explanation "because that's what you do!" Their behavior is governed by rules they know implicitly but which are not part of their awareness they can comment upon. Their awareness or knowledge of the rules is encoded within their behavior and not in any system of self-commentary upon their behavior.

The key issue is to comprehend the idea that latent within all social discourse may be found invisible texts that are only visible beneath or between the lines of the observable text. If the explicit text is difficult to comprehend, by unraveling the latent text it may be possible to notice links between parts that otherwise may appear uncoupled.

A key element of latent texts and ground rules is that they provide a powerful contouring of subsequent experiences. They give us a template, a type of master mold from which all subsequent experience is approached and upon which our perceptions are mapped. These templates, these latent scripts, serve as guides to action as powerful in their regulatory force as the rules of grammar are for the formulation of a verbal communication.

To provide an example of learning to look for the latent text beneath a set of surface exchanges I want to discuss something that happened to me during a lengthy study of a public school system in the New England town of Ashgrove (Smith, 1982a). For months I had been working as a participant observer in the system, tracing the relations among various groups such as the town politicians and the elected board of education, the superintendent's office, the principals in the high school, and the like. I had reached the point of having access to a tremendous amount of information, having sat for hours in clandestine caucuses in dark political crevices, read scores of files, and observed hundreds of hours of meetings, and so on. My presence had appeared to be accpeted and I no longer felt vulnerable to being excluded.

Then in quick succession I had two experiences with the board of education that raised the question as to the appropriateness of the open access I had been given. One was at a clandestine caucus of the Democratic board members being held in the early hours of the morning in one of their homes. The atmosphere was highly charged. They were hatching a scheme of enormous complexity. Suddenly someone became concerned that I was present. "Shred his notes," suggested one person. "That won't work. It's all in his head by now anyway," returned another. Suddenly, two of the board members, grown men, highly esteemed in the community, jumped up, put their fingers close to my scalp and chanted in high pitched voices, "scramble your brain, scramble your brain" as though they were ritualistically subjecting me to some exorcism or symbolic electric shock treatment that would eliminate my memory.

A few days later I was sitting as a lone outsider observing a closed meeting of the whole board of education, a practice that had been ritualized. My observing presence was as much part of the landscape as the old furniture that made up the board room—at least, so I thought. Suddenly someone suggested I should be asked to leave. A heavy debate continued around me as they examined the pros and cons of my being permitted to remain. I was rescued. "You've got to be crazy throwing him out of here. He's got the goods on every one of us," offered one of the Democrats. "Do you want to alienate him now? Lest there be any doubt, I've told him everything I think about every one of you in this room, things I wouldn't tell you to your face and my bet is he knows all of your reactions to me too!" This burst killed the discussion. They proceeded with their business, letting me continue my observation.

The two experiences puzzled me and caused me to look beneath the surface in what for me were new ways. What was happening to me was data about the board of education, but what was this data telling me? My surprise was not so much that I was nearly thrown out—I expected that and in fact was somewhat amazed I was not often asked to leave. But in each of these instances was the issue of timing. Why now? This was what was central. The experience and my subsequent struggles to deal with it taught me a new way to look at Ashgrove, and the board of education in particular, for the pattern I observed was intriguing. Once I had seen it clearly, it was easy to recognize from then on. The latent script was that whenever two internal factions within the board were about to engage in some horrendous fight, they as a whole first attacked some other group or person. If it was not someone else it was me. Living through this experience and allowing myself to generate new hypotheses directly from the experience made it possible to gather data of a quite different kind to check out my emerging suspicions about the covert rules of interaction that dominated the Ashgrove system.

THE CLOSE RELATIONSHIP
OF PROCESS AND STRUCTURE

At first blush organizations appear to have some structures and some processes. The structures seem fixed and given. The processes seem changeable and volitional. I would like to argue, however, that this is true primarily at the level of appearances. Dig underneath or go behind what we label as process and structure and we will see in large part that they are fundamentally the same. I want to be careful not to overstate the case. Hence let me concede that some structures, virtually by definition, are fixed. For example, water is always H_2O, made up of a very precise combination of hydrogen and oxygen. Alter the structure and you no longer have water. However, most of the structures we are dealing with in human organizations are not like water. Rather, they are processes that have been repeated so often that they have the appearance of being fixed.

To illustrate this point let's consider an example. In the earliest formation stages of a stream there is no structure. All we have are drops of water following a path of least resistance. However, if these drops always travel along the same route, in time the aggregation of the individual meanderings of the water drops creates what is experienced as a structure—a stream. Then other living organisms in the environs (plants, animals) come to count on the predictability of the water's behavior, and begin to act as though the stream were a firm structure. The act of treating the stream as a structure causes a secondary set of processes to emerge. Vegetation springs up around the water path, animals make tracks to the best drinking spots, and so on. In the process, another set of augmentary structures are created. That is, the process of the stream becoming experienced as a structure generates other processes, which in time also are repeated so often that they too seem fixed. In some cases the emergence of these secondary structures helps to reinforce the primary structure even more. For example, the development of vegetation around the stream heightens the regularity of the water cycle, thereby reinforcing the viability of the stream. In no time we have an interlocking network of structures that together make up what we may describe as a system.

It is very important for us, however, to recognize that these structures are actually processes repeated over and over again. Hence it does not really make sense to talk of the structures separate from the processes that constitute them. In fact, processes and structures are really one and the same thing. They merely become manifest in different ways depending on whether we are looking at their static or their dynamic characteristics. Bacharach and Lawler (1980) capture this reality for us nicely by defining structure as the crystalization of processes that have become repeated so often that their patterning appears fixed.

In human interactions it is not at all uncommon to have an event occur that does not appear to fit the prevailing structures. We usually label it as aberrant and see it as a process that is threatening the established structures. It would, of course, be more accurate to describe it as a process that is a little different from the other processes that have become repeated so often in homogenized form that they are experienced as structures.

When the "aberrant" occurs we can ask, "What is it about the nature of this event that makes it not fit the established order?" We may equally ask what is it about the established order (structure, crystallized processes) that makes it impossible to expand in order to incorporate the "aberrant," thereby treating it as a normal event? The point is that the "aberrant" is only aberrant because of the tightness of the definition of the structure (crystallized processes). If the structure were less homogeneous, the "aberrant" would be merely a part of the heterogeneity of a much looser structure.

Because structure tends to be viewed as given and because other processes have become linked to it, creating a "system of structures," and since individual acts appear as volitional, pressure is experienced by the individual actor (person, group, or whatever) to make its actions fit the structure rather than the other way around. This is especially so because it is so much more convenient. To have the new act destabilize the whole edifice of structured processes would require much more work. To deal with the nonfitting acts as deviance or error makes life more simple.

The particular relevance of this set of thoughts to our research endeavors is the following. As we draw maps of our observations of organizational actions, there are some events (interactions) that appear not to fit. At this point we confront a choice. Is there something about these particular events (acts, people, circumstances, and so on) that makes them unusual? Or is there something about the restrictions of the maps, contours, or structures that make these events appear as unusual? We can look (1) to the character of the aberrant, (2) to the tightness of the structure, and (3) to their relationship with each other as possible places for explanation.

All too often, however, we fall into the trap of looking only at the "aberrant." As a result we overlook the fact that the "aberrant" may fulfill a very critical function for the prevailing structures (crystallized processes). This has been elaborated for us in group theory (the functions of the social deviant—Dentler & Erikson, 1959), in intergroup theory (the role of the "out" group—Simmel, 1955), and in the family literature (the role of the "acting out" family member—Minuchin, 1974). What we need are much more general theories that provide automatic ways of examining the relationship of the "normal" with the "aberrant." And we also need to recognize that this will be the exact opposite of how the organization (its members, its dominant coalitions) thinks because to give credence to the aberrant would threaten the prevailing system of structures. And the very nature of organization involves the maintaining and elaboration of those structures.

SUMMARY

Thus far I have discussed four epistemological dilemmas that plague our understanding of human relationships. (1) The problem with typical organizational thinking is that it falls into dialectical binds. If A is defined as the problem, not-A is seen as the solution. This is faulty logic. (2) Relationships are easier to manage when they are stable. However, those that are built on the principles of stability may not be very resilient when conflict and turbulence arise. (3) While relationships may appear to be of a particular form when examined at the surface level, their texture is made up, in large part, of dynamics that are invisible. Seeking out the latent content and the hidden rules that drive relationships is an important element of organizational work. (4) Process and structure are two terms that evoke different images for the organizational researcher. However, they are tightly related to each other and in most ways are basically the same thing. Hence, when we are working on structures we are also working on processes, and vice versa. To treat them as separate or separable is a false dichotomy. These four dilemmas are merely a sample from the large array of concerns that need to be rethought as we push toward methodologies that will facilitate the development of an adequate theory of relationships.

NECESSARY SKILLS •

The question we are now confronted with is whether there are ways out of these methodological woods so heavily mined with epistemological dilemmas. To this I have no clear answer—at least not yet. But there are some starting points. I want to suggest the importance of three craft skills that I believe, if developed more fully and drawn together, may provide us with critical new possibilities. These are the following: the art of double description as reported by Bateson (1979); the art of contextualization (Jakobson & Halle, 1956; Christians & Carey, 1981); and the art of reframing (Watzlawick, 1978).

THE ART OF DOUBLE DESCRIPTION

The essence of the double description process may be seen in an examination of vision. If we had only one eye, the world would appear as two dimensional. Since we have a second eye it is possible to gain information about depth. If we look at the world with one eye *what* we see is the same as if we're looking with two eyes, except that as a consequence of the second eye we can see differently. The information added creates a different kind of picture than that generated by monocular vision. There is nothing more right about one picture or the other. It's just that the mere existence of two types of pictures (descriptions) of the one scene enables extra perspective, extra insight to be incorporated that would not be possible without the capacity to make contrasts.

Bateson (1979) provides a superb example of the increment of insight produced by a second language of description, without the addition of any extra so-called objective information, in his comparison of algebra and geometry.

In algebra we can say $(a + b)^2 = a^2 + b^2 + 2ab$. In geometry we can represent this same statement as follows:

	a	b
a	a^2	ab
b	ab	b^2

In one sense absolutely nothing extra was added by the geometric description; the second language added no new information. However, it did lead to an increment in understanding the relation of $(a + b)^2$ to its product.

Bateson (1979) further illustrates this issue by asking the question "what is the sum of the first ten odd numbers?" An individual could write out the series $1 + 3 + 5 \ldots + 19$ and add them. Or they could note that

The sum of the first odd number is 1

The sum of the first two odd numbers is 4

The sum of the first three odd numbers is 9

The sum of the first four odd numbers is 16

The sum of the first five odd numbers is 25, etc.

Soon the trick can be learned that "the sum of the first ten odd numbers must be the square of the ordinal name, which in this case is 10, hence the answer is 100." What has been learned here is the difference between the *ordinal* name of a given odd number and its *cardinal* value. The ordinal name of the number 5 in the above series is 3. Hence the sum of the first 3 odd numbers will be 9, and so on.

The addition of the second system of description that led to the pattern dealing with the ordinal names has enabled us to move from talking arithmetic to talking about arithmetic. The switch has been from numbers to attributes of numbers.

Double description, or better still, multiple description, enables us to create multiple maps of single observations. And these multiple maps facilitate contrasts that otherwise would not be possible. Since all science, in the final analysis, depends upon the information generated by differences and similarities, we as investigators must generate multiple observations. One way to do this is to observe the same phenomenon in multiple cases—the traditional view of the variable n in research. Another is to generate multiple perspectives on the same phenomenon, an alternate way of thinking about n, made possible by multiple description.

For our task of studying relationships the key issue is whether we can create at least one description (or a number) that casts our concerns in interactive terms. Again, Bateson (1979) provides a useful illustration of this basic process. He suggests we examine a dog and a rabbit involved in a game of chase. If we view them as separate entities, we end up asking questions such as, When does the dog chase the rabbit? and, What level of self/other knowledge does the dog have? However, if we view the whole dog-rabbit as a single system, the pertinent questions change, for now the only critical information is *relational.* We are no longer in the bind of whether the rabbit ran because the dog chased it, or whether the rabbit, by running, *told* the dog to chase it. Instead we have a system of A and B combined and our focus can be the patterns that characterize the A-B entity as a whole.

In this example we can see that by shifting the level of analysis from the entities A and B to the entity of the A-B interaction, we are forced to draw new boundaries that generate different patterns of similarity and difference, demanding in turn different types of descriptions. These new patterns are no more or less right than those noted when observations were made from a noninteractional frame. However, the extra description does force upon us a tension without which we could easily become locked into a single, reified interpretation.

THE ART OF CONTEXTUALIZATION

The importance of context in social discourse cannot be overemphasized. Since social entities (individuals, groups, organizations) all strive to give meaning to experience, their sense-making processes are very important.

The work of Jakobson and Halle on metaphor (1956) highlights the centrality of context in the creation of meaning. For example, the metaphor "blanket" as discussed by Jaynes (1976) evokes a very different meaning in the following two sentences: "The thick snow blankets the ground" and "The thick smog blankets the city" (Smith, 1982b). In the former context, the metaphor "blanket" conjures images such as protection and warmth until some period of awakening whereas in the latter case the images are of suffocation from which escape is desirable (Smith & Simmons, 1983).

There are many different levels of context that can be important. For example, an interpersonal exchange between two individuals may mean radically different things depending on the group, the intergroup, and the organizational context in which it is occurring (Alderfer & Smith, 1982; Berg, 1984). Two white males holding a conversation about what it means to be white in a group of workers where everyone else is black would be quite a different exchange than if all the other members were white. The meaning of the conversation would again be equally influenced by the larger organizational context if the setting in which this group of workers belonged were managed by only whites while all but these two workers were black.

Each level of analysis that we use as a context within which to set a relational event can create a different set of meanings. Set the event in five contexts and we may get as many as five sets of meaning validly attached to that which is observed.

An example of the relevance of the issue of contextualization can be seen in the following. At one time when I was observing an organization adjusting to a strike I listened intently to a lengthy conversation of corporate executives who were discussing structure. Their concern was that during normal times they had a formal structure for the organization's operations that really did not operate very effectively. In fact, they all agreed the organization remained viable because of the powerful informal structure that existed. Few obeyed the formal rules. There were a large number of informal networks that enabled managers and workers to get things done despite the system rather than because of the system. One perspective taken in this exchange was that the strike offered the opportunity "to clean up our act," expressed as follows:

"Let's take this chance to make formal many of those informal procedures we've agreed work so effectively; at least that way we won't have to
be always sneaking around behind the back of the formal procedures."
A counterperspective was offered. "No. That's a big error. You don't
seem to understand that the informal structure only works *because* it is
juxtaposed beside the formal structure. I wouldn't tamper with the
informal at all. In fact, if we formalize it we'll probably kill it off."

They debated at length. It was very sophisticated. The issue was
whether the informal processes that were so effective would be viable if it
were not for how they tied to the formal structure that in fact contextualized them. This latter thought prevailed in this situation with very
creative consequences. The executives agreed that surviving the strike
would probably depend on whether some new informal networks and
procedures emerged. They concluded that to tamper directly with the
informal networks would be an error. Rather, they saw their best option
to be to change certain elements of the formal structure, the domain over
which they had legitimate power, with the hope that their changes would
prompt the necessary readjustment in the informal system they believed
would be beneficial. They could not accurately predict what the new
informal system would look like, but they were able to press certain
structural levers that stirred a very creative period of informal
realignments.

THE ART OF REFRAMING:
BOTH A CONCLUSION AND A BEGINNING

In the above section, I pointed out the importance of context on the
meaning of an event. How the context is used as a frame for an exchange
influences the nature of the event. The context may exist ready-made for
the experience. No interpretation is required, for the context is self-
evident. More often than not, however, there is no immediately "right"
context available, or else there are numerous possible contexts, each
with validity, but also each generating its own meaning out of the event.
In this setting, the researcher has to choose the frame or frames to be
used and the choice will shape the meanings that will be infused into the
event or events being examined.

A great deal has been written on framing, especially in the family
therapy literature (see Watzlawick, 1978; Haley, 1973; Selvini Palazzoli,
Boscolo, Cecchin, & Prata, 1978). Hence, for the discussion here I will
limit myself to simply pointing out that the process of double/multiple
descriptions and thus our theorizing about relationships are primarily
based on multiple framing. Slot an event into a singular frame and all we

have is one description. Frame it multiply and then we have multiple descriptions, thereby creating the possibility of numerous meanings. This art of creating multiple meanings is as central to the clinical side of the research process as the concept of sample size is to the procedures of the logical positivist.

Some aspects of framing are self-evident. Other aspects are very complex. For example, it is not all that difficult to understand the multiple frames that can be created by mapping events into a variety of explicit external contexts, as I've discussed. However, events may also be framed by internal contexts—by what might be called the "inscape" (in contrast to the "landscape") for events that can be meaningfully framed by the dynamics latent within them.

Perhaps the best way to capture what I mean by this is to draw upon an analogy we can take from music—the concept of *voicing*. Hofstadter (1979) provides a wonderful description of the basic principles of voicing. A simple melody such as Three Blind Mice has a single theme, the line any of us would sing if invited to join in this song. This we think of as the main voice. This single theme, however, can be played against itself by having "copies" of the theme join in after a fixed time-dealy. The first voice enters with the theme, then a copy joins in a few bars later with exactly the same theme. Then after an equal delay a third voice enters, and so forth. In order for a simple round like this to work each of its notes must be able to serve in a dual or triple role. That is, it must be able to be simultaneously part of the melody and part of the harmonization of the same melody. In this sense, it is both a voice in its own right *and* a frame for another voice. In the triple round the same note must fulfill the melody (voice) and dual harmonization (two frames). This is the simple concept of voicing—that is, the delayed repetition of copies of the same theme.

There are numerous complex versions of voicing. For example, a second type of complexity may be introduced by staggering not only in time but in pitch. Thus the first voice might commence the theme in one key, the second voice joins in after an appropriate delay, not on the same note but five notes higher, while a third joins in later yet another five notes higher, overlapping the first two. A third type of complexity may be created by having the second voice singing twice as quickly or twice as slowly as the first, and so on. This is formally referred to as dimunition and augmentation, respectively, since the change in pace either shrinks or expands the theme. A fourth complexity involves the *inversion* of the theme. This means making the melody jump down whenever the original theme jumps up, and by exactly the same amount. A fifth complexity—one that represents a great deal of sophistication—is playing the theme backward in time. The complexities go on and on, with the elaboration of concepts like the "countersubject," and so forth. The details, for our purpose here, do not matter.

What is of value is to recognize that each event that we social researchers make into data for our theories has both context (settings in which it is embedded) and latent texts (scripts), which are the behavioral equivalent of musical voices. Hence the richness of the meanings of the data we are working with depends almost entirely on our capacity to see/hear/sense/intuit that which is beyond the manifest and then to make these into frames that will give us multiple descriptions to make into the fibre from which the fabric of our theories is constructed.

This, I would argue, is at the core of the clinical skills we must develop if we are to give ourselves a fighting chance of creating a theory of relationships. It is only when we have learned how to formulate anew the substance out of which we build our theories that we will be ready to generate epistemologies adequate to the tasks of understanding organizational relationships. I do not know what the journey will involve. But I'm convinced the foundation skills for setting off on the journey into this terrain are the skills of multiple description, contextualization, and reframing.

6

LOOKING AT RESEARCH IDEAS
AS BEHAVIORAL DATA

Stewart E. Perry

The first clinical demand of social science requires researchers to recognize their own humanity as it inheres in their basic research concepts. In this chapter, I want to suggest an intellectually respectable perspective for responding to that demand. I will do so by presenting the view that research ideas (like all ideas) are pieces of human behavior and therefore are themselves susceptible to scientific analysis and understanding in the same way as any other behavioral data.[1]

All too often in the course of research we as social scientists work with our scientific research ideas as if they had an existence and a meaning quite apart from the human beings who use them. We too often consider that our careful use of scientific techniques and methods somehow provides us with a means to transcend the common ground of frail humanity that we otherwise share with everyone. We are, in fact, apt to approach research as a way of shedding our humanity. It cannot be done.

Harry Stack Sullivan reminded his trainees that physicists (in the Einsteinian revolution) discovered themselves moving about among their own data (Perry, H., this volume). Thus psychiatrists (and, by extension, all social scientists) should not be surprised to find themselves as participants in all their observations of human behavior. Here I will suggest further that all of us engaged in research will discover ourselves embedded also in the midst of our working concepts. Although social scientists, like other scientists, have long since recognized that all our data are shaped by the concepts that we choose to use, we have not yet accepted the notion that in our ineluctable humanity we have not only chosen the concepts but have also shaped them to fit our human condition. In that manner we fashion both our ideas and any resultant information.

Let me jump in with a case illustration from the research in a major psychiatric hospital where I worked for five years in the mid-1950s as a participant observer studying the relationship between the social setting of the hospital and the theories, methods, and research problems of the researchers (Perry, S., 1966). I have recently learned that something odd has been happening in the intervening years at that hospital.

When I was there in the mid-1950s, the most significant mental health problems that the staff studied were defined mainly in the research frameworks of "psychotherapy," "social structure," "social epidemiology," and "cultural milieu." It is true that at that time the hospital also sponsored research in the biology and chemistry of both the normal and the disordered brain. For example, there was a lot of work on brain analogs to lysergic acid diethylamide (long before the hippies discovered LSD). However, the then preferred research frameworks 'had'[2] to be included in the brain chemistry projects. That is, concurrently with brain chemistry questions the researcher was strongly encouraged to consider social and psychological questions. Even if one was rather single-mindedly a brain chemist and not at all a Leonardo in the whole range of psychiatry, one was expected to link one's work somehow to the preferred framework.

During the intervening years in that same hospital, the situation has completely reversed itself. Now, as I have learned from current staff members, what is really valuable to research is generally cast in biological and chemical frameworks. Little goes on as of now that relates to the previously honored rubrics of "social," "cultural," and "psychotherapeutic." How has this come about?

Thomas Kuhn's (1962) work on the paradigmatic shifts in science might make this change recognizable. He has argued that new findings can pile up to such a persuasive degree that previous ways of thinking about scientific puzzles are jettisoned in favor of other ways that had been around for a good while but not accepted. But that is not true in this case. Nothing over the last twenty years in the results of psychiatric research either at that hospital or elsewhere provides the disinterested observer with a 'scientific' rationale for that shift. Indeed, at many other respected settings the social-psychological-cultural rubrics still hold sway.

TOOLS FROM DEVELOPMENTAL PSYCHOLOGY

To understand what has happened to the research ideas in this one case (and, by implication, in similar cases), I would want to seek tools for studying the behavior of the persons using the research ideas, rather than tools for studying the ideas themselves. I would want to begin at the beginning—the very beginning: How do children grow up to use ideas? That is, by looking at events in child growth and development one might find general processes that ultimately produce the researcher and his or her research ideas (Piaget, 1970). For the case of the research hospital, developmental psychology does not offer immediate explanatory assistance but it does provide the best overall entry into the perspective of the behavioral analysis of ideas and provides the bridge for moving on to sociological and political science tools that will aid in looking at the hospital puzzle. Along the way I believe it will become evident that anthropology, economics, and all the other social sciences can also be relevant to the study of ideational behavior in science and elsewhere.

So, to begin with, an idea is, after all, embodied in a word or phrase, and that would immediately suggest examining the process by which the child comes to learn and deal with words, shuffling and reshuffling them until they satisfy her or him as somehow referring to what she or he wants them to refer to. No matter how one might try to escape the constraints of relying on words—by using numbers, for example, as if these too were not simply a special type of word—we cannot elude all that learning to use words implies in human behavior. It is true that at least some physical scientists report that they tend to formulate their concepts in 'mental pictures' of 'physical structures.' Having done so, however, the physicist then faces the task of translating the internal images into socially communicable mathematical formulae and verbal expression.

Surely, the most limiting and at the same time most releasing of all the child's early learning experiences for developing ideas, including scientific ideas, is the language the child is brought up to use—and will manipulate for purposes of research reports. Consider only the simplest situation, in which the language of one's childhood is the language of one's scientific field. If this is one of the major European tongues, it is a magnificently flexible tool indeed. In one sense, a contemporary European language is inexhaustible, for probably any language can express anything if its users can coin new expressions, new terms.

By contrast, traditional literary Arabic does not permit language development. Partly this has to do with certain religious strictures about the number of words in the Koran; and thus there is a sacred speech and a secular one, the vernacular Arabic. For those of the Arabic cultures, the traditional literary language is the only language to be used for truly valuable ideas. That means that the advancement of science must take place outside the realm of "valuable ideas." Consider how this might constrain diplomatic communication among devout Moslems about the ethics of scientific technologies in nuclear energy and nuclear arms.

But even if a language is growing or, more to the point, because it can grow, the variety of ideas that *might* be expressed in it will never be mastered even in the largest dictionary. At the same time, each people and each person is constrained, as Whorf (1950) has made us well aware, from thinking certain thoughts and from expressing certain ideas because the language in current use lacks certain words and expressions. When we learn another language, we can begin to see that our previous world of ideas is only a limited sector of an unknown range or spectrum of possible ideas.

Schachtel (1947), the clinical psychologist, told us that the rich experience of children in their 'naive' interactions with the physical and interpersonal world is whittled down by the lack of appropriate words (or schemata) available to them, their parents, and their other associates for latching on to the experience. Without the linguistic schemata as vessels in which to catch the heavy rain of experience, all memory of the broad range of sensation, for instance, that is open to the child is restricted or distorted into a distribution that will fill the available words with the meanings that significant others assign to them. Children thus come to recognize and remember only those parts of the world that people in their culture group have recognized before. And if by chance a child has vividly sensed or felt something that does not fit the choice of words that is available, so that he or she creates new words or combinations of words, the child may be disciplined or subtly controlled to forget it. Gaps in memory, then, have a systemic source, Schachtel argued, far beyond the reasons for repression that Freud described. And experience in the present is subject to the same constraints as experience recalled.

One of the ways that later researchers have discovered that this is so is by the comparison of reactions of people, from different language backgrounds, to what the researchers call the same stimulation. A rather dramatic array of evidence occurs with respect to color. Color, in terms of twentieth-century Western science, is a combination of hue (that is, places on a spectrum measured within the range of 100 to 700 millimicrons); chroma (that is, saturation or purity); and brightness or brilliance (called *value* in technical colorimetry). True, those three dimensions constitute a very specialized language for technical purposes, but, after all, most readers of this book will recognize the concept of color and will be albe to discriminate red from orange, and so on.[3]

Color, however, is not a universal concept; and quite apart from so-called color blindness, not all people recognize what you and I might call the same colors. For example, the Haununóo, a central Philippines culture group, have no such concept, and it requires a special investigative technique in anthropology to discover exactly what elements they do respond to in the discrimination of something comparable to what Americans would call different colors (Conklin, 1955; Frake, 1969). It turns out that the Haununóo discriminate colors according to a four-way system of darkness or lightness and redness or greenness. The latter terms of distinction apparently arise from a rural perspective and imply dryness versus succulence, what one might discriminate by the state of the stem of a plant during different seasons of the year.

Thus the child in this Philippine culture can and must do different things in the recognition of coloration compared to the child in the United States. Similarly, U.S. children of different backgrounds will latch on to variant color distinctions. The child of artist parents may see something different in the tomato reds than the child of a farm family discriminates. But even Americans of homogeneous background can give corollary evidence of the influence of the conceptual categories of language upon perception. In American English there are some colors that can be identified with a one-word name; others need a phrase. It is harder for American college students presented with color chips to recognize colors that need a phrase; and they do not agree with each other as much on those colors as they do on the colors identifiable by one word. The same color chip study done with the Zuñi Indians, using the Zuñi language, gives similar results for responses to one-word colors versus those requiring Zuñi phrases (Brown & Lennenberg, 1954).

Such studies provide good evidence that language really constricts or opens powers of perception. That is, the world, as each person is able to formulate it, really is different depending upon the schemata that the person is trained to use to describe it. What is true for color discrimination is true for other sorts of experience. In growing up, one is taught to make only a limited number of conceptual discriminations.

TOOLS FROM OTHER SOCIAL SCIENCES

Because discrimination, perception, and conceptualization can vary so with early developmental experiences, including language, some specialists argue that the reason that people throughout the world can communicate at all is because some concepts are physiologically built into the body's equipment (Chomsky, 1971). Thus, in addition to tools in developmental psychology, physiology is another set of behavioral science tools to examine ideas as behavioral data. The special case of toxic hallucinations is only the simplest matter to be considered in that perspective. Much more intriguing and fundamental is the issue of the 'fit' between our body equipment and the physical world around us such that we *can* apprehend that world (Campbell, 1977). However, there are still other tools to consider before returning to the case of the research hospital.

Given the variations deriving from each person's own history, the research ideas in use or created by the person must somehow reach a shared core of meaning, however refined and simultaneously impoverished by the requirements of sharing. Only thus is the user accepted and heard in her or his social groupings, including academic departments and research laboratories. Ultimately, the user has to seek a minimum of consensus with others by which her or his ideas can be validated. At that point new social rules as well as interpersonal sensitivities come into play, and one would seek tools from social psychology, sociology, and political science.

Of course, philosophers and kings of many times and places have wondered how it might be possible to engineer a consensus (establish a set of shared rules) that would be dependable over the years and require acceptance on its own terms. That is another way of asking, as scientists do, how can we reach the truth about a certain experience? But truth itself is an idea; and as an idea it too has its own ties with the particular times and places in which it occupies attention. For example, Merton (1957: chap. 16) has suggested some reasons to suppose that science and its version of truth requires or at least flourishes best in a democratic setting. However, even in science, nondemocratic forms of behavior play a necessary role, as I will note later on.

Yet even a dictator may ask, How can I establish a criterion of true knowledge that is free of the ties of time and place and person, including my own time, place, and person? The person in authority may recognize his or her own mortality, so how will the truth live on after the ruler? One solution is to institutionalize a means of succession—the king is dead, long live the queen. Thus authority might survive human mortality, but of course the new monarch may turn out to have very different ideas. Then those who have lived under both regimes must ask themselves, Which one represents the truth?

In so-called Western society, it is very important to make the distinction between what is 'true' and what is 'untrue.' While other societies may have other priorities, in Western civilization a good deal of effort has gone into working out justifications for the label *true*. A whole set of different criteria have come to be recognized, and one may choose among them: Does it fit with other ideas held to be true (the criterion of consistency)? Is it a guide for successful action (the criterion of usefulness)? Does it produce dependable predictions beyond itself (the criterion of new knowledge or new truth)? Is it what some very trustworthy and expert person says (the criterion of authority)? Does it seem simpler and yet do the same thing as another more complicated formulation (the criterion of aesthetic economy)? And so on.

What makes us as researchers feel sure that the way we decide on the truth or falsity of an idea is itself the true way to do that? How did we learn to decide by that particular means? It may seem at first blush that science, dependent on so-called self-correcting research, is different from other ways of determining truth. Yet science as a system of ideas is, in fact, a very successful social institutionalization of authority about truth.

Very much like the temporal succession of other interpreters of truth, scientists provide for a succession that manages thereby in part to transcend place, time, and person. Some of the authority of science lives on in the succession of the particular scientist's students, some in acceptance of her or his students and ideas in other kingdoms and duchies—other laboratories. But it must be recognized that science is a human transmission of authority, even if one is thereby merely recognizing that no individual scientist can manage to retest all that has gone before, even in his or her own narrowly defined field. Thus all must take on authority that some other criterion besides authority was at one time applied.

The very humanity of science as revealed in its dependence upon its own system of authority makes it accessible to the rest of society. Science is vulnerable to competing views through its always-present loopholes, vulnerable to entry by the surrounding nonscientific environment that supports and defines its boundaries. This is so, even though the authority of 'science' may be accepted not only by scientists but also, to some extent, by most of the nonscientists in their environment. Acceptance occurs, however, only if it will not fundamentally interfere with the authority of the nonscientists. For example, South African political elites accept the truth of scientific statements except when those statements conflict with the implications of their racial views. So, generally speaking, science as a way of life and as a set of ideas is relatively acceptable to European-oriented people today so long as it does not interfere with their other ways of life and other views. And thus science remains enmeshed in the tangles of those other ways of life and other views.

Scientists, nevertheless, often claim stoutly that their activity is independent of the realms of political, religious, and other such competing institutions, ideas, and ways of life. After all, science as a way of life and as a way of determining the truth of statements has grown up on the denial of the relevance of social and cultural ties that might bind it to a particular moment in history. Thereby the authority of science—not linked to political or other authority, but only to its own standards—seeks to determine truth in a way that will live forever.

However, if we scientists and researchers are to give ourselves this special superhuman eternal status, we must have some superhuman means at our disposal, and that, so far, we have not been able to demonstrate. In fact, it is only religious or spiritual realms—so much in opposition to science—that have so far been able to 'demonstrate' superhumanity. So we, as scientists, recognizing the way human beings behave, will have to come to the conclusion that scientific ideas can no more escape their political environment, for example, than the political environment can escape the onslaught of scientific ideas. There will always be some sort of interchange between each pattern of social activity and any others within the tangent environment—a cross-cultural exchange, so to speak.

WORKING IN A RESEARCH SETTING

In our personal lives as researchers, then, we will encounter, wittingly or unwittingly, such exchanges. Sometimes the exchanges are very visible, and sometimes they seem to come upon us without our having recognized it until it has happened. In biology, one visible exchange was Stalin's decree on Lysenkoism in which Stalin underwrote the Russian agronomist Lysenko's scientific hypothesis that environment-induced changes in plants are inheritable. Somewhat less visible has been the exchange that became the reversal of what is more valuable science and less valuable science at my old research hospital, which, as it happens, is a mostly federally supported hospital.

I do not have sufficient careful information by which to explain that shift in valued research questions, but I believe the following is a reasonable hypothesis. Most observers will agree that federal policy, beginning in the Nixon administration, came to downgrade social science in general as not being a part of 'real science' and as therefore not deserving the same support. Under Reagan, the broad social forces expressed in his even more stringent policies are also expressed in the yardstick being used at the research hospital. Because of the hospital's virtually full dependence upon federal funds, it is especially vulnerable to the definitions of federal policymakers at the highest levels, and so the reversal occurred.

Eventually, of course, such pressures can generate their own resistance. Social scientists systematically entered the political arena as lobbyists in 1981 to protect their access to federal funds—and, ultimately, their status as a part of science. A lobbying organization now operates under the name of the Consortium of Social Science Associations.

Be that as it may, suppose you were a research scientist at that hospital in the early period and were a brain physiologist; or suppose you were a research scientist in this later era and were a social psychologist. In either instance, you could, of course, pack up your files and go to an intellectually more congenial research institution; and indeed researchers in all sorts of settings are doing this all the time.

The opportunity for that sort of mobility varies. On the one hand, for example, the choices tend to narrow as the scientist becomes older, unless she or he is of sufficient stature to create her or his own institutional setting. On the other hand, generally the older one is, the more likely it is that one has already found or created a congenial setting. Nevertheless, whatever the choice, to stay or to go, the research is shaped.

Do the ideas themselves get shaped in this situation or is this just a matter of more resources for selected research topics? Also, does the overall course of development of the ideas in the entire affected field get shaped? Such questions require their own systematic study, but they should sensitize the researcher to his or her own intellectual accommodations to the research work setting. Probably, the more uncongenial the environment, the more cautiously and carefully you will progress to protect your work against potentially well-founded criticism. So, what effect will that have upon the leaps of thought that mean so much in scientific development? What sort of person would you have to be to make those leaps when others in the setting do not share your perspective, when you are isolated by your choice of research topics? That suggests the matching of the researcher's personality predilections to particular social settings—still more sophisticated questions to be explored in the field of scientific ideation (Kohn & Schooler, 1983).

By contrast, the more uncritical and supportive the research environment, perhaps the more apt you will be to trade ideas swiftly and lightheartedly, and the more apt you are to be less self-critical in your own research and the conceptual definitions you formulate and use. Is the more congenial environment apt to perpetuate what in the long term will be viewed as a dead end, when the support group runs out of energy, resources, and, ultimately, members?

As soon as one no longer concedes a scientific idea as *essentially* having its own life apart from the human context in which it is grown, these and a whole host of other ideational behavior questions can be raised. And these questions can themselves be pursued according to the rules of scientific research.

I do not think it is too much to jump from the accessibility of such questions to the further issue of instituting new criteria for scientific truth. By that I do not mean to suggest that newer criteria would turn out to be better; but I do suggest that if our human environment is a part of scientific truth and knowledge, then somehow or another we as social scientists need to take that into account in our efforts to calibrate our research ideas and their results. Is it enough to say, "Well, the results have been replicated elsewhere, so everything must be okay"? The "elsewhere" may share some very crucial social and other behavioral characteristics that help to produce identical results. To counter this, one might wish to rely most upon an "elsewhere" that is quite different. But, what are the factors that should be varied for truth's sake? That is not at all clear; and that makes the relatively unexplored field of scientific ideational behavior that much more important to the social sciences researcher.

Explorations in the field can begin with examining the influential environment of one's own behavior in the research setting (Friedman, 1967). On the one hand, this examination can be considered merely, say, the sociology of knowledge, or perhaps merely as a radical empirical critique of one's methodology—simply taking one step further what the scientist has always insisted on: a careful and thorough description of research technique, now including hitherto overlooked behavioral parameters. On the other hand, if "methodology" or "sociology of knowledge" is the conceptual category for the study of ideational behavior in research, we may be using familiar categories of thought to isolate us subtly from an experience that requires other forms of formulation. We miss the point to which Schachtel alerted us and which we encounter mechanically in any computer today. Without a proper program, we can not accept data, no matter how valuable. The first step is surely for us to adopt the wonder with which the child encounters the world and engages ever anew in the struggle of discovery and formulation.

NOTES

1. This presentation attempts to provide in a readable format a sort of summary of a book of some ten chapters, now in process. I have indicated only a few exemplary references that might be consulted. The most rewarding and comprehensive approach to the problem presented here is Donald T. Campbell's challenging William James Lectures at Harvard University, 1977, still in manuscript form but available from Campbell at Lehigh University.

2. I will use single quotation marks as flags that the word is a troublesome gloss for something more complex—as a translator might signal that a word that has been selected does not adequately translate what is in the original.

3. The general point I want to make about variations in color discrimination does not depend upon choosing between Land's retinex theory of color perception or the more standard view (Ingle, 1985).

FEMINIST DISTRUST:
Problems of Context and Content
in Sociological Work

Shulamit Reinharz

We do not know exactly what is on the Other Side until we arrive there—and the journey *is rough*. (Daly, 1978)

CONVENTIONAL AND ACADEMIC DISTRUST

One of the hallmarks of both the modern attitude and the scientific method is distrust. We moderns do not trust one another because we see that self-interest takes precedence over other considerations. Skepticism also pervades our relation to scholarship. Science requires that we do not simply accept assertions, but rather that we seek evidence according to standardized criteria. We must question if the author employed the correct methods; if the interpretations of data reflect bias; if the instrumentation was appropriate, and so on. In addition, we have recently discovered that certain methodological, epistemological, and social psychological dilemmas are constraints in the production of social science knowledge.[1] Thus, a social scientist learns to compound conventional distrust with academic distrust.

We are also taught that distrust can be suspended when someone's work has been found acceptable according to certain criteria. True, at

AUTHOR'S NOTE: The following people provided helpful reviews of this chapter: Loraine Obler, Gordon Fellman, Barbara Gruber, Anne Mulvey, Margaret Fearey, Oliva Espin, Brinton Lykes, Hortensia Amaro, Tracy Paget, Maurice Stein, Irving K. Zola, Barrie Thorne and Liz Stanley. Evan Harriman typed the manuscript and helped prepare the references.

some later point we might uncover new criteria or evidence that force us to reexamine previous assertions. But this possibility should not lead us to a relativist position, wherein one says, "Since I can never know anything with certainty, nothing can be judged."

Conventional criteria for determining the worth of scholarship do not include the extent to which findings match one's personal experience (see, e.g., Toby, 1955). In fact, it is believed that there would be no unique purpose for scholarship if it coincided with personal experience. Experience, it is believed, is the foundation of idiosyncratic claims on limited instances. In sum, the attitudes of the modern scholar/scientist include distrust of others' work, belief in the value of particular criteria for judging work, and disdain for personal experience.

FEMINIST DISTRUST

Feminism adds another dimension to this modern attitude. It suggests that conventional and academic distrust are limited because, as Kuhn has discussed, they function within a dominant paradigm erroneously equated with reality (Brandwein, 1984, p. 5). Feminism proposes that this paradigm is not sufficiently recognized as a paradigm. Therefore, feminist distrust applies to work *within* the conventional paradigm compounded by distrust *of* the paradigm itself. Feminists have alluded to this problem when referring to "personal tension" (Westkott, 1979) or "ontological anguish and exile" (Vickers, 1982). Only rarely has the attitude been labelled *distrust* (Lugones & Spelman, 1983).

The anguish mentioned by Vickers refers to a related problem—the lack of a solution to the problem of distrust (see, however, Register, 1979, p. 8). Feminist theory and research should, of course, be the solution, but these are still relatively new and somewhat problematic. For instance, the degree and nature of feminist anguish vary among the disciplines (Stacey & Thorne, 1984). And even in a single field there is more divergence than consensus. Moreover, feminism includes a heterogenous set of beliefs ranging from radical and separatist to liberal, reformist, and even conservative (Firestone, 1970), resulting in minimal consensus about guideposts for research (Reinharz, 1981). Furthermore, it is somewhat dangerous even to discuss the topic of feminist anguish without jeopardizing the fragile hold feminist scholars have on their jobs as researchers and teachers (Westkott, 1979, p. 430; Bernard, 1981, p. 17). Feminists do not as yet have sufficient resources to own or control settings for research. Finally, because feminism provokes among those who think in its terms a reevaluation of all aspects of one's life, acceptance of a feminist perspective introduces self-doubt. Thus, feminist consciousness places added demands on the researcher.

FOREMOTHERS OF FEMINIST DISTRUST

Feminist sociologists' distrust originated in the awareness that sexism was pervasive in the discipline, making it wrong, conservative and embarassing (Friedan, 1963, chap. 6). Kate Millett, writing from outside the field, was one of the first to make this point: "Modern research . . . takes patriarchy to be both the status quo and the state of nature" (1969, p. 78). For the sociologists who wrote during the early phase of this second wave of the American women's movement (see Gornick & Moran, 1971), the capacity to articulate a feminist critique was rather remarkable. After all, these women had been socialized within the dominant paradigm (Bernard, 1981, p. 14).

Nevertheless, as they discovered that the scholarship in which they had been trained was embedded in a patriarchal paradigm, they began to claim that there was strain and even incompatibility (Wittig, 1982) between "their" academic discipline and their feminist consciousness. For example, Daly (1978) argued that reform of patriarchal scholarship is impossible unless new language is used. Stanley and Wise (1983) argued that patriarchy is so intertwined with heterosexuality that to eliminate the former would mean little without eliminating the latter, the prospects of which were nil. This argument has been applied to other components of the dominant paradigm—such as classism, racism, capitalism, ageism—all of which render conventional scholarship partial and leave attempts at generalization limited (see, e.g., Reinharz, Bombyk & Wright, 1983; Ladner, 1973; and Schwendinger & Schwendinger, 1974).

Furthermore, feminist scholars' thinking about method became influenced by the effectiveness of consciousness raising in generating a social movement and in forming the groundwork for the articulation of feminist theory (see Reinharz, 1983). Because of the central role of consciousness-raising in the history of contemporary feminism, some feminist scholars give it a central role in all forms of feminist scholarship (see, e.g., Lugones & Spelman, 1983). MacKinnon, a well-known feminist theoretician, has expressed this view:

Consciousness-raising is the major technique of analysis, structure of organization, and theory of social change of the women's movement. In consciousness-raising, often in groups, the impact of male dominance is concretely uncovered and analyzed through collective speaking of women's experience, from the perspective of that experience. . . . Its claim to women's perspective is its claim to truth. (1982, pp. 519, 536)

The adoption of this position, however, encourages a methodological and epistemological shift that seems to take us out of the tradition of sociology—and conventional science—altogether (see Smith, D. E., 1974).

A few years after the Millett insight, Daniels wrote that when a feminist perspective is applied to the work of sociologists, "we are forced to rethink the structure and organization of sociological inquiry" (1975, p. 340) in all its aspects. In other words, she implied that sexism in the *content* of conventional sociological research was part and parcel of the sexist *context* in which sociological research was done, in particular, the university and other "normal" institutions.

In both arenas—content and context—some feminist sociologists have come to feel that we have to begin again. We have made some strides with regard to content—textbooks that have a feminist, sociological orientation have begun to appear (Bernard, 1981; Andersen, 1983) as have guides to the elimination of sexism in teaching (Thorne, 1982) and in theory and research (Millman & Kanter, 1975; ASA, 1980; Bowles & Duelli-Klein, 1983; Roberts, 1981; Stanley & Wise, 1983). Feminist criticism of all the disciplines, not just sociology, has even broken into the public arena (Fiske, 1981; Howe, 1982) and projects have been funded to mainstream some feminist materials. But this is only a beginning.

CONTEXT: THE MALE-CENTERED INSTITUTION

Research is a socially organized activity done in the context of socially structured institutions such as universities, hospitals, and research institutes. From a feminist perspective, the university is male-dominated rather than woman-centered (Bart, 1971; Bernard, 1973; Rich, 1979). It is a place in which men dominate, in part because they predominate (only approximately 17 percent of university faculties are female; U.S. Department of Labor Statistics, 1979) and because they earn more than the women do (in 1981 women college teachers earned 80 percent of what their male colleagues earned; Kendrigan, 1984, p. 36; see also Ehrenreich & Stallard, 1982). And even though male faculty earn more than women on average, at all ranks, with the same length of service, and at the same age, courts have ruled that this does not constitute discrimination against female faculty members (see *On Campus with Women,* 1982, p. 5).

It is a place in which men who want to succeed marry, whereas women who want to succeed don't.[2] The same pattern holds for having children.[3] These patterns combine, so that "married women are substantially less likely to earn tenure than unmarried women who are still less likely to earn tenure than married men with children" (Hu-DeHart, 1982, pp. 8-9). Thus, it is less likely that research will be conducted by married women with children than by other groups. It is probably even less likely that research will be defined and conducted by gays or lesbians, or by people from racial and ethnic minorities.

The university, from the perspective of feminists, is a place where sexual harassment is common (Somers, 1982; Verba, 1983); a place where the names of persons found guilty of sexual harassment are not always divulged, thus allowing the practices to continue;[4] a place which is increasingly dangerous to women in terms of rape (*On Campus with Women*, 1982, p. 1); a place where there was so little attention to women's existence, that women's studies had to be created. It is a place where recruitment procedures have been demonstrated to be inequitable (Szafran, 1984); a place where as one goes up the academic ladder— from student to lecturer and through the professional ranks to the ranks of highest administration—there are fewer and fewer women (Committee to Study the Status of Women in Graduate Education and Later Careers, 1974); a place where there are more demands made on women than on men (e.g., affirmative action activities, sexual harassment committees, women's role conferences) and there are also fewer role models for women to emulate. It is a place where feminists, minorities, and women in general must compete with each other since there is little room to move up (for a discussion of this issue, particularly with regard to tenure, see Freeman, 1979). It is a place where textbooks and classics abound with sexist language. And finally, it is a place where most of these factors are not considered very important or where they are no longer considered important.

Although we may want it to be otherwise, this context is reinforced by the *content* of the work done within the university, including much of its research. This is because research is conducted within disciplinary methodological and theoretical *traditions* that act as constraints. Although the origins of the disciplines were developed at a time when society differed in major ways from the present, certain structures such as sexism were pervasive then as now, and through their influence on the tradition continue to influence the content of current research.

Generally, the methodological and theoretical traditions are learned during the socialization process; internalized, and then used and transmitted (Reinharz, 1979, 1983). Feminist consciousness raises doubts about these disciplinary conventions, particularly epistemology. Within sociology, this questioning of tradition calls into question the dominant positivist paradigm. It is to this that I now turn.

CONTENT: THE POSITIVIST PARADIGM

Modern social science is conducted in the framework of positivist philosophy (Alexander, 1982; Coser, 1975; Giddens, 1974; Polking-horne, 1983).

> Positivism stands for a certain philosophical attitude concerning human knowledge ... it is a collection of rules and evaluative criteria referring to human cognition: it tells us what kind of contents in our statements about the world deserves the name of knowledge and supplies us with norms that make it possible to distinguish between that which may and that which may not reasonably be asked. (Kolawowski, 1969, p. 2)

One of the key components of the positivist view is that knowledge must be concerned with *observable* phenomena whose explanations must be limited to forces that are not metaphysical or religious in nature. The explanations, however, need not consist of observable phenomena but can be ideas. In my view, the invocation of these explanatory ideas constitutes a defection from the very innovation that positivism was supposed to introduce. I will explain this problem in the context of feminist distrust.

There are three assumptions in the positivist paradigm. First is the assumption that there is a clear-cut distinction between observable phenomena on the one hand and metaphysical entities or religious phenomena on the other (Alexander, 1982). It is assumed that this distinction is obvious and not a result of human interpretation rooted in particular interests.

This assumption leads to the second underlying view: that there is a dichotomy between the object of study and the person who is conduct-ing the study. This distinction is referred to as the subject/object dichot-omy. It allows those who work in the positivist framework to believe that "the investigator's commitments have no influence on his or her data . . . [and that] generalizations are based solely on objective evi-dence" (Alexander, 1982, p. 6). The insistence on subject/object differ-entiation has been linked by feminist theories to the male child's need for individuation in relation to his mother (Keller, 1982). Feminists see in this insistence a defensive, even dangerous, need for differentiation, distance, and separation, which characterizes patriarchal culture.

In addition, positivist philosophy assumes that procedures can be applied to observable phenomena in a way that produces certain knowledge with which everyone is compelled to agree by virtue of rules of logic and mathematics. These three assumptions lead those working in the positivist perspective to disregard the context in which phenomena are embedded (Mishler, 1979; Cicourel, 1982), to believe that "facts" are unproblematic (Thomas & Edmondson, in press), to be disinterested in the unique human experience (Polkinghorne, 1983, p. 21), and to be intolerant of ambiguity.

Positivism is contrasted with speculative, introspective subjectivism, defined as prescientific, arbitrary, and incapable of producing lawlike generalizations from specific instances. Positivism posits that the rules that apply to the study of the physical environment can be applied to all phenomena, because human behavior, like nature, is law-like. Finally, positivism implies that because empirical observation is definitive, the certainty of science yields legitimate *power*. In their rejection of theology, positivists took the power from God and put it in the hands of scientists. The subject/object dichotomy inherent in positivist philosophy complemented the androcentrism of the culture in which it was formulated and the personal views of the people who worked within it. Together they formed a deep male-centeredness[5] which erased women's experience and set the stage for feminist distrust. I shall attempt to document this statement in the following section.

POSITIVIST ORIGINS AND SEXISM

A French male aristocrat, Claude Henri de Rouvroy de Saint-Simon (1760-1825), should be credited with having developed the framework of positivist philosophy. He also linked this philosophy with social goals. He believed that empirical social science could be harnessed for "organizing and rationalizing human relations" (Schwendinger & Schwendinger, 1974, p. 68). In other words, when speculation and philosophy were replaced by the scientific method, a positive society could be created.

Saint-Simon did not rid himself of religion, but instead attempted a synthesis of science and religion. Yet he called this positivism. Having been profoundly influenced by the French Revolution, his description of the ideal society which could be brought about through the application of positivist principles reflects a mix of protecting vested interests and supporting democracy:

> I believe that all classes of society would benefit from an organization on these lines: the spiritual power in the hands of the scientists, the temporal

power in the hands of the property-owners, the power to nominate those who should perform the functions of the leaders of humanity, in the hands of all; the reward of the rulers, esteem. (Saint-Simon, 1964, p. 11)

A student of Saint-Simon's, August Comte (1790-1857), is generally thought of as having defined positivism and having dedicated his life to its widespread adoption. He believed that the power of positivism was such that using its principles, social scientists could construct the ideal society free of social problems. Ironically, the ideal society envisioned by this French Catholic man was infused with religious symbols and rituals. For example, in the ideal society built on positivist principles, Comte believed women would play the role of "guardian angel" and would be worshipped. As for the reproduction of society, a Virgin Mother would give birth to children by means of artificial insemination (Kolawowski, 1969, pp. 62-63).

Historians of social science "explain" Comte's development of religious idealism from the foundations of scientific positivism by reference to his long periods of mental illness. This explanation avoids acknowledgment of the fact that positivism cannot escape being interwoven with values and pragmatics. However, studying the development of Comte's philosophy raises doubt about the ability of positivism to withstand the influence not only of individual psychopathology but also political ideologies, religious beliefs, and values of other kinds. Particularly apparent is the inability of positivism in general, and positivist sociology in particular, to withstand the influence of patriarchal ideology.

Emile Durkheim, an anticlerical French Jew, considered by most sociologists as a founding figure because he defined social phenomena and showed how they should be studied, stipulated rules that should be followed in order to discover empirically based knowledge. His book, *The Rules of Sociological Method* (1895/1938), states that all preconditions must be eradicated, thus assuming that they *can* be. Durkheim earns his place as a founder of sociology because he produced both a model and the standards for empirical research in his classic study, *Suicide* (1951). This study contains much material on the differential rate of suicide among men and women. As is well known, Durkheim used suicide statistics to develop his theories. But it is generally not discussed that he *inferred* or *speculated* about the motivations of the people who had committed these suicides. The inferences drew on ideas held subjectively by Durkheim, which may be referred to as *the ideology that underpinned a surface positivism*. For example, Durkheim's explanation of the greater rate of suicide among married women than among married men includes the following:

Women's sexual needs have less of a mental character because, generally speaking, her mental life is less developed. These needs are more closely related to the needs of the organism, following rather than leading them, and consequently finding in them an efficient restraint. Being a more instinctive creature than man, woman has only to follow her instincts to find calmness and peace. She thus does not require so strict a social regulation as marriage, and particularly as monogamic marriage. (1951, p. 272)[6]

This passage is one of many that illustrate how positivist philosophy and research procedures were unable to eliminate the influence of patriarchal social ideology.[7] What this means is that thought, which had been believed to be governed by the rules of objectivity, was not objective at all, but rather a reflection of the social relations in which it was produced. This link converted the liberating potential of positivism to a new form of tyranny (Myrdal, 1969).

THE SOCIOLOGY OF KNOWLEDGE AND SEXISM

The thesis that science, thought, and culture are mental superstructures that reflect the social substructure (Stark, 1958) is the central tenet of the sociology of knowledge, defined first by Karl Marx and elaborated later by Karl Mannheim, C. Wright Mills, Robert K. Merton, and others. This idea, sometimes referred to as "historical realism" (Suppe, 1977; Gergen, 1973), claims that "science is a human activity which takes place in various *historical* contexts and is not a process of formal logic attaining timeless truths" (Polkinghorne, 1983). Because the sociology of knowledge position represents a radical critique of science, it is a framework that feminists have found useful (see, e.g., Sherman & Beck, 1979; Bernard, 1981). Feminists have shown that it is not only the class structure of the historical period that influences the production of knowledge, but also the sex of the writer, because social conditions differentially affect men and women, making the perspectives of each a reflection of their sex-based ideology.

Mannheim, the man identified as the definer of the field, stated that the sociology of knowledge endeavors "to comprehend the theories and their mutations in close relation to the collective groups and typical total situations out of which they arose and whose exponents they are" (cited in Stark, 1958, p. 12). The whole point of this endeavor is to unveil the connection between social relationships and the knowledge accepted in a particular period. Essentially, the connection between the two rests on the values that underpin both. Unfortunately, however, these values are not easily recognized at the moment, but become more apparent with the occurrence of social change and social conflict (Merton, 1957; Shaskolsky, 1970).

Despite the sociology of knowledge, the relation between knowledge and the fact that it was produced by men in a patriarchal society was rarely, if ever, considered by scholars in this field, leading to extraordinary contradictions. For example, Stark devoted an entire book to showing that thought was rooted in social conditions, and that different people's perceptions of the "same phenomenon" depend on their interests. Yet, here is an example he offered in support of his thesis:

> When a man and a woman see a lady passing in the street, they will (unless the man happens to be a fashion designer!) receive different impressions and images of her. The man's mind is likely to register her features and bodily form rather than her frock, the woman's her frock rather than her features and bodily form because their order of values is in all typical cases different from that of the majority of males . . . men on the one hand, women on the other—are constituted by nature, not by social forces, and the eye-opening interest or value is rooted in the instinctual rather than the social life (though it certainly is not purely instinctual, as our reference to the dress-designer is sufficient to demonstrate). (Stark, 1958, p. 133)

Despite the author's commitment to the basic premise of the sociology of knowledge, he claimed that *sex differences* in the production of thought are *not* rooted in social circumstances, but are instinctual. Patriarchal ideology stood firm despite the sociology of knowledge insight because it was an integral part of the thinking of social scientists, characteristic not only of positivists but of their sociology of knowledge critics as well.[8] It was so taken for granted that it could not be seen.

This confounding of seemingly "scientific" assertions with ideological beliefs is a central concern of feminists. To explore instances of its occurrence is to engage in a kind of consciousness-raising about the discipline (Lopata, 1976, p. 176). Recognition of this interpenetration of social science and social ideology brings in its wake distrust of sociological theory, concern about the value of accumulated social science knowledge, and questions about the distinction between science and ideology. As Eisenstein argued, "to the degree that sociology is rooted in a male world-view, it is as much ideology as it is science. The dichotomization between science and ideology does not hold" (1982, p. 36). In other words, feminist uncovering of patriarchy suggests that both what was thought to be positivist and the supposedly scientific critique of positivism were ideologically infused.

A pure form of positivism could function only in a society that has no divisions or interests, including the interests of the social scientists (Berg, 1984). The feminist critique of social science supports the view that since interest-free knowledge is logically impossible, we should feel free to substitute explicit interests for implicit ones. Feminism challenges us to articulate our values and, on the basis of these, to develop new theories and formulate new research practices.

SEXISM IN OUR "TRUSTED" CONTEMPORARY CLASSICS

Cultural attitudes toward women at the time in which American sociology was being defined were also sexist (Schwendinger & Schwendinger, 1974, pp. 290-334). These attitudes became part of American sociology in terms of its body of knowledge and its professional associations (Deegan, 1981). As a result, the contributions of female sociologists were not acknowledged and had little influence in shaping the discipline. This pattern continues (Welch & Lewis, 1980).

Hand in hand with this discriminatory context was the pejorative writing about women among both positivist sociologists and their sociology of knowledge critics. I will clarify this statement by presenting examples from the writing itself. I located this material by looking at esteemed sociology books, not in terms of their major arguments, but rather in terms of their asides, illustrations, and examples. I looked not at what the authors thought needed explaining, but at what they thought did not—that is, their taken-for-granted assumptions. To me this is a first strategy for working away from feminist distrust—facing the preconceptions squarely. Examples writers use reveal the images with which they think and build their arguments. The examples writers offer can be likened to Thematic Apperception Test pictures used by psychologists to trigger their subjects' way of looking at the world.

For example, a much praised book still widely adopted in sociology courses, Peter Berger's *Invitation to Sociology* (1963), does not look very inviting to me when the images are examined. Upon reexamination, the fact that many sociologists accepted this book as a self-definiton is rather alarming.[9] Berger's use of analogies and images is extensive throughout the book. Here are a few examples at the start of the book:

> Perhaps some little boys consumed with curiosity to watch their maiden aunts in the bathroom later became inveterate sociologists. (p. 19)

> The geologist looks at rocks only at appropriate times, and the linguist speaks English with his wife. Anthropologists use the term "culture shock" to describe the impact of a totally new culture upon a newcomer.

In an extreme instance such shock will be experienced by the Western explorer who is told, half-way through dinner, that he is eating the nice old lady he had been chatting with the previous day—a shock with predictable physiological, if not moral consequences. (p. 23)

On page 44 we learn the "sociological principle" that men are happy when their families are not around so that they can conveniently "use marginal people for their pleasure." On page 45 we learn that Veblen was an inveterate seducer of other people's women. (People *are* men, they *have* women.) On page 55 we learn that youth ends when a man decides to join the church and remain faithful to his wife. Here is Berger's definition of middle-age:

The middle-aged Joe Blow, having accepted the fact that his wife will not get to be any prettier and that his job as assistant advertising manager will not become any more interesting, looks back on his past and decides that his earlier aspirations to possess many beautiful women or to write the definitive novel of the half-century were immature. (p. 59)

According to Berger, social mobility has occurred

when the girl of one's teenage daydreams is transmuted into an ignorant though pretty peasant, [when] even Mama, who used to be the orb around which the universe revolved, has become a silly old Italian woman one must pacify. (p. 60)

Whereas sociologists usually asserted that wives acquire their socioeconomic status through their husbands, Berger seems inadvertently to suggest otherwise:

Most individuals to whom an executive career is open marry the "right" kind of wife (the one that David Reisman has called the "station-wagon" type) almost by instinct. (p. 85)

Perhaps, as Berger suggested earlier, sociology is inviting to those boys who are titillated by watching others. In the following definition of sociology's power, the little boy who used to peep through the keyhole to watch his maiden aunt in the bathroom, now is seen observing couples in their bedrooms:

A sociologist can predict whether a man of a certain class has sexual relations with his wife with the lights turned on or off. (p. 81)

Sociologists may self-consciously claim that marriage and the family are the foundations of a stable society, but actually find them miserable institutions:

> The idea that a man should fixate his sexual drive permanently and exclusively on one single woman with whom he is to share bed, bathroom and the boredom of a thousand bleary-eyed breakfasts was produced by misanthropic theologians. (p. 85)

Berger concludes his "inviting" book by explaining that sociology is humanistic, even though it is so difficult to be a humanist in our culture:

> It is not easy to introduce a humanistic dimension into research designed to determine the optimum crew composition of a bomber aircraft, or to discover the factors that will induce somnambulent housewives in a supermarket to reach for one brand of baking powder as against the other. (pp. 169-170)

In my view, the problem with these excerpts is not eliminated by calling them a "writing style." Rather there seems to me to be a sociological vision that underlies the images. My point is that the writing of sociologists reveals their view of society, a view that sees women primarily as stupid, sexually unexciting wives *or* objects of sexual desire and violence.

Another "trusted classic" of contemporary sociology that defined the field and is in its seventeenth printing (at least) rarely used images that referred to women, but if so only as wives whose significance was as possessions that helped define the character of men:

> We ... want to know how much each is influenced by his contemporaries, and in which realms of life this influence is more important—in the choice of one's car, the books one reads, the wife one takes, the profession one pursues? (Inkeles, 1964, p. 53)

With Luckmann, Berger coauthored *The Social Construction of Reality* (1967), a work that represents a cornerstone of contemporary sociological theory in the sociology of knowledge tradition. In this book women appear only once in the index, referring to the ill effects on boys if their father is "absent" and their mother's and sisters' presence influences them to be effeminate. Women make their appearance here only as vehicles of potential harm. It is almost ironic that Berger and Luckmann end their book with this revealing conclusion:

Sociology takes its place in the company of the sciences that deal with man as man ... [the] object is society as part of a human world, made by men, inhabited by men, and, in turn, making men, in an ongoing historical process. It is not the least fruit of a humanistic sociology that it reawakens our wonder at this astonishing phenomenon. (p. 211)

Criticism of the limited view of women that is an integral part of structural-functionalism, one of the most widely accepted among contemporary sociological theories, is well known (Millett, 1969, pp. 310-329). Yet even critics of structural-functionalist theory, advocates of conflict models, may unwittingly integrate sexist imagery into their theory. Sexist imagery is present in the works of humanistic critics of mainstream sociology, just as sexist practices were prevalent in humanistic social movement organizations that attempted to alter American society before the resurgence of the women's movement. For example, here are some images used in Derek Phillips's *Abandoning Method*:

Imagine a situation where Mrs. Jones' husband has behaved toward her in an abusive and violent manner over a period of several years. Finally after he has pushed her down a flight of stairs, Mrs. Jones obtains a knife and kills her husband. We might want to say that this situation fits a typical formula of causal ascription: no B without A. Had he not been so violent and abusive, had he not pushed her down the stairs, she would not have killed him. However, to support such a causal assertion it is also necessary to show that, if A is not present, B will not occur, or that whenever A occurs B will follow. But B could conceivably occur without A; Mrs. Jones could have killed her husband for a great variety of reasons; he beat the children, or insulted her mother, or snored too loudly. And there are too many abusive and violent husbands for us to say with any degree of certainty that their behavior will always be followed by their wives' killing them. So concepts such as motive, reason, and purpose have doubtful and indeterminate application. (1973, p. 174)

The misogyny in this excerpt is apparent in the implicit ridicule of a woman whose murder of her husband could have occurred for four apparently equivalent reasons: her husband's violence toward her, his beating of their children, his insulting her mother, or his snoring. She becomes absurd if she is considered willing to murder for snoring. By casting doubt on her reasonableness, she is demeaned and he is almost excused. To me, this conjecture about her motive speaks louder than Phillips's explicit disdain for violent husbands.

In a previous discussion of the concept of probability, Phillips uses the following telling example:

> A man who "flirts" with a woman at a party by ripping off her clothes and throwing her to the floor will almost certainly be seen as exceeding the rules of flirting. (1973, p. 159)

These examples reflect the workings of a misogynist imagination in a patriarchal culture. Yet it is this same imagination that these writers think of as sociology and that has been legitimated as such. Violence toward women and the view of women as ridiculous, particularly in their evaluation of men, is embedded in the writing of people thought of as reliable interpreters of society. Recognizing that sociology written by men has been "male sociology," not "sociology," can be a way of sidestepping the problem of distrust (see also Patai, 1983).

SEXISM IN CONTEMPORARY TEXTBOOKS

Even contemporary textbooks contain pejorative references to females despite recent public recognition of the need to expunge sexist writing from publications (Miller & Swift, 1980). In my view, these textbooks reinforce prejudice against women and other groups even when they disparage negative beliefs about them. When illustrations are ostensibly directed at undermining associations between certain groups and negative traits, people are reminded of these associations. Again, this problem arises in the examples and analogies, not in the explicit argument of the books. For example, one of the most highly regarded textbooks in sociology contains the following:

> Suppose you were once cheated by a shopkeeper you thought to be Jewish. You might conclude from that one event that Jewish shopkeepers are dishonest in general. Subsequently you'd probably take special note of dishonest actions by other Jewish shopkeepers, while ignoring honest Jews and dishonest non-Jews. Some people take special note of all lazy blacks they come across and ignore energetic blacks and lazy whites. Others notice irrational and emotional women while overlooking stable women as well as unstable men. (Babbie, 1983, p. 12)

Babbie returns to a discussion of Jews, blacks, and women when explaining the principle of deduction:

> Suppose, for example, you had decided that all Jewish shopkeepers were dishonest, and then *one of them* walked four miles to return the wallet that you left on the store counter. What would you do? In *our* casual, day-to-day handling of such matters, we often make up information that

would resolve the contradiction. Maybe the shopkeeper isn't really Jewish after all. Or maybe the shopkeeper was just casing your house with a later burglary in mind. (emphasis added)

Perhaps that hard-working and energetic black at work is just trying to get promoted to a soft executive post. Perversely, people often doubt the general femininity of the woman who is tough-minded, logical and unemotional in getting the job done. Concluding that she's not really a woman protects the general conclusion that women are irrational and flighty. (Babbie, 1983, p. 12)

In this methods textbook, necessary and sufficient causes are explained by scenarios about anti-Semitism:

Let's postulate, for example, that being an anti-Semite is a necessary cause for murdering Jews in the streets. Non-anti-Semites don't do it. This causal relationship is not at all diminished by the fact that the vast majority of anti-Semites do not murder Jews in the streets. (Babbie, 1983, p. 58)

The racism and sexism that I believe pervade such examples begin with seeing certain groups as "them" rather than "us." Since pronoun use reveals the author's identifications, one strategy for dealing with distrust is to look specifically at the way an author uses pronouns. To do this means to treat scientific writing not only as a source of information as defined by the author, but also as a text revealing something about the author. Although the passive voice of much scientific writing hides the author's voice to a large extent, clues can sometimes be found in introductions, conclusions, and asides. The pronouns with which the author writes reflect the perspective through which the author sees.

Another window on the author's implicit sociology is the use of adjectives. In the passages quoted above, some groups are given adjectives and others are not. People who are black are called black because they are a kind of person, whereas people who are white are not called white. Blacks are shown to be a variation of people, whereas whites are the people of which other groups are variations. The objects of derision or violence are specified as blacks, Jews, or women, but the agents of prejudice are labelled vaguely as people, not as groups with characteristics of their own such as Christians, men, or whites. This language use conforms to what psychologists have shown—namely, that men are seen as the norm, women as the deviation. The strategy out of distrust that flows from this idea is to not label blacks as blacks or women as women unless everyone is labelled in terms of race and gender. In addition, one could eliminate adjectives altogether and write about women or blacks as if they represented the universally human (see Patai, 1983). Reading social science with these ideas in mind reveals the extent to which contemporary prejudice can be reinforced by contemporary social science.

Examples keep women pregnant, homosexuals feared (Rosnow & Rosenthal, 1984, pp. 137-138), and the elderly stupid. The metaphor of the witch/woman/bad as a contrast with science/male/good is common. For example, Rosnow and Rosenthal (1984) contrast an old woman with the implicitly normative young man and middle-aged male magistrate, casting her as a weird, benevolent witch. Abrahamson (1983, p. 12) does likewise in his reference to the Sphinx, who was part monster and part woman, slain by Oedipus (here a symbol of science) after he acquired knowledge. The scientist as Oedipus and woman as "other" is perhaps the most succinct clue to the paradigm from which positivism has not yet been freed.

The problem is not resolved by looking at qualitative research texts written by men. For example, when using metaphors to discuss the researcher's attitudes, Douglas draws on sexual/military imagery:

A research assault on a social institution is often analogous to a military assault on a nation. (1976, p. 31)

The researcher, like the wise lover, *never presses his* case to the point where an explicit "no" is possible—*unless his* situation is desperate or unless there is no tomorrow. (emphasis added; 1976, p. 32)

The feminist researcher is likely to feel alienated from methodological instruction such as this (see also Gurney, in press). In Douglas's world, researchers are men who ensnare other men into acknowledging their deviance vis-à-vis women. For example, he explains that his clever dinner party tactics enabled him to trick a businessman into revealing that his company kept a list of callgirls for special customers (1976, pp. 66-67). He explains the idea of self-deception by reference to a man who tries to convince a "friend" to give up a girlfriend because he "wants the girl." Women appear frequently in this text, but only as the duped party, the whore, or the girlfriend manipulated by others.

FINAL THOUGHTS ON REREADING SOCIOLOGY

A male sociologist in a patriarchal milieu sees the world not only as a sociologist but also as a male, oftentimes in aggressive, manipulative, sexualized ways (unless he has gone out of his way to change his consciousness and behaviors through specific feminist commitments). In addition, he writes for a male audience who sees the world in the same terms. If this is so, then the challenge for the female and/or feminist sociologist is to figure out how to use selectively the sociological tradition—that is, to determine what she can trust.

In the classic sociological texts women were perceived only as objects, if they were perceived at all. Yet women made up half the society the sociologists were writing about. Rereading sociology leads to the conclusion that male sociologists have been unable to transcend their society's commonplace ideas.[10] In addition, despite the claims of objectivity (a supposed product of positivist methodology), the attitudes apparent in the work of male sociologists are not unlike those of their class and gender. What Simone de Beauvoir said of society in general was also true of sociologists. Women were defined by male sociologists as "the other" or were not there at all. Hatred and fear of women has been given the label *misogyny*. Perhaps a new word—*gynopia*—is needed to point out the inability to perceive the very existence of women as fully human actors.

Feminist distrust of sociology stems from the insulting, inaccurate, and entirely "other" nature of much theory, methodological instruction, and even humanistic criticism. But then the question remains, What theory and method would be a useful alternative? If it were only a question of defining new topics relative to women's lives and correcting specific sexist biases in research (see ASA, 1980) or teaching (Gappa & Pearce, 1982) things would be *relatively* simple. But the problem seems deeper than that.

Perhaps the answer is that sociology can never be free of sexism in a world characterized by misogyny and gynopia. Positivist science did not free thought of prejudice. Rather, social movements, political power, and consciousness raising seem to have made the most significant impacts in this regard. In my view, there is a continued need for consciousness-raising among social scientists, focused on the questions, To what extent does our research incorporate the prejudices of the day, and to what extent does it transcend them?

Although I have focused on distrust, I have also mentioned some means of working with distrust. First is to reexamine classic and contemporary sociological texts written by men in terms of their gendered authorship in a patriarchal society. This reexamination should seek the implicit sociology revealed in asides, examples, and metaphors. The use of pronouns and the phrase "of course" are other clues. Second is to seek missing historical and neglected contemporary works written by women and use them to build a modern sociology. These two consciousness-raising strategies redefine "sociology" as "male sociology" and "female sociology" as "sociology" (Patai, 1983). Third is to search for a postpositivist paradigm based on feminist and other critical assumptions (for an example, see Thomas & Edmondson, in press). These assumptions include recognition of one's values and the extent to which one is embedded in one's research (see Reinharz, 1979, 1983). Fourth is the construction of new contexts in which we can do our postpositivist feminist sociological work. These new contexts include institutions that have been transformed from competitive and bureaucratic to cooperative and egalitarian. In these new institutions, knowledge producers would be demographically representative of the population at large. It goes without saying that these new institutions would be physically and psychologically safe. In the meantime, a sociology grounded in values other than those that define our society may have to be carried out in alternative settings alongside the university (see Nebraska Feminist Collective, 1983; Reinharz, 1983). Since the context in which knowledge is created affects the knowledge that is created, our attempts to develop an unalienating social science will always be linked to our ability to develop a fully humane society.

NOTES

1. See Rosnow and Rosenthal (1984) for a discussion of the methodological and epistemological problems of artifacts and values, and see Peters and Ceci (1982) for a discussion of the social psychologically based inconsistency in the evaluation of scientific work.

2. "Fewer than half of women academics are married, compared to almost 90% of the men" (Hu-DeHart, 1982, p. 8).

3. "About one-third of the women in academe have children, compared to more than two-thirds of the men, and these women tend to have fewer children than men with families" (Hu-DeHart, 1982, p. 8).

4. Names of sexual harassers are sometimes written in women's bathroom stalls as a way of alerting potential victims.

5. I am indebted to Barrie Thorne, who suggested this phrase (personal communication, 1984).

6. Part of this quote is discussed in Nebraska Feminist Collective (1983). To Durkheim's credit, it must be said that he did not lump all women in one category but rather recognized the differences among types of women, depending, in this case, on whether or not they were married. Similarly, Durkheim recognized that marriage has differential consequences for the male and female partner. He thereby implicitly accepted a conflict-of-interests model of marriage—a model that feminists are also developing in contrast with the structural-functionalist model.

7. See also, Durkheim, *The Division of Labor in Society* (1933/1964, pp. 55-63).

8. Anti-positivists, phenomenologists, critical theorists, and Marxist sociologists seem to have been similarly encumbered by and not cognizant of their patriarchal

assumptions. For this reason, although the feminist sociological critique has benefitted from these preceding critical perspectives, it has not been satisfied by them.

9. When I was preparing to teach an introductory social psychology course in 1982, I asked colleagues at various universities which books they thought were best and Berger's was hailed as a twenty-year-old classic worth using nowadays. I continously see praise for the book. For example, Westhues (1982), a humanistic sociologist, annotates a reference to it as "a little book that brims over with clarity and cordiality" (p. 32).

10. The extent to which this is true is continuously being discovered. For example, Charlotte Schwartz and Merton Kahne have shown that in the theorizing of medical sociologists there has been an unwitting and implicit assumption that the physician is a white male and the patient is a woman, child, or person compromised economically or socially (1983, p. 335). They show that these assumptions have almost undermined the theory built on them.

8

WHAT *IS* CLINICAL METHOD?

Rodney L. Lowman

This chapter and this book should not have had to be written in 1985. It is astounding and in many ways preposterous to imagine that those who study and attempt to change social systems should be oblivious and often downright hostile to the idea of "clinical" methods. That a collection such as this one will likely be at the fringe of social science studies is a sad statement about the narrow-mindedness of a field that potentially could do much to improve the lives of persons who live, work, and play in social systems.

But just as good clinical change agents must begin with clients as they now are and not as they would like for them to be, so too this chapter makes the assumption that its readers are persons for whom clinical method is a fairly recent, and in many ways still novel, concept. The chapter therefore asks and attempts to address such questions as the following. How does one think "clinically"? How does the epistemology of clinical method differ from that of more traditional approaches used to understand social systems? How can quality standards be applied to such methods to assure that they are rigorous? These questions, and others, will constitute the central themes of this chapter. True to its subject, the presentation incorporates my own experiences and perceptions to illustrate how social scientists function when they use clinical methods.

The term *clinical* originated with the medical profession. In medicine, *clinical* refers to those aspects of study that are based on actual treatment and observation of patients as distinguised from experimental or laboratory study (*Webster's New Twentieth Century Dictionary*,1971). Clinical methods of teaching or research therefore refer to those that are closely tied to the real-life manifestations of that which is studied or treated, as opposed to paradigms, models, or analogues from other species. *Experience-based* is an appropriate descriptor.

Although clinical methods are well established in the health care professions, the same cannot be said of those who study or attempt to change social systems. The animosity that has characterized the debates between traditional researchers and those more clinically oriented goes beyond the natural rivalry that might arise between proponents of different methodologies used to study the same phenomenon. Exemplary of the depth of feelings on both sides is the following anecdote. A fews years ago, a group of researchers were invited by the Industrial/ Organizational (I/O) Psychology Division of the American Psychological Association to present a symposium for its annual convention on the topic of "parallel processes in organizational research." The theme of similarities between the behaviors studied and those of the researchers was an old one for clinical psychologists but apparently a radical one for the I/O group, which, after soliciting the symposium, insisted that a critic be sent along to challenge the views to be presented (K. Smith, personal communication, 1984). At the sparsely attended symposium the critic proceeded to lambast the presentations, primarily on the basis that "parallel processes" had nothing to do with research. The critic went so far as to inquire of one member of the audience who had asked a sympathetic question of the presenters whether he was wearing beads. This experience suggests more than a difference of scientific paradigms: It implies a threat of some significance. One does not fight that which has no importance.

If animosity extends both to clinical methodology and to its substantive findings, it is useful to ask why. Part of the answer lies in a difference of abilities and of world views of the type of persons who are attracted to the two methodologies (which will here be called *traditional* and *clinical*). Traditional researchers bring a "scientific" orientation to their subject matter. They look at the world through representational eyes: The accurate symbolization of reality is more important than empathic understanding or learning through introspection or observation. This type of personality is probably best described by Holland's (1973) "Investigative" type: analytical, distant, asocial, more interested in working with ideas or things than with people (e.g., Osipow, 1973; Roe, 1961).

The person who studies from what might be called the *phenomenological,* or *clinical*, perspective, in contrast, is more likely to be at least as oriented to other people as to ideas or things. Intuition and the understanding of phenomena on the basis of experience form an important research tool for this type of investigator's approach. In Holland's terms, the typical "clinical" researcher probably has both "Social" and "Investigative" components. It is possible, particularly for those who study organizations and social systems, that those attracted to the clinical methodologies are persons for whom research methods are relatively sterile or "juiceless" unless they involve meaningful interaction with people. Clinical methods, in this view, may be one possible way of adjusting to a misfit between themselves and the general field of which they are part.

It is appropriate to speculate on the personal dynamics that cause one to be attracted to a field like organizational psychology. In my experience, graduate students in the area of organizational and social systems studies who have been attracted to clinical research and change methodologies have been those who have had some interest in working with people and who felt themselves alien to mainstream organizational research methods, yet who for one reason or another had seriously considered—and rejected—the more unambiguously "clinical" areas of study. Thus, individuals may choose such a field as a relatively safe way of handling personal conflicts. While something about psychology attracted and kept them (rather than choosing a field like business management), they chose a psychological specialty that is both applied and emotionally "safe." The ones who actively struggle with the "clinical" issues are probably those for whom the desire to help, to understand themselves, and/or to work with other people have not yet been fully suffused with intellect or power drives.

These divided loyalties, unassisted by a sympathetic audience of either faculty or peers, can make for considerable personal conflict. In my own case, for example, I trained in both clinical and organizational psychology and have struggled for years to find or create a setting compatible with what seem to me, if not the profession, to be complementary perspectives. I have learned to expect almost no understanding, much less appreciation, from the vast majority of my traditionally trained colleagues. The professional life of the clinically oriented social systems researcher or interventionist is, in 1985, a lonely one.

It would of course be bad psychology to pretend that career choice decisions are made solely on the basis of personal psychological dynamics, or that personality is the exclusive determinant of one's approach to research. One's abilities constitute another critical determinant. An intriguing work by Gardner (1983) presents a theory of "multiple intelligences." Gardner's work reminds us of the narrowness of our present concepts of what qualifies as intelligent behavior by identifying seven kinds of intelligence: linguistic, spatial, kinesthetic, musical, logical-mathematical, and two kinds of interpersonal intelligence. How abilities relate to personality and vocational interests is still an unsettled question in the professional literature (e.g., Osipow, 1973), but it is plausible that persons who are attracted to clinical methods in the social sciences are those whose abilities tend toward the verbal-linguistic and interpersonal, while those who are specialists in the traditional, quantitative methods are more skilled in the spatial and mathematical abilities. Such differences, if empirically confirmed, would likely result in very different approaches to both research and life, and could explain some of the hostility directed at clinical methodologists by traditional researchers.

Clinical method is of interest and importance, however, only if it illuminates and clarifies what cannot be accomplished by other, better-established methodologies. It is no good to develop clinical approaches if all they do is keep intellectual misfits less discontent. Clinical methodologies worth developing are those that uniquely add to understanding and that have widespread applicability. They are perhaps most useful as exploratory devices for those aspects of a field of inquiry that are uncharted; for studying complex social systems as a whole that cannot be examined easily, if at all, by the traditionalist's scientific scrutiny; and as the methdology of choice for interpersonally based change strategies.

WHY CLINICAL METHODS ARE NEEDED

The study of social systems needs clinical methodologies if only because so little has been learned from traditional approaches. As one example, Miner (1984) illustrates the limitations of many of the theories that have predominated in the literature in one area relevant to this discussion—industrial/organizational psychology. A similar concern was raised by Gordon, Kleiman, and Hanie (1978), who empirically demonstrated that few of the research findings of organizational psychology differed significantly from common sense.

Traditional I/O psychology, particularly personnel psychology, has most successfully created technically sophisticated studies of rather small subsystems of life in organizations, especially personnel selection and evaluation. In the day-to-day experiences of most organizations, these are important, but clearly delimited, concerns. Moreover, quantitative sophistication is no substitute for veridicality to experience. Studies in social systems of personality, emotions, and complex interactions of personal and structural aspects have been rare. Even case studies that accurately reproduce the real-life experience of members of an organization are few. It is as if Freud were to have attempted to understand neurosis solely by reference to intellect, ignoring emotions.

Since traditional methodologies have had over fifty years to apply their methodologies to the problems of social systems and have had such little impact on the day-to-day behavior of these systems, then perhaps it is time for other research methods to be given a real chance to explore the same territory. Such opportunity would require primarily the legitimization of clinical methods as proper research tools. Were clinical methods to be seriously integrated into the curricula of relevant graduate training programs, perhaps a new, more clinically sensitive, generation of scholars and practitioners with astute observational and change agent skills would become attracted to the field.

DIFFERENTIATING CLINICAL AND TRADITIONAL METHODS

"Clinical" methodologies differ from traditional ones in their perceptual and inferential processes, in what is acceptable as "data," and in the researcher's relationship to the phenomenon being studied. Clinical researchers include cultural anthropologists, scientifically oriented interventionists, and even some artists and novelists. A clinical researcher considers as a primary requirement that he or she have a basic, personalized, and ultimately well-integrated understanding of the phenomenon being studied. Whether the product be a therapeutic statement, a canvas, or a journal article, the effective clinical methodologist clearly conveys depth and complexity of understanding.

APPLIED SCIENCE

The distinction between the clinical and the traditional approaches is something regarded as the "subjective" versus the "scientific." This is misleading. As Herma puts it: "The real opposition is not between more or less scientific disciplines, but between a theoretical and an applied science. All practical applications of scientific knowledge introduce personal factors such as experience, skill, intuition, and invention" (1968, p. 122).

It is in these "personal factors" that organizational behaviorists are so inadequately trained. In contrast, psychotherapy provides an example of a field that is unabashedly "clinical" in orientation. Attention is directed both in training and in practice to the development of expertise in observation, interpersonal competence, and in the juxtaposition of theory with experience (e.g., Greenson, 1967; Paul, 1973). Observational skills, timing, intuition, and a comparison of the observed and the theoretical are obviously needed for success as a psychotherapist.

Clinical methods may be more suited for some undertakings than for others. Microsurgery and plumbing do not obviously lend themselves to clinical methods. It is likely that important criteria for determining whether clinical methods will be able to make a substantive contribution include that they be applied to phenomena that cannot adequately be represented by traditional scientific method alone (at least at that stage of the science's development), that the phenomena be directly observable by those with appropriate skills and training, and that there be sufficient complexity that traditional methods of experimental control are not applicable.

It is illustrative that one of the most important contributions to understanding psychopathology even today is the work of Freud. Those researchers who have tried to apply traditional methodologies to such constructs as unconscious processes (e.g., Silverman, 1976) have added rather little understanding when compared to Freud's. While not abandoning scientific principles, Freud used his investigative and observational genius to create methods appropriate to his subject matter. The technique of free association provided a relatively standardized method for observing and working with a great diversity of client problems. These methods were decidedly toward the "clinical" end of the "traditional-clinical" spectrum of research methods. Controlled studies with high interrater reliabilities were no substitute for the insightful observations by one man of his patients' behaviors.

By analogy, in the social systems area the researcher or interventionist might learn a great deal by the feel of an organization, its physical plant, bulletin boards, responses to an unstructured interview with a few representative employees, or through observation of the posture and voice tones of a supervisor and subordinate as they interact. Such a methodology might study the memoranda, advertisements, the financial history of the organization, and the nonverbal behaviors manifested by key organizational members in a meeting. For the clinical investigator *all* behavior is potentially important. The ability to observe, classify, and interpret behavior accurately rests critically on the skills and personality of the clinician.

SYSTEMIC PERSPECTIVE

The clinical methodologist is perhaps best able to view a complex social structure as a system. While heavily acknowledged as a desirable theoretical foundation for studying organizations (e.g., Katz & Kahn, 1978), systems theory has been adequately incorporated into relatively few empirical studies of organizations or social systems. The best examples of the application of systems theory to date are case studies such as those by Newhouse of the airplane manufacturing industry (1982) and Levinson's detailed case studies of organizations (1972), though the latter are tainted by a rather mechanistic fixation on psychoanalytic theory.

The clinical investigator is better able to examine behavior systematically because of not being bound to one research paradigm, which by its nature limits the number of hypotheses that can be measured or considered at any one time. The clinician is free to introduce hypothesized explanatory constructs without the necessity of having to measure such variables "scientifically." This does not mean that anything goes, but rather that the clinician may consider as explanations alternatives not empirically measured by the investigator, such as the relative influence on an organization of such events as the death of its founder, its recently having successfully marketed a new product, or a protracted strike that occurred three years prior to the study.

The clinical researcher is also free to examine many different types of data, even though some data sources may be less rigorously measured. For example, a psychotherapist may inquire in some detail about events that historically have been important to a client and may accept a subjective interpretation of the meaning of these events independent of their "objective" truth or falsity. The clinician can also observe multiple data sources simultaneously—the tone of voice with which a client speaks about her or his mother, the discrepancy between gestures and words, or the difference in the amount of time devoted to one subject rather than another.

THE PRODUCT

Traditional researchers seek to reduce information about social systems to quantitative data that can be analyzed statistically. Clinicians recognize that numbers are only one way to express knowledge and make liberal use of alternative ways of reporting findings. The case study and the qualitative description of clinical experience are regarded as acceptable forms in which to present results, particularly those of complex systems. Works such as those of Jaques (1952), Sofer (1961), Whyte (1948), and Watzlawick, Weakland, and Fisch (1974) are illustrative of good clinical writings (especially concerning social systems) and of both the values and the limitations of this approach.

DEVELOPMENTAL PERSPECTIVE

The clinician thinks in developmental terms in two primary ways. First, the age of a person or a social system provides a good indicator of the types of issues that are generally important at that particular life or developmental stage (e.g., Levinson, Darrow, Klein, Levinson, & McKee, 1978; Kimberly & Miles, 1980). The developmental perspective helps the researcher or interventionist tailor the inquiry or change project to methodologies that are likely to be relevant and important to the client.

Second, a developmental approach suggests the need for theories and observations that are dynamic rather than static, since change is recognized as being the natural state of a person or system. The clinical method pays special attention to events, not just to variables, in attempting to understand change in a social system, recognizing the importance of both historical happenings and of variables that can be expressed and analyzed mathematically. The clinical method values these views while also recognizing the inadequacies of existing theories of the developmental phases of organizations. Unlike the study of individuals, in which multiple theories of predictable life stages have been developed and tested in literally thousands of studies, we do not yet have comparable developmental theories for social systems and have virtually no empirical studies in this area. The clinical investigator must therefore be sensitive to patterns of growth and development without reliably knowing the stages through which the social system will predictably pass. It is precisely for a problem like this that clinical methodologies are best suited.

INFERENTIAL AND
EPISTEMOLOGICAL PROCESSES

Any method of inquiry must articulate methods for moving from the data collected to generalizations about the data. The traditional researcher characteristically moves from theory to data to statistical tests of theory. The clinical researcher moves from observation of behavior to interpretation to hypothesis generation. The traditional researcher relies on logico-deductive models of inference; the clinician, on intuitive models and on the interaction between the researcher and the object being studied. While in traditional research "truth" is established through the quantitative analysis of data, in clinical research other methods must be used. In psychotherapy, for example, the therapist's perception is a hypothesis whose accuracy or inaccuracy will be judged, among other things, by the response of the patient. Criteria have been developed by psychotherapists to determine whether or not an interpretation is accurate. For example, Malan (1979) asserts that accurate interpretation will be followed by an increase in the client's rapport with the therapist. What is important in this context is not the validity of this particular approach to establishing "truth" but rather the illustration of a method in which investigative approaches are carefully integrated with their subject matter.

Similarly, in working with an organization, a clinically oriented interventionist might conclude that an apparent problem of low productivity really stems from father-son rivalry and the owner-father's ambivalence toward giving up control of the organization (e.g., Levinson, 1983). Again, the interventionist translates client-presented data to theories or understandings that would explain the behavior and about which the client may be unaware. The veracity of the theory is confirmed, if at all, by the reception it receives from the client in an interactive process, as previously discussed. The clinical inferential process is therefore personalistic and highly related to the skill, intuition, and competence of the therapist or researcher.

WORKING ON MULTIPLE LEVELS

The clinical approach, at least to individuals, addresses its subject matter from multiple levels. It is not content to deal only with the surface manifestations of a behavior. Recognizing that behavior is determined by both conscious and unconscious factors, and that it is typically overdetermined by multiple sources of causality, the clinician seeks an understanding of both the rational and the irrational.

It is the unconscious processes that have largely been ignored by traditional researchers of organizations and social systems. Most of the theories of behavior in organizations are comfortable only with the most overt and "rational" causes of behavior, despite the fact that unconscious factors may, at least at the individual level, be highly deterministic of such behaviors as procrastination, goal setting, and work accomplishment. In the clinical approach, special sensitivity to the less easily measured aspects of behavior is stressed. Interactions among cognitive, affective, and value-related determinants of behavior are all taken into account by the clinical investigator.

ACTIVISM

The clinical researcher is a more active participant in the process of learning. Rather than rigidly controlling the type of data that is elicited or trying to minimize personal observations that might lead to alternative hypotheses to those originally considered, in the clinical approach the investigator is actively a part of the process of learning. The clinical investigator tries different types of interpretations and observes the client's responses. The clinical investigator also recognizes that his or her own behavior is always influential in determining what will be observed (e.g., Lowman, 1982b). It was one of Freud's important contributions to recognize that a separate psychology was not needed to explain the therapist and the patient: Similar concepts and principles apply to both. Researchers cannot act in isolation from what they research without seriously jeopardizing their understanding. Clinical researchers or interventionists recognize that they are necessarily part of the system they seek to change or to understand, and therefore make an active effort to integrate that reality into research methods.

EMOTIONAL DEMANDS
OF CLINICAL METHODS

Because the person of the clinical investigator is so prominent in the interaction, clinical methods are affectively demanding of the researcher. If, as was speculated earlier in this chapter, traditional investigators typically enter the field of research as a way of assuring predictability and order in their lives, clinical methods are a radical, and presumably unappealing, departure. The clinical researcher involves him- or herself in all phases of an investigation. Moreover, clinicians are sensitive to unconscious and well-defended explanatory causes, which may put considerable strain on their own defense mechanisms. The extreme ambiguity associated with experience-driven, as opposed to data- and theory-driven, approaches also requires expertise in coping with considerable uncertainty.

WHO CAN AND WHO CANNOT CONDUCT
CLINICAL STUDIES

Clinical methods demand far more of the researcher than do traditional methods. Clinical researchers place themselves in the thick of the data-gathering process and place their person on the line in the process of collecting data or making interventions. Because of these working conditions, clinical researchers or interventionists are far more likely to experience anxiety, intrusion into their personal dynamics and defenses, and, since depth rather than superficial understanding is sought, the arousal of anxiety in the persons being studied.

Curiously, the personal qualities, skills, and abilities required for the successful clinical researcher have been poorly researched. Berg (1980) and Sofer (1961) come closest, among existing literature. Table 8.1 presents a hypothesized and admittedly speculative listing of the job skills, knowledge, and desired attributes of the clinical researcher or

TABLE 8.1   Job Skills, Knowledge, and Attributes of the Clinical Researcher

(1) *Job Skills*
   A. Ability to establish relationships of trust, acceptance, warmth and concern
   B. Ability to diagnose a client's condition, to gather and interpret evidence from a variety of sources, to use oneself as a diagnostic instrument
   C. Ability to communicate at the level of the recipient, to give and receive feedback in minimally threatening ways, to communicate with a minimum of contradictory messages, to help others acknowledge ownership of their own ideas and feelings
   D. Ability to execute a well-developed sense of timing, especially when working under stress
   E. Ability to be pragmatic, emphasizing the applied and practical aspects of behavior
   F. Ability to work under conditions of high stress, high uncertainty and ambiguity, high frustration, loneliness and professional isolation

(2) *Job Knowledge*
   A. Organizational and interpersonal dynamics
   B. Principles of change and changing
   C. Individual personality dynamics
   D. Ethics
   E. Standards of professional practice

(3) *Personal Attributes*
   A. Cognitive complexity and high intelligence
   B. Interpersonal competence, including:
      B1. Openness and honesty
      B2. Awareness of and control over one's own personal psychological defenses
      B3. Cognitive flexibility
      B4. Self awareness and self acceptance
   C. Moderate needs for affiliation, achievement, and power
   D. "Helping" orientation
   E. High need for personal competence
   F. Comfort with intuitive methods
   G. Imagination and cognitive flexibility

interventionist. In this table there are numerous presumed personal characteristics that either should be made the focus of clinical methodological training or criteria of selection for those entering the field.

The skills outlined in Table 8.1 are primarily interpersonal. It is likely that the characteristics that make for a successful clinical investigator will rarely be found in traditional researchers. Miles (1979) makes the point that as qualitative methods increase in popularity, they may become an "attractive nuisance" to those unprepared by training or temperament for their complexities. Such individuals may do more harm than good by using these methods. The task for traditional researchers is not to abandon or even necessarily to supplement the methodologies with which they personally are familiar and skilled, but rather to encourage and support nontraditional researchers to develop outstanding examples of studies using their particular methods. Even more important, the traditionalist should attempt to learn from the findings of clinical studies—which is hard to do if personal aversion perverts interest or attention.

THE URGENT NEED FOR QUALITY CONTROL IN CLINICAL APPROACHES

When they are bad, clinical methods can be very bad indeed. They are more subject to abuse than traditional approaches. They may invite weak researchers or those who are simply in the wrong field. Because the role of the clinical researcher or interventionist is so much more personalized, there is far more need for checks on the quality of the work.

The controls and checks that a clinical methodology requires are different from those appropriate to traditional research. In training psychotherapists, for example, clinical supervision models make extensive use of one-to-one supervision with audio- and videotapes of actual trainee-client interactions. Supervision is regarded as a long-term process and an ongoing need beyond one's formal years of training. It is recognized that the opportunities for distortion of data based on personal needs or the therapist's own psychopathology are many; an external party to the client-therapist relationship provides a needed outside perspective to minimize possible negative consequences to the client.

In general, bad clinical methods are probably much worse than bad traditional methods. Because there is more agreement on the methodologies and rules of evidence for the traditional than for the clinical approach, inferior work of a traditional nature can more easily be discovered. Bad clinical research may be ignored or never presented so that there is no external jury or, worse, only sympathetic admirers to evaluate its merit. Since clinical research methods are still in their infancy, it is up to those persons who perform clinical studies, whether as researchers or as interventionists, to impose their own requirements for quality control. For those still in graduate school, the task will often be to seek out interested faculty and fellow students, perhaps those in other areas of study such as psychiatry or clinical psychology, to develop the supervisory and support relationships needed.

TRAINING CLINICAL SKILLS

Curiously, there has been rather little attention directed toward how to train clinical skills in the few applied behavioral science training programs that give any attention at all to clinical methods. Such programs would benefit first by providing comprehensive rather than piecemeal programs for training these skills (e.g., Lowman, 1982a). Second, such programs could make the assessment and development of the requisite interpersonal skills or aptitudes major criteria for the selection of students and faculty, and for the measurement of acquired competencies. There appears to be little awareness by students, faculty, or program administrators of more traditional programs of what would be required to train persons competent in clinical methods. A course or two tossed into what is essentially a research curriculum may be worse than no training in clinical methodology. Alderfer and Berg (1977), Lippitt, Watson, and Westley (1958), and Sofer (1961) are among the few authors who have demonstrated much understanding of what would be needed to train clinical skills. My own perspectives on training clinical skills in applied behavioral science settings are similar to those just cited. I would add the following additional recommendations:

(1) Responsibility. Medical training models impose, appropriately, a rigid system of control to assure the protection of the client. The concept of personal responsibility for the client is so strongly part of the culture that no one would expect to challenge it with impunity, and breaches are dealt with rather severely. There is no comparable ethic among those who would attempt to change or to study social systems. Such an ethos would require far more rigorous standards of selection than now exist, but also the creation of training paradigms embodying such standards from the very beginning of training.

(2) Personal self-awareness. To take responsibility for another implies the need to subordinate one's own needs, defenses, and conflicts to the needs of the client. To experience the client role firsthand is an appropriate adjunct to the training in clinical research methods. In my experience, personal therapy is especially needed by those attracted to the clinical study of social systems to address conflicts in the areas of counterdependency and in the experience and exercise of power. In addition, personal therapy can provide a better foundation for the ongoing examination of roles suggested by Berg (1980).

Self-awareness proceeds both by intensive self-exploratory methods and by examining one's cognitive and personal strengths and weaknesses. Clinicians have no monopoly on self-awareness, only models of training that give members of the profession explicit opportunity to discuss, and, if need be, to challenge one another's self-perceptions. Participation in intensive, personally intrusive laboratory experiences and completion of psychological testing can enhance self-awareness.

(3) Peer support. If my hypotheses of professional isolation, loneliness, and a basic desire for strong interpersonal relations by clinical researchers are valid, strong peer support may provide one mechanism for countering professional isolation. Group solidarity may be fostered by a number of well-established means that need not be elaborated here. Mentoring (Levinson et al., 1978), while important, should not be overemphasized since its contribution may be slight compared to the heady innervation that is precipitated by the discovery of psychological congruity with a relevant group of peers. Moreover, the peer relationship may be less prone to the apparently natural demise of the mentoring relationship. (For similar reasons, I have always favored sending teams rather than individual students into organizations to learn change methodologies. While intensive supervision by an experienced instructor is also provided and considered important, the team tends to be where the more long-lasting learning occurs.)

(4) Diagnostic and conceptual skills. Students of social systems are perhaps among the worst trained diagnosticians of any major helping profession. The scarcity of diagnostic theory severely limits the ability to acquire skills in social system diagnostic practice. Moreover, the weak understanding of individuals by those oriented to study or change of social systems does not facilitate the ability to think complexly in terms of individual-group-system interactions.

In the absence of adequate diagnostic taxonomies, the clinician may best proceed in developing an understanding of diagnostic principles by experience-based tutorage from those with relevant clinical experience. Matching learning to appropriate interventions by those so inclined would best, at this stage of learning, proceed similarly.

(5) Ethics. Existing codes of ethics of medicine and psychology provide reasonable bases from which to formulate guidelines for practice. Elaborating such codes to the practice of research and intervention in social systems (as opposed to work with individuals) is needed. Integration of ethical concerns with the training of social science inquiry is also important.

CONCLUSION

Clinical methodologies are not for everyone. They are far more demanding than traditional methods in terms of emotionality, activity levels, and in the need for observational acuity and technical integration. Clinical researchers will probably always, and perhaps even appropriately, constitute a minority of social systems researchers. Most persons with skills amenable to clinical methods will probably find more compatible settings with more and better role models in fields such as cultural anthropology, clinical psychology, or psychiatry. It is hoped that someday soon there will be a Freud of organizations, of communities, and of other branches of social sciences to exemplify fully the potential of clinical methodologies. In the meantime, such clinical researchers face a lonely undertaking.

While the need will always be there for the rational scientist, advances in clinical methods of social science inquiry and intervention must await challengers, people able to look at the field with new visions and new understandings, to say that what we know and how we know it is both personally and professionally insufficient. The task of the social sciences is to legitimize such methodologies of inquiry, to encourage those clinically inclined to approach their work with rigor and discipline, and to sanction the belief that there are multiple ways to study the same phenomenon. Like the unrecognized gifted artist, clinical researchers in social systems need also to be protected from the existential despair that may be an inevitable part of the legacy of the innovator and that may lead, prematurely, to abandonment of inquiry.

In the future, clinical and traditional research methodologies might best be combined, each making a distinct and complementary contribution. It is time to make respectable the work of clinical researchers and to realize the limitations of our traditional approaches. The field of applied social science studies is rather urgently in need of intellectual rehabilitation. As Robert Pirsig put it in a different context,

> Classic understanding should not be overlaid with romantic prettiness: classic and romantic understanding should be united at a basic level. . . . At present we're snowed under with an irrational expansion of blind data-gathering in the sciences because there's no rational format for any understanding of scientific creativity. . . . We have artists with no scientific knowledge and scientists with no spiritual sense of gravity at all, and the result is not just bad, it is ghastly. (1974, pp. 293-294)

Commentary

The common bond that draws the chapters of this section together is the underlying question of how our ways of knowing shape our understanding of the social world. When we take these chapters as a whole, it is possible to make some clear assertions. There are important differences among us that affect our judgments about what constitutes relevant data or valuable knowledge including our gender, our interest in social action or basic science, and our source of support. The list of factors that makes a difference is long, but the general point is straightforward. The knowledge we create is, in part, a product of the culture or cultures in which we live, the groups to which we belong, the institutions that support us, and the values we hope our knowledge will sustain.

The chapter by Cammann puts before us the central concern. Knowledge is not an island, absolute unto itself. It is a set of relationships that are tied explicitly to criteria we value. The very elaboration of different criteria forces us to "count" knowledge differently. In this case, Cammann is interested in knowledge that he describes as action usable in organizational change projects. He contrasts this type of knowledge with what is knowable via methods that require "detachment and objectivity."

In a way, the pursuit of "pure" knowledge is the pursuit of an illusion made possible by the protection of institutions such as wealthy private universities that do not ask that applicability be a key criterion for funding. This point is wonderfully illustrated by Perry's example of the way changes in what was viewed as acceptable knowledge in a psychiatric hospital mirrored almost perfectly the shifts in the economic and political agendas of the funding agencies on which the hospital depended. Devastating as the thought may be in some academic circles, knowledge appears often to be a pawn in the hands of public policymakers. We may not have evolved as far as we would like to think in separating social knowledge from the desires of those who, at a given moment, dominate our society.

The chapter by Reinharz is a stark reminder that knowledge is a product of intergroup relations. What has passed as knowledge has been a product of ways of knowing that contain within them dynamics that elevate men and preserve their power while devaluing women and denigrating their humanity. Had there been a chapter written in a similar vein by a black American we would see the all-pervasiveness of the problem of social dominance.

These chapters inevitably lead us to the question of what type of ordering process we might use to create alternative hypotheses about the world, or knowledge less truncated by a single way of knowing. In the answer to this question we can observe a similar pattern in each chapter. All the authors struggled with the issue of influence—the influence upon them of social and organizational forces and, in turn, the researchers' influence on how and what they know. All saw knowledge as a product of these influences. None of the authors seemed totally at peace with this realization. It touched something deep and catalyzed further struggle. Each needed to find some resting place, a touchstone that would provide a foundation for their assessments as well as some emotional comfort.

There were differences in where each author came to rest. Perhaps the place where these differences were most evident was in the writing style each used. Cammann, for example, used a very personal style to present his ideas. As he writes about his struggles, the professional angst he feels comes through on the written page. The writing style reflects the source of his understanding. Cammann writes, "If it's action usable for me in a particular setting, I'll settle for that as knowledge." A personal foundation presented in a personal style. In contrast, Smith went to the level of relationships, Reinharz to her group identification with women, Lowman to the discipline of his profession, and Perry to the domain of politics, culture, and the world of ideas. In each case the writing style seemed consistent with the content presented.

The overall gestalt of this section is that there are many ways of knowing. This recognition comes from looking at clinical issues in a systematic way. We can know by coming up close and seeing what works for us, by entering into relationships, by developing an awareness of our group and intergroup identities, by accepting the discipline of a particular field and by examining the way our knowledge reflects our culture.

The question may well be asked, Is it possible to know anything for sure? This may be one dilemma raised by this section. There is, however, another place to come to rest. Having established that different understandings arise from different ways of knowing, we now have many more hypotheses, ideas, and concepts to use as rival explanations for our research findings. This opens up the possibility of a much broader knowledge base. If our goal is richness and potency of explanation, the more alternatives that are rigorously mapped, the less likely we are to suffer the frustration of "significant" results with trivial importance.

SECTION III

Clinical Involvement

After reading the five chapters in this section, one is struck by the relationship between clinical involvement and self-scrutiny. One could argue that involvement is a powerful stimulus for self-reflection, but it is also apparent that the willingness to engage in self-scrutiny opens up possibilities for involvement and learning. In each of the following chapters the authors describe both their involvement (with themselves, with colleagues, with research participants) and their struggles to gain some self-understanding. Together the chapters support the contention that involvement and self-scrutiny enhance both researcher and research.

In the first chapter Hackman takes us through his struggle, still incomplete, to find his own clinical "voice." It is a deeply personal account of successes and failures, anger and hurt, pain and hope. As he describes this odyssey, Hackman offers us glimpses of the repercussions occurring in his significant relationships with colleagues who are strongly identified with the clinical tradition and with others who are skeptical of it. As Hackman finally completes a chapter he says he did not want to write, it becomes clear that the personal struggle and the professional relationships are closely linked.

The second chapter is concerned with the *researcher's* emotions during research with human systems. Berg's contention is that many of our research methods are designed to protect us from the various sources of anxiety present in social research. The chapter includes an analysis of two short cases that illustrate how important the exploration of the researcher's anxiety is to the conduct of research. Berg calls on us to examine and report the emotional dynamics of research relationships since they are an inevitable consequence of the researcher's involvement.

In the third chapter Louis helps Mirvis explore the transferential dynamics present in a research project and the impact they had on Mirvis's actions, perceptions, and research role. Mirvis takes the risk of showing us some of his family history in an effort to uncover its initially subtle but ultimately powerful effect. The chapter shows a researcher willing to explore how his *whole* self becomes involved in the research relationships that make up social research.

The fourth chapter describes how Kram's research on mentoring forced her to confront the influences of her own group memberships on her study. She takes us through numerous examples of research issues that led her through a process of self-reflection and then back again to decisions about the research. In

191

some cases Kram had not anticipated that the research would cause her to scrutinize the impact of her age and sex on *her* behavior as well as the behavior of the participants in her study.

In the final chapter, Peshkin recounts two fascinating stories about his ethnographic studies of the educational systems in two midwestern towns. Peshkin spent a year in each town and only *after* writing major research reports on both studies did he begin to realize that his findings were heavily influenced by the "persona" evoked by each setting. One of the central issues in both settings was the nature and function of intolerance in these communities. Peshkin slowly discovered that the *concept* of intolerance takes on very different intellectual forms depending on whether the researcher identifies himself or herself with the tolerant or the intolerant. The narrative itself is a marvelous description of self-discovery.

The five chapters in this section are filled with emotion. Each of the authors struggles to convey what research involvement *feels* like—the pain, the intensity, the dawning awareness, the learning. It is difficult to describe feelings with words, but the emotion, the involvement, and the commitment to self-scrutiny come through.

ON SEEKING ONE'S OWN CLINICAL VOICE:
A Personal Account

J. Richard Hackman

It probably is significant that I do not want to be writing this right now. Since it may help readers make sense of what I am about to say, let me take a few paragraphs to reflect on why I have put this paper off until the last conceivable minute—and still find myself less than eager to proceed with the task.

First, I have no special commitment to the promulgation and use of clinical research methods. Clinical methodology is one of many sets of tools, all of which are flawed in some ways, that are available to researchers interested in making sense of individual, group, and organizational phenomena. The clinical approach is one about which I have tried to do some learning over the last decade or so, and one that has proven helpful to me in my scholarly work. But I do not feel called to espouse or explain clinical methods; that can be done more appropriately (and better) by colleagues who are more experienced and expert in the use of these methods than I am.

Moreover, my dominant motivation right now is to get on with my research, not to write about methodology. I am trying to understand certain group and organizational dynamics, and I want to develop and frame my understanding so that it contributes to others' learning and, I hope, enhances their ability to act competently in pursuing their objectives. In short, I want to spend my time these days *doing* it, not writing about how one does it, and certainly not reflecting on how I happen to have developed my own ways of doing it. This chapter comes at the wrong time in the evolution and execution of my own work and I wish I had not committed to write it.

My continuing ambivalence about clinical methods has been evident to me (and to the editors) in thinking about this chapter—as the paragraphs above surely make clear. One of the ways I respond when I am feeling ambivalent about something is to wallow in it for a while, and then put my head down and charges ahead in one direction or another. I have wallowed in this project for many months now, and finally agreed with one of the editors that it is time to put my head down and charge—to see if anything worth sharing with others comes out. What follows is the product of that negotiated agreement.

OVERVIEW

If one can characterize my involvement with clinical methodologies as something of a struggle (as I have experienced it, this is not a bad metaphor), then it may be useful to discuss how the struggle began. Although one could reflect back well into childhood in attempting to trace the roots of any scholar's conceptual and methodological orientation, I will begin with my years in graduate school—for it is there that I learned what "research" meant and developed my initial approach to scholarly work. Then I will review a series of events that occurred as I was leaving graduate school and starting my academic career that provided the impetus for my engagement with clinical methods.

What I have to say about the process of seeking my clinical "voice" follows that introductory material. The theme I have chosen to use in organizing my thoughts about that process (and this should not now be a surprise) is ambivalence. As I made choices to engage with the clinical world, I found ambivalence everywhere I turned: on the part of my colleagues in experimental social psychology, on the part of colleagues who identify themselves with the clinical tradition, and (perhaps most of all) within myself. For me, then, to talk about the development of clinical voice *is* to talk about ambivalence—how it is expressed and how it is dealt with, by the learner and by his or her colleagues.

The essay ends with something of a balance sheet expressing my present view of the assets and liabilities of clinical methods for the kind of work I do. This provides me an opportunity to assess whether the time and emotional energy I have expended in beginning to learn clinical methods have been well spent (I conclude that it *has* been worth it). It also gives me a platform to express my present views about the value of clinical approaches for organizational research, teaching, and intervention (I conclude that these methods offer opportunities that are not otherwise available) and about the risks that inhere in the use of clinical approaches (I conclude that the risks are serious, particularly if clinical methods come to be seen as the only legitimate way to learn about and help people and social systems, but that they can be managed).

This essay is, of necessity, highly personal in character. As someone trained that the person and the personal pronoun have no place in writing intended for one's scholarly colleagues—and being someone who values his personal privacy a great deal—that necessity makes me uncomfortable. My hope is that by opening the curtains a bit on the experiences I have had (and the feelings that have accompanied them) in the course of my development to date as a scholar and teacher, I may be able to serve as a kindred spirit at a distance for others who are travelling the same road—and who may be feeling as alone on that road as I often have felt.

WHEREFROM CAME THIS CLOSET CLINICIAN?

To the best of my recollection, Freud was mentioned in class once during my four years as a doctoral student in psychology at the University of Illinois in the mid-1960s—and that was to identify him as a figure in the history of psychology of little relevance to contemporary psychologists. That was surprising to me. Although I had taken only a couple of psychology courses as an undergraduate (my major was mathematics), I arrived at graduate school with the impression that Freud was at the core of the discipline. But I adapted quickly to the highly quantitative and empirical orientation of my doctoral program, and found that I could "do psychology" pretty well.

I had what I believed to be (and still believe to be) superb training in experimental social psychology at the hands of people like Joe McGrath, Ivan Steiner, Fred Fiedler, and Marty Fishbein. We had to take two minors in those days, and mine were psychological measurement (a special strength of Illinois psychology) and sociology (just enough involvement to convince me that I was not a natural sociologist, and that I had little interest in becoming one). My only exposure to organizational psychology at Illinois was one doctoral seminar that was mainly spent trying to figure out if there was anything about organizations that might be interesting to study (I concluded there probably was not).

Quantitative data were at the core of the Illinois program in those days, and I learned well how to collect and analyze them in accord with state-of-the-art measurement and statistical techniques. "Dustbowl empiricism," a term sometimes applied to the kind of research that was done at Illinois, is an offensive term to me because it demeans the impressive capability those people had to use numbers and statistics to make sense of phenomena whose complexity defied comprehension in other ways. The psychologists with whom I worked were smart, thoughtful, and insightful; I admired them then, and I do today.

My dissertation research was squarely in the Illinois paradigm. Tony Morris and I collaborated to collect data on 108 experimental groups, each of which performed 4 of 108 different tasks we had written, yielding 432 transcripts of group interaction (the focus of Tony's dissertation) and 432 written group products (the focus of mine). The research design was beautifully counterbalanced, the analysis was sophisticated, and for some time thereafter I characterized the dissertation as "the best piece of research I will ever do."

Yet, even as I was preparing to leave Illinois, I experienced a vague and troubling disaffection with the work. I kept trying to figure out how to apply the dissertation findings, to use them to make a constructive difference in something I cared about. I could not come up with much, at least in part because I could not figure out from the data *why* our task manipulations had such large effects on group performance outcomes. Standard arguments about the inherent virtues of basic research provided little solace.

This uneasiness with my research may have contributed (although if it did I was not aware of it at the time) to my decision about which of three academic positions to accept. The options were Wake Forest College (which was appealing because of my interest in undergraduate liberal arts education), Carnegie Institute of Technology (which had a fine group of potential colleagues in experimental social psychology), and Yale (where I would have an appointment in something called "industrial administration" with a token secondary appointment in psychology). I went to the Yale interview mainly because it was Yale—and that seemed quite something for a kid from the Midwest who had never been east of Ohio. On the way, I tried to read a book by Chris Argyris (a senior faculty member at Yale of whom I had never heard) but I could not understand it. On the way back, I wondered why I was so engaged by what was going on in that strange department where people were looking at organizations and behavior within them using methods and concepts that were wholly foreign to me. A few weeks later, when I found myself fudging the numbers on my decision-making balance sheet so that Yale would come out a little higher than it had the first time, I decided to throw caution (and the balance sheet) to the wind and go east.

IMPETUS FOR LEARNING

One cherishes what one knows how to do, and I cherished my skills as an experimental social psychologist. I could barely wait to bring them to bear on the organizational issues that were so much alive at Yale. But it gradually became clear that I did not have all the skills I needed to do the kind of teaching and research I wanted to do, or to have the constructive influence on organizational practice I wanted to have. The signs that I needed some more learning came from diverse parts of my life at work, and their cumulative impact was powerful.

In laboratory research. Still smarting over my inability to comprehend fully the reasons for the large performance differences among groups in my dissertation research, I decided to do a careful reading of the group interaction transcripts. I reasoned that if one looked at what happened in high-performing groups and compared that to what transpired in groups that performed poorly, then surely one would discover what was *really* responsible for the observed performance differences. So I selected appropriate subsets of transcripts and (with considerable anticipation) carefully read and studied them.

When I finished, the anticipation had turned to dismay: I had no idea what to make of what I had read.[1] Despite the fact that I had available for my use one of the best data sets on group performance ever compiled, I was unable to frame a reasonable answer to the fundamental question in the group effectiveness paradigm: "How come some groups perform so much better than others?" Neither multivariate statistics nor verbatim reading of the interaction transcripts had provided much help. So how, I asked myself, *does* one understand a group, anyway? It was a most troubling question, and one I knew I would have to take on.

In field research. One of my early experiences in field research resulted (I believe) in a manager losing his job—a consequence of my good intentions coupled with inexperience, incompetence, and lack of supervision in managing field relationships.

The project dealt with shop-floor motivational questions, and involved collection of data using questionnaires and interviews. Early on, I experienced the project as enjoyable and relatively easy to manage. The top manager who had initiated the research seemed enthusiastic, it was exciting to learn about the organization and how it conducted its business, and data collection was going smoothly—although some people did seem guarded and uneasy about talking with me. (When I sensed uneasiness, I would let the individual "off the hook," even to the extent of ignoring the interview questions and filling the scheduled time with casual conversation with the interviewee.)

Things were not so smooth and relaxed when the time arrived to present the research findings to the organization. For one thing, the top manager seemed to have lost interest in the project (he claimed that pressing business matters were fully occupying him). And when I arrived for one feedback session, I found myself scheduled with the executive committee of the union (with whom I had not met as a group before, and who asserted that they were there to see which managers I had identified as incompetent). My protestations that that was not what the project was about fell on deaf ears, and when I refused to name names, they ended the session and left.

I kept trying to make contact with the top manager until, one day, I learned that he had dismissed the manager of the department where the research had been done—and, I was told, had used the research findings as part of his justification.

This shocked me about as profoundly as anything else I can recall in my professional work (even now, many years later, I find it hard to write about the events of the project). The only positive outcome of the research was that it jolted me (finally) into realizing how I and my research had been used, how unaware I had been of what was actually transpiring throughout the life of the project, and how grossly unskilled I was in comprehending and managing research in organizational settings. It was clear that if I was going to do research in the field, I was going to have to learn a lot of things I had not been taught in graduate school.

In teaching. One of my first teaching assignments was a large section of introductory psychology. T-groups were much in vogue at the time, and the staff (I was one of four) decided that everybody in the course should have a three-hour T-group experience. We scheduled hundreds of students into small groups, reserved rooms around campus for the group meetings, and lined up dozens of trainers to facilitate them.

On the evening of the event, one of the trainers failed to appear, and another instructor suggested that I substitute for him. I declined politely but I was aghast. I could not comprehend how a trained clinician could suggest that someone with no group training whatever lead a T-group— even if it was only a three-hour "demonstration." While the dubious worth (and the risks) of the whole enterprise of one-shot T-groups for all introductory psychology students was not something I understood at the time, I at least had enough sense to realize that one needed some training to lead such a group. I did not have it, I had serious reservations about the behavior of some of those who did, and I figured that it might make sense to learn a little about that stuff—considering that I billed myself as someone not only interested in groups, but knowledgeable about them.

In the department. The climate of the Department of Industrial Administration (subsequently Administrative Sciences) at Yale in the late 1960s provided persistent support for exploring alternative ways of behaving, teaching, and learning—and many of these explorations were rooted in the clinical tradition. It was impossible to be a member of the Yale organizational behavior group in those years and not be affected in some way by clinical thought and practice.

The events that affected me were separately of small consequence but collectively had great impact. For example,

— attempting to line up Fritz Steele's vote for an upcoming faculty appointment, and his using the occasion to inquire about my personal model of organizational politics. By the time the conversation was over, he had gently prodded me toward expanding my thinking about social influence in organizations, and had modeled for me an alternative way of being influential that I found as intriguing as it was unfamiliar;

— participating in a fairly intense debate with my faculty colleagues (at one of our evening discussions at Argyris's house) on whether or not there really is such a thing as "unconscious motivation," and finding myself disturbed at how my own thinking about human behavior was restricted by assumptions I had never thought seriously about, let alone questioned;

— trying to respond to concerns raised by graduate students about how "authority dynamics" might be affecting what was happening in my course, and not even being sure what it was they were talking about.

With all of these events and more, I increasingly realized that I was standing just outside the real inner circle. It was not the best of motives, but I wanted to be in the inner circle—and this, coupled with the experiences enumerated above, led me to decide to test the clinical waters. I had no idea at the time whether I could do even the basics of research and teaching using clinical methods—it all seemed mysterious, special, and (perhaps partly for those reasons) incredibly attractive.

TESTING THE WATER

There was (and is) no programmatic character to my explorations of clinical teaching and research methods. There were, however, some signal learning events and activities that helped me (1) see that I had overblown the mystique of group, clinical, and experiential methods; (2) discover that becoming moderately competent in their use was not out of my personal reach; and (3) learn some skills and develop some attitudes about research and teaching that were new to me. In no particular order, they include the following.

Engagement with Alderfer, Argyris, and Torbert. Clay Alderfer received his doctorate from the Yale organizational behavior program in 1966 and went off to teach at Cornell just as I was arriving in New Haven. Two years later he returned to Yale, and there was a clear expectation on the part of the senior faculty that he and I had some things to learn from one another. It was true. We jumped into collaborative work, starting with a jointly taught course on research methodology that attempted to meld clinical and experimental research approaches. A couple of years later, we wrote a joint research proposal (which compared work design and team building as points of departure for initiating organizational change) and began a lengthy (and ultimately unsuccessful) series of negotiations to find an organization where we could do the research. These activities provided many opportunities for me to learn about clinical methods—both cognitively and by observing (and, at times, modeling) Clay's behavior.

The intellectual pivot around which organizational behavior at Yale revolved in the late 1960s was Chris Argyris. Indeed, after Don Taylor became chairman of psychology and Wight Bakke passed away, Chris was the only senior faculty member in our group. He kept after me: reading my scholarly work carefully and commenting on it in ways that forced me to think hard about what I was doing, why, and how; and confronting me persistently and constructively about my research and teaching. His obvious commitment to learning and understanding was a model for me, and his high expectations of me helped keep my motivation and standards high. While my involvement with Chris was an important part of my development as a scholar and teacher, it also was highly frustrating: It seemed that every time I thought I was getting it, it turned out that I was not, and I began to sense how difficult clinical skills could be to learn.

Bill Torbert (a doctoral student at the time) seemed to "have it," but I could not understand exactly what it was he had—and I was supposed to be one of his advisors. We taught an experimental (and moderately experiential) undergraduate course together, and in some sense it was a miserable failure: Our attempt to promote self-directed learning turned out instead to promote disengagement from the course for many of our students.[2] Yet the course did help me understand better than I had before that one must behave in order to learn, that failure is a necessary part of the learning process, and that blind or unexamined behavior is grossly insufficient for someone who aspires to understand people and social systems.

A couple of years in a couples' T-group. Four couples (we varied in age, work situation, and experience in group training) decided to meet regularly to explore personal and interpersonal issues in marriage. The group became a supportive setting in which I could learn about (and practice dealing with) unconscious, emotional, and interpersonal phenomena that previously I had ruled out of consideration on the grounds that they accounted for trivial variance—or that they could not be addressed in a systematic, "scientific" matter. I discovered that some of my preconceptions were little more than defensiveness, and that maybe I even had some skill in dealing with issues that before had seemed either not worth the trouble or beyond my competence.

Half a year of individual "developmental" therapy. During one of my first official Yale leaves, I decided to do some personal emotional learning and signed up for a period of therapy with a highly recommended individual to "look inside." It was a glorious rationalization: In retrospect, I believe I actually wanted to get rid of some problems I was having with myself, and I acted as if coming in for fifty minutes once a week and letting the therapist do his good work on me would take care of it. It did not, of course, but the experience was valuable in helping me shed the view that this clinical stuff was somehow magic. Therapy was a constructive and worthwhile thing for me to have done (and something I have repeated), but for reasons different than those on my mind when I first signed up.

The Oshry power laboratory. Ken Smith (a doctoral student in our program) had attended a "power laboratory" led by Barry Oshry and came back enthusiastic about what he had learned. What he said and wrote about the experience fascinated me, so I decided to try it out. The laboratory helped me comprehend the full power of group and intergroup forces for the first time, and also forced me to acknowledge the ways I had kept myself from having to deal with them—both in my work and in my life. (To find yourself arm wrestling for real with a valued friend and colleague through a jagged window you have just broken to force your way into his residence tends to shake you up a bit.) Yet when I compared my ability to understand and deal with group and intergroup dynamics with that of the staff (and that of other participants, some of whom were repeat attendees), I felt naive and ignorant. This experience, as much as any other, hammered home the fact that I had to *learn* this stuff. I could not go on saying I was a psychologist (of all things!) interested in groups and organizations without opening myself to phenomena that can have tidal (rather than ripple) effects on what transpires within them. I needed to understand these forces, to figure out how to study them, and to discover ways to use them in studying other things. I was, I felt, ready for a major push forward in my learning about unconscious and group dynamics in organizational life.

GOING FOR IT—AND COMING UP SHORT

After deciding to try to expand and deepen my clinical skills (there was no exact date the decision was made, but at some point it became clear that I was going to proceed), I expected my learning to unfold gradually but consistently. I had not anticipated the ambivalence I would find on every side—and on the inside. Since I have come to believe that experiencing and dealing with ambivalence is an integral and necessary feature of such learning, I will describe my encounters with it below.

THE CLINICAL ESTABLISHMENT

I imagined that once I presented myself for learning (I was motivated and reasonably well prepared, surely an attractive student) I would be welcomed into the fold of those interested in clinical and experiential methods of research and teaching. I was wrong. Those in a position to teach me tended instead to reject me, something they had not done before I implicitly "announced" myself as a serious student. (That the announcement was implicit may have been part of the reason for this— and a sign of my own ambivalence about proceeding.) The rebuffs came from a variety of sources, ranging from an organization dedicated to experiential education to students in our program at Yale. For example:

— National Training Laboratories (NTL) rejecting my application to participate in a workshop on experiential approaches to job design (an area in which I had done quite a bit of empirical and conceptual work) on grounds that I was unqualified to attend. (I had not previously taken their basic human interaction laboratory.)

— Offers to participate in teaching our experiential introductory master's course, and to apprentice myself in our group dynamics course, being ignored or rejected by my clinically oriented faculty colleagues.

— As I began to experiment more with experiential and clinical method-ologies in the classroom, students identified with that group doing things to keep me in the "traditional" camp—and, occasionally, to encourage conflict between the two groups. When I did a classroom session on field diagnostic methodologies, for example, one such student wondered aloud to his colleagues (within my earshot) how much of what I covered would "have to be un-taught" the next semester in the experiential course he would be helping with. (Students identified with traditional teaching and research methodologies have engaged in similar behavior, although aimed in the opposite direction. Apparently some students feel it is in their best interest—or, perhaps, they are just more comfortable—if faculty stay in their historically proper places.)

Events such as these keep happening, and they frustrate and anger me. On the one hand, some of my clinically oriented colleagues claim that their approach is where the *real* learning about people, groups, and organizations is to be had. This, they say, is where the action is in our field, and the presence of a clinical stream of teaching and research in our program is one of its most distinctive and attractive features. On the other hand, they behave toward me (and some other interested faculty) in ways that preclude our becoming involved with them in these cutting-edge activities. The message, as I receive it, is that I am not ready (or, perhaps, not able—it has never been clear) to learn what they have to teach.

How is this to be understood? From the point of view of the clinical establishment, Hackman's interest is surely a compliment: He says that what we do is sufficiently interesting and important that he wants to learn more about it. But perhaps it also is a threat: If Hackman learns how to do it, our comparative advantage diminishes—particularly if he should turn out to be a good student. So we find ourselves ambivalent about helping him learn.

That is, of course, raw speculation—I cannot speak for my colleagues. My response to what I have encountered has been to learn as best I can on my own, with lots of trial and error, and to work with students who "straddle" the two groups whenever appropriate and possible. And I believe I have learned some things that are both interesting and different from the core doctrine of the clinical cohort in organizational behavior. That is one of the advantages of doing it on your own—you discover what *you* discover. But it has created even more problems with the clinical establishment: Hackman is not only *doing* it, he's getting it *wrong*. (But maybe he's getting it right. How are we ever to tell if we keep him at arm's length?)

THE SOCIAL PSYCHOLOGY ESTABLISHMENT

Colleagues identified with mainline social psychology seem to harbor a wish that I would continue to be the same guy I was when I left Illinois. The signs of this are subtle, but they also are plentiful and they keep coming. For example:

— A former Yale colleague calling to tell me (with a chuckle) that there is controversy in the social psychology world about what my name is. This individual (who knows me as "Richard") was at a conference heavily attended by experimental social psychologists, including colleagues from my Illinois days (who knew me as "Dick"). When my work was discussed at the conference, he reported, there was explicit and occasionally vigorous disagreement about my name: Is he Richard, or is he Dick?

While my colleague called because he thought it was funny, his interpretation was that my social psychologist colleagues *really* wanted me to be the person they used to know, the one who did things the scientifically correct way, rather than the one who may have been led astray by his more clinically oriented colleagues out east.

— A faculty member on the West Coast who writes me shortly after I have delivered a paper at a university near her own proposing some new approaches to methodology for group and organizational research, telling me that she heard that Hackman has "thrown over all his previous work, and is starting over with some really far-out methods." She wanted to know if it was true. Hackman had, of course, done no such thing; indeed, he was trying to *build* on what we have learned about theory and method to date, to take the next incremental step in improving our scholarly tools. Is it an expression of ambivalence that the presentation was coded as a wholesale switching of sides?

— Social psychologists writing or calling about my work on groups, inviting me to be on review boards, to speak at conferences, to consider applying for grants they know about, saying "these new directions you are taking are just what we need, just the way the field should be evolving." Yet, some of them see in their own work little movement in the directions they applaud in mine. Is it that I am to serve as the point person in edging toward new kinds of methods and theories so that they do not have to?

In all, I sense among my colleagues in social psychology some gentle encouragement for me to come back home. I feel they would welcome me, forgive me for the errors of my recent ways, and even give me back my old room. In fact, I do want to reengage with mainline social psychology. These people are my friends, and in a real sense my professional family of origin. Moreover, I am encouraged by what seems to be a renewed interest in relationships and groups among members of the social psychology establishment. But the guy who is coming back is different from the guy who left—and he is returning with some new tools and with a belief that the old homestead might be more interesting and durable if a few structural modifications were made. I wonder if the welcome mat will be kept out once that is realized.

MYSELF

Part of the ambivalence I receive from my colleagues—whether of the clinical or the social psychological persuasion—has been internalized, and part of my ambivalence is wholly self-generated. While I cannot sort out the sources, here are the signs I see:

— Getting a tiny rejection (e.g., having an offer to co-teach a course declined) and turning that into a major event. This allows me to continue to feel virtuous without having to actually do what I hesitantly suggested

I'd like to do. It is characteristic of me, and one of my unattractive features: Someone puts my nose a little out of joint, I put it the rest of the way out of joint and work to keep it there. I am a great victim.

— I do not know how good I really am at using clinical methods, and I may be behaving in ways that keep me from finding out. When I have worked collaboratively with clinically oriented colleagues, for example, I invariably wind up taking greater responsibility for the conceptual part of the activity, while they manage the experiential part. I have resented that—but I also regularly have colluded with it (and on occasion have even suggested such a division of labor). How worried am I that I will, eventually, discover that I am not very talented in the use of clinical and experiential methods? To what extent does that fear keep me from putting myself squarely on the line?

— There are numerous learning opportunities open to me that I have not accepted, such as finding an appropriate time to participate in a Tavistock conference. Given my interest in groups and in the exercise of authority as a way to create conditions that foster work team effectiveness, I need the learning that a Tavistock experience could provide. Moreover, my clinically oriented colleagues have actively encouraged me to enroll. Yet things keep getting scheduled in a way that makes it impossible. How am I to understand that in the context of my avowed commitment to learning clinical skills?

— I find it far easier to help and nurture others than to be helped and nurtured by them. I spend a great deal of my professional time teaching others, and almost none of it in a student role. Indeed, I get reasonably uneasy when I am being taught or helped, when I am dependent on somebody else for something I want or need. When I learn, I *prefer* to figure things out for myself, even if it takes longer or is more painful. If I am going to become expert in clinical methods, at some point I am going to have to come to terms with this issue—and I am still unsure how willing (or able) I am to do that.

— When I am with "traditional" colleagues I often espouse the clinical view of things, but when I am with clinically oriented colleagues I often raise questions that imply that I favor more traditional methods of research and teaching. This may merely reflect my tendency to behave in a counterdependent fashion on occasion, but it also has a self-protective character that can inhibit learning. That is, if I play the role of skeptic (regardless of the group I am with), how seriously will members of that group take my espoused wish to learn from them? Does my probing, skeptical stance (something I generally value in myself) actually cover resistance to learning new and potentially anxiety-arousing material?

SUMMARY

Happily, despite all the ambivalence listed above, there are some things that are relatively unambiguous—things that have made it possible for me to continue learning, despite the opposing pulls I have experienced and my personal conflicts about moving further toward developing my clinical voice.

For one, a handful of colleagues have consistently supported my attempts to learn new skills. I will not embarrass them by giving their names here, but it pleases me that they include people from both sides of my professional life, people with strikingly different professional values and personal orientations toward research and practice. Their support and encouragement have made it possible for me to stick my neck out on occasion in ways I probably would not otherwise have done.

Moreover, I have finally learned what it is I do well—and that provides a solid base from which I can take some risks to expand my knowledge and skills. What I do best, it turns out, is *neither* (1) designing clever experiments or doing powerful multivariate analyses of massive datasets, nor (2) probing deeply submerged emotional dynamics or reaching out for remote but fascinating possible interpretations of what might *really* be going on within a person, a relationship, a group, or an organization. Instead, my particular specialty is *inductive conceptualization*. I can take massive and confused sets of materials (virtually any materials) and make sense of them. I do this relatively effortlessly, and generally I do it well. The point is that this skill is useful both in making sense of massive tables of data *and* in comprehending seemingly chaotic transpirings in groups and organizations. The movement I have made is not so much away from data tables (I still enjoy studying and trying to make sense of them) but toward using my skills in new ways in researching, teaching about, and intervening with groups and organizations.

Knowing what it is that I can do well has made it easier to keep trying to develop skills and methods that I can use in exercising my specialty. Even if I come up short in learning activity, or if I try a new method that fails, I have something that I and my colleagues value to fall back on. I need that, and I have great admiration for people (such as some graduate students) who are able to engage in personally risky skill-development activities even before they have a good sense of their core professional competence.

CONCLUSION

Let me conclude by reflecting on some of the lessons I have learned thus far from my engagement with clinical methods. First I discuss why I have come to believe that the struggle to develop a clinical voice is ultimately worth the effort it takes, and then address some aspects of clinical methods (and some behaviors occasionally exhibited by clinical researchers) that I would like to avoid in my own work.

WHY THE STRUGGLE IS WORTH IT

Moving away from either/or thinking. Most of us trained in scientific methods have long ago adopted the "hypothesis testing" way of thinking about research: Either you reject the null hypothesis or you do not, and the numbers that emerge from the research design and statistical analysis tell you which is correct. "Don't give me any of this 'significant at the .06 level' nonsense," we admonish students in our research methods classes. Follow the formula, and truth will be revealed as a binary state. It is a neat, clean, either/or way of thinking. There is no messy middle to worry about.

Despite the fact that we regularly violate our own admonitions when we need to understand some particularly complex phenomenon or data set, most of us have either/or thinking well ingrained in how we comprehend and explain our phenomena. "Is this theory or that one correct?" we ask, and then proceed to design a horse-race study to compare them. "Does variable x cause outcome y, or doesn't it?" "Is the leader's style democratic or is it autocratic?" And the list goes on.

If social systems were binary, traditional research methodologies (and the kind of thinking they promote) would be appropriate. But organizations are more complex than that: There are multiple routes to the same outcome, causes often are intercorrelated and have redundant effects, a single event can result in a variety of different outcomes (some of which are not predictable from things we can measure beforehand) and occurrences in organizations often have multiple meanings even for the same observer (let alone for people with different stakes who watch from different perches). Either/or thinking invites us to overlook such complexity and messiness, or to suppress it, in the interest of experimental control. And, unfortunately, what is overlooked or suppressed may be near the heart of the phenomena we are trying to understand.

Clinical methods, when appropriately used, offer a way to avoid getting trapped by our own methods and cognitive styles—not merely by acknowledging that the world is more complex than either/or thinking suggests, but by providing a way of understanding multiple causes, effects, perceptions, and realities. It is hard to imagine how one could develop and test a rich and useful understanding of behavior in organizations without clinical methods.

Learning more from fewer cases. While I would not argue for a fully idiographic approach to group and organizational research, my guess is that we will learn more about our phenomena if we spend more time gathering better data about fewer cases—something for which clinical methodologies are particularly well suited. Consider, for example, an organizational researcher who is interested in understanding how white males in organizations accommodate increasing numbers of women and blacks in their midst, or one who seeks to identify the conditions required for decision-making groups in organizations to become more effective. If one of these researchers had some time and energy available to use in enriching his or her repertoire of research skills, which of the following would you recommend—(1) learning LISREL and collecting the large quantities of data required for appropriate use of that methodology, or (2) learning clinical methods and using them to study intensively a smaller number of cases? Is there any contest? Then why do so few of us do the latter and so many of us do the former?

Developing better ways of communicating research findings. One of the rarely acknowledged virtues of clinical methods is that the findings they generate often defy being placed in the format normally used for presenting the results of scholarly research. If, for example, one has large amounts of qualitative data (perhaps including data about the researcher's own involvement with and reactions to the organization), how can that material be presented in a method-results-discussion journal format? And what if one's conclusions are based on a large number of small and specific observations, each of which provides frail support for any conclusions, but which collectively provide a sturdy interpretive base? How does one write a results section containing such material in a way that allows readers to see and test for themselves the link between data and conclusions?

Problems such as these require that nontraditional ways of presenting what we learn in our research be explored. And that, of course, raises some fundamental questions about how we come to believe what we think we have found, how we can best teach others (including people whose skills and scholarly orientations differ from our own) what we have discovered, and how we can present our findings in ways that invite constructive use of the lessons learned.

Some might view these questions as illustrating problems with clinical methods; one cannot, after all, apply a standard template to the analytic results and crank out a journal article. I prefer to view them more optimistically, as occasions for addressing matters that *should* be on a scholar's mind much of the time but that usually are not—precisely because we have available to us widely accepted methods for doing and writing up research. To be involved with clinical research methods, then, requires that one worry a lot about how to communicate one's findings to others. That is, in my view, a worthy use of a scholar's time.

Moving toward new kinds of theories. Using clinical methods to study organizational behavior involves much more than simply applying concepts and methods developed in traditional individual and group clinical work to organizational phenomena. Such concepts and methods generally do not sufficiently take account of contextual and structural factors. Indeed, they often center our attention on phenomena that may themselves be derivative (or even epiphenomenal) in organizational settings (e.g., on aspects of group interaction that are far more significant for self-analytic groups than for teams operating in social systems where there are tasks to be performed, clients to be served, bosses to manage, and organizational control systems to contend with).

Using clinical methods in organizational settings, then, invites us to conceptualize group and organizational phenomena in ways that address both (1) the unconscious and emotional dynamics that are prominent in the work of clinical psychologists, and (2) the contextual and structural factors that powerfully shape what happens in purposive social systems. Such conceptualizations surely would be richer than those favored either by orthodox clinical psychologists or by students of organizations who rely on traditional research methodologies—and they just might turn out to be more valid and useful as well. While it is hardly new to notice that the methods one uses affect what one chooses to study (as well as the kinds of interpretations and conclusions that emerge) it is important nonetheless—and it is one of the advantages of clinical methods for organizational research.

TRAPDOORS AND MINEFIELDS

Glibness. A number of people who claim to be clinical researchers have this talent, and it is one that I share. It worries me about them, and it worries me about me. How can we distinguish genuine clinical insight from mere personal impressions glibly presented? How can we protect ourselves, our students, and the participants in our research from findings dressed up in the language of clinical interpretation that are, in fact, little more than unsupportable speculations?

Particularly distressing to me are clinicians who arrive on the research scene (virtually any research scene) with a ready-made interpretive apparatus (for example, involving authority dynamics or "basic assumption" behavior) that they then tailor to fit whatever group or organizational situation they encounter. Worse, such devices can be used by a facile commentator in a way that defies rebuttal (e.g., by characterizing attempts at disconfirmation as evidence of defensive resistance to accepting what is really going on and, therefore, as additional evidence for the validity of the interpretation).

It is *hard* to generate clinical interpretations of behavior in social systems that can be tested and disconfirmed with data, and too many researchers who don the clinical cloak are unwilling (or unable) to do the intellectual and methodological work required to protect themselves from the temptation to engage in glib, seamless interpretation.

The priesthood. To this outsider, the clinical establishment seems to have the quality of a priesthood: You are either in or out, and if you are in you have to accept the doctrine. While I acknowledge and accept the need to establish high standards of excellence for those who would use clinical methods (or any other research method, for that matter), I disagree with those who insist that using clinical methods requires one to accept a certain system of beliefs and values. I am also too old to be as respectful as perhaps I should be of the gatekeepers of clinical methodologies.

It should be clear from this chapter that I want to be an "associate member" of the priesthood—welcome at services, allowed to do a baptism now and then, encouraged to continue my studies, but free to be heretical and to practice other religions as well. That seems to me an altogether reasonable aspiration. Yet I also must acknowledge the possibility that my feelings about the matter (which, obviously, are strongly held) are simply one more sign of a deep-seated ambivalence about what I am studying—and the fact that in this arena I am a novitiate rather than a priest.

Failure. I am generally against it—particularly when it makes me look stupid, hurts others unintentionally, or results in research reports that are incorrect or misleading. Yet failure is an important component of learning—and learning is obviously something I am for. This dilemma can loom large for the student of clinical methods, because the stakes are high both for the learner and for the organization where the learning activities take place.

How can the essential opportunities for learning from failure be provided without either (1) placing ourselves or the social systems we are studying at greater-than-necessary risk, or (2) cutting the level of risk to the point where we neither fail *nor* learn? Teachers of clinical methods have thought hard about precisely this question and have come up with pedagogical devices that appear to chart a reasonable course between the horns of the dilemma. But it can be troublesome nonetheless when one is just starting to learn clinical methods, particularly for those of us who have difficulty finding colleagues who are willing to teach us.

Risking the core scholarly values. I have little patience for people who make clinical interpretations of events and, when asked for the data and the logic of inference used to generate those interpretations, respond with a statement such as "If you know how to look you can see it." Such assertions (which I have heard far too often) combine the worst features of glibness and the priesthood, and I find them wholly at variance with the core values of scholarly work.

Whatever clinical methods I wind up using in my future research, I am reasonably certain that they will seek to promote (rather than dismiss) three core values: (1) trustworthy, verifiable data as the basis for interpretations and inferences; (2) means of assessing the meaning of those data that are accessible to other scholars; and (3) sound logic of inference in drawing conclusions from data.

Clinical methodologies greatly expand the kinds of data that are available for scholarly work, and may unearth hypotheses that otherwise would go unnoticed (including hypotheses that centrally involve the person of the data collector and his or her relationship to the data source). That is all to the good—but it is also insufficient. In my view, those of us who use clinical methods are obligated to subject our data and inferences to the same skeptical scrutiny we would apply to a layperson's interpretation of what is going on in a group or organization.

SUMMARY

This chapter has charted my halting and tentative attempts over the years to expand my repertoire of research tools by learning something about clinical methods for organizational research. Having summarized above my present assessment of certain benefits and risks associated with the use of those methods, let me close by posing a question that surely is on the minds of at least some readers: Why in the world would Hackman ever write an essay such as this?

It is a question I have asked myself more than once—particularly when I found myself putting events and feelings on paper that I would prefer to keep private, or when the account of my professional development bored even me. My answer has much less to do with any imagined virtue of self-disclosure than with the loneliness of learning clinical methods. Often, when feeling incompetent, rejected, or unsure of just what it was I was doing, I also felt professionally alone. There were few people around who could help me make sense of what was happening, or to reflect with me on whether or not my explorations were worth the trouble.

Ironically, the process of writing this chapter has provided such colleagueship in good measure—from the editors of the book especially, but also from others. That fact suggests that I could have obtained more support along the way if I had more actively sought it. Moreover, it highlights an unanticipated function the chapter has served: It has provided an occasion for reengaging with colleagues on both the clinical and social psychological sides of my professional life about what I have been doing and how they have been reacting to it. After writing a rough draft of the chapter and discussing it with the editors, I realized that I also had to show it to Joe McGrath and Clay Alderfer—because they are important actors in the events recounted here, certainly, but also because my attempts to learn clinical skills are entwined with and consequential for my relationships with them. In their reactions, both provided not only helpful substantive suggestions but also (and more important) personal reflections and challenges that reaffirmed their importance to my continuing development as a scholar.

So writing this essay has served more functions than I suspected it would when, a few months ago, I set my ambivalence temporarily aside and began to put words on paper. To the extent that some readers may be dealing with issues and feelings similar to those I have experienced, I hope they find an instant of recognition (and, perhaps, a bit of encouragement) in the words of someone who has been travelling a similar path.

NOTES

1. It never occurred to me at the time, despite my finding that task factors controlled considerable variation in group performance, that I might be looking in the wrong place—that the clues I was seeking might lie outside rather than within groups. Only much later, when I began observing groups operating in their natural organizational habitats, did I come to entertain this possibility.

2. What we did and what we learned are described in Torbert and Hackman, "Taking the Fun out of Outfoxing the System," in Runkel, Harrison, and Runkel, *The Changing College Classroom* (1969).

ANXIETY IN RESEARCH RELATIONSHIPS

David N. Berg

The methodological appendix has a long and illustrious history in social science field research. It is often the section of the report in which we learn the real story about the researcher's discoveries and how he or she felt during the months or years of field research. This appendix, often titled "Method," contains a rich description of the research procedures, the relationships formed with the people who participated in the study, and the dilemmas or problems faced by the researcher along the way. It is the story behind the story and, ironically, it can become the central feature of a research report (e.g., Dalton, 1959; Whyte, 1955) long after the findings have been updated.

The value of the appendix is in the insight it provides about the struggles—emotional and intellectual—that make up field research. The fact that these accounts and insights are often appended to the main text testifies to the belief that the information in the appendix is tangentially germane to the knowledge reported. Other evidence suggests that social scientists are not particularly interested in the role research relationships play in developing our understanding of social systems. A recent volume on organizational assessment, for example, included new articles on a variety of research methods, but adopted a fourteen-year-old article on the effects of research relationships on behavioral science knowledge (Lawler, Nadler, & Cammann, 1980). Yet the frequency with which authors feel compelled to include such appendixes and the interest with which we all read them suggest that the appended information plays an important role in how we understand the body of the text.

This chapter begins with the assumption that the information found in methodological appendixes is too important to be relegated to the

AUTHOR'S NOTE: I would like to thank David Morgan, Jeff McNally, Vicki Van Steenberg, Cortlandt Cammann, Leroy Wells and Richard Hackman for their helpful comments on an earlier draft of this chapter.

very end of a research report. In particular, the emotional as well as the intellectual consequences of research involvement need to be described and examined because of the influence they exert on the development of both theory and method (Devereux, 1967). For the participants, the emotions generated by research involvement include fear, mistrust, anxiety, apprehension, excitement, interest, dependency, and reactivity. Some of these emotions have been studied by social scientists in an effort to learn how to minimize their influence on the research process. Much less attention has been paid to the emotions generated within researchers as they conduct research. It is a startling omission (albeit with some notable exceptions) considering that once one has participated in field research it is impossible to overlook the powerful emotions stirred by the undertaking.

When a description of the emotional dynamics of the research relationship is missing from a research report, the reader is denied access to the researcher's perception of the emotional context in which the study was conducted. This is important information because no matter how hard researchers try to wall off their emotions—whether in the lab or in the field—they are rarely, if ever, successful. The absence of a description and analysis of these emotional dynamics in our research reports does nothing to diminish the effects of these emotions, it merely hides them from systematic scrutiny. A piece of the framework necessary to interpret the findings is lost.

When attention has been paid to the role of emotions in social research, interesting questions and dilemmas have been raised. Anthropologists have struggled with the effects of the researcher's ideology and culture on his or her fieldwork (e.g., Von Laue, 1975; Mead, 1973; Freeman, 1983). Fieldwork in ethnography has sought to define a role for the researcher that provides the ethnographer with a "native's" view of the culture while maintaining a certain reflective distance from that culture. The process of deepening emotional involvement happens gradually as the representatives of two cultures come to know each other. The question of interest to the social scientist is how and in what ways this emotional involvement influences the conduct of research (Devereux, 1967).

Research in the psychotherapeutic professions has also attended to this question—specifically, to the effects of the therapist's emotional relationship with the patient on his or her understanding of the patient's situation. The emotions involved in the therapeutic relationship may derive from unconscious personal, interpersonal, or cultural factors and often exert a powerful influence on the therapist's behavior. The example of countertransference in psychoanalysis (the analyst's reactions to the patient, which originate in the analyst's unconscious reactions to relationships in early childhood) has not only identified this phenomenon, but also provided other social scientists with a strong rationale for attending to the effects of their own emotional involvement. This work has made the examination of these questions a domain of inquiry in its own right.

George Devereux, an anthropologist and a psychoanalyst, also explored in great detail the emotional consequences for the researcher of conducting behavioral science research. His example of a European anthropologist observing a castration ritual in a tribal setting makes poignantly clear the possible emotional influences on the collection, analysis, and interpretation of behavioral science data (1967). Devereux was particularly interested in the anxiety that was aroused in social research. One of his conclusions was that the development of research methods that specified a distant, uninvolved relationship between researcher and research participant was an unconscious attempt to defend the researcher against the anxiety aroused in behavioral science research.

Whether one agrees with Devereux or not (I confess I do) his work serves as a point of departure for this chapter. In it I will explore the role of anxiety in social research. The first section discusses possible sources of anxiety in the research process. The second examines two short cases to illustrate the influence of anxiety on field research. The final section addresses the implications of the previous two sections for social science research.

The focus of this chapter is anxiety. It is not the only emotion that attends social research and it may not be the most frequently experienced, but it is arguably the most troublesome and therefore the most rewarding for examination. Unlike some emotional reactions to research relationships, anxiety often provides its own veil—a veil that is neither transparent enough to allow easy access nor opaque enough to allow easy dismissal. We know, however vaguely, what is behind the veil. We know what it feels like. But most of us have only a clouded understanding of the role it plays in our research.

ANXIETY

An examination of the sources of anxiety in research relationships begins with a working understanding of the concept of anxiety in general. For an individual, May (1977) defines anxiety as "the apprehension cued off by a threat to some value that the individual holds is essential to his [or her] existence as a personality" (p. 180). In his discussion of anxiety May raises the following points:

(1) the diffuse and often vague sense of apprehension is associated with a threat to "core" patterns of security each individual develops;

(2) when the security base of an individual is threatened, and since it is in terms of this security base that the individual experiences himself or herself in relation to other objects, the distinction between subject and object breaks down;

(3) the reaction to the threat is disproportionate to the objective danger because some internal conflict is involved (i.e., it is the subjective experience of threat that determines the level of anxiety);

(4) repression, or the unconscious removal of the source of threat from conscious awareness is a central feature of subjective or neurotic anxiety;

(5) the capacity for anxiety is not learned, but the quantities and forms of anxiety in a given individual are;

(6) fear, as distinguished from anxiety, is a differentiated emotional reaction to a specific, "objective" danger that is external to the individual (pp. 180-199).

He concludes with a statement about threats to a culture that exacerbate the anxiety experienced by individuals: "The[se] threats . . . are not threats which can be met on the basis of the assumptions of the culture but rather are threats to those underlying assumptions themselves." (p. 212) If we substitute "group" for "culture" May has provided us with a definition of group-level anxiety which is consistent with other work in group dynamics (Bion, 1961). This group-level anxiety adds to the anxiety experienced by individuals.

What then are the sources of anxiety in research relationships and what individual values or group-level assumptions might be threatened by research involvement? The following discussion is based on the view that research relationships have the potential to arouse some degree of anxiety because the relationship is felt to be the source of threat in three areas: personal, professional, and group-level. Personal anxiety is aroused by threats to the individual's psychological identity—that is, by threats to the way he or she responds to the surrounding world. Professional anxiety is aroused when the researcher feels there is a threat to the research itself. Group-level anxiety is aroused in the special case where research is done by a team and threat is experienced as a result of the emotional dynamics of groups. These three areas are not independent since one could argue, at a minimum, that personal anxiety will influence both professional and group-level anxiety, but it is also true that each of the three makes a unique contribution to the anxiety experienced in social research. For that reason we will examine each separately.

Personal anxiety. There are a number of sources of personal anxiety in research relationships. First, unlike research in the physical sciences, the study of human behavior involves researchers in self-study. Whether or not the social scientist is motivated to study human behavior in order to gain some measure of self-awareness (as some have argued), the act of studying human behavior has an element of self-analysis. The social scientist often confronts the difficult task of self-scrutiny without conscious awareness or choice. Anxiety may surface because the research relationship "forces" the researcher to confront personal weaknesses, unconscious conflicts, or current struggles in the development of his or her identity (Balmary, 1979; Devereux, 1967).

This anxiety is like that of the painter who undertakes a self-portrait and finds that it is much more difficult than painting the portrait of someone else. The artist is simultaneously painting an image and his or her relationship to that image. In the case of a self-portrait the work involves "staring into" the artist's relationship to him- or herself. Whatever anxiety is inside the artist is now made a part of the work process. In addition, self-analysis always brings with it the threat that the "patterns of security" developed to protect an individual's identity will themselves be questioned.

Second, as with any relationship, research relationships include transference and countertransference reactions. Since most field research involves complex authority relations (e.g., inside the research team, between the research team and numerous levels of the system being studied) it provides fertile ground for unconscious reenactments of parental and familial conflicts. Since transference reactions are unconscious, the anxiety that attends them is not easily traced to its source and may be misattributed to other events in the research relationship.

A third source of anxiety comes from the group identities the researcher brings to every research relationship. Each of us is not an anonymous scientist in the relationship with research participants. We also carry with us a variety of group memberships that contribute to our identity: race, gender, age, ethnicity, and social class (Alderfer, 1977). These group memberships can be a source of anxiety in two ways: (1) The groups to which the researcher and the research participant belong may have a history of conflict, hostility, or suspicion that may, in turn, affect the level of anxiety for one or both. The uncertainty surrounding these intergroup relations and the unspoken norms that make it difficult to discuss the effects of intergroup history on interpersonal relations heighten this anxiety. (2) The salience of a particular group membership (e.g., ethnicity) in a research relationship may raise unresolved issues in the researcher's own identity (e.g., whether, or how much, to identify with an ethnic tradition) that may cause anxiety (McGoldrick, Pearce, & Giordano, 1982; Babad, Birnbaum, & Benne, 1983).

It is possible to consider these three areas as representing anxiety that springs from our present, our individual histories, and our collective histories. For each of us, these anxieties are different but are evoked by the relationship with individuals, groups, and organizations who participate in the research.

Professional anxiety. Doing research with human systems also brings with it different kinds of professional anxiety. In the course of a research project researchers may face situations that question their professional abilities or competencies as well as the assumptions underlying the research itself. To the extent that research is an important part of the researcher's identity, this anxiety can be strong. A few sources of professional anxiety are discussed below.

Multiple responsibilities—especially responsibilities to the participating social system—can cause anxiety. No longer do researchers' actions influence only their findings, publications, or careers. Research conducted with the active participation of a social system necessarily involves the needs and objectives of that system and obligates the researcher to consider these in the course of the research. The researcher's actions can and do affect individuals and organizations. When information is fed back or discussed with an organization, for example, the possible consequences carry with them a significant responsibility. This responsibility may overlap with other professional or scientific responsibilities (e.g., measurement standards, confidentiality) but it may also involve decisions not covered in professional manuals (Mirvis & Seashore, 1979). The increased uncertainty and the risk of failure caused by multiple responsibilities can be potent sources of anxiety.

Control is another source of anxiety in field research. Field settings increase the complexity of the scientific tasks. There are more uncertainties, more potentially relevant factors for explaining events, and more activities outside the control of the researcher. In addition, researchers often share what control they have in order to design a project that is useful for the participating social system. The objective in moving from the laboratory to the field is to gain insight into human behavior in nonlaboratory settings. Yet research methods transferred from the lab often work at cross purposes to this objective, urging the researcher to assert quasi-experimental control so that the influence of specific variables can be isolated and cause-and-effect relationships inferred. The researcher in the field may struggle to retain control in the belief that this is the only way to produce and publish scientific research. As the researcher's control seems to slip away, so it seems does his or her opportunity for theory building that is predicated on control. The attendant anxiety is especially troublesome since it involves the individual researcher's relationship to social science as a profession.

Research with social systems invariably involves a relationship with an existing authority structure. A research "contract" is often drawn up between the researcher and representatives of one or more authority structures (e.g., labor and management; paid and volunteer staff; physicians and patients). In these situations the values, expectations, and desires of the social system's authority structure must be examined, understood, discussed, and reconciled (if possible) with the values of the research project. There always exists the possibility that misunderstanding or differences can lead the authority structure to undermine the research activities. It is also possible that the researcher will need to confront the authority structure with unpleasant or unwanted information. The fact that research projects often originate near the top of the authority structure means that researchers inevitably attract the prevailing attitudes toward those with authority. Since these processes are ongoing over the life of the project as new dilemmas and decisions are faced, managing the relationship with the authority structure can be a source of anxiety.

A researcher's professional investment in a project can also be a source of anxiety when combined with uncertainty, multiple responsibilities, and shared control. Consider a young assistant professor on the verge of producing his or her first major theoretical contribution who is one year away from a tenure review. Under these conditions a great deal more anxiety may attend every unexpected event in an important research project. In fact, the position of the researcher may actually imbue a research relationship with the career anxiety he or she is experiencing. It is misleading to assume that because researchers are scientists they are not human beings. Research is an activity embedded in a profession. Most of us earn our living or part of it doing research. As a result, all of the anxieties associated with earning a living (e.g., advancement, security, recognition) are also part of the research process. Uncertainty in our research relationships can threaten not only our research but our lives as well.

A final source of professional anxiety has been suggested by the work of Jaques (1955) and Becker (1973). Both of these authors argue that social institutions (organizations, rituals, traditions) are the means by which individuals and groups defend themselves against certain forms of anxiety. In Jaques's (1955) view, social systems play a role in defending the individual from paranoid and depressive anxiety; in Becker's (1973) view, culture in general is a collective way of managing the anxiety associated with death. If it is true that social systems have a role in defending their members against anxiety, then researchers who seek to understand these social systems may be treading on very sensitive ground. The process of looking into a social system (the thoughts and feelings of its members, their frustrations and satisfactions, the meaning of their participation) may increase the anxiety experienced by the participants, which in turn may increase the anxiety experienced by the researchers.

Group-level anxiety. Teams or research groups raise the possibility of a third type of anxiety in social research. Strictly speaking, most of these anxieties stem from the tensions any team encounters as it struggles to become an effective group (Bion, 1961; Bennis & Shepard, 1956; Smith & Berg, 1984) and would occur during any kind of research. These sources of anxiety include (1) *individual differences*—the anxiety that arises from the exploration of individual strengths and weaknesses; (2) *trust*—the anxiety associated with learning to trust others while protecting oneself from exploitation; (3) *conflict*—the anxiety derived from the fear that conflict will destroy the group, no matter how strong the espoused belief that conflict is necessary for group development; and (4) *leadership and authority*—the anxiety born of the emotions surrounding both leading and following, fears of being misled, or fears that whatever authority structure is adopted will become tyrannical.

These are only examples of the anxieties that accompany the development of a group. A research team that works with a living system can develop additional sources of anxiety rooted in its relationship to the social system it studies. As the research team develops its own group identity there is inevitably some degree of ethnocentrism with respect to other groups (e.g., the site organization). This ethnocentrism can cause the research team to project its own internal hostility and anxiety onto the site organization, subsequently experiencing this organization as a source of threat and anxiety. And while it is possible that research teams meet with hostile or mistrustful reactions from research participants, it is also likely that these reactions are exaggerated by the ethnocentric tendencies of the team itself.

The use of a research group also carries with it the possibility of mirroring or parallel processes in its relationships with other groups involved in the research (Alderfer et al., in press; Ekstein & Wallerstein, 1958; Berg, 1980). Parallel process (described in the opening chapter of this volume) refers to the tendency of living systems in a relationship to develop internal, emotional dynamics that parallel each other. As a result, research teams may experience whatever anxiety exists in the participating system, often mistaking this anxiety for their own. In this case the research team's anxiety can be used to develop hypotheses for understanding the dynamics of the research site.

CASES AND CONSEQUENCES

We have examined anxiety as an example of powerful and complex emotions that can be engendered by a researcher's involvement with a social system. But of what consequence are these emotional effects? Do the emotional dynamics of a research relationship create different data? Would we be justified in interpreting "findings" differently if we knew the emotional characteristics of the relationship that spawned the findings? It is to these questions that I now turn. In the following two cases, anxiety stemmed from specific characteristics of the research relationship and in each case the effects of the anxiety were analyzed as part of a postmortem on the events described.

Case 1. I (white, male researcher) approached a predominantly female public relations firm with a proposal to study the influence of ideology (feminist) on organization. I was interested in learning how an organization committed to an "alternative" structure and value system differed (if at all) from a traditional hierarchical organization in the way it handled a range of issues common to organizational life, (e.g., accountability, decision making, control, evaluation). After some discussion to which I was not privy, the president reported that the study could proceed but that the firm was very busy and could not devote a great deal of time to the project. I planned an entry phase designed to acquaint members of the organization with the purposes and activities of the study. At the conclusion of this phase it was my intention to draft a "contract" between myself and the organization describing the expectations and responsibilities of everyone involved. The study was to be totally voluntary, but a minimum level of participation was necessary for the study to have any validity.

After some initial, short interviews with a cross-section of organization members, I became aware of a number of tensions between various groups in the firm: feminists and nonfeminists; upstairs (clerical) and downstairs (professional); black and white. Initially I succeeded in recruiting representation from each group for a liaison system (Alderfer,

1980a) to help manage the research, but soon a number of people (feminist, upstairs, black) began to withdraw. In spite of this I continued to plan the project, concentrating on those people who remained interested. I solicited reactions to my ideas and drafted the contract. Finally I distributed the draft contract to everyone in the firm and invited them to see me or call me at an office set aside for this purpose. No one called or came by.

This unmistakable expression of a lack of interest and involvement was very disturbing. I called a colleague and asked for help in analyzing the situation. That discussion and subsequent reflections on the evolution of the project led me to some conclusions about my own actions during the entry phase.

(1) Lack of involvement in the project had been characteristic of the firm's reaction to the study from the beginning. I *knew* that this lack of involvement needed to be examined during the entry phase if there was to be a successful project since the richness of the case study would depend upon the firm's willingness to become active partners in the research. But I feared that the lack of involvement might also mean that if the project became at all troublesome, the firm would simply terminate the research. Without realizing it, my anxiety about the project's possible termination led me to avoid any actions that might produce disagreements or conflict in the firm. One of the issues avoided was the apparent lack of interest in the study.

(2) The tensions between internal subgroups in the firm became increasingly important during the entry phase. I *knew* that the project was becoming enmeshed in the existing intergroup conflicts—if one group was in favor of it, the other group was not. The conflicts in the firm about ideology, work delegation, and treatment of minorities began to play themselves out around the question of the study. I felt some responsibility for stirring up this conflict, especially in an organization that took pride in its solidarity and struggled to survive in a business environment that was hostile to the firm's avowed ideological goals. In spite of the fact that these conflicts threatened to engulf the project, my anxiety moved me *away* from discussing these issues with the firm's staff. The anxiety about being responsible for igniting these issues combined with the fear that any disruption would terminate the project caused me actively, albeit unconsciously, to avoid these issues and their potential influences on the study.

(3) When first contacting the organization, I was concerned about the implications for the research of a male researcher doing a study with an almost all-female firm. I realized that the absence of a woman on the research team would seriously affect the data collection and analysis, but hoped that an internal liaison group might address this problem.

When, at an introductory meeting, no mention was made of this issue except in a joke ("Can he type?"), I assumed that the firm had decided that sexual dynamics were not an issue. Upon reflection I began to understand my quick acceptance of this explanation.

It seemed that sexual dynamics were important in two ways. First, my identity had been influential in the firm's decision to go ahead with the study. (I learned about this when papers of mine that had been circulated during the entry phase were returned to me along with a "comments" sheet.) Because I was male, the firm reasoned, my research results (assumed to be laudatory about the firm) would be more acceptable to the larger, male-controlled society. In this way, I was treated as a representative of men who could communicate with his own group in ways that women could not. The decision to allow the study was based partly on the belief that the researcher, *by virtue of his male identity*, could be used to influence men. My anxiety about the intergroup aspects of a male researcher working in a female organization led me to accept the belief that gender would have no effect on the project. From the beginning I had been curious about the apparent lack of attention to gender issues and I suspected there were concerns not being expressed, but I decided not to push it. What would I do if a number of women in the firm resented my presence? What if some of the women did not like me? The anxiety raised by these questions led me away from the topic and from any actions that would have raised the issue of sexual politics.

The second influence of sexual dynamics was more personal. Only upon reflection did I realize the role of sexuality in the project. My attraction to some of the women in the firm and my desire to be liked by them seemed so unprofessional and engendered so much anxiety that I could not admit or examine these feelings. I subsequently discovered that these feelings influenced my choice of whom to interview, which in turn influenced my perception of the firm. Although the influence was subtle, with hindsight it is clear. The topic was so fraught with anxiety that I was totally unaware of most of the sexual aspects of the project until over a year after its conclusion.

The project ended when I decided that the divisiveness in the firm threatened the participation rate in the study. It was almost certain that a significant number of people would refuse to participate and the validity of the diagnostic goals of the study would be seriously undermined. The research relationship was terminated.

Case 2. Two black men and three white women chose to work together on an organizational diagnosis (Alderfer, 1980a) with a nonprofit service organization (NSO). The five-person team was part of a graduate-level course and the team members were students. The purpose of the course was to learn about the theory and practice of organizational diagnosis and to provide interested organizations with some help in understanding their problems and their potential. NSO was a predominantly black organization that served a predominantly black constituency although, like most organizations of its kind, it was embedded in a white community. The executive director asked the class instructor if a student team could come to explore the possibility of a diagnostic project.

In a class of twenty-two students only three were members of a minority group and two of them chose to be on the NSO team. This was noticed and discussed in class. Both black members of the NSO team said they felt some pressure from the class to join the NSO team since an all-white team could not do a diagnosis in an all-black organization. Each had chosen the NSO project for personal reasons, but both felt this pressure and expressed it to the class. The discussion was a difficult one for the class, and the process whereby the project teams were chosen was not extensively examined.

The team sent one black man and one white woman to the initial meeting with the executive director, a black, female Ph.D. in psychology, to discuss the possibility of a project. The students reported that the meeting was an uncomfortable one. The executive director, not the team members, controlled the meeting and asked a lot of questions. In particular, she had asked the team about how they were handling the topic of race relations in their team. She also asked how the team was handling male-female relations and pointed out that the combination of black men and white women had historical meaning in the black community and might affect the diagnostic team's relations with NSO. The executive director was also clear that she thought it was absolutely crucial for white students to be involved since NSO existed in a white world, depended on that world for support, and had to manage its relationships with that outside world as did any other nonprofit organization. The students came away from the meeting feeling that they had been on the defensive most of the time.

In reviewing the meeting, the entire team became increasingly alarmed at what they perceived to be their loss of control of the entry meeting. The agenda they had prepared had quickly dissolved and the students who had met with the executive director felt they had been unprepared for the discussion that she had initiated. At one point the team members who had *not* been present at the meeting blamed their representatives for losing control. At the end of the review meeting the entire team was wondering if they could handle the power and obvious competence of the executive director.

A few days later the team met with the instructor of the course to discuss a draft of the "contract" between the diagnostic team and NSO. The students had drafted the contract. The instructor was struck by the formal, legalistic style and language of the draft. It began: "The diagnostic team, hereafter designated 'Team' agrees to . . . " and proceeded to outline the rights and obligations of the parties involved. The aims and goals of the diagnosis were obscured by the language and the impression left by the document was one of mutual mistrust. As the instructor read the words back to the team members, they began to discuss the emotional aspects of their relationship with NSO and its effects on them.

(1) The initial meeting with the executive director had shaken the entire team. They had entered the meeting feeling in control and believing that they should control the entire project since the diagnostic expertise rested with them. The loss of control during the meeting caused anxiety about the whole project. One reason for the formal, controlling contract language was to reassert the team's control. The team realized it had been unprepared to share influence with the executive director. When she asserted her willingness to take control, the team feared that the project might be taken away from them.

(2) The initial meeting also created anxiety about race and gender relations. The team had not confronted these issues among its members during its formation meetings—perhaps because it felt a necessity to present a united front to the rest of the class—but the meeting with the executive director made it much harder to avoid the racial and sexual dynamics inside the team. This very difficult and anxiety-producing set of issues, coming as it did in the early stages of the team's development, threatened the group's cohesiveness. Although the team discussed race (individual feelings and experiences), in a way it seemed that the team's survival as a *work* group depended on not probing too deeply into the topic of racism because this might uncover feelings that could not be managed easily. The executive director had identified precisely those issues that had the greatest potential for fragmenting the team (and thereby jeopardizing the project and the course). In part, the team's reaction provided the group with an external "threat" that helped build the team's cohesiveness.

(3) Finally, the experience with the executive director caused the team a great deal of anxiety about its competence. Team members voiced concerns about their skill in managing unpredictable, emotional situations. The "contract" they had drafted attempted to specify the behavior of both parties in a variety of possible circumstances in order to reduce the likelihood that the team would have to struggle with unforeseen issues and the trust, or lack thereof, in their relationships

with each other. It was the instructor's belief that the draft contract would have decreased the chances that the project would proceed, perhaps unconsciously saving the team from an experience that might have forced them to struggle with the issues of competence and race.

Eventually the team rewrote the contract and conducted a diagnosis with NSO that was praised by the executive director for its accuracy and thoughtfulness. Throughout the project the team did struggle with its own process, racism, sexuality, and scapegoating—topics that, according to team members, never seemed to be "worked through" satisfactorily.

Reflections. It would be a mistake to label these two cases "bad" field research or the work of neophyte researchers. It is possible that these examples are oversimplified in the service of illustration, but the theme presented in both cases is an important one. In each case, anxieties arising from the research relationship influenced the researchers' behavior. It is difficult to assess how these experiences influenced the researchers' understanding of human behavior, but there can be no doubt that this was the case. We can be sure that there would be differences in the theories that might have evolved had the researchers' reactions been different or been managed differently. Although it is tempting to try to evaluate which reactions are "right" and which are "wrong," the unavoidable descriptive statement is that our understanding of human behavior is embedded in a particular relationship with the human systems in which the research is conducted.

IMPLICATIONS

The implication of this discussion is that the emotional dynamics in research relationships are an important variable in the social science research process. They are not merely sources of bias or reactivity, but rather the context in which research happens, influencing both the process and the outcome. This suggests that the field needs to pay more attention to this variable.

Specifically, we should begin to *examine* more closely the effects of research relationships on researchers. Just as the examination of countertransference is an integral part of psychoanalytic practice, the examination of the researcher's reactions to the research relationship should be an integral part of field research. We need to struggle to identify the ways in which we choose methods, topics, and activities that help us to defend ourselves against the feelings generated by research in and about human systems. Perhaps most important, we need to entertain the hypothesis that these feelings are an inevitable part of social science research—especially when we use ourselves as the research instrument. Our understanding of human behavior will be very different if we merely "cope" with our reactions instead of examining them and attempting to learn about ourselves and about human behavior through this examination.

If we are to examine the research relationship we must *train* applied behavioral scientists to be able to face and to struggle with the difficult personal, professional, and group issues that arise in research. This kind of training requires supervised experience in the exploration of unconscious processes at the individual and group levels. As this chapter suggests, the struggle to understand the role of anxiety in one's research involves both self-examination and the examination of relationships in which the researcher is involved. We must learn to design our research based on an awareness of the inevitable presence of anxiety in our work rather than on the wish that it could be eliminated. We must be willing to examine our involvement in our profession, including our satisfactions and frustrations and the role professional achievement plays in our lives at various stages of the life cycle. If we conduct ourselves and our research in flight from the anxiety that is part of our work, we will produce knowledge that is an artifact of this response.

Perhaps even more important, we must strive to develop researchers who are able to use the experience of anxiety to guide and enhance their understanding of social systems. Most often, the emotions generated by research relationships are not merely the expression of an individual researcher's personal history. Instead, they are the product of a specific human being engaged with others in the study of social systems. These emotions can be a window into the researcher's internal dynamics, but they can also broaden his or her understanding of the social world by providing additional kinds of data from which to construct hypotheses and, in some cases, by providing different kinds of hypotheses. Anxiety in particular, because of its roots in the unconscious experience of threat, may alert us to some of the more powerful forces affecting the social system we study and our work with it.

Training also raises the issue of supervision. I do not believe we are currently training researchers to make the examination of difficult emotions part of their research work. If we believe such an examination is important and useful for the development of meaningful theories about human behavior, then our desire to provide training in this area may outstrip our ability to do so. We, the generation responsible for the training of future social scientists, may find it necessary to train ourselves first. We may have to learn to learn from each other in ways that are neither familiar nor comfortable and we may find it necessary to look outside our particular disciplines for the supervision and guidance we need.

Finally, it is important that we begin to *report and describe* the emotional dynamics in the research relationship when we publish our findings and our theories. Just as scientific standards urge us to publish our F-tables so that readers can check our data or draw their own conclusions from our presentations, it is important that we report the relationship context and not bury it in a footnote or an appendix. Especially because we are usually so close to this particular variable, we should require ourselves to examine it and describe it so that others might observe its possible effects. Only by reporting these relationship variables can we begin to develop theories about the effects of certain kinds of research relationships on the research process.

CONCLUSION

Every theory that emerges from field research has been constructed in the context of a research relationship. Often we do not know as much about this relationship as we do about the "findings" that grow out of it. Sometimes knowledge of the characteristics of this relationship would powerfully influence our understanding and critical evaluation of a theory. Sometimes the influence would be trivial. To know more about these relationships we must make a commitment to examine, describe, and report them in our work. This commitment would further add to the complexity of social science research, making it a personally taxing endeavor far beyond mere hard work and intellect. It could be argued that the relatively minor role given to the study of research relationships is designed to spare us this pain.

CHAPTER 11

SELF-FULL RESEARCH:
Working Through the Self as Instrument
in Organizational Research

Philip H. Mirvis and Meryl Reis Louis

This chapter recounts conversations between the authors to illustrate how the self enters into the research process, where and why, and even when it should; hence the title "Self-Full Research." It considers the study of a corporate acquisition and focuses on Mirvis's work as an "instrument" in the research. For the past eight years, I (Mirvis) have been studying the impact of the acquisition of DC, a 1000-person manufacturing firm, by a conglomerate called GrandCo. Meryl Louis has studied how newcomers bring their needs, values, family histories, and interpretive frameworks to the task of making sense of a culture new to them (Louis, 1980). We talked over this study of DC, and my needs, values, family system, and sense of things, in search of ways that my self, and therefore other selves, can influence organizational research.

Meryl and I first talked about DC and me. The case study concerned a "white knight" acquisition: DC had been the target of an "unfriendly" takeover bid by an unwanted, some said unscrupulous, buyer. GrandCo had saved DC by outbidding this firm and securing majority ownership of DC's stock. It had become DC's new "parent" company. I felt the impact most immediately and fully through my relationship to DC's chief executive. Lester Richardson, DC's head and son of its founder, was called a "wounded leader" following the acquisition. He had fought to keep DC independent but had failed and been forced to turn to GrandCo. He was depressed after the sale. His wife reported that he did not want to face work, that he could not rid himself of his disappoint-

AUTHORS' NOTE: We would like to thank Joan Sieber and the editors for their assistance with this chapter.

ment and pain. My mother had once said this about my dad. My father, a business executive, lost his job in a corporate acquisition in the early 1970s. He, too, became depressed. He died a short time later—unemployed.

So Meryl and I talked about families and growing up. I still see myself as a child of the sixties, then at the fringe of the antiwar movement, at the core today, continuing to question the place of politics, business, war, and injustice in the society and in my own life. GrandCo had come to the rescue of DC. It was also big business and, in DCers' eyes, full of aristocrats who expected people to knuckle under, bureaucrats who expected people to follow their rules, and politicians who knew how to get people to play the game their way. In my story of the acquisition, these characterizations served to focus observations and interpretations. GrandCo became a symbol; and DCers took on personae based upon the way they related to GrandCo, its bigness, its values, its badness.

Our talk came back to concepts. My initial conceptions of myself in the research focused on the inner me, neglecting other facets of my self, as well as the research participants, the family system in DC, indeed the context in which they and I lived and worked. Conversation led to the realization that my self and their selves together shaped the research. "Sounds like transference and countertransference," said my clinically minded self, "or boundary relations." We laughed at this. I added, "In this paper I want to communicate my own selfness as a kind of affirmation of personhood or of universal self-fullness. That sounds trite. But I am fearful that in communications about who I am, what truths I find, how I get screwed up . . . I will only introduce a bunch of concepts." Meryl replied, "I have less concern. Your selves, their selves, make up multiple stories. We'll tether concepts to experience."

SELF AS INSTRUMENT

"Have you seen the movie *Silkwood*?" Meryl recalled an image of the lead actress putting her arms through a glass and into long, thick, rubber gloves while handling radioactive material. The material could be seen, even touched with rubber gloves, but as the hands became an instrument, they were demonstrably and intendedly separate from the material in their grasp. What was the reason for this? Clearly, to protect a self from radiation. Did this not also protect the material from contamination? We then conjured the material, aware of the separations and protections, winking at a handler. Suppose instrument is persona: Would it do to study responses to a thick, rubber glove?

I related a story Charles Perrow had told me of how merchants in the Middle Ages had turned "souls" into "hands." The Christians of that time had many holidays and worked in cottage industries. The merchants, seeking greater output for trade, organized them into factories and gradually eliminated most of the religious holidays. "Hands reach, grasp, mold, form," said I. "I see souls with wings, more ethereal, not really a body part, or else maybe in the form of a heart." Meryl countered that the self lives in many realms. There is the self as the secular, pragmatic actor in life space. Then there is the more spiritual self, maybe—in deference to me—with wings.

After the meeting, Meryl prepared some notes that began:

> Phil . . . Help. What are we arguing? Try this: It has been widely assumed that the researcher should "stay out of the way," bracket his or her self aside with a narrowly circumscribed research/scientist role.

> We are (are we?) arguing, however, that: (1) This *does not* happen and we are going to highlight ways and places that the self sneaks into inquiry, wanted or not; (2) Further, it *should not* happen (this total bracketing of the self) for "good" research occurs when the self is there in more than a narrowly defined role; "good" research comes about from managing the way the self enters in, beyond the research role.

> So we hope to show (don't we?) that it is neither possible nor desirable to screen out the self; but you gotta pay attention to how and when the self shows up.

Neither of us subscribes to notions of value-free science. Many have shown how personal and societal values are deeply embedded in what researchers study, how they study it, what conclusions are drawn, how their work is used. Nor can we accept the idea of self-less research. To do so is to accept mechanization of the research, alienation in research relations, and ultimately the absence of identity for the researcher. This simply does not match our research experience.

The self is, of course, bracketed in research. The case study here involves research in an organization by a university-based researcher. That establishes a context that defines the research. The study was to focus on the impact of the acquisition on DC executives, the workforce, and, more broadly, the DC culture. Its purposes were for scholarly research and to contribute to DC's learning. My self, therefore, would be put into focused and purposeful research and action roles. Such role definitions narrow and channel the ways that the self enters into the research effort. Futhermore, I was an outsider to DC. People were eager to tell their story of the acquisition, but also protective of their privacy and unsure how the information would be used by the organization.

Such defensiveness constrains self-expression in research relations (Argyris, 1952).

Mirvis and Seashore (1979) use concepts of roles and role systems to explicate research relations and call upon researchers to work jointly with research participants in negotiating and implementing research roles. This was accomplished in the initial contracting meeting for the acquisition study. I also sought to work openly with DCers to examine personal values, purposes, thoughts, and feelings as these are expressed in the research effort (Mirvis, 1982). That much is essential for researchers who make use of clinical research methods (Berg, 1980). These prescriptions loosen brackets on the research/scientist role and the role of research participants. They free people to be more effective as "secular, pragmatic actors in life space." Our concern here, however, is with the nonconscious, historic, symbolic, even universalistic brackets that, much as rubber gloves, protect the self but also intrude on the research process, interpretations, and recommendations. Our concern is with developing an awareness of those parts of the self and the need to examine openly, and tighten or loosen, their bracket in the conduct of self-full research.

The canons of clinical methodology can be a bane or boon to self-full research. Through the method itself, the self experiences past, present, and future, the good and bad, the essential and nonessential. Self experiences itself and the experience can be "irradiating." The canons prescribe that researchers objectify themselves, as in the classical bracketing of clinical therapy. This can provide an informative diagnostic data base about behavior in organizations (Alderfer, 1968), but it excludes some significant insights into organizational dynamics by keeping the researcher, figuratively, behind the glass (Mirvis, 1980). The alternative is to subjectify the self, and thus intensify and personalize experience, but that risks contamination (Evered & Louis, 1981). The self as instrument must be both subject and object, clinician and in the clinic, to meet the demands of self-full clinical research. The gloves must be removed; the handler must wink back. This requires introspection, reflection, self-awareness and mutuality, empathy, the capacity to share. The stories of the acquisition, of DC, and of me reflect my efforts, in the course of everyday fieldwork, to put myself clinically into research. Conversations with Meryl took place on holidays. They are our sharing of souls.

RICHARDSON

I first met Richardson when I was a student at an American Management Association seminar for college students. I was searching for career direction in my life and attended the seminar to learn more about business. This was a difficult time in my life as I was in a stage of rebellion anchored in maturation but focused on the outside world of Vietnam, capitalism, the military-industrial complex. The dreaming, achieving, powerful side of me envisioned and embraced social change. The vehicle, I reasoned, could be the work organization if only more participative, democratic, humane practices could be introduced and sustained. "Not that this would end the war," I told Meryl, "but that it was a place to begin and one where I could assume a place."

That Richardson was a father figure for me was not in my conscious awareness at that seminar. I was in a rough relationship with my father at that time as he had become the embodiment of some of the evils I saw in the world. Still, his ways and values and warmth also led me to want to understand more of the business world to see what it might hold for me. Richardson was an image of possibility. He was an advocate of humanistic business values and linked them with participation, delegation, and group effort in his stewardship of DC. He described his management philosophy and DC's practices in the language of behavioral science. After the seminar he urged me to learn more about behavioral science at Yale and to come and visit him at DC some day.

My father died later that year. Several years later, as a graduate student, I began a study of work life in DC. Richardson was the sponsor of the study and saw it as an extension of his philosophy and the DC way. The study took on added dimension following DC's acquisition. It was agreed that a chronicle of the acquisition, based upon clinical interviews with key executives, analyses of memoranda, and careful listening to tapes of key acquisition-related meetings, could help DC to learn from its experiences. I did some background research and then met with Richardson. There my identification with this father figure hit me.

Richardson was the wounded leader at that time and I had heard from others of his depression and withdrawal following the sale to GrandCo. I asked him first about his current career situation. He clarified that things were status quo—he hoped to become a group vice-president in GrandCo but it looked as though he would have to report to a GrandCo official named Schmidt, a man he neither liked nor respected. I then asked if he had any contingency plans and he stated, "In my view, my career planning is off the subject" and cautioned me against taking any "sidepaths." The interview became contentious. I was accused of asking many "loaded questions." My experience was of playing "gotcha games" with my father as we discussed politics, business, and values in that stormy time of my life.

Out of the blue I told Richardson about my father, his firing after an acquisition, his death, all with my voice cracking, tears in my eyes.

Richardson, arms folded in his lap, head bowed, just nodded. A month earlier, in negotiations about the study, Richardson had warned me that careers could be at risk in this study of the acquisition. I sensed his wounds during the interview and felt that more than a career might be at stake.

In my briefing of top DC executives following the first round of data gathering, I focused on the death-and-dying imagery many had used to describe reactions to the sale. There were the denial and anger they had expressed at a key in-house meeting and the lingering tensions over who was to blame for the failure to prevent the sale. We talked openly about Richardson's culpability and all agreed that his guilt was baseless for it was impossible to stop a "speeding truck." There was a strong consensus that Richardson's wounding had left managers uncertain of his career plans. This uncertainty—never discussed between Richardson and top managers—was proving to be a drain on their energies. It was agreed that in the next months Richardson would have to get on with his career planning and DCers with their own.

THE SELF SYSTEM

I followed Richardson's advice after the management seminar and explored the behavioral sciences at Yale. My first professor was Richard Hackman and he turned me on to McGregor, Likert, finally Argyris. Richardson knew of all their works and had worked with Argyris in crafting the management system at DC. The behavioral science courses I took, including a T-group and a seminar on Freudian psychology, provided an inspiration. Now, I went back to reread the papers I had kept to look at myself from that period.

One of the papers addressed boundary relations.

The logic of my paper followed the lines of object relations theory and addressed libidinous tensions arising from fears of abandonment. My tendency had been to intellectualize relationships with the T-group leader and hold on through attention-gaining comments and insights. In this study of DC, I recognized my intellectual bonds to Richardson, which we had talked about in negotiating the study. Part of my role was to offer a distinct perspective on the impact of the acquisition—one that Richardson did not see or could not grasp. My insight was that Richardson's wounding was a source of anxiety for all DC executives and clouded their relations with him. That insight seemed to match the experience of DCers and stimulated career planning in DC.

The other paper covered identification with my father. Periodic cuts to the finger are sufficient data for this male to accept the ubiquity of castration anxiety. I had studied internalization of my father's moral values and masculine role. The paper covered what was accepted and what was rejected—from my vantage in college days. My link to my dad had brought me to the management seminar where I met Richardson. Resolution of conflicts with my dad was, sadly, cut short by his death. With Richardson I could grow to full manhood. I hoped to work with him and learn with him in this study of DC.

My identification with Richardson and the transference of love focused on his masculinity, his values, his intellect, his fatherliness. His wounding was akin to the wounding of my father. I did not want to lose him either. My researchings helped to unearth the tensions that his career uncertainties were creating in DC. At the briefing meeting several began to talk about his leaving and how DC would get along without him. Richardson went to the window. I stated, "Don't throw him out," then sheepishly mumbled something about the need to think through executive transitions, to let Richardson make up his own mind.

The coincidence of Richardson's life story and of my own father's makes the intensity of the identification with a research participant in this instance unusual. "But wasn't it Richardson who brought you into DC's world?" It was, and that alone augurs for some mutual identification among the research self and the other selves in the organization. Meryl noted, too, the potential for countertransference. Indeed, Richardson had treated me like a son, a good son at that. It is understandable that a young man would link his soul to a competent, mature male. And Richardson was half-Jewish. I am half-Jewish too—on my father's side. The tapes of our conversations show that I said that Richardson's mother was a Catholic. That is wrong. My mother was the Catholic. From her I learned that souls have wings.

GRANDCO

GrandCo was set up from the first research negotiations. Richardson felt it was "damn near suicidal" to involve them in the study, despite my research inclinations. According to him, GrandCo's "protect your ass" orientation would quash the study. They were not open to data; they were not willing to problem-solve the problems of combining the two firms. Their style was to be "nice and genteel" and "to sweep problems under the rug." I pressed. He said,

> I am reluctant to come to this conclusion because I really place a value on informed choice. . . . In effect, I'm saying I'm going to deprive GrandCo of a choice [to be in the study]. . . . It's a choice I don't want to bother them with. . . . We are so deviant already. . . . We have to use our shots carefully.

It was recognized that this would limit the validity of the study. There would be no data gathered from GrandCo and no chance for GrandCo people to become involved in the study at all. I would be hearing only one side of the story, and likely a side slanted to "fit people's needs." Richardson was afraid of GrandCo and felt that the risks of involving them in this study were too great to take.

Relations between DC and GrandCo had been bad from the start. When Richardson was wounded another DCer set the combination strategy. He saw GrandCo as a "technostructure" that would enslave DC, an octopus that would engulf them, an amoeba that would absorb them. He urged DC executives to "repel all borders" and to "avoid kissing the enemy's ring before the results of the battle were announced." He set the strategic tone for months of conflict that would follow between the two firms.

There were many levels to the conflict between the two firms. One conflict was between Richardson and his boss at GrandCo. Schmidt was described by Richardson and others as a bastard who worked through henchmen and who was thoroughly unprofessional. Another was between the business systems of the two firms. GrandCo was financially oriented, tight on controls, organizationally bureaucratic. DC was product oriented, loose on controls, less policy driven, more open and flexible. The deepest conflict, the most troubling to DCers, concerned the value systems in the two firms. Here DCers made distinctions between the authority of knowledge and the power of aristocrats, the political environment and the family feeling. GrandCo people were Theory X, technocrats, turkeys, whereas DCers saw themselves as Theory Y, people oriented, just good God-fearing folk.

SYMBOLIC SYSTEMS

It was this latter conflict that hooked me. No doubt characterizations of GrandCo as an octopus or amoeba are archetypal images. I used them to convey the depth of DCers' anxieties about joining with GrandCo in my briefing meeting. They were not my images, however, for I never experienced GrandCo in that way. No doubt, too, my absence of contact with GrandCo people, based in Richardson's fears, led me to stereotype GrandCo. Maybe Schmidt was the bad father. Maybe GrandCo was like that bad company that took the job away from my dad. No doubt that my sense of GrandCo's size, DC's account of the "wars," and DCers' descriptions of those technocrats led me to picture GrandCo people as strong, tough, and skilled—the same muscle crowd that wreaks havoc in the world today. But all that did not hook me; what did was values.

Symbols are expressions of the self. To a God-fearing boy like I was, prone to intellectualization, values become a common language to talk about, think about, often be myself. Values were a common bond between DCers and me. We used value talk to express our purposes and what we were doing with the research. In the contracting meeting Richardson talked about evangelizing GrandCo. That failed. Following the sale to GrandCo, DC executives had prepared a list of twenty-five values to be preserved in the combination. My researchings were to help DC "keep religion"—to learn from its response to the acquisition in service of maintaining its values.

My briefing on the results of the first round of data gathering shows me unhooked from the amoebas, the parents, the wars, even the technocrats. I focused on the roots of DC's stategy in DCers' anger, reactiveness, and wounded leadership. All agreed that the strategy of resistance had been self-defeating. I traced conflicts to commonplace emotions and to the natural happenstance of an acquisition. By the time of the briefing DCers recognized all of that as well. Finally, I mirrored for them their perceptions of GrandCo as ethnocentric, polarizing, and evaluative. They knew as much and said so; although some belittling was justified, their views had surely been tainted. DCers left the briefing in collective spirit. Richardson was asserting himself again and vowed to at least work more openly with Schmidt. The strategy of resistance was abandoned and DCers agreed to work more authentically with Grand-Co, to test their perceptions, and to avoid fights for fighting's sake. I felt great about the briefing. Full of myself. But myself was not fully in *what I said*.

"You seem angry at GrandCo, seem to be stereotyping them." What I had left unsaid but was just below the surface was my feeling that GrandCo's values were potent and bad. Meryl drew a distinction between ethnographic and phenomenological ways of knowing. In the former, one learns by taking others' perspectives—those of different insiders or native groups. In the latter, one learns by putting oneself in the live situation and reflecting on one's own experience—something like "going native" and reporting on one native's perspective. Where was I actually and ideally in those terms?

In my briefing, I could take DC's side and see GrandCo in one way, but I could also take GrandCo's side and in that way help DCers better understand GrandCo's point of view. As DCers stepped back from their relationship with GrandCo, they could see the two perspectives too.

"But how did you experience GrandCo?" "I didn't," I stammered, for I never met any of their executives. I had read a book about the firm and talked to a former employee; I did not really like any of what I had heard or read. "So," Meryl said, "whatever GrandCo is for you is really what comes from DCers' experiences of GrandCo and your experience of DCers." "Mmmmm." "Are values a shorthand for whatever GrandCo means to you?" "Mmmmm." "Why values, Phil?" Maybe I was "externalizing" myself. We had never heard of such a concept and agreed that Freud would likely turn over in his grave. "I really wanted DC to hold onto its values—I was an evangelist, too, and GrandCo people were heathens." Then I called them callous capitalists with no sense of human feeling: "Those fucking bastards were kicking my boys around." Meryl asked who I symbolized in the story. Talk turned to families.

BATES AND DAVIS

Bruce Bates was a role model for me—maybe an ego ideal. He was the Human Resources Officer in DC and chief implementer of the DC philosophy and value system. I first worked with him when the studies of worklife began in DC and he was a strong backer of the acquisition study. Like Richardson, he too voted against GrandCo's involvement in the study. He could find no evidence that GrandCo was interested in learning about the acquisition and DC's reaction; he saw no prospects for GrandCo people mutually addressing problems that might be unearthed by the research. He could not keep his "integrity" if GrandCo was in the study so long as the relationship was that way.

Bates was a great conceptualizer and reader of organizational process. I once told him that a part of me thirsted for the day-to-day impact and family feeling that a business position should provide. He seemed to embody an ideal businessperson cum social scientist. Bates was my guide through the first round of data collection on the acquisition. He had thought of "jumping ship" after the sale but stayed on to protect DC's interest. He had fought against the reactive strategy, but his efforts to promote a more proactive strategy had failed. Bates proposed several concepts that were useful at the briefing. One was the death-and-dying model used to characterize DC's denial of the legitimacy of GrandCo and their anger at losing their independence. His concepts, his guidance, and the change in his own approach to GrandCo helped reshape DC's strategy and set DC and GrandCo on a more cooperative track.

Richardson's career planning speeded up after the briefing meeting and it became clear that DC needed a new executive vice-president. The decision was to be made using DC's participative selection system and, in recognition of GrandCo's interest and in the spirit of cooperative relations, Schmidt of GrandCo was asked to join the selection committee. It was quickly agreed that several internal candidates were qualified for the job. Following months of interviews with the candidates, analysis of ratings of their peers and subordinates, and discussions within the committee, the field narrowed to two. One was Bates. He was distinguished by his intellect, his leadership in participative management, and his human relations management style. The other was Robert Davis, head of the major operating divisions in DC, and known for his line experience and financial acumen. His was the traditional route to the top in DC.

The committee was divided over the candidates. Then Schmidt announced he was in favor of looking for an external person, maybe someone in GrandCo. Richardson flew to GrandCo headquarters to meet with him. One week later Davis was named DC's new executive vice-president.

The second round of data gathering began shortly after this announcement. Amongst interviewees there were varied opinions as to how the decision had been made. Some saw it as an honest business decision—that the "best man" had won—and pointed with pride that GrandCo could be involved in this participative way. Others said that Bates's conflicts with GrandCo during the first year of combination had hurt him, that GrandCo needed to find a guy who could play the game more in their way. Still others said that "the deck was stacked" and GrandCo's power made the decision in Davis's favor.

Interviewees reported a surge of momentum after the decision. They had moved into the acceptance phase in the death-and-dying sequence and had established parameters of control with GrandCo. Business was improving and many sensed a stronger pace in DC. As I prepared my report, a major business decision was made. Several divisions in DC were combined and Bates, the human resource man, was named the new general manager. Davis had initially been against his appointment. The selection committee saw it as a "natural," however, and Davis and Bates met to "get the bugs out." This decision was hailed throughout DC. The family feeling was back again.

FAMILY SYSTEMS

The vice-presidential selection had been a real battle. As I told Meryl the story, we agreed that it sounded like the description of a family system. Meryl wondered where the researcher was in that family system: Where were the indebtednesses, alliances, conflicts, vendettas, and whatever else? Battles can be embedded in the experience of being in a family. "How do you feel about Davis?" "A fair amount of ambivalence." "You have an older brother, don't you?"

Bates was "pissed off" by the vice-presidential decision. So was I. As I reentered the room I mumbled that my brother was more like Davis than Bates—"In some ways," I added. "And aren't you more like Bates?" Meryl wondered. My brother had been a Junior Achiever, a business major in college, a Harvard MBA. He had taken a T-group course and hated it. I had never fit into Junior Achievement and had eschewed business training. I was reminded that I had characterized Bates as Richardson's "son" in DC; so who was Davis? We swirled awhile. Meryl recalled that I had forecasted an impending bloody battle between Davis and Bates in a cautionary note attached to the first round briefing report. "Impending; but you already know it's bloody, don't you?" I let out a moan. "What's the struggle with the brothers?" At the oddest times the fire in the wood stove needs tending, so I took out the poker and tended to it.

I still have a hard time talking about myself in relation to my family and my brother. Brotherly rivalries are not uncommon, and I may have carried such a rivalry into my relationship with Davis. I identified with Bates's ways of thinking, his style, and his appreciation of life. In Davis I saw confidence, groundedness, a sense of responsibility—all aspects of my brother that I admire and resist in myself. The rivalry may be linked to family position. Older brothers show Davis's traits, and also tend to value property, to get along with authority figures, and to have a taste for running a business. Second brothers do not. We tend to be more spirited, more quixotic in thinking, and centered upon people; we may talk but never seem ready to run the show.

Now, these traits are not ascribed to Davis or Bates. They do fit with my own family system. In DC, Davis was older than Bates and clearly the more experienced manager as he came from a line position. His was also the traditional route to the vice-presidential post. All of these criteria stick in my brotherly craw. Bates's obstinate manner estranged him from GrandCo and, curiously, his orientation to people was seen as softness, which hurt him as well. Those same curious traits cohabit in many second brothers. We resent them used against us by impersonal authority figures and institutions.

The second report intimated that the struggle between the brothers was not resolved. There was the possibility that Bates would leapfrog Davis and examples were drawn from GrandCo to explicate the likelihood. Younger brothers have such wishes; Meryl sensed that mine were farfetched. What is more, I cited Davis's promotion and the organizational structure decisions as signs that DC was abandoning its value system and that true family feeling was being lost. In the report, I asked managers to consider whether DC risked deculturation. I urged them to rededicate themselves to their old values and to seek to integrate the changes.

The report was read with interest. Richardson and Bates wanted to meet as we had done after round one and discuss the report and its action implications. Davis and other officials in DC, members of his alliance, felt that a meeting was unnecessary. For them the report slowed progress and my warnings seemed vague and without action implications. Months went by. Then I got a letter from Richardson saying a decision had been made that no briefing would take place.

It's one thing to not put your heart into things. Emptiness and futility are its companions. But I had put my heart and soul into the second round report. And it was not recognized; it did not make a difference to anyone. The symbol system went to work. GrandCo, Schmidt, Davis, a hidden subculture in DC were in cahoots. "With whom?" "Well," I said, "I guess the military-industrial complex doesn't map very well to reality." Then, I added,

> With the contingency crowd, the crowd that questions the "sufficiency" of participative management in a world of rock throwers; I went after them in my dissertation; the crowd that says tough, rationalistic, autocratic management fits well in certain environments. Whose ends are served by that? Makes more sense to be tight, kick ass when the environment says. . . . Says who? That damn competing values crowd. . . .

DISINTEGRATION

Richardson left DC before the third round of data gathering. We talked before his leaving. I asked him whether my story was wrong, whether I had lost all objectivity, whose issues were being worked in the story: DC's, his, or my own. Heady, warm, but inconclusive. I then asked him about DC's future. He was of two minds. He was a strong believer that the culture of a company takes on the values of its leader. With a new man heading DC, the culture could change and change fast. At the same time, Richardson also believed that cultures are ingrained in people, ideas, functions, rituals, traditions. DC people would influence the new president. DC's way of life would resist disintegration and assimilation into GrandCo.

Davis was named the new president of DC. The transition was handled well. Richardson went to all DC locations to say goodbye and was followed by Davis, who met with all DCers and presented himself to them in customary group, family-style meetings. Interviewees made no comments on the reasons surrounding Richardson's departure. My sense was that it was better left unsaid. They did express loss—of their own father figure—and of the family symbol he set for DC. Interviewees also commented on some changing norms amongst top management, less process discussion, less extensive participation in decisions, less joking and horseplay. Many commented as well that GrandCo was having a greater influence over some decisions in DC.

Nonetheless, there was also keen excitement, a sense that DC was moving again. New products were being developed, the market was coming out of the recession, profits would be up again. Bates was doing a "super" job; Davis was full of energy; the company was healthy again.

There was a briefing following the third round of data gathering. No report was requested; I was just asked to give my impressions in the context of reviewing the worklife data. I talked about the disintegration of DC and urged top managers not to resurrect the old culture but rather to reculturate and set a new path. One said we were all "feeling the elephant." So an elephant was drawn depicting cultural options. One option was for the elephant to sit on the people; another was to use its trunk to call attention to new challenges. One option was for the elephant to stand on its hind legs and lead the herd; another was for it to listen to people and to use its head. The elephant had to walk through tall grass to sustain profitability. It also had to carry people—all DCers—on its back. One stated that the group was like blind men each feeling a part of the elephant. They had to share their feelings; give the elephant a heart.

The elephant was presented to all DCers at worklife briefing meetings. So was the task of reculturation. Meetings were held throughout DC to the end of feeling the elephant and giving the elephant a heart. A new statement of beliefs and values has been drafted and is circulating through DC today. Davis is meeting with DCers at all locations in group, family-style meetings to learn their reactions.

MYTHIC SYSTEMS

Acquisitions and mergers beget myths (Hirsch, 1980). There is the "war and western" genre with battles, bombings, shootouts, and ambushes. These have heroic referents in raiders, the big hat boys, gunfighters, and the tombstone makers. There are nautical myths, with pirates and safe harbors, and gamesmanship, with moves, countermoves, and strategy plays. There are the courtship myths with wooing, playing hard to get, marrying, and the afterglow.

Many myths surfaced around the acquisition of DC. The company that sought to take them over was seen as a "rapist." GrandCo, in traditional chivalry, was cast as the white knight that rode to rescue. DC was, of course, the damsel in distress. Following the sale, many in DC referred to it as a marriage.

DCers had their own myth born at the time Richardson assumed leadership of the company some eight years before the sale. The top management went on a retreat, talked over their values, visions, hopes, and selves, and embarked on a path toward more participative, soulful stewardship of the corporation. They saw their realm as Camelot, with Richardson as Arthur and top managers as Knights of the Round Table. Their rites included poetry, skits at management meetings, a sense of themselves in a holy crusade.

I felt a part of this myth, like another member of the realm. I was the kingdom's scholar, its storyteller. I wrote an epic poem about the acquisition. In the land of Camelot there lived a princess, it began, and traced the preacquisition history to the point of the threatened rape. It celebrated the beneficence of the white knight but warned of the covetous nobles and grasping beast in its castle far away. The financial people and technostructure were symbolized that way. There came to pass months of struggle, with jousts over principle and skirmishes over power, the poem read, tracing the roots of DC's combative strategy and the consequences. Then came the visit to the Land of the Scholars, the new strategy, the new relationship, later the new realities. The final stanzas read:

> Kingdoms come and Kingdoms go, Princesses marry and marriage means change. Beasts do battle and nobles count money, but battles do end and more than gold makes a reign. The days of Camelot are passing, what call ye the next days? Will harvests still flourish? Will the princess still shine? With the old spark gone, will a new one arise?
>
> Scholars can ponder and knights dream of glory. But the answers to these questions await the princess's story.

I do not know the princess's story today. I have lost touch with the reality of DC. A story *could* be written about a security-driven man, Richardson, who installed a Mickey Mouse system, participative management, who was not man enough to handle an acquisition, who had a namby-pamby human resource director; and now some real men have taken over the business, who are realistic about participation, who know what business is all about, who have gotten the place cleaned up. A story about war or a western, of the forces of light and darkness, could be the tale. "It ain't my story. I do not see that story in DC, I do not experience that myself," I told Meryl.

"What was your experience?" "I am losing touch with myself." My father was gone at DC, my values were being recast, the big villains were wreaking injustice on my boys, and maybe my brother was trying to keep the whole thing together. Bates was writing poetry about his search for the "path with the heart." I was blathering to Meryl.

We then talked, necessarily so, about clinical supervision. Researchers who use themselves as instruments need that in the field. Ken Benne

(1959) has done some thoughtful writing on neurotic anxiety as it expresses itself in organizational research and consultation. Needless to say, I have my neuroses and my normal anxieties as well. Benne makes a distinction between neurotic anxiety and rational fear "based upon the sober fact that both 'change agent' and 'client' change during a process of consultation. And change may involve disintegration of a self and its associations without valid re-integration and rebuilding" (p. 63).

TURNING TO OTHERS

There was another person working with DC, another man I identified with, another man who guided me along the way. Garfinkle, a clinical psychologist, worked with DC to implement its management system alongside Richardson and Bates. He has met Schmidt, knows the people at GrandCo, and does not think my anxieties are neurotic; he is feeling them himself. Garfinkle participated in the executive vice-presidential decision committee. He discussed values and character with Davis and cast his lot with Bates. Garfinkle finds GrandCo to be "benevolent/ authoritarian," as he is wont to say, and committed to conventional business wisdom.

Garfinkle believes in octopuses and amoebas as valid psychic images and metaphors for corporate behavior. He finds GrandCo's values to be antithetical to genuine concern for people and, thus, to DC's participative systems. He is not sure whether DC's value system can be preserved. Garfinkle, more deeply than I, feels the loss of Richardson. He, more so than I, feels the loss of value of his work in DC. He told me, sadly, that he would never again find a client like Richardson and an organization like DC used to be.

Our earlier discovery that DCers, their selves, histories, and situations, shaped my self in the research process comes back to me now. As I live the DC myth through Richardson, Bates, even Garfinkle, the story reads one way. By contrast, the new human resources man at DC, after a discussion of my current views, tells me he believes that DC's Camelot is ahead. Richardson's predecessor had his myth, Richardson had his, and the new generation will have their own. He believes that Richardson's legacy will live on in DC through its rituals and its practices, newly defined in a new culture, but at core, at the level of value, the same. A professional colleague to whom I described DC's current efforts at reculturation said it sounded like organization development in the 1980s. He said I had to "let go" of my sixties' images, get with today. So I told Meryl, "I am not sure what is going on in DC; I am not sure of my self."

TURNING TO SELF

We then talked about the therapeutic aspects of doing particular forms of social science—as therapy for the self. Certainly researchers study topics that envelop personal life issues and characters that bring to the fore central life themes. Such encounters can enable the self-minded researcher to gain insights into ways the self influences the research process and, perhaps, work through some of the issues in the successful management of research relations. We then kibitzed about power mongers who study power, the brains who study things like sense-making. It seemed the powerless, isolated, and brainless studied these too. Thus, we concurred that there is always some pathology in the self-selection of a field of study, an area of inquiry, a line of interpretation. "One reason people study particular issues, interpret data in particular ways, even make interventions of a particular sort is to maintain an issue, to keep it fixed, to make it legitimate," said Meryl. We noted that that could normalize experience, even reveal a universal in life drama. It could also be a sign of pathology.

My psychodynamic self found certain psychodynamics in DC. The issues were of authority, manliness, weakness, models of leadership. My symbolic self found symbolism in GrandCo's power and values, in DC's Camelot and conquest, totems of goodness and taboos of badness. My familial self found family feeling, then upset; a place for me, then betrayal. Those selves intertwine an instrument, shape it and are shaped by it. My relations with DCers, the setting, the circumstances, and my self activated all these self systems in my data gathering, interpretations, and interventions. I was intertwined with all the selves in DC too, and in this sought the universal self. "Hadn't my story of DC's acquisition, the myths and all, revealed something about all of us? About people in transition? About the meaning of life—for DCers? for me?"

"So where's the pathology?" I hollered at Meryl. Silence was the reply. I told her of the latest developments in the story. I have been talking to Bates about the research, talking about the ways I portrayed him, confessing that Davis was being cast as something of a bad guy, little more than a caricature. Bates suggested I talk to Davis, let him know my feelings, see if we could get a better fix on each other. At this writing it has been three weeks and I still have not called him. One more thing. Bates, Davis, and I agreed that it was time GrandCo knew about the study. I had some worries that this would create problems in DC, but both assured me that the relationship, at this point, could withstand them. Schmidt now has several draft papers about the history of acquisition. I have not called him to learn of his reaction either.

"What are you afraid of?" "I do not want to change the story at this point!" It will be a fuller, richer, more valid story once I learn more about Davis and learn more about GrandCo; I know that, but I certainly am hesitating. "Would it mean more than giving up the myth, the aesthetic of the story?" "Mmmmm." "Is there another danger?" "I'm afraid of losing my anger," I said. "Suppose these guys are not caricatures, suppose values are relativistic, suppose I do bring their world into me? I would lose my anger." "Then there's the pathology."

Therapy for the self in the research process must be premised upon not only the limits of the self but also of its possibilities. In this study, and in this dialogue, I am seeking my self of being and becoming. It is a developmental task. My brother and I are really connecting of late. We have talked about our dad, what life is like for him as the older brother, and what life is like for me. I find myself more conscious of ways we are similar as well as our differences. I am dealing better with my anger, fear, and tightness around corporate "big boys." Some of this has to do with my own maturity; some comes from growth experienced in preparing this work! I am also letting go. Not of the core; but I am trying out a new identity, less judgmental, narrow, and exclusive, and more accepting, broad, and inclusive. I am planning to let go of the story soon. Oh, I will continue my research in DC. But I will be listening more openly, more aware of my own self, more responsive to what DC really might become.

These selves of being and becoming transcend the other self-systems and gain expression in instrument, too. The systems of self, family, symbol, and myth to live in these selves and, in the experience of being and becoming, can be developed. I am developing in my life and in my research world, too. Progress is slow; but talking about it seems to help.

As we concluded our conversations we thought about constructing one of those strips that turns over on itself and then returns back. "What do you call that damn thing, Meryl?" "A Möbius strip." It might go from the self into the research, the research into the self, the research letting go of the self, the self letting go of the research. "Seems a technocratic image to me." Meryl agreed, offering Eliot instead:

> We shall not cease from exploration
> And the end of all our exploring
> Will be to arrive where we started
> And know the place for the first time.

> (T. S. Eliot, *Four Quartets*, 1971)

ON THE RESEARCHER'S
GROUP MEMBERSHIPS

Kathy E. Kram

The primary purpose of this chapter is to draw on my own experiences to illustrate the potent effects that one's personal characteristics have on the formulation and implementation of social science investigations. Through a discussion of two major research projects I will highlight how my age, gender, and professional group identifications shaped both the definition of the problems that I studied and the manner in which each study was carried out, as well as the nature, quality, and validity of the major findings. On the assumption that such self-understanding is a necessary prerequisite for the development of effective clinical field skills (Berg, 1980), I will also identify several strategies for achieving awareness of how one's group memberships influence the research process.

In my attempt to understand how my personal characteristics have shaped my research endeavors, I have found that an intergroup perspective on the research process is extremely useful. This theoretical perspective suggests that individual, interpersonal, group, and organizational relations can be understood by examining the group memberships of the parties involved and the relationship among these groups in the broader social context (Alderfer, 1984; Alderfer & Smith, 1982; Rice, 1969; Smith, 1977; Smith, 1982a). Thus, for example, my interactions with the individuals that I interviewed for both studies were shaped by the group memberships that each of us brought to these interpersonal transactions. In addition, my formulation of the research problem and my interpretation of the data were shaped by my memberships in particular age, gender, and organizational groups. This theoretical orientation provides a framework for exploration of how one's personal identity shapes the research process.

HOW GROUP MEMBERSHIPS AFFECT
THE RESEARCH PROCESS

An intergroup perspective suggests that the behavior of the researcher, the relationships between researcher and client, and the relationship between the researcher and the data that are collected can be understood by considering the groups that each of the actors in the research process represent (Rice, 1969; Alderfer, 1984; Alderfer & Smith, 1982). The basis of this claim is that all individuals are part of collective social processes that shape their behavior through the groups to which they belong.

The effects of these group memberships on the research process are found in first considering which group membership may be shaping the behavior of the researcher as well as the transactions between researcher and client system members. Once these salient group memberships are identified, intergroup theory suggests that the relationships between these relevant groups in the larger social context will parallel behavior at the individual and interpersonal levels (Alderfer, 1984; Alderfer & Smith, 1982). Thus, for example, the impact of being a young female researcher in a male-dominated setting can be best understood by considering the well-documented dynamics of token women in all-male work groups (Kanter, 1977; Wolman & Frank, 1975), and how these may be operating in the research setting. Similarly, the impact of being an academic researcher in a corporate setting can be understood by considering the nature of ongoing relations between industry and university groups. In both examples, relevant factors to consider are the nature of group boundaries, power dynamics, affective patterns, cognitive formulations, and leadership behavior manifested among the groups of interest (Alderfer, 1984).

In practice, this conceptualization requires the researcher to ask several important diagnostic questions during the research process. First, how are my group memberships shaping my perceptions, behavior, and affective reactions as I formulate the research questions and move forward to data collection and analysis? Second, how are my group memberships shaping research participants' reactions to me and their willingness to respond authentically to questions and probes throughout the data collection process? Third, how do the group memberships of all parties involved in the research process shape the nature and quality of data that are finally collected? Fourth, how do my group memberships shape the interpretation of findings at the conclusion of the investigation?

Discussion of two major research projects serves to illustrate the value of attending to the researcher's group memberships. The first involved a biographical interview[1] study of pairs of junior and senior managers in one corporate setting; the primary purpose was to investigate the nature of mentor relationships. The second study, which evolved directly out of the findings of the first, involved a biographical interview study of relationships with peers that managers experience at three different career stages; the primary purpose was to investigate alternatives to hierarchical relationships that might provide critical mentoring functions. In both cases, retrospective analysis of how salient group memberships shaped definition of the research problem, design and implementation of data collection, as well as interpretation of findings, has illuminated how my personal characteristics and those of the research participants shaped these endeavors.

STUDY 1: MENTOR RELATIONSHIPS IN MANAGERIAL CAREERS

The study was designed to explore the nature of mentor relationships, those relationships between junior and senior adults in a work context that are perceived as being supportive of individual development. In one corporate setting 18 pairs of managers were interviewed individually about their career histories and about their relationships with each other. Analysis of these interview data resulted in a conceptualization of the range of developmental functions that are provided in these relationships, a dynamic view of how these relationships unfold over time, and a delineation of the psychological and organizational forces that limit the value of these development alliances (Kram, 1983; Kram, 1985).

At the conclusion of this study, much progress had been made toward understanding the nature of mentor relationships and defining a broader conception of developmental relationships. The critical role of relationships in adult and career development was confirmed, the complexities of cross-gender relationships were illuminated, and new questions about the role of peer relationships in career development provided the impetus for the second study. The content and context of this project determined that my age, gender, and graduate student role would significantly influence definition of the problem, collection of the data, and interpretation of the findings.

DEFINING THE PROBLEM

Attendance at a seminar on adult development led by Daniel J. Levinson was a major catalyst for choosing the topic for my dissertation project. This intellectual experience was critical because it introduced me to a conceptual scheme that would guide my research for years to come (Levinson, Darrow, Klein, Levinson, & McKee, 1978). I now realize how much my own stage of development shaped my decision to do research in this area and to define the focus and scope for the study as I did.

I found the seminar particularly relevant to understanding the course of my own life during my early adult years. At age 27, I had encountered several hurdles in my professional and personal life that I was able to address effectively because, in part, of several important relationships with more senior colleagues. Although unconscious at the time, a primary motivation for pursuing this study was to better understand the role of these relationships in my own life. The adult development perspective not only legitimized the challenges and crises that I had experienced, but provided some insight into a kind of adult relationship that was key to their resolution in the early adulthood period (Levinson et al., 1978; Erikson, 1968; Jung, 1933).

My age also affected how I defined the methodology for studying the nature of mentor relationships. Pairs of managers in a corporate setting were identified by first approaching juniors in the age range of 25-35 about their significant relationships with seniors, and then inviting those significant others to participate in a parallel interview sequence. Intuitively, I felt more inclined to approach the juniors first; this reflected my relative comfort and identification with this group, in contrast to the group of mentors who would later be identified. This early choice had unanticipated consequences for the range of data that were collected and for the analysis of both groups' personal accounts. For example, I learned very little about the multiple protégés that a mentor may have at a given point in time since I contacted the seniors about the relationship identified by the junior. In addition, my tendency to identify with the juniors made it more difficult to develop insight into the seniors' experience of the mentor alliance.

My gender appears to have influenced the definition of the project in two major ways. First, the decision to study relationships and their role in adult and career development, rather than some other feature of the developmental perspective, reflects the strong relationship orientation in my own life. This is consistent with my sex role socialization in earlier years as well as with my contemporary experiences (Gilligan, 1982; Baker-Miller, 1976). Clearly, the study of subjective and personal experiences in relationships attracted my attention far more than the study of more objective organizational processes.

My gender also influenced the definition of the research sample. I was compelled to have women in the sample so that I could examine sex differences in patterns of individual development and in relationship dynamics. The demographics of the research site made it impossible to find more than one female mentor, but I was able to locate eight cross-gender alliances in which the junior was female. These gender comparisons were a high priority for me in this study, and continue to be a theme in each successive research project that I design. It is interesting to note that race comparisons were not included in the study; had I been other than white, I suspect this oversight would not have occurred.

My organizational role and affiliation affected the design of this project in two ways. First, my graduate school mentors encouraged me to utilize a biographical interviewing methodology; this was clearly most appropriate for the task at hand, but also frequently discounted in traditional academic arenas as not sufficiently rigorous. Most certainly the freedom, guidance, and encouragement that I received as I learned the methodology and implemented it influenced the course of this study. The findings are rich, and they clearly strengthen conclusions drawn from more traditional research methodologies.

Second, the location of the research site was facilitated by my dissertation chair and mentor. His ongoing relationship with a local corporation enabled easy access to this site, and minimized my initial anxieties about entering the field for this study. While I did explore other options, I chose to work at the site where the positive reputation of my mentor preceded me. With my increased knowledge of the dynamics of mentoring, I now understand why at this point in time I chose to follow in his footsteps. While the research relationship was an extremely positive one, I gained insight into the organizational influences on mentoring alliances from a particular setting. Hence the findings are limited by this design choice.

Finally, it is interesting to note that my age, gender, and organizational role significantly shaped my working hypotheses about the nature of mentor relationships. First, I suspected that these developmental alliances were primarily beneficial to the junior in the pair because of my own experiences to date in which I was yet too young to appreciate how my mentors benefited from teaching and coaching me. Second, I suspected that cross-gender alliances would be somehow different from same-gender alliances, based on discussions that I had had with my male peers about their relationships with their mentors; those hypotheses that emerged from the research were far more comprehensive than I could begin to articulate at the outset of the study. Third, I wrongly assumed that mentor relationships would look just like the ones that I had experienced during my academic career; variations due to organiza-tional setting, nature of the profession, and individual differences had yet to be identified through the research process. These working hypotheses, shaped by my group identifications, could have posed threats to the validity of the data collection and analysis; with the aid of clinical supervision (discussed later), I was able to acknowledge them and continue to generate alternative explanations and interpretations.

COLLECTING THE DATA

In this phase the intergroup perspective suggests that the group memberships of both researcher and interviewees are relevant. Group memberships of both parties shape key elements of the interview, such as rapport building, information sharing, and termination processes.

First, it was easier to build rapport with individuals of similar age to me than it was with the senior managers who were identified as mentors. I found myself far less anxious in approaching a young manager in his or her late twenties than I did in approaching a manager in his fifties. My own historical attitudes toward those older and in positions of authority were idealization; I assumed that they would not be interested in talking with a novice researcher. My anxiety and discomfort delayed the rapport-building process. As I examined familiar feelings from the past and questioned their relevance in the present, I was able to challenge these preliminary assumptions. With this increased self-awareness, I became less anxious about asking those in authority positions to take the time to participate in the interview sequence. I also had a sense that I became more credible and easier to talk with for the senior managers; data collection proceeded more openly once this age barrier was overcome.

Similarly, my age enhanced my ability to understand and empathize with the junior managers' experiences, making it relatively easy for me to ask relevant, probing questions. In contrast, interviews with senior managers were sometimes more stilted; I was unable to identify with their experiences, my empathy was more limited, and hence I was more often surprised. My questions to the seniors were not as finely tuned, and indeed I learned from them which questions needed to be asked in order to obtain adequate understanding of their points of view.

Gender similarities and differences had parallel effects on the interview transactions. Membership in the same-gender group facilitated rapport and identification, while membership in opposite-gender groups frequently created sexual tension and/or the lack of empathy or rapport, particularly early in the interview sequence. In my interviews with female research participants, I found it quite easy to build rapport and to empathize with their personal accounts. The corresponding threat to valid data collection, however, was the degree to which I identified with many of their experiences. Frequently I found myself pursuing tangents to the predesignated questions because of personal interest in their comments. Or, my strong identification with their accounts caused me to project some of my own reactions and experiences rather than listen openly to theirs.[2] Thus, while similar gender group identifications facilitated rapport, they simultaneously presented a threat to the validity of the data.

In my interviews with male research participants there were both advantages and disadvantages resulting from our gender group differences. On the one hand, sexual tensions and awkwardness frequently hindered the interview process, particularly when I asked male mentors about their relationships with female protégés. On the other hand, if these tensions could be managed over the course of the interview sequence so that sexual attractiveness was enhancing rapport rather than threatening it, here and now data on cross-gender relationship dynamics could be observed. While identification and rapport were more difficult to achieve in cross-gender interview transactions, the potential benefits of these encounters were great.

Age and gender group differences between researcher and participants provided several opportunities to learn from the transferences and countertransferences that evolved during the interview sequences (see Chapter 1 for definitions). I hypothesized that the senior male managers' reactions toward me were, in part, a replication of their feelings toward their junior female colleagues. These transferences were very useful in developing insight into sex role dynamics and intimacy concerns in cross-gender mentor alliances; when I experienced their attempts to keep me in a "one-down" position or their flirtatious behavior as a distraction from the interview task, I suspected that this same behavior might occur in their roles as mentors. Similarly, my reactions to these same male senior managers provided insight into the authority dynamics in mentor relationships. By comparing these countertransferences with the personal accounts of junior managers, I was able to further understand how attitudes toward authority shape the phases of a mentor relationship.

Finally, to a lesser extent, my role as graduate student also influenced this phase of the research process. This organizational group membership, given its low status, low power, and transient nature, contributed to feelings of uncertainty about my own competence and the likelihood that I would complete a project of significant merit and importance. At the same time, I can hypothesize that research participants frequently wondered whether this study would have significance and whether I had sufficient experience to conduct the interviews and analysis effectively. This particular barrier was surmounted during the interview sequences as I demonstrated competence, answered relevant questions about me and the study, and became aware of how my own performance anxiety was shaping the interview process.

ANALYZING THE DATA

In practice, the analysis of interview data cannot be entirely separated from the collection of the data. In clinical research of this kind, these two phases of the research process are intimately intertwined. As interviews are conducted, initial insights emerge about the phenomenon that is being studied. These new insights influence the kinds of questions that seem important to ask in subsequent interviews. This inductive process is characterized by continuous movement between data and concepts until the time when sufficient categories have been defined to explain what has been observed. This methodology is described by Glaser and Strauss (1967) as the "constant comparative method of analysis."

Clearly, in this kind of inductive and "messy" process, there are many ways to cut the data; and the researcher's perspectives on the world, shaped by his or her group memberships, will determine which course is chosen. In delineating the functions of mentor relationships, I identified two types: career functions and psychosocial functions (Kram, 1985). Whereas other studies of mentoring have tended to emphasize the career functions (Missirian, 1982; Kanter, 1977; Clawson, 1980; Phillips-Jones, 1982), I paid particular attention to how these developmental relationships supported psychosocial growth as well as career advancement. In retrospect, this is a reflection of what I had recently experienced in my own professional life; several relationships with senior colleagues that extended support beyond instrumental advancement concerns to broader personal and professional dilemmas.

Second, in delineating the phases of a mentor relationship (Kram, 1983) I devoted considerable attention to the separation phase of the relationship. This was undoubtedly due to the fact that at the time of the study I was beginning to anticipate leaving graduate school and separating from several people who had provided a variety of mentoring functions. The complexity of feelings that I experienced, including sadness, appreciation, anger, and excitement as I began to say goodbye to a most significant mentor, fueled my desire to understand intellectually this critical relationship phase. Clearly current developmental concerns in my own life (e.g., whether I would continue to flourish apart from my mentor) shaped which categories were emphasized in my analysis. It was only after I completed my own separation that I could expand my analysis to present a more comprehensive description of all of the relationship phases.

In a similar fashion, my work offered a much more comprehensive picture of the juniors' experiences of the mentor relationship than it did of the seniors' experiences. Even with arduous analysis of transcripts and interview notes, the juniors' personal accounts were more fully brought to life in the written analyses because I was able to empathize and identify with many of their experiences. It was only through extensive discussion with my senior colleagues and further informal interviews with age peers of the seniors in my sample that I developed a full appreciation for the significance of assuming the role of mentor. From this experience I learned that more consistent effort and extra grappling with the data will be required to develop adequate understanding of personal accounts from people with vastly different group memberships than those of the researcher.

As in the interview phase, the use of self in the analysis is a critical resource for the researcher. Organizing themes and categories emerge in the interaction between the researcher and the data that have been collected as one's own reactions to the data and to the interview phase of the project are examined. Thus, whenever I had strong affective responses to the data as I was studying interview transcripts, I referred back to personal reactions that I had noted during the interview phase as well as to my own experiences in mentor relationships for further insight. I then had three sources of data rather than only one to draw upon in formulating new interpretations.

The most vivid example of this use of multiple sources of data from self and research participants is found in my analyses of the dynamics of cross-gender mentor relationships. I noted that my relationships with male mentors and peers had been somewhat guarded as they and I experienced both the excitement and threat of increasing intimacy. I, and I suspect some of them, avoided frequent one-on-one contact. And, in some instances, I felt trapped in stereotypical role relationships where I played the "helpless" student and they "rescued" me, or I played the "cheerleader" while they expressed their knowledge and creativity. These stereotypical roles minimized discomfort with sexual attraction but they were extremely dysfunctional since they reduced my competence, intellectual contributions, and sense of autonomy.

The downside risk of using one's own personal reactions and experiences in efforts to understand the data of research participants is that analysis of their accounts will be distorted by the researcher's own projections and transferences. Indeed, I had to reassess my analyses of cross-gender dynamics when I noted that only the junior women's points of view were well articulated; this indicated to me that my interpretations of these relationships were significantly biased by my age and gender group identifications.

Finally, as the analysis phase is completed, implications for research and practice are identified. As with the choice of categories and themes for analysis, this "choicepoint" is also shaped by the personal character-istics of the researchers. As one who, at the time, was moving out of the role of graduate student into the role of professor, I was particularly intrigued with how organizational circumstances shape the course of a mentor relationship. Similarly, as one who would be leaving several significant relationships with senior colleagues, I was interested in the findings that suggested that relationships with peers might provide critical alternatives to the hierarchical mentor relationship. Finally, as the solo woman entering an all-male work group, I remained curious about how organizational contexts shape the dynamics of cross-gender alliances. Each of these has become a focus of inquiry for me since Study 1 was completed.

STUDY 2: PEER RELATIONSHIPS AS MENTORING ALTERNATIVES

This study was designed to explore the nature of relationships with peers in work settings that support individual development. The first study indicated that while mentor relationships provide critical develop-mental functions in both early and middle career years, they endure only a few years and they are relatively unavailable to most people in organizations (Kram, 1985). I decided to explore relationships with peers in work settings because they were frequently mentioned by participants in the first study as providing a variety of supportive functions, particularly in the absence of mentors.

In order to investigate the role of peer relationships in career development, 15 individuals spanning three age groups (25-35, 36-45, 46-64) were interviewed about their career histories and about relation-ships along the way that had supported their development. They were asked to describe in depth two such relationships with peers. These significant others were then invited to participate in a parallel interview study about the relationship and the personal and organizational context in which it evolved. The majority of the original 15 research participants identified two peer relationships, 3 identified only one, and 1 identified none. Thus 25 relationship pairs were studied, and they were all located in one large *Fortune 500* manufacturing firm.

This study resulted in the delineation of a continuum of peer relationships that extend across a lifetime, providing unique functions at different career stages (Kram & Isabella, 1985). The results highlighted how relationships with peers can provide critical mentoring functions (Kram & Isabella, 1985).

The similarities between Studies 1 and 2 are readily apparent: a biographical interview methodology was utilized; the unit of analysis was the relationship; personal and organizational factors that shaped the evolution of relationships were examined; and the critical role of each kind of developmental relationship in psychosocial and career development was investigated. Given these similarities, it is not surprising that many of the group membership influences outlined in the discussion of Study 1 also characterized this second study. I discuss Study 2 in order to highlight several striking differences in each major phase of the research process due to variations in age and organizational group memberships. These comparisons reinforce the potent effects of personal characteristics and intergroup forces on social science investigation.

DEFINING THE PROBLEM

A number of interesting questions evolved from the mentoring study that defined several options for future research. Indeed, in seminar discussions of the findings, colleagues frequently pursued those that further explored the potential negative consequences of mentoring alliances or, alternatively, those that would illuminate differences in these developmental relationships across organizations and the practical implications of such variations. While these areas piqued my interest, and have subsequently become subjects of investigation, at the time that Study 2 was defined, relationships with peers presented the most intrigue for me. This choice was clearly shaped by the age- and career-related developmental tasks that I faced at the moment.

Four years had passed since the inception of the first study, and I had experienced many personal and professional changes during that period that influenced the kinds of relationships that I needed and that were available to me in my new work setting. At age 32, I had a strong desire to experience greater mutuality in my relationships with colleagues, and even early images of providing mentoring functions to my junior colleagues. I was aware of missing my graduate school mentors, and yet I also sensed that I was too old to recreate such relationships. This transition period, in moving from student to professor, from my twenties to my thirties, and from single to married provided the impetus to explore the potential of peer relationships in a work context.

Growing older and experiencing these major transitions also compelled me to develop a far more complex view of relationships. Whereas I entered the mentoring study with a working hypothesis that individuals generally have one mentor who guides and supports them, I could now see how relationships change, personal needs change, and, more often than not, individuals have a variety of hierarchical and peer alliances within and outside the work context that support their development. This increasing awareness of the complexities of relationship dynamics was a driving force behind investigation of other types of developmental alliances.

My organizational group membership significantly shaped the design of this project. As a junior professor, I felt a sense of urgency to conduct new research and very little time in which to do so, given the varied responsibilities of the role. In addition, the need for ongoing colleagueship on research endeavors sparked my interest in working with others on the study rather than recreating the solitary dissertation experience. Finally, in the role of teacher and scholar, I wanted the opportunity to guide others in learning about research. These forces contributed to my decision to put together a team of two doctoral students and myself; this team not only shaped the course of data collection and analysis, but it also provided an opportunity for me to experience many of the mentoring and peer dynamics that were the subject of my ongoing investigations.

At this point in time, I was acutely aware of how changes in organizational position and age are catalysts for changes in relationship needs and possibilities. Thus, I was convinced that the study should include individuals at early, middle, and late career stages rather than just a sample of juniors who are launching new careers. The mentoring study provided the opportunity for me to develop greater capacity to relate to and understand those at other stages than my own. Ideally, our research team would have representatives from the three major career stages; however, the graduate students with the interests and skills to participate were about my age with several years of work experience outside of academia. Awareness of the effects of group memberships on each stage of the research process would at least enable us to be aware of the limitations of our age homogeneity.

The research team did provide one dimension of diversity that was absent in Study 1; we were two women and one man. Thus, we had constructive counterpoints on gender-based issues, the capacity to conduct same-gender and cross-gender interviews, and the opportunity to examine—within one research team—how gender affects mentoring and peer alliances in terms of power relations, affective responses, competition, and intimacy. Because we were age peers but not organizational peers, my relationships with my colleagues had characteristics of both mentoring and peer alliances.

COLLECTING THE DATA

In this study, most of the interviews were conducted by the doctoral students on our research team. My organizational role as professor and teacher prompted me to give up total immersion in the data collection process in order to adopt a clinical supervisor role. I negotiated entry into a research site, conducted several exploratory interviews and then through the remainder of data collection met with the team on a weekly basis to discuss their experiences in the field and to set up data analysis procedures.

It was during this phase of the project that we began to utilize our own experience to learn about peer relationships. First, there was considerable ambiguity about the boundaries and definitions of our interpersonal relationships. While organizationally I was to serve as a mentor in conducting research of this kind, at least one member of the team felt more comfortable with me as a peer rather than as a supervisor. I contributed to the confusion in the situation by feeling some ambivalence and anxiety about assuming the expert and mentor role for the first time. Gradually, as we took the time to process our experiences working together, we learned about the difficult dynamics—competition, resentment, struggles for control—that frequently emerge in peer relationships and in mentor relationships during certain phases. These were also the dynamics that were less likely to surface in our interviews, where we were primarily investigating the supportive nature of peer alliances. In retrospect, this self-study was essential to overcoming significant obstacles to getting our work done well. At the same time, attending to these process issues significantly enhanced our understanding of the relationships that we studied.

As in Study 1, age and gender group memberships of researchers and participants shaped the data collection process. In general, similarities promoted empathy and rapport during the interview sequences as well as threats to valid interpretations due to researchers' projective identifications. Differences, on the other hand, promoted the opportunity to learn firsthand how such differences shape the relationships that were the focus of investigation, as well as threats to valid data collection posed by predictable resistances, transferences, and countertransferences. These group and intergroup forces are significant, and would be even more so if the population studied were also characterized by socioeconomic, racial, or cultural backgrounds that were vastly different from those of the researchers. It appears that one way these complexities are managed is to choose (albeit unconsciously) to do research in settings where group membership differences between researcher and participants are minimized.

ANALYZING THE DATA

The process of analysis proceeded in a similar fashion to that described in Study 1. The team of researchers proved to be invaluable at this phase to the extent that the range of possible organizing categories and themes was quite extensive and each of us could bring our own perspective (and group memberships) to bear on the interpretation of the data. Most threats to validity were minimized by the active involvement of three researchers, each of whom had unique contributions and questions; tendencies to distort the data as a result of particular group memberships and associated projections or transferences were checked by our colleagues on the team.

My previous work on mentoring unknowingly presented a threat to valid interpretation of the data because I was inclined to use concepts from the first study to organize the data in the peer study. Fortunately, my colleagues pushed me to search for categories and concepts that were truly grounded in the interview data. The "messy" process of reviewing transcripts and trying to make sense of them was even "messier" with three sets of eyes. At times each of us wondered whether the struggles and disagreements over interpretations would result in greater insight and understanding at the completion of the project. In retrospect, it is clear to me that our gender differences enhanced our understanding of same-gender and cross-gender relationships; and our similarities in age, but differences in organizational group memberships, enabled us to define the continuum of peer relationships and to identify unique forms of these developmental relationships at different career stages.

Our own efforts to be an effective team enhanced our understanding of the "underside" of peer relationships. Whereas our interviewees focused almost entirely on the contributions that their relationships with peers made to their development, our conflicts, competitive dynamics, struggles for control, and difficulties in establishing open and trusted communication produced another set of data that provided a balanced view of the benefits as well as the limitations of peer relationships.

The most unanticipated consequence of this phase of the research project was the additional insight that I developed into what it is like to be a mentor. During this project, I began to truly empathize with the mentors that I had interviewed years before, and to understand more fully the range of challenges and affective experiences that characterizes this generative stance toward junior colleagues. Changes in my age and organizational group memberships were a catalyst for this increased awareness and insight.

IMPLICATIONS

This retrospective analysis from an intergroup perspective offers several guidelines for future research endeavors:

(1) At the outset of a study, the salient group memberships shaping the research process should be identified so that they can be consciously managed. These will depend on the content and the context of the study. It is not difficult to imagine how the questions, methods, and obstacles encountered during the research reported here would differ if I had had other personal characteristics.

(2) It may be necessary to modify a research strategy in order to increase the likelihood that group membership influences will enhance rather than interfere with the research process. Comparisons of the two studies of developmental relationships indicated that the introduction of a team of researchers enhanced the research process by creating diversity in gender and organizational group memberships. Both studies would have been strengthened by the inclusion of researchers who were older and/or of a different racial group.

(3) If the relevant group memberships appear to create insurmountable obstacles to valid data collection and analysis, then the research endeavor should be discontinued or significantly modified. When group memberships are such that little empathy and rapport can be established between researcher and participants, or characteristics of the researcher make valid interpretation of the data very unlikely due to a frame of reference that distorts rather than facilitates insight, professional integrity can only be maintained by a decision to discontinue the project and to pursue questions that can be adequately addressed.

(4) Systematic study of group membership influences is necessary at the outset of each new research endeavor because the complexion of these forces will undoubtedly differ from one project to the next. While certain group memberships of the researcher never change (like gender or race), organizational memberships change as one's career evolves, as illustrated in my transition from student to professor. Each study presents a context with new actors; even if the researcher's group memberships are stable, unique dynamics are created by their interaction with those of a new set of research participants.

(5) The potent influences of group memberships necessitate the use of finely tuned clinical skills. Self-awareness, relationship skills that enable effective management of field relationships, and the diagnostic skills to understand and manage these inevitable intergroup forces, are absolutely necessary to complete a project that meets the standards of valid investigation (Isabella, 1983).

MANAGING GROUP MEMBERSHIPS EFFECTIVELY

I conclude that managing group membership influences is a primary responsibility of every individual who is engaged in social science investigation. Three major vehicles exist for supporting efforts to identify and consciously manage these intergroup forces: systematic self-study, clinical supervision, and the use of a research team.

SYSTEMATIC SELF-STUDY

Understanding the effects of one's own group memberships on the research process is not an easy task. It requires inquiry into one's past to discover how identity group memberships have shaped current values and perspectives that are brought to one's work. In addition, it requires observation of one's current experiences and interactions in order to develop insight into how both identity group and organizational group memberships are affecting one's relationships and activities. Such self-awareness is difficult to achieve, and frequently a painful rather than enjoyable experience.

There are several solo activities that can support productive self-study. First, keeping a personal journal on a regular basis facilitates insight into one's reactions to events and the forces that are contributing to them. In essence, the same skills that are utilized in the research process can be applied to the study of self. Data is collected in a systematic way and then analyzed using concepts and themes that aid organization and insight. Often this is facilitated in personal therapy, where self-analytic work with a trained professional supports the ongoing process of inquiry. Second, taking field notes during a research project enables systematic study of self as one is engaged in the research setting. More focused than the personal journal, field notes attend to specific events related to each phase of the research process. Here, reactions during interviews and during periods of data analysis can be recorded and then referred back to as one attempts to understand the projections and transferences that may have shaped the study as it unfolded.

These solo activities are often difficult to perpetuate, particularly when there are so many external demands taking energy and time that could otherwise be used for systematic self-study. Another avenue is collaborative study with others who have similar aspirations to achieve self-awareness as well as personal and professional effectiveness. Experientially based courses in interpersonal effectiveness, group dynamics, and/or clinical field methods provide a context in which such learning can occur. Not only does this kind of structure facilitate regular self-study, but it provides an opportunity for individuals to get feedback from colleagues that is likely to enhance self-understanding. In addition, these learning contexts provide discussion of relevant conceptual frameworks that can be utilized with colleagues or in solo pursuits to develop further understanding of how one's personal characteristics affect one's experiences as a researcher.

CLINICAL SUPERVISION

A one-on-one relationship with a more experienced teacher, colleague, or mentor, provides the opportunity for an individual to enhance self-awareness, relationship skills, and diagnostic skills that are needed to identify and manage group membership influences effectively, especially since individuals are limited by blind spots, biases, and resistances. Berg (1980) describes this as an apprenticeship in which a young researcher can learn the requisite clinical field skills by working closely with another who is both well-trained and interested in the student's continuing learning and development. In this context, the student has the opportunity to develop his or her identity as a researcher by examining personal values and skills, and to expand self-awareness and a range of clinical field skills through the supervisor's role modeling, coaching, and counseling.

Clinical supervision includes ongoing self-study, study of the here-and-now relationship between student and supervisor, and study of the experiences one has in research sites in ongoing projects. Thus, three opportunities are created for identifying salient group memberships and how they influence one's activities in research endeavors. Through self-disclosure, feedback from one's supervisor, and joint exploration of both parties' experiences in their relationship, psychological processes of projection, transference and resistance are examined, the impacts of particular group memberships are discovered, and personal, relationship management, and diagnostic skills are further developed (Berg, 1980).

Clinical supervision serves different purposes at each stage of the researcher's career. Early it is likely to be a mentoring relationship—later it will be more peerlike.

CREATING A RESEARCH TEAM

This vehicle serves several of the functions provided by clinical supervision: colleagues can act as sounding boards for each other, they can provide feedback on particular methods of data collection and analysis, and, through joint investigation, they can enhance each other's learning as well as the scope and quality of the research project through each colleague's unique contributions to the team. As long as members have the needed skills and a commitment to building effective working relationships among themselves, a research team has great potential to reduce the threats to valid data collection and analysis discussed earlier.

The composition of a research team can be designed to enhance group membership influences. First, by creating diversity in identity group and organizational group memberships, a collective wisdom is generated that prevents narrow thinking, obstacles to rapport in data collection, and distortions in analysis. Second, where homogeneity does exist, representatives of the same groups have an opportunity to learn more about the meaning and impact of these memberships by exploring common experiences and perspectives. Finally, to the extent that representation among team members resembles the population of research participants, it is more likely that parallel processes will evolve. Thus what occurs in the team can be analyzed and related to what goes on in the field, and vice versa. This helps generate appropriate questions, causes data collection to be more open, and allows analysis to reflect more accurately participants' accounts.

One difficulty is that research teams are not readily available; it is frequently difficult to find individuals with the requisite skills and schedules to launch a collaborative effort. In addition, this vehicle requires a range of clinical skills to manage the group process so that the team enhances rather than detracts from the research process.

CONCLUSION

A researcher's group memberships always shape his or her investigations; systematic understanding of these influences is essential so that they can be managed effectively. The discussion of two studies of developmental relationships illustrated how gender, age, and organizational group memberships affected each phase of the research process.

In some instances these personal characteristics enhanced the effort by facilitating rapport and empathy. In other instances, these same factors created limitations and threats to valid data collection and analysis.

The clinical skills necessary to identify and manage effectively group membership influences are not easily attained. Just as training in theory and method generally takes years of intensive study, so do skills in self-awareness, building and managing field relationships, and diagnosing how one's identity in the role of researcher affects the process of inquiry. These skills cannot be developed fully within the context of a graduate program; more likely than not, the foundation is created during this training and socialization period. From then on, however, systematic self-study, clinical supervision, and the use of research teams will be essential to facilitate ongoing understanding and effective management of these potent forces.

NOTES

1. Biographical interviewing is a data collection methodology designed to reconstruct research participants' life or career histories. It is like a traditional interview method in that there is a list of topics to be covered and questions to be asked. However, each interview is different from the others because unique questions and comments are utilized in response to the individual's way of telling his or her own story. This flexibility facilitates joint investigation by enabling the interviewee to manage his or her personal exploration. Comparisons across interviews are based on an integrated understanding of each person and each relationship. For further explanation of this method, see Levinson et al. (1978).

2. Projective identification is an unconscious process by which an individual projects parts of his or her self onto another. This process facilitates empathy and rapport; however, it poses a threat to valid data collection and interpretation because what are noted as attributes of the research participant may really be characteristics of the interviewer that have been projected.

VIRTUOUS SUBJECTIVITY:
In the Participant-Observer's I's

Alan Peshkin

A way of seeing is always a way of not seeing.

(Kenneth Burke)

It is psychologically impossible for scientists' perceptions to be uncontaminated by social conditioning.

(Henrika Kuklick)

Quidquid perciptur, runs the Thomistic adage, *per modum percipientis percipitur:* Whatever is perceived is perceived through the character of the one who perceives.

(Michael Novak)

Subjectivity, so it is thought, compromises a researcher's most faithful rendering of a phenomenon because it leads to emphases and omissions that result in skewed portrayals. Nonetheless, these days researchers report their subjectivity with a straightforwardness bordering on aplomb. In this chapter, I discuss my personal encounter with subjectivity, which Webster defines as "the quality of an investigator that affects the results of observational investigation," and, I would add, other types of investigation as well. This quality I take to be an amalgam of the dispositions stemming from one's class, statuses, gender, and values. To me, the issue is not whether subjectivity is a persisting aspect of social research—it undoubtedly is. The issue is subjectivity's variable nature at the hands of the very same researcher. The question to consider, I now realize, is, Which of the researchers' personal qualities will a research experience elicit? This realization arose in the course of working as a participant observer in two different field settings where I pursued my studies of the school-community relationship.

AUTHOR'S NOTE: I am indebted to Elliot Eisner, Walter Feinberg, David Spain, and Robert Stake for usefully critical comments on this chapter.

ON SUBJECTIVITY

Like good soldiers imbued with their side's truth, social scientists may align themselves in opposing camps, so taken by the orthodoxy of their own perspective that they scorn those with contrary views (see Phillips, 1983, and Eisner, 1983, for example). The contending—and contentious—true believers may identify themselves as realists or empiricists, on the one hand, and idealists, on the other. As generally defined, these two traditions are in conflict (for example, see Riley, 1974), whereas in the actual practice, as opposed to the abstract discussion, of social science, researchers seldom are struck by the ineluctability of either one. They tack, so it seems, between alternating—even simultaneous—understanding and awareness of their own project in terms of the realist's objectivity and the idealist's subjectivity. Even those who unequivocally endorse an idealist orientation would be embarrassed by a critic's claim that prejudice so dominated their work that what they had seen was primarily in their beholding eye. Those oriented toward idealism do not want to exalt prejudice, subjectivity's stepchild; their orientation derives from a recognition of the impossibility of value-free research, the consequent inevitability of researcher-object interaction in social research, and, most important for my purpose in this chapter, the sense that subjectivity is the salt of creativity.

That personal factors penetrate all points of the research process is a matter of record (Peshkin, 1982a). Although it would be farfetched to claim that we could predict what researchers would study if we but knew enough about them, their choice of topics for investigation is far from random. Notwithstanding the opportunism generated by the availability of funds, we are generally attracted to a limited, if not a narrow, band of topics. Choice of topic is a starting point for the interplay of subjectivity in social science inquiry.

In this regard, note the acknowledgments of several sociologists. Shulamit Reinharz, reflecting on her choice of dissertation topic, writes,

> In the subtle matter of selecting a research problem and site, the researcher's conscious and unconscious needs seek fulfillment. . . . I plunged into the study of a mental hospital . . . to grapple with the personal pain of having friends of my own recently hospitalized for psychiatric problems. (1979, p. 141)

Reisman observes that Lazarsfeld

> used to remark that he undertook the Teacher Apprehension Study because it gave him a chance to put to work his passion for newly

discovered contextual analysis. But . . . it was no accident that the subject
was academic freedom: he cared about that. (1979, p. 226)

Of course, our personal proclivities do more than incline us to investigate certain problems. They lead us to take sides—Stein chooses that of
gypsum workers, not their boss's (1971, p. 143); Metz, whose work
focuses on schooling, concludes, "I did have a personal predilection
favoring the side in the debate which gave more rights of participation to
children" (1981, p. 13). And they lead us to make decisions that we see,
usually in retrospect, were not governed by strict concerns for objectivity and dispassion. For example, anthropologist Morris Freilich writes,

The biases which stem from the personality of the researcher are many
and include the selection of a given type of community to study . . . and
selection of given types of natives as key informants. (1970: 568)

An Indian anthropologist, Madan, reports that in his study of Kash-
miri Brahmins he obtained data on conflict among kinfolk from some
families who chanced—again, the personal factor—to take him "into
the domain of their privacy" (1975, p. 151).

Although it may be no serious matter that what we choose to investigate derives from personal inclinations, we would take as serious the
charge that our conclusions are subjective. But can subjective factors be
removed from the social scientist's conclusions? Can we claim to set
aside our personal orientations at the end of our studies any more than
we did at the beginning and thereafter? I think not. Sociologist Daniels
writes, following her procedurally difficult study of the American military, "If women can study male societies from which they are specifically
excluded," it may be useful to think of the value of other "alien" persons
studying other groups. "It is not argued," she says, "that such observers
will learn the same things that less alien persons might. Some perspectives will be lost, others will be gained" (1967, p. 267). When English
sociologist Roy Wallis says that other investigators of Scientology could well reach conclusions different from his (1977, p. 164), we
must wonder what, indeed, we should make of Wallis's conclusions
about Scientology, or, for that matter, of Daniels's about the military.
Does anything go? Is social science reduced to mere personalistic
wallow? These questions will be answered in the course of this chapter,
but first I will discuss my personal experiences that prompted this
reflection on subjectivity. These experiences made me realize how
abstract my previous understanding of subjectivity was, and they
provided the basis for the particular point I intend to make about
subjectivity.

TWO STUDIES, TWO VIEWS:
WHOSE OX IS GORED?

Some insights and understandings may be acquired by virtue of the experience of others. As parents, we often hope this will prove true, trusting that our children will profit from what we know and thereby forego the anguish of what we have experienced. As adults, we acquire some insights and understandings vicariously through the graphically portrayed documentation of others. We may continue believing that we have grasped what they have communicated until we come to deeper belief through personal experience—as I did in the case of subjectivity.

I have been investigating the relationship between schools and their host communities in a variety of environmental settings. Among other sources of data (interviews, questionnaires, and documents), I learn about the phenomena that interest me by taking the role of participant observer, thereby becoming a resident in the site of my study for an extended period of time (12 to 18 months) and living the life of the community's residents to the fullest extent possible for an outsider.

Underlying the distinctions different definitions of participation-observation contain is the critical fact that in this data-collecting mode researchers are immersed in the lives of others whose behavior and beliefs are the essence of their data. Notwithstanding this personal immersion, sociologist Gans notes about participant observation that "it requires surrender of any personal interests one might have in the situation being studied in order to be free to observe it" (1968, p. 304). These "personal interests" are the basis for the "*human* participant observer" who, along with the "*research* participant observer," is present as we conduct our studies (for elaboration of this distinction see Freilich, 1970, pp. 535-536). Thus, fieldworkers each bring to their sites at least two selves—the human self that we generally are in everyday situations, and the research self that we fashion for our particular research situation. In reality, much as we may intend to surrender our personal interests, Gans's ideal remains out of reach because participant observation, especially within one's own culture, is emphatically first person singular. The human *I* is there, the I that is present under many of the same political, economic, and social circumstances as when one is being routinely human and not a researcher.

Behind this I are one's multiple personal dispositions—the result of the aforementioned amalgam of one's class, statuses, gender, and value orientations—that may be engaged by the realities of the field situation. Because of the unknown and the unexpected aspects of the research field, we do not know which of our dispositions will be engaged, but they are likely to be our enduring ones, those invested with the greatest affect. If we knew in advance which personal factors would be engaged and what selectivity would result, our studies might turn out differently.[1] But we do not know, at least not always, and not with certainty, and thus I come to Mansfield and Bethany.

THE STUDY OF MANSFIELD[2]

The midwestern village of Mansfield is on no one's list of quaint, charming villages, of places one must visit. Because of its isolated location, Mansfield is usually reached only by intention. I went there because it was truly a rural community, shaped essentially by the requisites of the corn and soybean fields that make it an island, contiguous with no human settlement of any size. Of course, its adults not employed in agriculture commute to factory jobs in small cities (the nearest approximately 45 minutes away), places where Mansfielders also do their major shopping, take their recreation, and receive their medical services.

Mansfield's school district population of about 2200 people contains a native-born majority who married locally and stayed to raise their children in these quiet confines. In the course of two years in Mansfield—one spent living in the house of an 84-year-old widower, a former coal miner and farmer—I learned many intriguing things about village life. Before coming to Mansfield, I thought of such places as interruptions on the way to somewhere else, places that I could not avoid because no expressway skirted their grain elevators, dying Main Streets, and obtrusive stop signs. Their two-story, white frame houses looked like a movie set for a film I would not want to see, somnolent settings the world had passed by, as would I once I got beyond their reduced speed zone.

As researcher, not motorist, in Mansfield, I asked students, teachers, and parents to tell me about their community. "I'm from Chicago, a city boy," I'd say, "so tell me what it's like to grow up here, to live here," indeed, though I never asked, to die here. And they did. Mansfield was not every resident's favorite place, but it was to the village's mainstream majority about whom I wrote my book (Peshkin, 1978). They told me that privacy was scarce in Mansfield. It was like living in a fishbowl. They explained, however, that it was caring, not nosiness, that motivated them to be informed about their neighbors. When someone dies, neighbors close in with a level of support that moderates the impact of death's loss. Old folks have their caretakers, a nearby family that voluntarily looks after the aged who live alone and have no one to shovel their snowy sidewalks or haul out their garbage. I heard a great deal about shades being watched—if an oldster's shades are not raised by the usual time, concerned neighbors call to be sure that everything is okay; and also about chimney smoke in winter—neighbors check (just a quick glance out a window) to see if smoke is visible. As long as it is, the furnace is working properly.

When young Mansfielders grow up, they stay at home or close to it, notwithstanding their adolescent impulse as high school seniors to depart for distant shores, fed up with the village's intimacy and nurturance. Yet, when they do leave, it is most often to another small town located within the area they knew while growing up. When they move farther away, they often return for the high school's annual homecoming celebration, because this ritual roundup includes everyone, not just the members celebrating their fifth or fifteenth reunion. And when they retire, those who had moved away often move back to spend the rest of their lives where they feel most at home. This idyllic picture, presented without the blemishes, was basically confirmed by my questionnaire data and by readers of my Mansfield study who said they thought they were reading about their own home towns.

In regard to their school system, Mansfielders usually elect school board members who are both natives and farmers. These gentlemen operate as guardians of their community, hiring teachers and administrators who, in their terms, are "country." The more I learned about Mansfield High School, the educational focus of my study, the more I realized that through local control it had developed into an effective means for reproducing local values and behavior. In short, Mansfield High School fit Mansfield: the level of academic discourse, the many extracurricular activities, the models projected by teachers, and the emphasis on volunteerism and athletic competition—all reflected the lives of those adults who felt they belonged in Mansfield and who comprised their school system's host community.

THE STUDY OF BETHANY

Fundamentalist Christian schools are newsworthy these days, their numbers reputedly increasing in recent years by two, then three, and finally four newly opened schools per day. They open in small towns and large cities; they open in places where public schools are closing due to declining enrollment. Together with their expanding churches and popular television preachers, and their religiously oriented New Right politicians, they form a fundamentalist trinity. I thought it important to understand the fundamentalist's role in contemporary education.

For my study, I gained access to Bethany Baptist Church and its K-12 Bethany Baptist Academy (BBA). As in Mansfield, I focused on the academy's high school, concerned about the relationship between BBA and its host community encompassed by Bethany Baptist Church's 1500 members. I moved to Hartney, the city of approximately 50,000 people in which Bethany's church and school are located, and found an apartment in the home of a Bethany church family. They were stalwart Christians and kind, generous people who accepted me as a family member during my 18 months with them.

Bethany Baptist Church is run by Pastor Muller. He built its membership, its church building, and its school by attracting a large core of dedicated followers; they volunteer when work needs to be done, recruit new members in response to their scriptural imperative to proselytize, and aid their troubled brethren with money, time, or prayer as needed. As I sensed when I conducted interviews, and verified when I administered a questionnaire, a large majority of parents, teachers, and students center their away-from-home life around church and school activities.

Bethany Baptist Academy is physically separated from its church only by a parking lot. Otherwise, church and school are not separate in any way: The same interpretation of scripture underpins both institutions. Church leaders consider the school as integral a part of the church's establishment as its Sunday morning services. This is the basis for their argument that Christian schools, except for health and safety standards, are no more rightfully subject to state control than churches.

In its advertising brochure, BBA presents itself as "a school with a difference"; it means to be distinguished from its public school counterparts in terms of its philosophy, the conduct and appearance of its students and teachers, and the "integration," as they call it, of scripture and all subject matter, whether English, social studies, or mathematics.

Bethanyites claim their academy is a God-centered school, a necessary alternative to the Man-centered public school. They support this claim in several ways. Every person the academy hires in any capacity must already be a born-again Christian and willing to become a member of Bethany Baptist Church. Teachers, students, and their parents pledge themselves to observe church and school regulations. The student pledge is notable for its 24-hour coverage that requires students to obey the rules all the time, wherever they are; the same coverage applies to teacher behavior. The librarian censors what the library acquires in order to keep out doctrinally unsafe materials. Moreover, fully persuaded that scripture is God's word and, accordingly, absolute, eternal, and universal truth, Bethany's church and school strive to indoctrinate their beliefs. Their doctrine is not merely school stuff to be learned for recitation and tests and then forgotten; it is meant to be the foundation for their entire life, ideally for the life of all people everywhere.

Spirituality pervades the school—in its daily, pre-class devotional session, its prayers said at the outset of each class, its daily Bible study class, its thrice-weekly chapel, and its requirement that students always carry a Bible except during physical education. Informal social groupings tend to bring together students of equivalent degrees of spiritual commitment. When asked about their futures, the vast majority of students affirm they will attend a Bible-believing Christian college, marry a born-again Christian, send their children to Christian schools, and live with the Bible at the center of their lives.

In every respect, Bethany Baptist Academy is fully the agent of its church community, its educators neither allowed nor willing to differ in any way from what fundamentalist doctrine endorses. As in Mansfield, a sense of community prevails in Bethany, and its school provides welcome recruits to its community.

TWO VIEWS

One primary legacy of my study at Mansfield was an enhanced awareness of my own commitment to community. This community-supporting I was, in fact, the primary I who shaped the data collection and developed the interpretations in preparation for the resulting manuscript. In the span of years from 1972 when the project began to 1978 when the manuscript was published, I reinforced my a priori commitment to community. I believe this happened because of continually making manifest in my analysis and writing what previously had been latent. In retrospect I can see that this element of subjectivity that served and directed me at Mansfield was a potential obstacle to seeing in subsequent studies because my community orientation had become accustomed to center stage. It was the veteran I, practiced in directing my efforts as I pursued, across different settings, the common issue of the school-community relationship.

Another legacy from Mansfield was the understanding that local schools do more than help children develop their social skills and economic potential; and they do more than politically socialize them. In stable, basically homogeneous places like Mansfield, schools also contribute to the viability of their communities by providing an often critical set of community maintenance functions (see Peshkin, 1982b).

The title of my book about Mansfield conveys the story I meant to tell: *Growing up American: Schooling and the Survival of Community.* Its conclusions celebrate Mansfield and its high school, both flawed in several ways, clearly not meant for everyone, but comfortable and comforting places for Mansfield's aforementioned mainstream majority. I liked Mansfield and its people. In a world rife with alienation and insecurity, the Mansfields of America strike me as special places, worthy candidates for survival. When I drew my conclusions, I identified Mansfield's racism, which I muted by calling it "anti-black sentiment"; I identified its limited capacity to socialize adolescents for a world exceedingly more complex than its own little cosmos; and I identified its tendency to exact conformity as the price of belonging. I noted these attributes because they are important concerns to me and to our society. I also wanted to preempt the accusation that I ignored Mansfield's negative side. But, having stated the negative side, I could then send up my linguistic signal—"nevertheless," which indicates a shift in directions—and proceed to assert what I felt most strongly:

> Bearing in mind the dilemmas they raise, cannot a nation's Mansfields be nurtured rather than threatened by modern society? Must one equate goodness with largeness, mindlessly allowing all the dimensions of life to increase without regard to the quality of life that results? (Peshkin, 1978, pp. 209-210)

I entered Bethany's world expecting to find a sense of community— and I did; I expected to find a school that accurately reflected and reinforced the dominant behavior and values of its community—and I did. Mansfield prepared me for Bethany. However, Bethany provided me with more than just another manifestation of the school-community relationship; indeed, Mansfield's school-community relationship is loose compared to Bethany's nearly perfect fit. I was able to see in practice that an institution based on absolute truth of necessity strives to be a total institution (Goffman, 1961). No less a degree of control is congruent with the organizational imperatives of absolute truth.

In addition, my fieldwork there was an unexpected occasion to be defined, labeled, and judged, and, therefore, to learn unexpected things about myself. At Mansfield, I was the child of the city exploring the *terra incognita* of rural life, the white, academic urbanite who was not directly threatened by the village's racism and cognitive insularity. Mansfielders were content with my self-definition. They needed most to know not my antecedents but whether I was trustworthy and would hear their paeans to the rural life. At Bethany, much as I wanted to be the non-Christian scholar interested in learning about the fundamentalist educational phenomena that was sweeping the country, I discovered, so to speak, that being Jewish would be the personal fact that would bear on my research; it became the unavoidably salient aspect of my subjectivity. Bethanyites were content for me to define my research self, but could never rest easy with my unsaved human self. I became forcibly aware that the threats to my identity as a Jew were not just a matter of history.

For, in the course of inculcating their adolescents with doctrine and the meaning of their Christian identity, Bethany's educators taught us both that I was part of Satan's rejected, humanist world; I epitomized the darkness and unrighteousness that contrasts with their godly light and righteousness. They taught their children never to be close friends, marry, or go into business with someone like me. What they were expected to do with someone like me was proselytize, share their Truth, so I, too, by accepting Jesus as my personal savior, could be born-again and escape an eternity in hell. Although the children did not proselytize me, their mentors frequently did—over a bowl of soup in the lunch room, in the hall after leaving a meeting, but mostly in the course of our interview sessions.

The experience of Bethany's church and school as a total institution, and my perception of their evangelism as arrogance, turned my focus away from the very facts at Bethany that had so impressed me at Mansfield: its nurturant community and efficacious, community-maintaining school. Why? Because Mansfield had not gored me, and Bethany did. Thus, in the first paper I wrote about Bethany, called "Fundamentalist Christian Schooling: Truth and Consequences," I discussed the costs to its participants and others and I concluded as follows:

> I hope the day never comes when our society—feeling threatened by the success of Christian schools—believes that they must be suppressed or curtailed in any way.... I trust that my concern, and that of others, about their costs never exceeds the level of concern abolitionist Wendell Phillips expressed in his 1852 speech.... Studying Bethany Baptist Academy has rekindled my appreciation of Phillips' wise call for "eternal vigilance" if a nation is to preserve its liberty. (1983, pp. 23-24)

The academy's fundamentalist orthodoxy made me concerned about the resultant insularity of its students; its unrelenting evangelical efforts made me concerned about a future society (like those my persecuted ancestors lived in) that contained no place for me *as I am*. To repeat, Bethany gored me.

Given my differential reactions to community in Mansfield and Bethany, I was compelled to reflect on who I was and was not at Mansfield, whose racism I euphemized and toward whose intimate community I urged respectful consideration, and on who I was and was not at Bethany, whose evangelism I deplored and toward whose community and educational juggernaut I urged eternal vigilance.

I had indeed discovered my subjectivity at work, caught red-handed with my values at the very end of my pen—where I believe they belong. For example, if I were a black American studying Mansfield, would I, could I, moreover, should I have been able to see beyond its obvious racism in order to exalt its uncommon sense of community? And would I have been free—Is not one subjected to those personal factors composing one's subjectivity?—to learn how schools function to maintain such communities? My commitment to community—helped by being white—directed my attention to the school's nonacademic, community maintenance functions. Without understanding these functions, we do not fully grasp what schools mean to people in many villages, small cities, and stable urban neighborhoods. If I were a black American in Mansfield, I could find other true things to write about, other stories to tell.

Furthermore, if I were a born-again Christian studying Bethany's school, could I, would I, moreover, should I have been able to see beyond the extraordinary contribution it makes to my well-being as a Christian in order to identify how its teachings threaten outsiders? And would I have been able to spot Bethany's paradox, one likely to disturb nonfundamentalists? Bethany's school legally exists because our pluralistic society has laws that secure the private, religious school's right of establishment. Yet nothing in BBA's educational policy and practice supports pluralism. Both school and church are doctrinally monolithic. If I were a born-again Christian studying Bethany, I could find other true things to write about, other stories to tell.

Of course, as a white researcher I still see Mansfield's racism, and as a Jewish researcher I still see Bethany's successful school and community. Seeing, however, is not enough; it leads me merely to point out, not focus on, Mansfield's racism and Bethany's community. I concede that subjectivity need not blind me to perspectives other than those following naturally from my subjectivity. However, since these other perspectives are not reinforced by my personal dispositions, they fail to get the same attention as those that are. They fail, therefore, to be explicated and connected to other aspects of the phenomenon under study, and expanded so that the promise of the perspective is most fully exploited.

I do not dwell, for example, on Mansfield's limited social opportunities that preclude knowing almost anyone unlike themselves. As a result, I do not explore how tolerance and certain types of community are inversely related. There is a story worth telling about this inverse relationship; I did not so much reject telling it as I felt drawn to tell the one I did. I feel at liberty to spin a particular story—the gift of my subjectivity—but not out of thin air; my story must be borne out by facts that are potentially available to any other researcher. I do not ask, however, if it is the best story, as though there invariably is just one story most worth telling. I do strive to relate the story that best follows from my construction of a setting. This construction results in my particular perception and ordering of facts, and my particular interpretation.

The failure to exploit fully other themes than the one I have chosen may be seen as a shortcoming, but I see it as the reality of social research conducted in complex settings. Such settings support many stories, so to speak, not all of which can be told—or told most effectively—by any one researcher. Thus, my subjectivity is simultaneously enabling and disabling, as it impels me to entertain and develop some research possibilities and restrains and delimits me from developing others.

Subjectivity has assumed a usefully concrete form to me as a consequence of my participant-observer experience in Mansfield and Bethany. So informed, I may more consciously take account of its effects on my research procedure, from its beginning to its end, rather than just writing the after-the-fact, *pro forma* section in one's manuscript that says, "This is who I am. Reader, beware!" Such sections should be written, but their writing should not be the first occasion for considering how subjectivity has encroached upon one's research process. After all, if my subjectivity grants me a license to pursue a certain line of thinking, it does not warrant the self-congratulatory conclusion of, "Eureka! This is it!" The virtue of subjectivity is that it concentrates and focuses attention; and it produces an "it." Since in doing so subjectivity has also narrowed my perception and awareness, I need to know both what has moved me and what has not; I need to discover what interpretations I slight or ignore in the course of exploiting the ones that I favor.

CONCLUSIONS

As noted, my subjectivity narrows what I see and shapes what I make of what I see. By disposing me to choose, I select from the array of N possibilities those that I will make something of. I bring my biases or inclinations to my research. Unlike clothing, they are preexisting states that cannot be shed and thereby prevented from interacting in some way with the objects I study. That they will interact is unavoidable; just how they will do so is uncertain. My subjectivity, furthermore, is one basis for my distinctiveness, although not a unique distinctiveness, peculiar solely to me. Otherwise, my work would be marked by idiosyncracy that locates what I have seen exclusively in my eyes and in those of no other's. If my work is to become acceptable to the corpus of social science, it should not be the product of hallucination, delusion, or illusion (Polanyi, 1958, p. 302). That is, if what I see cannot be squared with the real or imaginable perceptions of others, I may have had an interesting personal experience but I have missed the boat.

If subjectivity is both unavoidable and virtuous, does this make objectivity avoidable and unvirtuous? I think not. My *Webster's* circularly defines objectivity as the state of being objective, and defines objective, more usefully, as "independent of what is personal or private in our apprehension and feelings; expressing or involving the use of facts without distortion by personal feelings or prejudices."[3] Because objectivity directs attention to the relationship between personal dispositions and distortion, it is a good thing. Distortion is bad; we all agree. Shaping is good, at least better than distortion. Passion and prejudice distort, while values and other personal orientations shape, or so it seems as I think of these terms.[4]

Objectivity, however, does more than alert us to the potential association between distortion and personal dispositions, and most assuredly between distortion and prejudice, a distinction that *Webster's* fails to make; the above definition wrongly presents personal feelings and prejudice as identical. This pertains to my central point: The mistaken notion that "true" science is value-free has compelled even those who know better to feel guilty about the legitimate role of subjectivity in the course of their research. Personal dispositions, what I have defined as subjectivity, are the researcher's allies. If you stand where I do, and think, or understand how I think, as I do, then you may see what I see: a community in Mansfield and a total institution in Bethany. Not thinking as I do, but in ways that I find imaginable, you may see misery in Mansfield and blessings in Bethany. Both sets of outcomes are warrantable. The researcher's prejudices are not allies; nor is the belief that every aspect of a phenomenon is fair game for his subjectivity. Objects do have attributes that are generally singular in nature—that is, about which one true or fitting statement can be made using the linguistic conventions peculiar to the observer's culture. Included in these attributes are traits denotable by number, sex, and color. If I am subjective, if personal states affect how I represent denotable qualities, then I have erred.

One can find good company for the belief that there is no value-free social research, and no less good company for the insistence that there is no virtue in a runaway subjectivity that has become subjectivism, defined as the view that attaches "supreme importance to the subjective

elements in experience" and also as the belief that "individual feeling . . .
is the ultimate criterion of the good and the right." By exalting one's
singularity, subjectivism gives no scope for verifying one's perceptions
and interpretations by the generally accessible experience of other investigators. Subjectivity is not subjectivism. When others agree with my
perceptions and interpretations, I believe I have achieved a creditable
intersubjectivity, not a discreditable group illusion.

From those who accept their subjectivity but abhor subjectivism, one
hears an abundance of injunctions that reflect a concern to keep the
former from deteriorating into the latter. Nadel espouses teamwork in
anthropological research as "a means of overcoming the limitations of
the personality" (1951, p. 50; see also Diesing, 1971, p. 281). Becker
urges researchers to avoid that sentimentality which hinders them from
investigating "some matter that properly should be regarded as problematic" (1974, p. 119). Barzun and Graff emphatically advise that what one
knows as a consequence of one's subjectivity be tested in all ways
possible with the evidence available to competent scholars (1957, p.
146). Eisner elaborates an argument opposing the view that subjectivity
is tantamount to relativism. Among the six points he would have us ask
of theories or interpretations are the following: Do they have "instrumental" utility? Are they consistent with other theories or interpretations?
And do they offer economical and elegant accounts of the data? (1983, p.
4). These many injunctions attest to the seriousness of the researcher's
concern to preclude the dysfunctional consequences of passion, prejudice, and subjectivism.

My subjectivity is functional and the results it produces are rational.
But if they are rational only to me and no one else, not now or ever, then
I have spawned illusions and my views are bound to be ignored. When I
disclose what I have seen, my results invite other researchers to look
where I did and see what I saw. My ideas are candidates for others to
entertain, not necessarily as truth, let alone Truth, but as positions
about the nature and meaning of a phenomenon that may fit their
sensibility and shape their thinking about their own inquiries. If, somehow, all researchers were alike, we would all tell the same story (insofar
as its nondenotable aspects are concerned) about the same phenomenon. By virtue of subjectivity, I tell the story I am moved to tell. Remove
my subjectivity and I do not become a value-free participant observer,
merely an empty-headed one (Diesing, 1971, p. 280).

Since I know now which I's were most tellingly present at Mansfield
and Bethany, I am alerted to these, which *might* be present in my next
study. But, in fact, I do not know which of the possible configurations of
my personal dispositions will be most engaged when I next assume the

role of participant observer and immerse both my human and research selves in someone else's life. When I do know, I will perhaps then be aware of what force has shaped my research procedure from beginning to end. I may also be aware of what I have not seen or seen imperfectly, for these are the costs virtuous subjectivity exacts for its particular perceptual gifts.

NOTES

1. It is inaccurate to compare methods in terms of engagement-nonengagement, since one's data, however collected—by telephone or face-to-face interviews, by observations of naturalistic behavior behind one-way mirrors or of behavior in a staged setting, or by library research—end up as data in hand. They become stimuli to the researcher and, accordingly, can engage some aspects of the researcher's human selves. The participant observers' proximity to their data sharply accentuates this process.

2. This and all other names mentioned in regard to Mansfield and Bethany, the site of the second study described here, are pseudonyms.

3. This definition, and all others quoted in this section without citation, are from the *Webster's Third New International Dictionary*.

4. There is an Orwellian Newspeak here that I must acknowledge—I shape, but you distort.

Commentary

In the introduction to this section we suggested that one theme common to each of these five chapters was the experience of pain. The authors, either explicitly or implicitly, point to how the pain surfaced and how it influenced their lives. There is also some additional pain in acknowledging, retrospectively, how their response to the pain clouded their perceptiveness and led to actions that might have been different "if they knew then what is clear now."

In both the Hackman and Berg chapters the pain emanated from sources inside the researcher. Anxieties that threaten are first defended against and then, as the defenses are noticed, attempts are made to understand the source of these internal reactions. The pain becomes the stimulus for the self-reflection process. In the chapters by Mirvis and Louis and by Kram, the self-reflection is focused primarily at the level of the interaction. The pain triggered an examination of the relationship with other people and with the research topic itself. Peshkin focuses at a different level. He noticed how the two communities of Mansfield and Bethany evoked very different responses in him, creating an imbalance in his sympathies. He saw the positive side of the community dynamics in one setting and the negative side in the other, using benign language in one study and malignant language in the other to describe processes that at their core were similar.

The pain described in each of the five chapters was both a consequence of and a contribution to the deep levels of involvement the researchers experienced in their investigations. Kram expresses this most clearly when she identifies that her interests in researching first mentor and then peer relationships grew out of her own experiences with developmental relationships. The very recognition of her involvement meant that she expected that scrutinizing her personal reactions would yield worthwhile data—not only for the purpose of minimizing bias, but as a valuable source of insight. Thus committed to self-scrutiny, Kram was also committed to struggling with what she uncovered about herself and her research relationships, and this in turn heightened her level of involvement.

The levels of involvement, the commitment to self-scrutiny, and the pain were emotionally costly, but there were also significant gains. In each of the chapters there is a sense of rejuvenation. In Hackman's experience it is clear that his struggles are, in part, a consequence of his desire to push important relationships to greater levels of significance. This may involve pruning relationships he has grown beyond, or it may mean incorporating parts of himself he has not wished to accept. In any case, the tone is one of a desire to live his professional life in a fuller way. Even the choice of his title suggests a voice that has been present but underdeveloped.

Learning how to reframe anxiety as the possibility of new figures emerging from undifferentiated backgrounds is the key to Berg's chapter. Instead of staying with the posture of defending oneself against the pain of anxiety, the reframing has a vitalizing quality to it. This is also seen in the Mirvis and Louis account of how much Mirvis was reliving the pain of his relationship with his father when dealing with Richardson at DC. It could be argued that the pain was worth it, for through his examination of the transference process Mirvis was aided in understanding better his father's experience and thereby their relationship as father and son. Mirvis was also able to appreciate more fully some of the problems for Richardson and some of the human costs brought about by the merger.

For Kram, the benefits that came from the pain included her ability to take on new roles. Her struggles to understand the mentor-mentee relationship brought her to the inevitable position of taking on the mentor role herself, a position that seemed so foreign to her just a few years earlier when she began her own work. Peshkin's chapter is a rich description of the process of reclaiming parts of ourselves that we leave behind or split off in the service of "objective" research. From reading the chapter we have the sense of a person whose awareness of his own involvement in research deepened as a result of what he learned from the pain of self-scrutiny.

Another theme that cuts across the chapters is the struggle with ambivalence. Hackman makes it the centerpiece of his chapter, but throughout the section there are signs of deep reluctance on the part of each researcher. Despite this reluctance, each moved ahead in some way, somehow making the ambivalence a companion in work. We argue that perhaps the central clinical skill is learning how to see ambivalence diagnostically, without becoming paralyzed by it and without blaming others for its existence. Perhaps the most powerful critique of positivist methodologies is that they funnel experience into either/or frameworks. Contradictions demand resolution. Something is either true or false. The clinical approach suggests that it is possible for seemingly contradictory data to coexist and to express a truth. In fact, the clinical perspective reminds us that data often appear contradictory because of the way we frame them. It is in the nature of the question that one determines the nature of the answer.

Taking an intellectual position that allows and encourages us to frame issues in "both/and" ways triggers deep emotional ambivalence. It is stressful to live with contradiction. If we cannot change this ambivalence internally, our predisposition to reduce it may cause us to prematurely "choose" one side or another. No one is equipped to attend to the clinical side of research until he or she has begun to learn about ambivalence and is willing to scrutinize its role in social research.

The issues addressed in Section III feel to us to be at the heart of the clinical method. In many ways Section II is the head and Section IV is the body. Each part, of course, has no existence or meaning without the others, but the heart feels special.

Clinical Methods

The first four chapters in this section examine the application of a clinical method to a variety of research activities: archival analysis, interviewing, historical analysis, participant observation, and biographical research. The question addressed by these chapters is, How does a clinical approach change our theories about data collection and our methods of doing it? The final chapter presents a model for managing the process of analyzing and presenting qualitative data. All five chapters attempt to come to grips with the implications for research methods of clinical involvement.

In the first chapter, Simmons describes her experience reconstructing an organization's prehistory. Initially the work involved extensive archival analysis and interviewing. In the second phase, however, Simmons struggled to reconcile seemingly contradictory descriptions of events, actions, and chronologies. The "method" she developed for understanding what these contradictions meant grew out of her willingness to treat contradiction as evidence. Gillette, too, is concerned with history. He provides us with a definition of history and a role for historical analysis in social science research. In examining the assumptions underlying the historical and social scientific perspectives on "here and now" behavior, he finds them distinct but complementary and concludes his call for more historical analysis with some cautions about the demands it places on the researcher.

Perry's chapter is a reflection on a twenty-year process of creating a biography. In particular, she examines the way in which she evolved a participant observation method for studying the life of Harry Stack Sullivan. At critical phases of her research Perry found that her ability to open *herself,* emotionally and intellectually, to *his* environment provided valuable insight into Sullivan's life. By examining her own reactions and those of the people around her, she was able to piece together some of the powerful forces that shaped Sullivan's life.

Early in the chapter by Sutton and Schurman we read about an interviewer who calls a respondent to schedule an interview only to receive an angry and abusive reaction to this apparently innocent request. The rest of the chapter describes what these two ISR researchers learned about conducting interviews on "hot" emotional topics. As they learned about respondents' reactions to layoffs and plant closings, they also learned about research relationships. The chapter concludes with an analysis of the ways researchers might handle emotionally "hot" topics and the ways interviewing methods must change to accommodate such research.

The final chapter deals with the inevitable dilemmas facing qualitative researchers who must record, analyze, and present an overwhelming amount of data. Huberman and Miles argue that this process is constantly being shaped by the researcher's latent theories about the social system. They believe we must allow these theories an explicit role in the data reduction process so that both the theories and the reductive analysis can be scrutinized by the researcher and the research participants.

The chapters in this section point to the many clinical choices present in all research activities. Facing these choices, making them, and understanding them fully is an essential part of a clinical method. These choices are often made difficult by the emotional and intellectual risks they present, but to avoid or finesse them can imperil the validity and integrity of the research.

RECONSTRUCTING AN ORGANIZATION'S HISTORY:
Systematic Distortion in
Retrospective Data

Valerie M. Simmons

I expected to be bored. I could already picture myself sitting in a bleak, bureaucrat's office, hunting through file after file of dusty documents, reading the six hundredth memo, stopping to worry the paper cuts in my cuticles, yawning.

I was after information about the history of "Dexter" (a pseudonym), a public service organization we (Kenwyn K. Smith, Terri B. Thames, and Judith Marx) had been studying for nearly two years. Our research team had been trying to understand how a new organization develops (see also Smith & Simmons, 1983), and had started daily partici- pant observation soon after the first staff were hired. Spurred on by Sarason's (1972) admonition that a new organization's early develop- ment could be understood *only* in historical context, I had taken on the investigation of Dexter's "prehistory" for my dissertation research.

I had not expected to be drawn back through time some fifteen years, back to when Dexter was only a glimmer in its parents' eyes—nor that Dexter would turn out to have had so many parents. I had not thought that it would be so hard to find the beginning of planning for an organization only two years old; perhaps the metaphor of the human life cycle increasingly applied to organizations (Kimberly & Miles, 1980) had led me to expect a gestation period only nine months long.

Certainly I had not expected to relive those fifteen years of planning history with an intensity and vividness that took over my life. For the six months it took me to reconstruct the history of planning for Dexter, I lived my here-and-now life only as a shadow, drifting off in the middle of dinner conversations to ponder the day's new data, or in the midst of intimate moments with friends to think about relationships among the people I'd met in search of Dexter's past.

Reconstructing the past brings about a peculiar relationship between the researcher and the *time* she or he relives. I found that historical research demands that we understand how the complex cognitions and emotions experienced *at* an event—already an imperfect representation—become further degraded and reinterpreted over time in the memories of those who were there. But an understanding of cognitive/emotional distortion is not enough. Historical research demands that we acknowledge the central role of empathy—the researcher's empathy—in that reconstruction process.

In historical research, the only data available are the memories of people who participated in the history, tapped through retrospective interviews, and surviving paper records produced by participants at the time. Using empathy as a method is to use these memories and documents as the grounding for building a model of a particular history, reconstructing the gestalt from which those writings and memories emerged. The researcher must conduct a dialogue with the experience (of others) and with social, clinical, and cognitive psychological theory, gradually coming to see the raw data in light of those ideas that make it make sense.

But empathy is a process during which the researcher becomes increasingly involved with the past and must scrutinize the emotions of that involvement as second-order data—a kind of validity test—of the completeness of that empathic understanding. As I came to know the participants in Dexter's creation, through pieces of memories and fragments of interactions recorded on paper, I came to feel what it *must have been like* for those people to be invested in creating Dexter. As I reconstructed the network of relationships among these people and, using general theory about groups, began to see which investments and perceptions were shared, I began to feel for the groups, and then for the intergroup interactions across boundaries, and finally for the system as a whole.

Organizational research, even in the present, involves internalizing the conflicting perceptions of participants. This process can be an emotionally risky undertaking, as an introjection of a system in full-blown conflict feels just as awful as a raging inner conflict. A system researcher must suffer the conflict until a transcendent theoretical/emotional framework emerges that makes it *all* make sense (Marshall, 1981).

Such a framework must *order* empathic insights correctly in time, so that the development of emotional attachments and the progression of events feed into one another as the history actually unfolded. I found that the single most valuable method of historical research was to read through the data from the beginning after every datum had been painstakingly located and placed in proper order. It was only then that I could make sense of the inconsistencies, and only then that I could feel the first stirring of an idea, the coincidences of fragments of ideas about Dexter, the churning of political organizing in the community, the grim grinding processes of the bureaucracy, the tragedies of conflicts in the making, the casualties of those caught in the explosions of system conflict, the powerful cathexis of planners to an emergent dream, and the pain of being severed from that dream, leading inevitably to the recent past, when the Dexter *I* had lived during the just past two years finally made sense. When I finished that chronological pass through history, I felt I had myself given birth to Dexter. I was not bored.

In this chapter, I present some ways in which I learned to think about distortion in retrospective data, including the constraints on encoding an event in memory when it happens, the further distortions of memory that may occur with the passage of time, and the difficulties in interpreting self-report data. I then describe the gradual evolution of a model of Dexter that helped me understand *how* each person's data was distorted and which was a tool for using both distortion and "truth." Then I address the ways in which I came to deal with some of my own distortions and how I came to trust the experience of empathy as a final validity check. The chapter concludes with a discussion of how we might meet the overwhelming demands of such methods.

RECONSTRUCTING A HISTORY OF DISTORTIONS

When I began this research, I intended to use both retrospective interviews and archival documents as data but fully expected that the interviews would yield the richest and most reliable data—memos and official planning documents are known to be carefully crafted public presentations that often bear little resemblance to the complex realities out of which they emerge. I found exactly the opposite: The gestation of Dexter was preserved in those dusty files in a form that allowed analysis of the fictional nature of documents and insight into the reality behind them, but human memories of events stretching some fifteen years into the past were so degraded and distorted that only a sophisticated application of clinical rigor could sort out what they actually represented.

DISTORTIONS IN ENCODING

I have always tended to take cognitive psychology seriously, and if there is any single message from recent work in cognition and perception, it is that the simple act of perceiving an event is greatly constrained by our cognitive capacities and that the representation that gets stored in memory is a highly interpreted one. When an interviewer asks, "What happened at that committee meeting in January of 1975?" she or he must keep in mind that several factors intervene between the event and participants' perceptions of that event: the opportunity to observe, selective perception, and interpretation.

Participants' memories of a single event seem to differ systematically with controversy and investment in the *meaning* of events. With the passage of time, initial perceptions of an event are likely to change even more as participants "forget," or get the chronological order of events confused, or reinterpret past events every time a new event intervenes and clouds original interpretations with current dynamics.

DISTORTIONS IN REPORTING

Finally even these highly degraded and distorted memories of an event are available only through the interview process so that both the interviewer's cognitive limitations and the dynamics of the relationship between interviewer and informant intervene further between past "reality" and current understanding. Retrospective interviewing is not just a simple matter of deciding whether the informant is telling the "truth."

THE LIMITS OF "TRUTH"

Although I thought that I understood the dynamics of interviewing and the highly interpretive nature of self-report, an event early in my interviewing process reminded me how easy it is to mistakenly trust memories reported by a key informant. I had accepted an invitation to

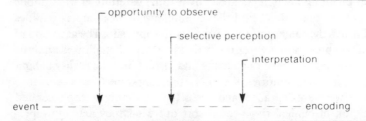

Figure 14.1 Factors Intervening in the Encoding of Events

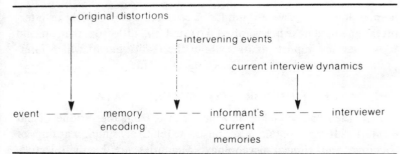

Figure 14.2   Factors Intervening in the Reporting of Events

lunch from a Dexter woman I had grown to know and trust through the two years of participant observation of Dexter's present. When I arrived at her house, the table was laid and a good bottle of Cabernet open to toast our friendship; as the bottle was consumed, we talked as women often do, and my informant revealed intimate, risky details of her private life. I recall reflecting to myself that I really trusted Carol to tell me the truth, and her revelations about her private life were evidence that she trusted me.

We were talking about recent events at Dexter, so I decided to probe to see what she knew about the recent firing of an employee. I knew, through other sources, that the employee had been fired to avoid a scandal of some proportions from the employee's activities outside Dexter. I recorded that event in my journal:

> I probed once about D.L.—she didn't bat an eyelid. She said that she got fired for being ugly and obnoxious. I'd bet money she doesn't know.

I was congratulating myself on the richness of my informant system and feeling pretty smug about knowing "the truth" when my complacency was shattered by the realization of what this analysis implied for historical interviewing. Even if I could assure myself, as I could with Carol, that the informant was doing his or her best to tell me the truth, I might have a seriously misleading version of "truth." *And I would have no way to know.* Carol, like all of us, had filled in the simple "fact" of a firing with an interpretation that made it make sense to her. Had I not held a privileged piece of information, I would have recorded Carol's interpretation as the truth.

This event gave me a paranoia that was to serve me well throughout my restrospective interviewing: a test of rigor that demanded that every "fact" be seen as the informant's interpretation of events to which she or

he may have had severely limited access and about which an interpretation might have been crafted. I trusted very little from then on, and
took interview reports as data about the reality out of which interpretations emerged rather than as "objective" facts.

THE VALUE OF DISTORTED INTERVIEW DATA

How then can valuable data be gleaned from the residue of old
memories? It requires taking seriously the relatively simple warnings of
cognitive and clinical psychology: Memories are highly selective,
opportunistic, contextually encoded, and frequently reinterpreted fragments that represent the factual "truth" only slightly. But had I stopped
there, I would have thrown out a lot of good data. I recorded in my
research journal that I did not trust my interview data and was reluctant
to include them:

> It's slowly dawning on me that I just don't have much confidence in
> people's ability to reconstruct a chronology—they just can't seem to be
> very accurate about dates, and it seems hard—impossible—for them to go
> back to prior emotions. The latest ones leave too heavy an imprint.

> I feel confident in getting a general feel for the reality set of their role, but
> I'm reluctant to pin it into the very specific time frame of my archival
> chronology. Interviewing people is frustrating—they just don't have good
> enough memories. This past is more important to me than it is to most of
> them.

It was only after I turned in desperation to a closer examination of
archival data that I was able to construct a framework of people and
groups, changing through time, that enabled me to move from rejecting
interview data as "distorted" into building a Dexter-specific model of
distortion that enabled me to make sense of both distortion and fact.

BUILDING A MODEL OF DISTORTION

Although knowledge of the kinds of distortions that can occur is
necessary to retrospective understanding, it is not sufficient. Knowing
only that memories about Dexter were distorted was no help; such
knowledge is paralyzing (which may be why so many people choose to
deny the inevitable subjectivity of data). The only way out of the
wilderness for me was to construct slowly a Dexter-specific model of
events and people's emotional investments as a guide to sorting out *how*
data were distorted—what was "true" in what context at what time for
each person.

DISTORTIONS ABOUT INVOLVEMENT

I had begun retrospective interviewing with current Dexter employees who had participated in Dexter's planning. I was using a nomination technique, asking each informant, "Who else was involved in Dexter's planning?" I began with A.L., a current Dexter administrator, who told me of endless committee meetings with representatives from community groups and public agencies who had a stake in Dexter's creation. When I asked A.L. who had represented the local criminal justice system in meetings, he drew a blank. For long minutes, he had a puzzled look on his face, as he searched his memory without success.

I knew, from minutes of meetings, that A.L. had sat through many meetings with representatives of the criminal justice system, people whom he knew well; yet he had "forgotten" them. Triangulating A.L.'s self-report against archival evidence, I was able to form hypotheses about the reasons for this peculiar distortion. Perhaps the criminal justice system had been shut out of the real action; perhaps the real planning took place behind the scenes, so that the committee meetings were only a charade of participation; perhaps A.L. had been involved in conflictual interactions with the representatives of the criminal justice system, so that he wished to "forget" that they were present. These hypotheses, formed out of an analysis of distortion in self-reports, led me to seek evidence about the relationship between A.L. and the criminal justice system and about behind-the-scenes planning activities. Some hypotheses turned out to be supported, others contradicted. None would ever have been formed had I not taken "forgetting" as potential data.

My Dexter-specific model of distortion evolved through this research, gradually refining my research techniques. For example, while I originally set out to use informant "nominations" to tell me who else had been involved in the planning process, I changed my technique to first probe for self-generated (systematically distorted) nomination lists and follow up with questions about who else was peripherally involved but not important, who represented the most deviant perspective, or who might disagree most with the informant's perceptions.

Thus, self-report data were valuable not only for what was there but for what was left out. When I interviewed G.D., a man who had been centrally involved in ten years of Dexter planning, he could not remember many names. Since I knew from committee meeting minutes how many long hours he had spent with these people, I tried the hypothesis that his "bad memory" was saying something important about his relationship to these others. After this interview, I recorded in my journal my

> overwhelming sense of G.D.'s isolation (self-imposed)—he's just not attuned to others—he forgets names and the contributions of others.

From this observation and an evolving model of distortion, I was able to generate and test the hypotheses that G.D. felt himself to be the real central planner, that he engineered a sham of participation in public meetings, and that he was personally deeply invested in Dexter, so deeply that he was blind to the investments of others.

DISTORTIONS OF TIME

This interview contributed another corollary to my evolving model of distortion. As I listened to G.D. tell the story of Dexter's planning history, I got the impression that for *most* of the years of planning, G.D. had worked in a warm, collaborative partnership with B.K. G.D. spoke of his friend B.K. with great warmth and affection, and described at some length the plans they made together. I recorded in my journal that "from G.D.'s eyes, he and B.K. were the whole show."

Piecing together a chronology of events and actors from archival documents, I was surprised to learn that G.D. and B.K. had worked together for only six short months. Setting this partnership in the context of an accurate time frame, it became apparent that G.D. had distorted his encoding of the passage of time to *expand* the length of a warm partnership and *shrink* the time during which he had been dealing with other relationships of less importance to him personally. Eventually, this piece of "distorted" data led me to understand how terribly conflictual the planning process had been for participants and how they sought relief from the stress of conflict by retreating to behind-the-scenes planning and cooperative relationships. Intervening events (i.e., the more recent warm relationship between two actors) had further distorted memories of the stream of time.

DISTORTIONS VISIBLE IN THE INTERVIEW

In the first half-hour of talking with G.D., I thought that he had played a relatively uninvolved part in the Dexter story: He did not remember much about the details of the history, he claimed not to know much about Dexter present, and he did not seem to care that its administration had been taken away from his agency. Only when I began asking about archival records did I get clues that his detachment might be misleading. G.D.'s files on Dexter were not packed away in storage (as one might have expected from a project over five years dead); they were within arm's reach of G.D.'s chair. At first he had denied me free access to the files, but he offered to go through them to pull out relevant documents. I watched his final expressions as he leafed through files; his brow wrinkled with concentration, a wry smile flashed across his face, he sighed deeply, closed his eyes, shook his head, and suddenly turned to start piling files in my arms. "It's just too depressing—it all comes rushing back," he sighed. "I couldn't stand to go through these papers again."

That brief glimpse of emotion was the first clue I had that G.D. had had a more deeply personal investment in Dexter than he would admit; it was the data from which a hypothesis eventually emerged suggesting that G.D.'s identification with Dexter planning was shared by a small, cohesive group of planners, each of whom came to identify more strongly with Dexter planning than with the agencies that each represented. This was a conceptual breakthrough in understanding how planning proceeded in the midst of constant community chaos.

RECONSTRUCTING NETWORKS

When I began this historical study, I began keeping notecards, one for each person, to note official job titles and agency affiliations; when I had enough information, I began drawing charts of the system, placing each actor in his or her proper position. My "errors" troubled me; I would think that I had placed a person correctly, only later to find contradictory evidence—a different job title, or even worse, a "mistake" in agency. Just about the time I was ready to start all over, despairing at the many such "errors," I realized that in a system as political as the one I was studying, promotions and transfers must have been a consistent phenomenon.

I started over, this time noting *dates* carefully, and was unable to construct a series of system charts, showing not only the configurations of actors and interest groups in each slice of time, but also the movements of each actor through promotions, demotions, transfers, and relocations to a new agency—data that again helped me to "make sense" of some anomalies: A "state" person who seemed to take the perspective of "county" people was no longer puzzling when I learned that he was a former county politician; a psychiatrist's virulent animosity toward the "medical model" suddenly made sense when I learned that years before he had been forced out of the state psychiatric group which had planned Dexter on a medical model.

In these ways, I gradually moved from a bare bones outline of people and agencies into an understanding of individual and group investments in Dexter planning; I began to understand why their actions were reasonable, given the total reality from which they operated.

EMPATHY AS A VALIDITY TEST

I do not know when it was that I realized how emotionally involved I was becoming in the Dexter history, nor when I became self-conscious about using my own emotions as a test of validity. Despite my training in clinical aspects of qualitative methods, which taught me to pay attention to my own emotions as an interviewer and participant observer in the present, I had not expected to become emotional about the past.

One of the most important intergroup conflicts in Dexter present was a well-developed antagonism between county and state, both of whom funded and held Dexter responsible. I felt myself originally to be relatively neutral in this enthnocentrism, but as I talked to people and read documents, I noticed that I was constantly being drawn into judgments about who was "right" and who was "wrong."

When I realized how long and hard state bureaucrats had worked to get legislative approvals for the plans, I respected the state position, and saw the county as ungrateful for the state's "gift" to them. When I interviewed people in the county who had volunteered their time for grass-roots organizing and lobbying, I began to understand their feeling that the state had "grabbed the control and the credit" for Dexter. I admired county efforts to gain local control, the struggle of the "little people" against the huge state bureaucracy, and despised the state's sham of encouraging "community input." When I interviewed state bureaucrats, however, I shifted position again when I realized how community protests actually endangered the funding and construction of Dexter's buildings. After spending a rainy Saturday in the local newspaper office, leafing through old papers for stories about Dexter, I was

> struck by the prevalence of county protests to *any* project—freeways, housing developments, on and on. It seems the essence of the bored rich-meddling syndrome. I went away feeling what a pain in the ass those county people are—all those whining letters about not being included!

But a few weeks later, following a trail of official letters between the state and the county, promises given and forgotten, I began to see again how "the state really led the county on—I'm beginning to see how the county felt screwed by the state."

Only after riding this emotional roller-coaster several times was I able to integrate my own feelings about county and state into an intergroup framework that allowed me to take account of both perspectives on the struggle: I could understand how county and state people justified their own feelings and how they came to despise the other group, without myself judging one perspective to be "right." I wrote in my journal, "I've gone back and forth so much with emotional identifications so many times that I now feel very sympathetic to just about everyone. I think I've got it."

However, the most biasing emotional attachment I had was still hidden to me: Having become so close to current Dexter employees, and having lived through the intense emotions of their early confusion and fights, I *blamed* the planners, both county and state, for having botched the planning and caused Dexter so many troubles after it opened. Sarason's (1972) proposition that new organizations inherit conflict from the planning history was emotionally convenient for me; it allowed me to give academic respectability to my own emotional agenda of absolving the Dexter I knew and loved from responsibility for its early failures. Only a coincidental event saved me from my own bias.

PHYSICIAN, HEAL THYSELF

About the time I had finished gathering data and placing it in proper time perspective, I had to stop thinking about Dexter's history of unresolved conflicts to prepare a speech for the American Association of University Women. I had been selected "Woman Scholar of the Year" by the local chapter of AAUW and was to accept the award at a banquet.

I was struck by the juxtaposition of "woman" and "scholar" and began thinking about my own life, how I had struggled with the contradiction of being "smart" and a "girl" during the 1950s, when those two images were mutually exclusive. I traced my life history through phases of trying to be a woman (giving up my intellectual promise) and trying to be a scholar (giving up my feminine promise) and saw that I had flipped back and forth several times, each time trying to resolve the conflict between woman and scholar by denying the need for one or the other.

As I worked on my speech, I began to realize that just as the old societal images of women and of scholars had begun to loosen and shift, so had I begun to integrate the previously contradictory images in my personal identity: I was a woman scholar, and although the *external* world still did not welcome women in academics, the *internal* conflict was slowly being resolved. My inability to resolve the woman/scholar conflict had slowly resulted in a new internal image that transcended the split. I decided to title my speech "The Value of Unresolved Conflict" and congratulated myself on being able to tolerate the conflict, unresolved, for so long.

When I returned to work on the Dexter history of conflicts, I realized what I had done. Working through my own emotions in another context had allowed me to see the possibility that unresolved conflict, no matter how painful, might have long-term benefits in creating something new. I could not allow myself to draw a conclusion about myself that I refused to consider for Dexter, so I examined the hypothesis that the planners' inability to resolve conflicts had been good for Dexter too. I had to admit that it was so. Despite the pain of conflicting images of what Dexter should be, Dexter had indeed begun to evolve into a public service agency that transcended previously contradictory images, no matter how awkwardly. I began to forgive the planners, and with that emotional breakthrough, I could begin to craft theory about conflict in the creation of new organizations without making emotional attributions of blame.

HISTORICAL SENSE-MAKING

So, given the logistical problems and emotional demands of reconstructing history, was it worth it? Did my hard-won historical understanding make Dexter's early development make sense, as Sarason (1972) had claimed?

It did, beyond my expectations. I had selected, from Dexter's first year, five key conflicts, issues with which Dexter struggled and by which it was nearly destroyed during those early months:

Which referral agency's needs was Dexter to serve?
What population was Dexter to serve?
What would constitute "success" for Dexter?
Who would pay for Dexter?
Who would Dexter be controlled by—county or state?

My historical search was focused on trying to find whether those conflicts had arisen during the planning and, if so, how planners had dealt with them. When I began searching for Dexter's planning history, I looked first to find its beginning. I began nearly every interview with the questions, "When do you first remember hearing any mention of Dexter?" and "Who first thought of creating Dexter?" They turned out to be very difficult questions.

After months of investigation, I began to think that *any* "origin question," even for an organization as young as Dexter, was doomed to be clouded in myth. It turned out that at least four separate groups thought that *they* had first thought of Dexter, and furthermore, that it was their hard work that brought Dexter to life. Along with feelings of parenting came feelings of ownership, and each group was certain that its needs were most pressing, knew which population was most appropriate for Dexter to serve, and who should pay for Dexter.

The irony of Dexter's beginning was that while conceptions that arose simultaneously in separate parts of the community flowed into a wave of demand sufficiently powerful and persistent to overcome bureaucratic inertia and bring Dexter to life, the divergent perceptions of origin coexisted without resolution throughout the planning, almost guaranteeing that Dexter would later be torn apart by its identity crisis.

A CHRONOLOGICAL PASS THROUGH TIME

After I had finally assembled papers and notes from archives and memories, I began the most painstaking task of my already obsessive venture: Beginning with the first myths of origin, I worked my way slowly through time, picturing events, trying to imagine feeling as the participants did, slowly building an image of the reality out of which each person and group produced documents, took stands, responded to others, and made decisions.

It was only then, with all data available to me simultaneously, that I was able to play memories against each other, make sense of the divergence between private opinions and public documents, and finally gain empathy both for participants and, in a new and startling way, for the actions of the system as a whole.

The emotional impact of making a chronological pass through time was powerful. In the early years, I felt the hope and determination of those many parents of Dexter, and could see how they all were part of a more general wave of belief sweeping the country during the sixties, a belief that all social problems could indeed be cured, given enough money and ingenuity. I felt them struggle with each other, and watched with feelings much like those of the audience to a Greek tragedy as the separate realities began to clash with one another, at tremendous human cost: public and private arguments, escalating into conflicts that ruined some careers and may have been responsible for a suicide. In the most conflictual periods of history, when people were behaving in the most unkind ways to each other, I hated them all; I was disgusted with the history, and had to force myself to sit down at my desk to continue working. I noticed that the planners of that era were avoiding work, too. My emotions paralleled theirs.

After participating empathically in such ugliness, which I could then see was a nearly inevitable result of so many diverse interests claiming legitimacy to participate in planning Dexter, I began to doubt my own conviction that participation was necessarily a "good" way to run society. Again, my feelings paralleled the planners'. Only by achieving a state of simultaneous empathy with clashing segments of this system could I at last understand *why* the planners had chosen to avoid conflict, to postpone resolution of such vital issues, and to withdraw behind walls of secrecy, creating a sham of public participation. For several years, progress and withdrawal from controversy were directly related. I began to think that this was the only way Dexter could possibly have been brought to life.

From the hard-won perspective of the historian, I could at last "see" the staggering cost of creating Dexter—the thousands of hours of time put into meetings, preparation of memos, telephone calls, lobbying (one single public hearing included the participation of 109 agencies and 37 individuals, with a transcript running several volumes). I had touched the emotions of only a few of the people who lived that history, yet I sat at my desk and wept for their humiliation, their hard work, and their failures. When I finished the history, I felt I had lived through those years of struggle and had myself given birth to Dexter. I was not sure it was fair to bring Dexter into a world so harsh and inevitably disappointing.

And yet with a longer range of vision, I was able to see that Dexter was not doing so badly after all. I could see that those long years of conflictual relationships among those who felt they "owned" Dexter had slowly, painfully, set the patterns for relationships in the present; conflict that had been chaotic in the early years was still present in current relationships, but more regulated, more manageable, and with some hope of benefit. Dexter present was managing, albeit with struggle, to meet some of the needs of all of its parents, to fulfill some of the dreams of integrating fragmented services into a single setting, to serve (with uncertain success) the populations whose need had stimulated planning fifteen long years earlier.

I finished my work (Simmons, 1983) with a profound respect for the difficulty of creating new life forms in a world set up for old ones and with a sense that change might indeed be inevitable, but only in retrospect. In process, to those participating in change, there are only hard choices and the limits of human perseverance.

THE CLINICAL DEMANDS OF HISTORY

I would advise anyone contemplating historical work to first read Lawrence Durrell's *Alexandria Quartet*, a series of four novels containing so much truth about social realities that it is fiction only in the most trivial sense. In these novels, Durrell leads the reader through a complete explanation of the meaning of a series of events, only to reveal how totally wrong we can be when we understand social reality from only a single perspective.

I struggled with Durrell's lesson during this research and constantly warned myself that no matter how thoroughly I thought I understood Dexter's history, I might get a totally different understanding if I talked to just one more person or searched through just one more set of files. I recorded this constant anxiety in my research journal:

> As I reach the end of the history, I keep getting exhausted—but there's still more data to be gathered! Going to the state offices sucks the life out of me. I just can't deal with any more commissions or task forces. I noticed _____'s office today, but I couldn't bear the thought of learning more, so I just walked away. I feel *bloated* with data, and nauseous because it's squirming around in a confused tangle. It's as if there are zones of data, with infinite confusion at the most distant points gradually giving way to a patterned understanding at the core. But because this network stretches outward (and deeper) endlessly, I *always* feel the anxiety of that outer rawness, and I try to find form in it, and if I get more data, I *do*, but that just moves the circle farther out into the void. I want to stop—I'm overwhelmed.

Although reconstructing the Dexter history was an obsessive act unequalled in my experience, I was constantly plagued with the certainty that it was "wrong." This was not just scientific caution—I knew that many of the people who had lived this history would eventually read my account, and I worried both that they might be hurt, embarrassed, or angry and that they would make fun of my "erroneous" conclusions.

It is no wonder that people do not use historical methods more with in-context phenomena. I would be willing to bet that I know as much as anyone has ever known about a particular set of events, but I *still* feel acutely ignorant about the full historical context of Dexter's beginnings. In retrospect, my single most valuable scientific safeguard was that continuous paranoid voice in my ear, telling me "You don't *know* that—you might be wrong!"

To make use of that vague anxiety, that epistemological paranoia, is a methodological task of the greatest demands:

- to acknowledge, fully and shockingly, the highly degraded, distorted, and constantly reinterpreted nature of human memory;
- to build, with the aid of theory about how humans construct realities for themselves, setting-specific models of distortion that help us to make use of both the "fact" and the "fiction" of human perception;
- to acknowledge, deconstruct, and make use of the emotional involvement of the historian as yet another participant in the construction of explanations for events; and
- to trust the guidance of those vague feelings of anxiety, using emotional empathy as a final test of validity.

ARE WE UP TO THE DEMANDS?

There seem to be three major sets of demands for doing research with attention to the complexities presented in this chapter: the demand that we be broadly educated in the social sciences and that we personally overcome the fragmentation of disciplinary boundaries in doing methodical research; the demand that we become personally educated about our own psychological processes, both as they affect our interactions with "subjects" and as they affect our own interpretations of the world we study; and the demand that we develop and disseminate methodological knowledge—not just methods, but rather understanding *of* method—far more sophisticated than our current prescriptions for research. A fourth is a meta-demand: that we alter the system of professional expectations to support and allow research which may be less "certain" than we are led to believe should be the case, legitimating the attendant anxieties of both researchers and the scientific community.

In this chapter, I have mentioned only two areas of psychology that I used extensively in this work: clinical psychology and cognitive psychology. It is exceedingly rare for an organizational researcher to receive training in the fundamentals of human cognition and human emotionality, along with organizational theory, yet these are only two areas among many that enrich a researcher's perspective. Since all disciplines in the social sciences and the humanities deal with human behavior, can we afford to pretend that these diverse disciplines do not all tell us something essential about humans? I think not, yet the pressures in higher education for increasingly differentiated, specialized, and narrow training are in sharp conflict with the pragmatics of institutional resources and the limits of human endurance. To "know" in the abstract, too, is not the same as "knowing" for oneself, and the demands of self-understanding suggested by this chapter mean that researchers should seek understanding of their own biases, blind spots, and cognitive limitations with as high a priority as theoretical knowledge. The anti-clinical bias in much of "scientific" psychology, which worships at the altar of detached objectivity, must be confronted directly as a defense against the implications of applying theory to oneself. The stigma of entering into individual psychotherapy must be transformed to a routine and essential part of graduate training, as must "consciousness raising" at the social level; we must come to understand how all of us are encased in the perspective of our ethnic, gender, and class backgrounds, as well as our own psychodynamic histories. The need to transcend all such filters is, sadly, mired in the impossibility of understanding the social world without them.

Our work as researchers must be supported by methodological theory that is informed by social theory, so that our methods do indeed take account of subjectivity as an inevitable, evolving social construction. These paradigmatic conflicts—the need for certainty against the impossibility of certainty—have seemed unresolvable, but after a long period of defensive prescriptions in methodological literature, we are finally beginning to see literature that takes on the challenge of methods for people studying people as they really are (e.g., Putnam & Pacanowsky, 1983; Morgan, 1983; Reason & Rowan, 1981).

The demand that we begin to make use of the ephemeral experience of empathy as a validity check is perhaps risky, as one person's empathy is another person's projection. No one but I will ever come to know the Dexter history as I have known it, nor come to have the same "making sense" of it as I. I must live with the anxiety that my hard-won understanding may be yet another, deeper fantasy to fulfill some personal agenda. I face that agonizing conflict with every word I write, resolving it only temporarily.

At heart, perhaps the conflict is one between the ideal that our intellect tells us must be found if we are to keep from fooling ourselves about what we know about the social world, and the reality that none of us is quite up to the challenge. There are limits to my capacity to endure internal conflict without fleeing into dissonance-reducing simplifications, but these limits are expanded when the intensity of the struggle is legitimized in the community of organizational scholars, and shared as an integral part of the process of research.

HISTORY IN THE HERE AND NOW:
The Development of a Historical Perspective

Jonathon H. Gillette

Recent organizational behavior literature reflects an emerging concern among social scientists that current scientific methods are failing to capture the dynamic qualities of organizations. A particularly frequent criticism is that researchers ignore past events and assume that they can understand a system by examining only the present (Kimberly & Miles, 1980).

While a review of the literature basically confirms this view, there have been some attempts to take into account the influence of an organization's past. Sarason (1972), for example, focused much of his attention when examining new organizations on their "prehistory." Some have proposed development models that, by definition, attend to the passage of time. (See Levinson et al., 1978, for individuals; Bennis & Shepard, 1956, for groups; and Kimberly & Miles, 1980, for organizations.) Others have done longitudinal studies (Lawrence & Dyer, 1983). Finally, a number of social scientists have examined an organization's past while researching its here-and-now dynamics through examining archival material and reconstructing past events in interviews. All these methods attempt to gain an understanding of the present through a greater sensitivity to the past (e.g., Alderfer & Brown, 1975). Their techniques, however, are often mentioned only in passing and have not been clearly connected to the social science methodology in use.

What is lacking is an explicit formulation of an interdisciplinary approach that brings together the historical and social science paradigms of analysis. Such a formulation would contain a specific set of constructs to guide the historical inquiry and its interpretation. It would mean that the researcher attended to the past as an integral part of any analysis of an ongoing system.

The development of an interdisciplinary perspective is not an easy task. History and organizational behavior have distinctive world views. Each has traditions that emphasize different foci and methods and, in some basic way, deny the validity of the other (Lifton, 1974). Bringing them together is analogous to trying to be simultaneously a member of two separate and distinct groups. Consider the following chart in which each field is presented as an ideal type:

Social Scientist/O.B. Practitioner   Historian

Praises

The scientific tradition   The literary tradition
- theory based   - data led
- replicable   - written in narrative form
- objective   - personal, subjective

Attacks

The non-scientific tradition   The historical tradition
- no explicit theory   - theory driven
- data arranged to suit end goals   - failing to deal with unexplain-
- missing data   ed variance
- no system of replication   - preserving false dichotomy be-
                                                   tween data that can and cannot
                                                   be counted
                                                 - acts as if past has no influence

What the chart makes clear is that the two fields are in many ways polar opposites. It is not hard to imagine a social scientist dismissing a historian's work as "novel," or to imagine a historian dismissing a social scientist as having "good numbers that mean nothing." Any interdisciplinary formulation would need to contend with these polarities. Is the evidence presented in a scientific or literary mode? What are the criteria for selecting evidence in the first place? What are the standards for distinguishing good work from bad? Further, these polarities are not likely to lead to a resolution that eliminates the tension between the two perspectives. Rather, any resolution will have to carry, as its price, some form of internal tension.

The goal of the particular mix of history and social science offered in this chapter is to gain a greater understanding of the present through an increased sensitivity to the past. This mix is new. Others, in particular the psychohistorians, have used an interdisciplinary mix of history and social science. Their process has involved doing traditional historical research through the lenses of new social science theory. They have sought to reinterpret past events through newly developed paradigms (Lifton, 1974). This particular model of uniting history and social science does not help a researcher studying present events who wishes to become sensitive to influences from the past. Such research requires an opposite resolution: the conduct of social science research through the lenses of a historical perspective.

This chapter attempts to take the first steps in developing such a historical perspective within social science research. Part one of the chapter examines the discipline of history, outlining the main components of its perspective, and describing the modes of historical inquiry. Part two proposes two steps in the development of a historical perspective: acquiring an understanding of historical works and doing actual historical research in an ongoing organization.

WHAT IS HISTORY?

At its simplest, history is the systematic study of the past. Its roots are in a literary tradition, and many of the great historians of the past were also great writers. As writers, they have struggled to recreate the past in a form accessible to readers in the present. As historians, they have a perspective that includes events preceding, during, and after the time of events studied. It is a perspective that seeks understanding across time boundaries.

The historical perspective consists of a number of different elements. These are (1) a basic assumption, (2) a sensitivity to context, (3) a narrative form, (4) the temporal position of the researcher, and (5) levels of analysis.

BASIC ASSUMPTION

Historical perspective has at its core a basic assumption that guides the inquiry. Phillip Rieff (1974), a psychohistorian, articulated it as follows: "The past is not simply dead weight to be cast off by enlightened minds, but active and engaged, threatening to master the present." Such an assumption is woven into the fabric of historical exposition, affecting its interpretation of individual behavior. Consider this passage from Trotsky's (1932) *History of the Russian Revolution*:

> Foremost in our vision will stand the great, moving forces of history, which are super-personal in character. . . . Moreover, we hope to show in what follows, partially at least, just where in a personality the strictly personal ends—often much sooner than we think—and how frequently the "disturbing traits" of a person are merely scratches made by a higher law of development.

Individual behavior and personality are influenced by the past: What is often interpreted as personality may instead be a reflection of the forces of the past. The historical perspective is based on the assumption that individuals are affected by events over time. Historical research, then, provides not just a tour of the past, but a method for understanding the past's relationship to and influence on the present.

This basic assumption requires a researcher to look beyond the experiences of any single individual. Just as social scientists have explored collective behavior as something distinct from any individual's behavior, so the historian seeks a perspective that interprets interconnections across individual time periods. Thus the historian is able to understand events and behaviors in a way that is unavailable to the individual participants.

A SENSITIVITY TO CONTEXT

A historical perspective is built on a belief in the importance of context. The emphasis is on building interpretation from the contextual ground up; there is an accompanying skepticism concerning theory. Both of these components have important methodological consequences, as noted in Lipset and Hofstadter's (1968) comparison of history and sociology:

History must be concerned with the analysis of the particular sets of events or processes. Where the sociologist looks for concepts which subsume a variety of particular descriptive categories, the historian must remain close to the actual happenings and avoid statements which, though linking behavior at one time or place to that elsewhere, lead to a distortion in the description of what occurred in the set of circumstances being analysed.

This skepticism of theory exists despite many historical works that present large theoretical statements. Historians would argue that the process used to develop their broad interpretations was qualitatively different from the social science process of generalization in that theories simply follow the data and any large conclusions are solidly based on specific contextual data.

In the final analysis, historians contend that there are elements of understanding that will always evade any theoretical application.

Most important, historians must always appreciate the limitations of using a single interpretive point of view.... Every model, by scaling down reality into a series of more easily comprehended components, inevitably reduces the complexities of history. Even when our models have accounted for goals, strategies, SOPs[Standard Operating Procedures], political influence, and outcomes, there remain those pieces of the picture which are still irreducible. . . . Some elements of history will always remain stubbornly intractable, beyond the reach of the model builders. (Davidson & Lytle, 1983)

THE NARRATIVE FORM

Key to a historical perspective is the creation of the narrative. A critical element is that the narrative flow from the events themselves rather than from a theoretical model. Tuchman (1981) notes,

As to treatment, I believe that the material must precede the thesis, that chronological narrative is the spine and the bloodstream that bring history close to "how it really was" and to a proper understanding of cause and effect; that, whatever the subject, it must be written in terms of what was known and believed at the time, not from the perspective of hindsight, for otherwise the result will be invalid.

The narrative is richly descriptive, and presents conclusions only after building the contextual fabric of the era for the reader. It is a collection of data, arranged through a literary medium and tolerating the use of imagination as long as the presentation remains rooted in the data.

The validity of a narrative lies in its ability to incorporate both previously known and newly discovered data. Historians have nightmares about discovering a relevant piece of research that has been left out of their analysis. From the data, the narrative must develop a perspective that makes sense of individuals and their behavior in the context of their time. The reader can, with this perspective, understand events in a way that no individual participant could. Validity is literary rather than scientific. It is the compelling nature of the narrative that distinguishes good work from bad: how tightly argued it is, whether it takes into account all the relevant information, and whether it evokes an instinctively believable image of the past.

THE TEMPORAL POSITION OF THE RESEARCHER

The above criteria for validity must themselves be understood as a product of their temporal position in the discipline of history. That is, judgments concerning validity shift as time passes. Historians fifty years ago interpreted the American Revolution as a radical break from the past, while more recent reinterpretations see it as a means of conserving that past. Every historian's interpretive lens, its selection and interpretation of data, is influenced by the time in which the historian lives.

Thus, historical perspective not only requires that we attempt to understand others in the context of their times, but that we begin to understand ourselves, including the influences of our present on our theories and interpretations. Threats to validity can arise either from a failure to account for the specific historical context of the events being described, or from failure to recognize assumptions of our own research framework that are based on our historical rootedness. In fact, historians also study themselves; the field of historiography attempts to examine how historians have been influenced by their circumstances.

LEVELS OF ANALYSIS

One of the difficulties in discussing history is that the same word is used whether you look at individuals, organizations, or society as a whole. Each has its own history. In order to clarify what is being analyzed, history can be conceived of as having a number of different levels. The word *level* comes from social science and is used to differentiate work done on individuals, groups, and organizations. Having a clear sense of these different levels can greatly aid in understanding how past events combine and interact. It makes it possible to differentiate between, for example, whether people find themselves unemployed during the Great Depression at the beginning or the end of their working lives.

Hareven (1977, 1982) was the first to begin looking at historical levels. She attempted to examine these differences by organizing history into three levels of time. One is *individual time*. This is essentially an understanding of the developmental stage of any single individual, including both chronological age and relationships to others (e.g., marriage, adolescence). Another is *organizational time*. This refers to an organization's developmental stage—for instance, whether it is expanding or bureaucratizing. A third is what Hareven calls *historical time*. This represents the overall social, economic, institutional, and cultural context of the larger society.

Despite the confusion of having the third level called "historical," this framework begins to bring together a number of theories to enrich and deepen each other. The various developmental theories noted in this chapter's introduction can all plot their particular dynamics on a single chart, each line of which represents a different level of analysis. Individual, group, system, and societal dynamics may cross over, pull at, intensify, or smother each other. This structure allows us to frame an analysis that keeps track of changes that have taken place at a particular level simultaneously with changes that have taken place in the context surrounding that level. It provides the opportunity to see a connection between changes within an organization and changes within the larger society.

In summary, history has a simple definition: It is the study of the past. It has a basic assumption that the past is actively engaged in the present. It is context sensitive and has a skepticism of theory. It relies on a narrative as its main form. In addition, it operates at a number of levels simultaneously, challenging us to understand both the past and ourselves.

DEVELOPING A HISTORICAL PERSPECTIVE

Given an accurate and thorough understanding of history, the task still remains of training the researcher to be sensitive to historical influences while examining ongoing systems. The goal is for the researcher to develop a historical perspective as an additional way of understanding the here-and-now.

This chapter suggests two actions through which an increasing historical perspective may develop: studying current historical works and conducting historical research within the organization under consideration. These actions incorporate all the elements of history that were outlined in the previous section, as well as having implications for how research is carried out.

STUDYING HISTORY

Studying current historical works helps in understanding the historical forces that are influencing one's working theories and one's role as a researcher/interventionist in a system. Social scientists have not been particularly interested in such an examination (Gergen, 1973; Schlenker, 1974). It is one thing to acknowledge history as something that needs to be controlled for internal validity (Campbell & Stanley, 1963). It is quite another to accept a relationship between history and the development of particular general theories.

The purpose, then, is to try to understand our historical position as researchers. This is clearly an ongoing task, one that seeks *understanding* of historical forces rather than elimination of their influence. The first step is to examine what assumptions in one's own set of theories remain unexplored and unchallenged. A great deal of recent work, especially by labor historians, is relevant to studies in organizational behavior. These writings discuss work structures (Friedlander, 1975; Hareven & Langenback, 1978), workers' control (Montgomery, 1979), bureaucracy and complex organizations (Clawson, 1980), scientific management and work designs (Noble, 1977), and corporate welfare programs (Meyer, 1981).

These works challenge social science researchers' assumptions about the nature of a research relationship, raising important questions about the system theories most investigators learn early in their training. Historical attitudes toward three major topics stand out as important challenges to conventional social science assumptions: views on the nature of bureaucracy, the nature of a research relationship, and the scope of a study.

Bureaucracy. It is a commonly held assumption that bureaucracy is an inevitable form that results when organizations grow in size and complexity. Katz (1971), however, finds compelling evidence in school systems organized in the early 1900s that "bureaucracies are bourgeois institutions designed to repress working people." His evidence on school systems is extended by David Tyack (1974), who states,

> Bureaucratization was *partially* a response to the complexities of urbanization and population growth *but* not the result of a preordained imperative. Rather the drive to bureaucratize urban schools, which flowered after 1890 in cities across the nation, was part of an effort by elites and educational professionals to turn political questions into administrative issues by removing decision making from the public arena to the hallways and offices of bureaucratic organizations where educational experts could operate free from the pressures of public opinion.

Dan Clawson (1980), comes to similar conclusions by examining the metal working industry. He analyzes a little-known form of production known as "inside contracting," a form he claims is craft centered:

> A distinction can be made between craft and bureaucratic forms of production; in craft production most or all of the basic decisions about how to produce a product are made by persons who are themselves directly involved in physically producing it; in bureaucratic production these decisions are made by people not in the work crew.

Eventually, inside contracting was abolished and replaced with a bureaucratic form. Clawson finds no evidence to support the traditional justification for bureaucratic forms:

> Why was inside contracting abolished? The two most important reasons were, first, the attempt to shift income from contractors to the company and second, the wish to establish and maintain an "acceptable" social hierarchy. Neither considerations of efficiency nor dissatisfaction with inside contracting's technical capacity to perform the work were significant issues at the time.

Research relationship. The second major challenge historians pose to social scientists concerns the forces shaping a researcher's relationship with an organization. A number of historians have pointed out the ways in which the relationship between corporations and academia has shaped the nature and scope of research questions, and that this relationship changes over time (Perrow, 1973). Consider the work of

Noble (1977), which focuses on technology and the rise of engineers and engineering schools.

As Christopher Lash writes in the preface to Noble (1977),

> The notion of technological determinism has dominated popular understanding of the industrial revolution. Changes in technology are assumed to have been the principal cause of industrialization, and the whole process is seen purely as a technological revolution.

Noble challenges that assumption by examining the rise of industrial engineering. He argues that engineers, and their choice of technology to develop, were dominated by the imperatives of economic and social control:

> In short, they ventured to design a new (yet old) social order, one dominated by the private corporation and grounded upon the regulated progress of scientific technology. Forces of production and social relations, industry and business, engineering and the price system—the two poles in the dialectic of social production—collapsed together in the consciousness of corporate engineering under the name of management.

Social scientists, especially in organizational behavior, have origins that parallel engineers and can, in some way, be seen as social engineers of organizations. Their ties to management and management science are reflected in their research topics and their location in management schools. This creates a "form of consciousness," to use Noble's phrase, that prevents a close examination of the ways intervention may be colluding with the forces for social and economic control.

It is important to note that the image that emerges is not one of social scientists harking to the beck and call of corporate greed. It is, instead, more an image of researchers who do not engage in a process of self-reflection. Concepts such as the "free flow of information" become valued because they are thought to be neutral or value free. The consequences are not always so neutral. Consider the consequences of the children's television show, *Sesame Street*. It was originally designed to provide key skills to those who were entering school with the lowest levels of competence. The results were intended to bring the top and the bottom closer together, by starting them in school with the same basis of skills. However, just the opposite happened. Since those at the top had a built in higher learning rate, exposure to *Sesame Street* put them even farther ahead. While all children's skills increased, parity decreased even further.

Scope of the study. Another prevalent assumption about organizational research is that the dynamics inside the system drive the behavior of its members. In essence, the belief is that one can understand behavior in organizations by restricting the scope of the study to the inside of the organization. Recent historical work by Gutman (1976) and Montgomery (1979) points to the importance of understanding working class culture inside *and outside* the factories. They refute the traditional historical interpretation that it is the factories and the bosses who are responsible for primary socialization into the workplace. Workers socialize other workers, both inside and outside the factory walls. My own work on New Haven Italian workers in a metal working industry confirms this interpretation. The metal workers sought to bring their larger community values into the factory (Gillette, 1983). An understanding of this interpretation might enable researchers to see how "resistant" behavior in the workplace may be a statement of community values, rather than just a battle with the boss.

DOING HISTORICAL RESEARCH

The second step in developing a historical perspective is to do actual historical research. This step influences both the processes of diagnosis and of intervention.

Diagnosis. A historical perspective can be developed while analyzing an ongoing system. The work involves examining past documents and interviewing members of that system about the past. The goal is to be able to put together time lines, sequences of events over time, for each of the levels outlined earlier in this chapter. The analysis seeks to understand events by looking at behavior among levels, connected across time.

It must be pointed out from the start that each source of historical data has some strengths and weaknesses. Documents are often easy to obtain but notoriously inadequate in describing the emotions and, in many cases, the exact actions taken by members of a system. Oral accounts are fallible because of memory loss and personal reinterpretations of past events. However, these two sources, taken together, can begin to help the researcher understand events of the past and how the current dynamics are connected to them.

As each level of time—individual, group, organizational, and societal—is charted, the power of this form of analysis lies in the new diagnostic insight the interaction of different levels of time lines provides. Consider the following case as an example of how various levels of time can be brought together:

In the late 1960s, a large manufacturing company decided to set up an independent subsidiary—one that would be structured differently—to attract what they thought would be a different kind of worker and a different kind of customer. The plant was small, run by the workers (who rotated the managerial duties) and emphasized increased contact between workers and customers. Despite a general shift in the larger society away from alternative structures, the subsidiary was successful and popular through the 70s and into the early 80s.

In 1982, the plant's environment changed, in that two similar subsidies were established in the same area. No longer a monopoly, the plant had to define more clearly just what made it special. The organizational structure had already moved toward a more traditional management structure. The physical plant had been redesigned to make the space occupied by workers and managers more differentiated. The process of manufacturing had originally been run by teams of four, but now most workers worked alone.

There was a variety of data available to them as they faced their re-examination. They were still turning a good profit and attracting highly skilled, highly motivated workers. Yet some of the new workers were experienced in more traditional forms of manufacturing. Among the old workers, some had strong feelings about the team method while others were worn out by it.

The plant decided to become more traditional. The question, then, is how to understand that decision. Certainly, the changes in the plant's environment are a factor, along with a trend that had been developing over time toward a more traditional structure. Theories put forth by scholars such as Dimaggio and Powell (1983) analyze similar trends by pointing out the tendency in organizations to conform to a standard structure over time. But is this analysis sufficient to explain the phenomenon? What is taking place at the other levels of the system?

At the individual level, all of the workers were between 35 and 42 years old, with the vast majority having worked at the plant since its opening and, in fact, never having worked elsewhere. Thus, for many of these individuals, issues of mid-life transition were powerful and disturbing. Many talked about leaving, but few had clear ideas as to what else they would do. For many, the financial stress of educating their children was increasing while their pay continued to be near the statewide low.

At the group level, two major factions had existed within the plant for most of its history: one that had always sought a more traditional approach, and one that had always pushed for alternatives. Since the plant was small, conflict between the two groups had often been seen as a clash of personalities. As long as the two groups remained in some state of parity, the system was able to satisfy both groups with small adjustments. However, in the last three years the traditionalists had gained dominance by securing the leadership position for one of their members and by the departure of a major leader of the other group. Developmentally, the traditional group had gained greater cohesion, while the alternative group unraveled more and more.

Finally, fiscal pressures that had been building up inside the parent company for a number of years began to influence the plant. Its original justification, as a choice based on its production structure, was replaced by a justification based on money. The plant, since it had fewer managers, had a lower per unit cost. In other words, what had made it legitimate to members of the system hierarchy changed.

Thus, the plant's movement toward a more traditional program was not just a function of events on any one of these levels; rather, each made an important contribution the rest. The decision can be seen as a synergistic response to a number of historically based patterns that reinforced each other.

The above case illustrates how one might interpret the historical data available in a system, as well as giving a sense of the kind of information one might need to seek. An additional factor must be kept in mind. The historical mind holds to the notion that the narrative or story follows wherever the data leads. To implement this aspect of historical research, a social scientist must be willing to expand, alter, or even contract the original parameters of a study. It is quite possible that the organization can be understood without seeking data outside the system. But it may also be true that some understanding of the larger system, such as the neighborhood from which the members originate, may be essential. The experience of historians is that the scope of the study is determined through the process of the research itself.

Intervention. The inclusion of historical research may also influence interventions in a system and may alert practitioners to the insufficiency of a here-and-now analysis as a guide for change. Consider the following example:

A group of inner city high school teachers was meeting regularly with an outside consultant to learn how to integrate theories of group dynamics into daily classroom management. In one particular session, the consultant's agenda was to demonstrate that the teachers were consistently acting as if they had no power or influence. He used, as an example, the issue of how dirty the building was, and refused to accept the teachers' refrain that they could not change that aspect of the school. In the process of resisting the consultant, the teachers became more aware of their denial of their own authority and power. The consultant left the session feeling that he had made an important contribution to their learning and had made an appropriate intervention.

The consultant had correctly analyzed their "acting as if" mode and was able to show it to them in a way that they accepted and which elicited a commitment to change. But he did not understnd the historical aspect of their resistance to taking power, particularly in relation to the upkeep of the building. His failure to do this meant that he had no sense of the utility of the particular resistance that emerged. In fact, that resistance was an important defense for those teachers and enabled them to work effectively in their classrooms. Time and time again, the system as a whole had threatened to drown them with its needs. Within a year after this particular program, two significant teachers left, suffering from burnout.

These teachers had, over time, created a boundary between themselves and the rest of the system, in order to prevent the system from overwhelming them. Historically, this boundary had served them well. They had done a number of projects that had accomplished some reform, while managing to continue teaching. The consultant had no sense of their previous interaction with the system, nor did he have a sense of how the myth of total powerlessness had emerged within the group. An alternative intervention might have been to build a boundary that was based on a more accurate sense of reality. This might have enabled the myth to be examined, lessening its deleterious effects on their performance, while preventing the removal of the myth from opening up the floodgates. This type of understanding would only have been possible if the history of that system and group had been examined.

IMPLICATIONS

The development of a historical perspective has a number of implications. First, the researcher is more likely to enter an organization with an expanded set of alternative hypotheses. This is especially beneficial if the research goal is to understand the multiple perspective in an organization. Here, knowing the history of the various groups may allow for their viewpoints to be recognized, then understood. Since most researchers are not from the same group or class as many members of the organizations they study, understanding other group history is a way to have some empathy even before entering an organization.

Second, new ways of interpreting data collected from an organization may open up. It is one thing to come up with information, for example, that workers in a garment factory are taking home unused pieces of fabric. However, it is another thing to interpret or even label it. The management might call it "stealing" and, to most outsiders, this makes sense, since it is assumed that the material bought by management belongs to management. But there is also an alternative interpretation: The workers have, by tradition, been granted ownership of any bolt of cloth they worked on, so that any charge of stealing would be a change in the way the cloth has been accounted for in the past.

A third implication concerns the process of generating and interpreting theory. To some extent, all theories seek to portray root processes that would take place no matter what the historical setting. In order for this to be true, the theorist must be able to distinguish historical content from theoretical process. Lifton (1967) raises this issue in his examination of the work of Freud:

The central dilemma here for depth psychology is its extreme susceptibility to specific historical imagery and conflict. That imagery, moreover, directly reflects the prevailing sense among the people of a particular culture and epoch of their own nature. . . .

The fact that Freud's model of libido and repression of the instinctual sexual impulses was put forth during the late Victorian era, at a time when society was struggling with these issues, does not invalidate the generalizability of his ideas; their power lies precisely in that generalizability. But it does raise the important point—not only for Freud but for our own work now— of the influence of historical forces on the psychological theories we choose to develop.

Lifton goes on to argue that, today, the fear of death is the content that has replaced the position held by sexual repression in Freud's day. The root psychological dynamics remain, while the content shifts according to culture and time.

Finally, all of this is not without some cost to the researcher; the demands of this type of work are heavy. Interdisciplinary work has been said to be "the process by which the unknowns of one's own subject are multiplied by the uncertainties of some other science." Venturing into a new field where there are no set guidelines creates internal tension, especially when that area is bounded by two competing perspectives. In this particular mix, it is hard not to lose one's sensitivity to unexplained data while doing social science research. Maintaining a tension between the two is essential.

Additional difficulties arise. The method requires the researcher to start off with, and to retain longer, more alternative hypotheses of behavior. This is not the traditional scientific method of narrowing possibilities toward the most likely answer; rather, it consciously seeks to widen the field of possible answers. This increases both the uncertainty any researcher has concerning the ability to understand a complex system and the volume of data that needs to be examined. Few have the resources or, more especially, the time to carry out a full historical examination.

The process of challenging one's own assumptions requires navigation between the two extremes of self-doubt and self-righteousness. Basic philosophical issues that challenge the ability of researchers to know themselves, much less an organization, remain. And, certainly, nothing is more infuriating than being told, "I am self-conscious of my history: you are not." However, between these two poles lies an opportunity to gain a richer perspective on oneself and the forces that influence one's theories. In turn, the investigator can develop a greater sensitivity to the system's memory as well as its here-and-now dynamics.

USING PARTICIPANT OBSERVATION TO CONSTRUCT A LIFE HISTORY

Helen Swick Perry

"Imagine the embarrassment of the physicist to have found that he was among his own data," Harry Stack Sullivan observed in a 1943 lecture to students in the Washington School of Psychiatry. He was reminding his audience, most of whom were psychiatrists in training, that they were engaged in participant observation in their work with patients and that they, too, were among their own data. Twentieth-century physicists had been forced to this realization by the discovery of relativity; they could no longer deal with absolute "truth." The student of human behavior had been struggling much longer with this blurring between the observer and the observed. Even the biographer, as I was to discover in constructing the life history of Harry Stack Sullivan, is forced into the role of participant observer.

When I began in the 1960s to gather data on Sullivan's early life in Chenango County, New York State, with the idea of writing his biography (Perry, H., 1982), I thought of my task in formal terms; I was in search of facts, correspondence, pictures, and interviews with relatives and friends. Yet almost immediately I dimly perceived that I had begun a new look at my own early life in ways that would extend far beyond my formal encounter with psychoanalysis some two decades earlier. As a female biographer of a male subject, I had to begin at a new level to cross the gender gap in much the same way that a therapist of one sex undertakes work with a patient of the other sex. Although my beginnings were superficially different from Sullivan's in important ways, I shortly discovered that "we are all much more simply human than otherwise," as Sullivan (1953a, p. 16) noted. In unexpected ways, I

AUTHOR'S NOTE: An earlier version of this paper, entitled "A Methodological Approach to Interpersonal Biography," was presented on January 26, 1980, in New York City at a symposium on "Psychoanalysis 1980: Converging Views," sponsored by the William Alanson White Institute of Psychiatry, Psychoanalysis and Psychology.

kept finding strange islands of similarities in our encounters with family, friends, and community, although Sullivan was born almost twenty years before me. And I learned to understand that differences in ethnicity, religious identification, and gender paled before the similarities of our human existence.

As I measured my own life and the lives of people in Sullivan's early background against the development of his life and his "durable achievements as a contributor to culture history" (Sullivan, 1947), I found myself, during the period that I worked on the biography, becoming much more sophisticated about the use of participant observation. Yet I had already used that tool for over a decade before in studying patients in three mental hospitals and in making a community mental health study of the Haight-Ashbury district in San Francisco (Perry, H., 1970). It is one thing to ferret out the current life and meaning of an ongoing social setting; it is another to reconstruct the life of a child growing up in a rural community at the turn of the century, over fifty years before my study began. Participant observation was a crucial tool for both kinds of endeavors.

The formula for writing an interpersonal biography, which is another term for the use of participant observation in gathering data for a life history, came from Sullivan himself. During his brief but productive life, Sullivan got around to commenting on many facets of society, including the writing of biography. Only a small portion of his writings are in book form and indexed, so I had forgotten that he had ever mentioned biography.[1] Only after I had already completed a good part of my research and an appreciable amount of the writing did I happen on his formula for writing biography, and I was astonished to see how I had operationally been forced into the avenues that he had so succinctly defined. The passage—which I used as an epigraph for the biography—comes from Sullivan's review (1947) of Ruth Benedict's book on Japanese society, *The Chrysanthemum and the Sword:*

Biography usually fails to integrate its subject person with the significant others who facilitated and handicapped his durable achievements as a contributor to culture history, and rarely indicates whence came his skills and limitations in the interpersonal relations which made his contribution effective. A survey of at least the near past and present of the culture-complex which he influenced is required to validate this sort of biographical data, to give it dependable psychiatric or social psychological meaning. The phenomenon of Freud without its setting in the contemporary society of Vienna has been followed by the phenomena of Freud's evangelists and Freud's detractors, also without sensitivity to the nuances of cultural differences within the major context of the Western world.

It is difficult to picture in diagrammatic fashion the intricacy and range of this process, representing as it does an important amalgam of the methods of social anthropology and the particular insights of dynamic psychiatry. When one begins to apply this approach in a systematic way, new insights and exciting connections appear as if by magic. The task becomes increasingly complex as one proceeds. Thus I had to inform myself in detail on the lives of more than a dozen people in Sullivan's early environment in order to have some idea of how their lives intertwined with his and helped to define him. Eventually I had to reconstruct his interaction with several friends and colleagues in his adult life and examine both the overlapping similarities that initiated the interaction and the differences that enlarged the scope of Sullivan's thinking.

In beginning with his early life, I first had to look at the geography and history of the area in which he grew up; his limited access to mass communication, which was mainly the daily newspaper published in the county seat; and the economic conditions, the mental health, the religious tensions, and the educational facilities of that time and place. All these factors affected the personalities that most intimately impinged on his early life. I also had to be alert to the anxieties implicit in those people I talked to, emergent from their own particular life histories, as measured against the impact of the general culture. There is no way to do a complete examination of all these factors, but after one has immersed one's self in reconstructing this kind of intimate data on the people and the culture-complex that surrounds any child in the process of growing up, certain obvious insights appear that can be verified, mainly by the way the assets and limitations of these early encounters are played out in the later life.

On my first field trip to Chenango County, I did not immediately recognize that I had any particular interest in studying the community intensively or my own interaction with it, although I was familiar with William Foote Whyte's classic study (1955) of an Italian-American urban community. Whyte set out to study the values of that community with the specific goal of understanding and defining the life-style of that group; from the outset this necessitated an evaluation of his own values and social class. Unlike me, he began his task by looking at the neighborhood as a whole, but eventually he had to concentrate on how these values were reflected and played out in the lives of particular people on whom he focused. I was originally intent on establishing one important fact about Sullivan's early life that I needed for an introduction to the collection of Sullivan papers on which I was then working— documentation for his hospitalization with a schizophrenic break, which he once mentioned to me (Perry, H., 1982, pp. 3-4). Although I was never able to find documentation for this—in hospital records, for instance—I began almost immediately to sense the input of the community into the mental life of its inhabitants. Thus I was confronted with cogent information on the life of the community over a period of many years. I was faced with vital information on what it was like to grow up as an outsider (the grandson of Irish immigrants) in this tightly structured and still remote part of the Eastern United States. Even though I arrived on the scene over a half-century after Sullivan had moved away, I began to relive the world in which he found himself, through interviews, through information that I found in the daily county newspaper for that period, and through the entire life of the county as reflected in the newspaper. Preeminently that included clear clues to patterns of mental disorder in the county. Shortly I was to discover through U.S. Census Bureau reports that Chenango County had the highest suicide rate for all rural counties in the United States in 1908, the year Sullivan graduated from high school. Out of such data I was forced to move from the particular career line of one person into a wide look at the total picture and then back again.

Either a study of a person living in a culture-complex or a study of a culture-complex as it is filtered through a variety of people is defined quite precisely by Sullivan (1947) in his review of Benedict's book:

> Any *person* is to a great degree a function of his past interpersonal history, the immediate present, and the well- or ill-foreseen neighboring future. Any *people* is an interlocking dynamic network of a great many contemporary persons, each with past, present, and neighboring future with considerable identities and similarities—roughly equaling the culture—and some significant differences [emphasis added].

Sullivan is here using the word *people* to represent what the anthropologists usually call *society*. He is making a contrast between the word *person* and the word *people*. This interplay of the two approaches to human behavior reached its highest point in a series of articles written by Sullivan near the end of his life, one of which was called significantly "Towards a Psychiatry of Peoples" (Sullivan, 1948).

Benedict, by a so-called coincidence, grew up in the same county as Sullivan, although the religious, social-class, and ethnic identification of their families set them apart, and they never knew each other in those years. During World War II, Benedict used this dual approach of person and people in her book on the Japanese. In making a wise recommendation to the United States government on the necessary retention of the

Japanese Emperor in the postwar period, she began by analyzing the complex meaning of the relationship of the people to their emperor through the use of literature, historical studies, and interviews with Japanese-Americans living in this country at the time of World War II. She herself had never been in Japan, and because of the war, she had no access to people living in Japan during the course of her study. Her role as a participant was therefore extremely difficult as she had to acquire a sympathetic feel for values so different from her own, with no firsthand contact with the then current situation in Japan and no firsthand knowledge of the country itself. Yet the Japanese people themselves feel that her study is one of the best ever done on their life and values.

As I went along in my task of trying to figure out what early experience had informed Sullivan's theory, I became more and more aware of my own experience in growing up and to what extent I had assets and liabilities for my participant observation of Chenango County in general and of Sullivan in particular. Partly I underwent a kind of personal sociological analysis, which became an important expansion of my earlier psychoanalytic experience. For the first time I had to face the fact that I had the bias and the blind spots of a WASP. I had never considered that I could be defined as belonging to an elite class. Indeed, partly in keeping with the ideas of the Society of Friends, in which my maternal grandfather had been raised, I was well acquainted with the belief that all men are equal in the sight of God and felt that I accepted this formulation in my daily life. For a variety of familial and personal reasons I was identified with the underdog on most political issues. Yet this was essentially an elitist attitude in which I felt that I must be generous with those who had less.

My own father and mother had been raised on farms in Niagara County, not too distant in social values from the WASPs in Chenango County, including Ruth Benedict. As a child I had spent vacations on relatives' farms in Niagara County, although I myself was raised in a small, largely working-class town just outside of Washington, D.C., where my scientist father had a government job. So, many of the people in Chenango County were much like my relatives; I felt comfortable talking to them.

I also slowly made friends with some of Sullivan's cousins and other Irish-Americans in the county, most of whom were Catholic. Only slowly and painfully did I begin to realize that my unconscious feeling of superiority to Catholics in particular and, more generally, to people who were closer to immigrant status than I was represented a considerable handicap in my explorations.

I had made several brief visits to the county early in the 1960s, but in 1963 I decided that I must make a more formal study of Sullivan's early life and that I would spend a month in the county. Through an Irish-Catholic friend, Miss Loretta Macksey—someone who had known Sullivan as a child—I found a rooming house near where Miss Macksey lived. On my first Sunday there, my (Protestant) landlady asked me which church I went to, and I immediately surmised that it was inconceivable to people in that area that as an adult I had given up attending church. I told her that as a child I had gone to the Congregational church, but that my mother was Quaker on her father's side and Methodist on her mother's side, and that my father was raised as a Baptist. She smiled knowingly—this pattern of different Protestant sects was well known to her, and she was sympathetic. She thought that I would be comfortable in her church, which as I remember was Methodist, and I dutifully accompanied her to church each Sunday. Miss Macksey, the Irish-Catholic neighbor, queried me about my religion after the first Sunday. She told me that I was so sympathetic to the Irish people that she had assumed that I must be part Irish. I told her that I had a great grandmother on my father's side who was Irish, but I had never known her at all; she asked me whether she was Catholic, and I told her that I really did not know.

Subsequently Miss Macksey, who was related to some of the Stack cousins, made arrangements for me to spend an evening with these cousins who happened to be on a visit from Brooklyn, N.Y., to this village where they had grown up. The visit supplied me with new understanding of Sullivan's general background, but I was also questioned by them. One of their main questions centered around whether Sullivan had really been buried by the Roman Catholic Church. When I said that he had and that I knew because I had attended the funeral, they challenged me sharply: How could I know if I were not a Catholic? At some point, Miss Macksey intervened for me; she told them that I was very understanding of the situation of Irish Catholics in Chenango County—"we were treated like skunks at a Sunday School picnic"—and she said that my own grandmother (exaggerating the immediacy of the relationship) was born in Ireland—but in the "northern part," she noted. This was news to me, but I was too startled to protest; so I simply accepted this interpretation, which, I understood, was given in good faith.

I finally recognized that Miss Macksey had explained my not being Catholic, though partly Irish in background, in such a way that my acceptance in the Irish-Catholic part of the community would be expedited: That is, I had the understanding of the Irish through my "grandmother" and the only reason I was not Catholic was because that part of my family had come from the "northern part" of Ireland where Protestants had dwelt for many centuries. That is, my ancestors in Ireland had not turned coat during one of the famines in Ireland, which would have been the worst possible explanation. During the great potato famine in particular, the inhabitants in the south and west of Ireland, far from the cities, were in most danger of starvation, and the English charitable organizations fed thin soup to the Catholic farmers only if they would renounce the Catholic church; the people who succumbed to this temptation were termed "soupies" by their neighbors. In Chenango County, by contrast, some of the Irish Catholics had become Protestant with much less of an excuse; no one had to starve in America, staunch Catholics noted, and therefore the tendency to become Protestant here as a way of making it faster up the ladder was a sign of an even greater weakness. So it was that Miss Macksey had carefully defined me in such a way that I would not be subject to such criticisms (even about my great grandmother) and that I would be accepted in the Irish-Catholic community in Chenango County.

This encounter also provided me with some insight into why Sullivan had specified that he wanted a Catholic funeral—a fact that caused a good deal of questioning among his psychiatric colleagues, most of whom had abandoned the religion of their own childhoods. They felt that Sullivan saw formal religion as often antithetical to good mental health and as a potential problem, particularly during adolescence. How could he specify a Catholic funeral? I understood his decision completely only after I had spent considerable time in Chenango County. They were keeping score there. The community's questioning continued indefinitely: Was a convert, in either direction, punished by God? And did someone, no matter how far he wandered from the teachings of the Catholic church, finally come back to the fold at the end? Regardless of all else, some church had to provide burial services; it was inconceivable that it would be omitted. In the end, Sullivan remained true to the expectation of those Stacks and Sullivans who were still Catholic. From these two experiences, I had a clear view of the importance of religion in the life of the county.

I would like to mention two other happenstances that were critical in my work. On one of my first visits, I discovered in the county newspaper for 1908 an item on Harry Sullivan's taking a state scholarship examination for Cornell University. He won a scholarship and attended there for less than a year. My father, a farm boy, had also won a state scholarship to Cornell five years earlier and had graduated from there. In my family, there was a story told by my paternal grandmother of how homesick my father had been in the metropolis of Ithaca so far away from home, and of how he had packed his trunk and returned home at Thanksgiving time in his freshman year, determined not to return to Cornell. His paternal grandfather had talked him into going back. A Sullivan cousin remembers that Harry as a freshman had not wanted to go back to Cornell after his first trip home at Thanksgiving. There was clear evidence here of the culture shock of a farm boy encountering a more sophisticated and complex community and of the significance of travelling even fifty miles in that period. But over time and after making some blunders, I found out that there was a difference between the homesickness of my father and that of Harry Sullivan.

To begin with, my father's family belonged to the farming community in which they lived—they were Protestant, lived on a fruit farm in the most lush section of Niagara County and had a substantial house and farm buildings. The family did not consider it essential at all that my father go to college, nor were they particularly impressed with the fact that my father had won a scholarship. Thus his return from college, not wanting to go back, was treated matter-of-factly by his parents; indeed, it was only his grandfather who encouraged him to return and lectured my father's parents on the fact that they should make more of an effort to go down to Ithaca on the train and visit their son. By contrast, Harry's reluctance to return to Cornell was completely unacceptable to his mother. She felt that Harry's only hope was education; even though he was not yet 17 years old when he went to Cornell, she would not accept the possibility that he could not make it at college. It was in that first year at Cornell that Harry's marks begin to fail and he was finally placed on probation for almost a year; he never went back to Cornell. However limited my father's encounter with larger centers of population before he went to Cornell, he had gone to market in Buffalo many times as a boy to sell farm produce and had looked with awe and wonder on the houses along Delaware Avenue. Moreover, he was almost three years older than Harry was upon entrance. My father, having been kept out of school each fall to help with harvesting, did not finish the required work in high school until he was 19 years old. The very similarities of their backgrounds underscored the differences.

Another area for participant observation emerged as I began to hunt for Sullivan's preadolescent chum—a formulation peculiarly evocative for me, as for many of Sullivan's students. In 1947, I first heard him lecture about the importance of the chum in the years just before adolescence. A person might suffer considerably, he said, from losing the companionship of a chum, through death or through the family's moving away. Although I had had considerable analytic experience by then, I had never explored the impact of a chum in my own growing-up years. That night at home, I wrote, almost automatically and entirely autobiographically, a short story entitled "The Lost Chum." For the first time I recognized why I had lost my best friend; she had moved not too far away but into a better neighborhood than ours, and her mother wished to terminate all contacts with the old neighborhood. Thus I had a strong personal interest in locating Sullivan's chum, even many years later.

As I talked to teachers, neighbors, and relatives who knew Sullivan as a child, I began to ask, "Did he have a particular friend in school or near home?" From all of them there was a consistent answer—it was Clarence Bellinger, the boy who lived on the next farm. He was Sullivan's *only* friend. They were both living on farms and attending the village school, and they were not totally accepted in that society made up of village children; so they clung together and dreamed together. They had handicaps for the true friendship of peers, for Clarence was five years older than Harry. Yet this relationship was a good deal better than nothing. They were both only children, with mothers who insisted on their becoming famous. The first one to become a psychiatrist was Clarence, and eventually Harry followed suit. Both of them had their first mental hospital experience at St. Elizabeths Hospital under William Alanson White, who himself was more than familiar with Chenango County, as I shall comment on shortly.

Finding Sullivan's chum opened up new avenues that I could explore participantly. For Clarence and Harry were both outsiders in the village school, partly because they were both living on farms. But Harry was the only Irish-Catholic boy in the village school, and Clarence's family did not go to any church—an even more unusual deviation from the norm. Thus Clarence's position was even worse than Harry's. In another dimension I too was an outsider in the school that I attended as a child; my parents arranged for their children to attend the city schools because they were better than the local schools, so that we were rejected by the children in the local schools as being high hat and yet were outsiders in the city schools. Such stories are often a significant part of growing up in the diverse society that is America, so that we peculiarly need the comfort of a chum in whom we can confide with impunity in the delicate years of transition to adulthood.

I shortly began to be aware of many other apparent coincidences as I proceeded with my task. In every significant relationship that Sullivan had, whether in childhood or adulthood, and that I explored, there were strange bands of commonality that one might term, in a mystical sense, auspicious coincidence, as if Sullivan were fated to find this or that person in his journey through life. I would like to redefine these so-called coincidences. I would posit that in a diverse society in which there is still relatively a good deal of chance for upward mobility, all of us have areas of experience that one can think of as almost isolated strands of life. Many of these experiences are kept well hidden in order to protect self-esteem. All of us who manage to survive become adept at locating the person whose experience at some critical point produces a situation in which we can confide within that delimited area; or, equally true, we withdraw because we become acutely sensitive to the anxiety in the other person that triggers our anxiety in the same area of experience, either because we have had the same experience and are trying to forget it or because the other person's experience is too different and unsettling. Because Sullivan's early life was peopled with an unusually small number of significant people, he seems to have had an uncanny sense for finding these bands of commonality and these areas that aroused anxiety in him.

I would like to begin by examining one simple basis for common experience—time and place (or geography). At the turn of the century, geography in rural United States was a much more important variable than it is now, selecting a limited range of people and experiences. When one adds to that variable another dimension—that of the mental health problems that exist in a particular community—then one has a strong common basis for understanding in general the problems of mental health there. One can talk with another about a similar population, with the same general problems of ethnicity, economics, religion, and so on. Having established some consensus, then one can pool one's knowledge with another's to extrapolate from this a common statement about mental health and disorder. The overlap of time and place in the lives of William Alanson White and Sullivan offers an example of this phenomenon.

In the same year that Sullivan was born, White came as a young physician to Binghamton State Hospital in Broome County, adjacent to Chenango County. This hospital was the usual resource for mentally disturbed patients in Chenango County. A few years after White left Binghamton in 1903, Ross McClure Chapman became a staff physician there and then later became superintendent at Sheppard and Enoch Pratt Hospital outside Baltimore. Sullivan's first hospital work was as a liaison person to St. Elizabeths in Washington, D.C., under White; his first important post as a psychiatrist was under Chapman at Sheppard. In other words, all of these people—Bellinger, White, and Chapman, who were each in his own way notable influences on Sullivan's life—had been exposed to the mental health problems of the same geographic area at about the same time. The difference was in the nature of the exposure: White and Chapman were exposed as young adults and professionals; Bellinger and Sullivan were 16 and 11, respectively, when White left Binghamton for St. Elizabeths, where he began a brilliant career as superintendent. For White, Binghamton was his only intensive work with patients on the wards; he reports that after he left there, he never again had the same opportunity to spend time with patients on the wards. But his view of patients had the same experiential flavor as Sullivan's, partly because they both had knowledge of the same kind of mental health problems in all kinds of people as they existed in that period in the environs of Binghamton State Hospital. Thus both White and Sullivan articulated the same feeling about patients. White (1938, p. 58) wrote of his Binghamton experience as illustrating that "these patients are very much more *like* the rest of us than they are *different* from us [emphasis in original]." Sullivan was more poetic in stating the same observation: "We are all much more simply human than otherwise, be we happy and successful, contented and detached, miserable and mentally disordered, or whatever." White's experience of that area of the country was not limited to the hospital. He writes of riding through the same countryside during the period that Sullivan was growing up:

> As I read over the pages of this book I am reminded of my experiences in Binghamton as a consultant. These experiences took me in many instances to near-by small towns and to the outlying districts, and I became acquainted with the country doctors, men who studied medicine and started their practice many years before and who, as a result, were schooled by experiences of the most varied kind. The country doctor then spent most of his time in his buggy making his calls, sometimes miles apart. . . .

> As I traveled with the country doctor along the roads on the way to and from his patients he talked to me confidentially about his work, and as we passed houses and people he would often note that here was where so-and-so lived and there was such-and-such a person. He knew about them and he knew about their families because he had lived with them or as their neighbor for years, had been their principal adviser. . . . He knew that if one of the members of such-and-such a family sustained a fracture that there would probably be delayed union. He knew that in another family a moderate temperature usually resulted in delirium. And in this family that we were passing he knew the husband and the father to be a shiftless, irresponsible and unreliable person and the oldest son to take after him very much in these respects, whereas the daughters were very much more like their mother, who was a substantial and stable woman, because it was the mother in this family who had the ability to hold the little group together and hold them to constructive ends. (pp. 270-271)

Thus geography and an overlapping time frame tended to create a commonality for White, Chapman, and Sullivan—and to a certain extent for Bellinger. But a similar commonality at another level existed for the Swiss psychiatrist Adolf Meyer and Sullivan; the ingredients of their common experience were more complex than what I have just described. That is, Meyer, born in Switzerland, came to the United States as a young man and had his first experience as a neuropathologist in a state hospital in Kankakee, Illinois. As a young immigrant who had suffered in transition to the new society, Meyer found himself losing interest in the examination of the brains of dead patients and turned to searching out the stories of these patients before they died. Many of the patients had been immigrants like himself, and they had lost their way in a new country. Under the influence of the founders of Hull-House in Chicago, Meyer began to develop a knowledge of the whole person and of the social stress of transition.

Thus the bond between Meyer and Sullivan did not come from geographic commonality but from the experience of being an outsider as it related to schizophrenic problems. They both recognized the need for a preventive psychiatry in order to minimize the impact of transition in this diverse society. Moreover, both of them had some firsthand experience with mental illness in the family: Meyer's mother suffered a serious mental illness after her oldest son left for America; she was then alone, a widow with all her children gone from home. Her illness had a profound effect on Meyer, since he had always considered her one of the sanest people he had ever known. And Sullivan's own personal bout with mental illness had its beginnings in part in the lonely and disturbed life of his mother, as both of them tried to cope with being outsiders in a WASP community.

Finally, White, Sullivan, and Meyer began their careers in psychiatry in mental hospitals that cared for a wide spectrum of patients of many different social classes and ethnic origins. White, Meyer, and Sullivan were all skeptical of psychoanalysis as *the* answer to mental health problems in a democratic and diverse society; it was an important tool, but the real answer would depend on developing data on the recurring problems in the general society that could be tackled scientifically—that is, by developing *life histories* on a wide spectrum of people. It seems significant that in 1938, Meyer cited Sullivan as being the person who had been active for years "in bringing anthropology and the study of personality together under a lead of psychiatry" (Meyer, 1952, p. 452).

To delineate adequately the use of differences in order to enrich the total experience of both persons is a much more complicated task. In brief, to the extent that one makes skillful use of areas of commonality with a stranger, one can proceed to learn about a wide gamut of experiences from the other person that are different from one's own. That too is exemplified over and over again in Sullivan's life. Thus his early and close collaboration with Edward Sapir brought together two people who varied in their ethnic, religious, and social class identities. Sapir, at five, came to this country with his mother, a Lithuanian Jew, and his father, an itinerant cantor; his father shortly disappeared, and Edward, as the only surviving child, was raised after the age of ten in New York City where his mother devoted herself to expediting his career as a student. He won scholarships to the Horace Mann School, followed by a four-year scholarship to Columbia University, where he did graduate work under Franz Boas in linguistics and cultural anthropology. Sullivan's education, by comparison, was spotty and casual, and largely obtained from long hours in libraries while he earned his way through a second-rate medical school in Chicago. It was the situation of their first meeting in 1926 that provided an immediate commonality. Sapir had sought out Sullivan in order to gain some understanding of the tragic illness and death of his first wife; she had suffered a mental disorder—emergent, again, from too many cultural transitions: from the role of outsider in her move as a teenager from Lithuania to the United States where she attended Radcliffe College, and finally, after marriage, travelling to Ottawa in Canada, where she found herself often alone with her young children while her husband was away engaged in his fieldwork. In this early encounter with Sullivan, Sapir gained a new understanding of the tragedy that had almost overwhelmed him. And Sullivan found a gifted thinker who understood in a participant way the importance of Sullivan's clinical insights. They could then go on from there, exploring for the next decade, until Sapir's untimely death in 1939, the richness of their differences, so that the differences in themselves became the source of new intellectual adventures.

So it is that beyond the theme of commonality, which appears over and over again in Sullivan's life and work, there is the stronger theme of using participant observation to overcome one's own anxieties in meeting a stranger, so that one can move from some slight area of commonality to the larger realm of differences in experience and life pattern that make each stranger an opportunity for growth.

In 1946, Sullivan summarized his approach to the field of psychiatry and psychiatric research; he might have used the same words in alerting anyone engaged in research into human behavior:

Individual differences, especially those which are principally matters of language and customs in people from widely separate parts of the world, may be extremely impressive and may present great handicap to discovering the significant differences in relative adequacy and appropriateness of action in interpersonal relations, which constitute extraordinary success, average living, or mental disorder.

The therapist or the research psychiatrist, however, participates intelligently in interpersonal relations with his confrere only to the extent that these handicaps are successfully overcome or evaded and finds opportunity to gain skill in this particular in his dealings with any stranger. (Sullivan, 1953a, pp. xii-xiii)

NOTE

1. At the time that the review was written and published (1947), I was working for Sullivan and was responsible for preparing the manuscript for publication; while I remembered some thirty years later the general content of the review, I was astounded to discover the reference to biography while I was sorting out Sullivan's professional relationship to Benedict.

ON STUDYING EMOTIONALLY HOT TOPICS:
Lessons From An Investigation Of
Organizational Death

Robert I. Sutton and Susan J. Schurman

We anticipated that a study of organizational death would require us to face strong emotion. This research entailed interviews with decision makers who had been in the thick of organizational death. Their reports were needed to help generate a theory of this organizational transition. We felt ready for this challenging fieldwork because of lessons gained from prior research with relatively benign topics. But we were unpleasantly surprised by the level and diversity of emotion encountered during initial efforts to interview managers, administrators, and union leaders. These expeditions into the real world at first strained our research skills, as well as our self-esteem. Later, they enlightened us about the unique demands of studying topics that evoke red-hot emotion.

Consider two of our early adventures. Schurman tried to call an informant at her home; the informant's husband answered. Schurman's field notes reveal,

> His response caught me completely off-guard. First he started yelling (literally) at me about graduate students, worthless social science research, voyeurism, etc., and assured me that his wife would have no interest in talking to me. Gradually, as he discovered a receptive audience, he turned from his tirade on grad students to the topic of the closing, which he termed 'the greatest screw job in the history of the state.' During the conversation the informant's son was standing in the background stirring his father on to further grievances about the closing. We were on the phone about 50 minutes.

Schurman was shocked by the conversation. She and Sutton spent an hour talking about the episode in an effort to make sense of it, and its implications for subsequent data gathering. Schurman also complained that working on this study was turning out to be far more effort than she bargained for, primarily because of the amount of emotion evoked by organizational death.

Anger was expressed by other gatekeepers, as well as by many informants with whom we spoke. One informant whom Sutton telephoned, for example, was a well-educated professional. Sutton expected at least the pretense of courtesy. He explained the nature of the research and asked if the informant wished to participate The professional told Sutton that he was a "mother-fucker." The informant got over his anger, however, and eventually participated in a series of enlightening interviews. Sutton worried about this conversation. He worried that, because of the level of emotion associated with organizational death, the research would cost more money, take more time, and cause more stress among members of the research team than first anticipated. He also worried that collecting quality data about this topic would be hampered by this red-hot emotion.

These two examples illustrate angry responses, and their influence on two researchers. Other profound emotional responses were also encountered throughout the research. One informant, for example, placed extreme and unwarranted faith in our ability to help him understand what he had just endured in the management of a dying organization. Another informant was very calm, but persistently lied to us, as well as to others, about his intentions and past behavior. Still other informants were so depressed that they reported feeling "numb."

The profound threat associated with this topic is illustrated by questionnaire responses of 23 informants who had been members of the eight defunct organizations. These managers, administrators, and union leaders were asked to compare the closing experience with five increasingly threatening life events: (1) receiving a parking ticket; (2) an argument with a friend or relative; (3) a serious illness; (4) a divorce; (5) the death of a spouse. On the average, the 23 former members reported that involvement in the closing was somewhat worse (3.39 on a five point scale) than having a serious illness. That organizational death can entail a profound strain is accentuated by the responses of 9 of the 23 (39%) former members. These 9 people revealed that the closing was comparable to divorce or the death of a spouse.

Working with these distraught informants taught us some important lessons. Perhaps the primary methodological lesson is that studying hot topics requires a more complex exchange relationship between researcher and informant. In return for providing data, informants expected us to listen, give them feedback, or give them advice—in short, to provide them with social support (House, 1981). Our experience with emotionally cold topics (e.g., a study of personnel practices) and warm topics (e.g., quality of work life) had not sufficiently prepared us for the strength and range of this need.

The remainder of the chapter explores this and other lessons gained from our research on organizational death and extends them to additional topics that arouse strong emotion among informants. We first consider conditions that give rise to hot topics. Then we describe the altered exchange relationship that arises when working with distressed informants, the influence of this relationship on the researcher, and coping techniques for the researcher. Next, the third section explores methods for enhancing the quality of data collected from distraught informants. Finally, the fourth section introduces some sticky ethical dilemmas that arise in high temperature research.

CONDITIONS THAT GIVE RISE TO EMOTIONALLY HOT TOPICS

Predicting which topics give rise to red-hot emotion is important: They place unique demands on the relationship between researcher and informant, and a special combination of methods is required for gathering high-quality data on such topics. Conditions likely to give rise to emotionally hot topics are proposed in Figure 17.1. The figure builds on the Institute for Social Research's model of social-environmental determinants of stress and health (Katz & Kahn, 1978). Starting from the left of the figure, distraught informants may be encountered when studying profound transitions at four levels of analysis: community, organizational, work group, and individual.

The purpose of this model is *not* to offer a formal theory of stress, strain, or disruptions, although it does have some elements of such a theory. Rather, its purpose is to provide researchers with indicators or "tip-offs" that the topic is emotionally hot. Thus, the presence of these disruptions does not assure that one will be working with distraught informants; nor does their absence make certain that one will not be working with such informants. In addition, these transitions are interdependent rather than independent. In our study of organizational death, for example, an economic depression in Michigan led to more frequent organizational deaths, which in turn led to the demise of more work

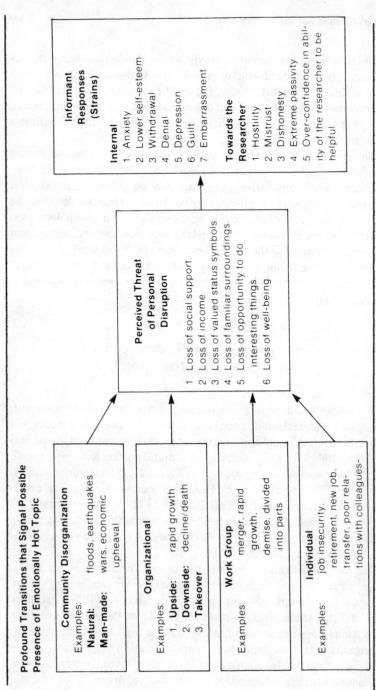

Figure 17.1 Conditions that May Give Rise to Emotionally Hot Topics in Organizational Research

groups. These social system transitions increased the occurrence of individual job loss, transfers, and early retirement.

These transitions, separately or in combination, may cause the informant to perceive (and objectively experience) personal disruption. The researcher is studying a hot topic to the extent that a high proportion of informants will experience or have experienced the threat of personal disruption. Disruption of organized response appears to be stressful for all organisms (Mandler & Watson, 1966).

These profound disruptions have two varieties of effects on informant responses that are relevant to our discussion. These informant responses (see Figure 17.1) include internal reactions to stress, such as anxiety, lower self-esteem, withdrawal, denial, depression, guilt, and embarrassment. These are typical reactions (usually labelled strain) to occupational stress (see, for example, Cobb & Kasl, 1977; Katz & Kahn, 1978).

Yet informant responses are not exclusively internal. These strains spill over to the informant's relationships with other people, including the researcher. Hostility, mistrust, dishonesty, passivity, and overconfidence in the researcher's ability to help the informant are thought to be common responses to this disruption. These and similar responses place unique demands on the study of hot topics.

This model for predicting the presence of a hot topic may prove helpful, but it must be used along with practical research skills. It is important, for example, to ask colleagues for advice about the topic that one is studying. Moreover, preliminary expeditions into the real world are essential if a high temperature topic is suspected. Such expeditions enhanced our research. Sutton interviewed several informants, and most were distraught. He did not fully appreciate the distinct demands of emotionally hot topics immediately, but these expeditions did improve the research design. These early warnings were also helpful because they encouraged him to seek people for the research team who had strong field skills.

Finally, the research worker must also consider the content of the data collected and the research methods employed. Strong emotions should be expected to the extent that informants are directly queried about threats of personal disruption. Thus, in our study of organizational death, questions about organizational size rarely evoked strong emotion. In contrast, questions about the fate of employees or decision makers were often followed by strong emotion. In addition, the strength of emotional responses is linked to the data-gathering methods used. Qualitative methods that entail working closely with informants create arenas in which strong emotional responses toward the investigator are possible.

THE RELATIONSHIP BETWEEN RESEARCHER
AND INFORMANT

This chapter has a persistent theme: Working with distraught informants requires special skills. The investigator studying a hot topic is compelled for ethical reasons, and forced for practical reasons, to enter into a different kind of relationship with informants than is customary for research on cold topics. Investigators conducting cold research have generally not had to give much in exchange for what they get. The price of data is usually the intrinsic satisfaction the informant gains for contributing to the lofty, but intangible, goal of scientific knowledge.

Upset informants expect more in exchange. They often expect the researcher to abandon the traditional, emotionally neutral posture and adopt a more clinical posture. This section describes the altered exchange relationship, its influence on the researcher, and coping strategies for the researcher.

THE ALTERED EXCHANGE RELATIONSHIP

A variety of authors have prescribed a reciprocal relationship between researcher and informant (e.g., May, 1980; D'Aunno & Price, 1983; Cassell, 1980). These recommendations are usually based on moral and epistemological considerations. In contrast, we found that a reciprocal relationship was unavoidable for studying hot topics. Many informants simply would not tolerate an asymmetrical relationship. They usually expected, and sometimes demanded, greater than ordinary inducements in exchange for participating in the research.

The additional inducement expected most often by the upset informants we worked with is best described as social support (Cobb, 1976; House, 1981). House's four dimensions of social support are useful for illustrating the range of help that distraught informants can be provided:

(1) *emotional support:* providing empathy, trust, and simply listening to the informant;
(2) *appraisal support:* providing data that allow the informant to compare him- or herself to similar others;
(3) *informational support:* providing information that allows the informant to cope with problems, usually information that helps people help themselves; and
(4) *instrumental support:* instrumental actions that directly help an informant in need.

The exchange relationships in our research extended to the first three forms of support only.

All informants expected us to provide them with some emotional support. In exchange for providing us with data about the closing, they expected us to listen attentively when they discussed personal problems. We had to be careful to strike a balance between how much we should gently prod informants back to the content of our questions and how much we should simply listen. Although this is always a challenge for interviewers, the magnitude is far greater when working with distressed informants. It was not uncommon for our gentle prods to be answered with hostile comments such as, "So I thought you wanted to hear my story." And many other informants simply ignored our efforts to structure the conversation and continued to talk about whatever they wished.

Some informants sought appraisal support. This is consistent with research suggesting that human beings in distress have a strong need to compare themselves to similar others (Singer, 1980). Singer proposes that social comparison allows humans in distress to evaluate and adjust their responses. Informants often asked us, "What did managers in other closings do in this situation?" Although we often sidestepped such questions, we sometimes felt it was appropriate to respond; it would help informants who had done much to help us. The ex-president of a defunct hospital (who had been extremely helpful) questioned us persistently about efforts other dying organizations had made to help displaced employees. His organization provided assistance for the unemployed that was superior to the other organizational deaths we had studied. We felt compelled to tell him this fact.

In contrast to emotional and appraisal support, we gave little informational support to informants. We did not give specific advice about managing closings, for example. Nonetheless, the feedback that we gave in exchange for participation included not only a complete journal article on "Managing Organizational Death" (Sutton, 1983); it also included a complete copy of the special issue of the journal in which the article appeared, which was on "The Management of Organizational Decline." This was provided because so many informants insisted that they had better get plenty of feedback about our findings. Finally, in looking back, we should have arrived at interviews with a list of therapists or at least referral agencies. Such information might have been needed by those who were suffering profound psychological distress.

Social support is a resource that those who study emotionally hot topics may exchange for data. We found that listening and understanding, rather than making judgments (which are so rampant in organizational death), was what informants wanted most often. The pressure of managing these responsibilities can be difficult for the researcher. This problem is addressed next.

THE INFLUENCE ON THE RESEARCHER OF WORKING WITH DISTRAUGHT INFORMANTS

The members of our research team responded in a variety of ways to working with informants who were angry, depressed, confused, distrustful, or otherwise difficult. Anger and guilt were perhaps our most common reactions. Our anger tended to arise in response to informant anger. At times, we would have to work very hard not to lose our tempers at informants who attacked us personally. Sutton, for example, was tempted to holler at the foul-mouthed professional described in the introduction to this chapter.

Perhaps the greatest anger, however, was evoked in response to the head of a dying organization who lied about us behind our backs. This administrator never directly refused to be interviewed. Instead, he always claimed "I'm too busy, call me back later." His superior was one of the informants in our research. The superior contacted the administrator and asked if he had any knowledge of our research. The administrator claimed he had not heard of our study and expressed anger at us for studying the organization without his permission. Yet, he had heard of the study *and* given us permission. Sutton and two other members of the research team were very angry at this dishonest informant who made them look bad. Moreover, we were extremely frustrated because we perceived that it was not possible to tell the superior the "true" story because of research ethics. This incident took much time—we held many meetings to decide how to handle this fellow. Our anger toward him was so strong, however, that most of the meeting time was spent complaining about this "liar," which hindered the progress of the research.

Guilt was also a common response among those of us on the research team. We worried that the fellow who accused social scientists of voyeurism was correct. Moreover, we often worried that participation in our research increased the work load of informants who were already overwhelmed with hundreds of tasks. Sutton worried about his impact on an informant who had a heart attack shortly after participating in the research. Sutton had put much pressure on this distressed fellow to produce archival data about the closing, and the informant had complained a great deal about the extra work.

The distress evoked within us by these emotional episodes sometimes interfered with our performance on subsequent research tasks. Some members of the research team responded to their own guilt and anger with psychological detachment from informants and with procrastination. The psychological detachment made it more difficult for us to feel and act concerned in response to the troubles of other informants. Such responses may have interfered with our performance, particularly because social support (which requires the expression of concern) was the primary resource expected by informants.

A second response to this stress was procrastinating about telephoning potential informants. Sutton, for example, put off planned phone calls to other informants for several weeks after he was verbally assaulted by the professional.

Clearly, not performing research tasks interferes with the quality of the research. But psychological and behavioral detachment are not without virtue. These "time outs" helped us to continue our long-term efforts. Despite the widely advertised evils of procrastination, putting off phone calls for a few weeks helped us regain our ability to be supportive and reduced the probability that we would abandon the research. Other coping strategies for researchers who study hot topics are explored next.

COPING STRATEGIES FOR THE RESEARCHER

Our experience suggests some steps that can be taken to manage the negative influence of distraught informants on researcher well-being and performance.

Anticipate the emotional temperature of the topic. As suggested above, forecasting that the research topic is hot helps eliminate a poor study design. The model presented earlier can help researchers anticipate emotionally hot topics. When an initial assessment suggests that the topic is hot, a research strategy may be needed that is appropriate for the special demands of gathering data from distraught informants.

We learned a variety of ways to plan for strong emotion. Sutton enlisted the help of a clinical psychologist after his first encounters with distraught informants. Following from the psychologist's suggestions, Sutton designed an "initial observation form." The form included open- and closed-ended questions about the potential informant's emotional responses—including anger, depression, and denial. This form prepared us for the crucial first few minutes with informants. It made salient the importance of initial contacts (usually telephone calls) and it prepared us to expect profound affect.

As implied above in the discussion of procrastination, we also learned not to contact people when we were distracted or distressed. We noted a positive correlation between our psychological preparedness and our success in obtaining informant participation. Similarly, we found conducting interviews when tired or upset to be an error.

Develop necessary clinical skills. The implications of our experience are clear: Greater skill at providing support increased the chances of informant cooperation and satisfaction, and reduced researcher stress. This suggests the research team studying a hot topic should be composed of people who can provide support. This means not only selecting people with such skills, but also using techniques such as role plays to help interviewers learn how to cope with upset informants. In our research, the degree of a researcher's clinical skill often determined failure or success at gaining entry to a research setting.

Build in a social support for the researchers. Studying hot topics increases the researcher's own need for social support. After our initial encounters with informants revealed the emotional intensity we would be facing, we found ourselves relying on each other for emotional support. Later, as additional researchers were added, we adopted regular meetings in which part of the time was devoted to discussing difficult encounters with informants. While this kind of research can certainly be conducted by solitary researchers, we recommend collaboration as a means of obtaining social support.

METHODS FOR ENHANCING THE QUALITY OF DATA COLLECTED FROM DISTRAUGHT INFORMANTS

Studying hot topics may require abandoning the "standard rules" of the research game derived from the traditional scientific method. This notion was suggested above and will be explored further in this section. Specifically, we consider (1) retrospective data; (2) nonparticipants; and (3) deviations from common field research practices.

RETROSPECTIVE DATA

The use of retrospective data is usually discouraged by methodologists. The negative effect of "history" (Cook & Campbell, 1979) on efforts to specify causal relationships is widely known. Similarly, research on shortcomings in human inference (Nisbett & Ross, 1980; Fischhoff, 1982) suggests that human judgments about the occurrence and causes of past events confirm the definition of *recollect* from *The*

Devil's Dictionary (Bierce, 1911): "to recall with additions something not previously known."

Our research concerned organizations that had recently closed and thus used much retrospective data. And our concern about the hazards of relying on human recollections influenced the research design. Effort was put forth to interview multiple informants with diverse perspectives in each closing. Moreover, much time was spent gathering pertinent organizational records, which provided prospective data. Finally, we attempted to study two closings prospectively: One attempt was moderately successful, but the other was terminated by management before much data could be gathered.

A primary lesson for studying emotionally hot topics is that, in contrast to cold topics, retrospective research has distinct strengths. When people are trapped in the turmoil of an organization closing or other profound transition, they often do not have either the time or the inclination to speak with a curious behavioral scientist. In the aborted effort to study the large department store, for example, the research was terminated partly because the management was so busy orchestrating the complex transition that they did not have time to speak with us. Management also worried that we would leak information to the press about the closing that could damage the reputation of the parent organization. In this closing, and other ongoing closings, we were told to call back after the crisis had passed because people would have time to participate only after it was over. Moreover, fears about leaks to the press would be less salient to management after the closing was complete.

Several potential informants also asserted that it was rude to study them during the throes of distress. One woman (a gatekeeper) told Schurman that it "was outrageous that you people would call at a time like this. Don't you have any idea what an upsetting thing this is?" Similarly Wortman and her colleagues (1980) report that it is impossible (and insensitive) to study rape victims immediately after an assault or to interview victims of spinal cord injuries while they are suffering acute pain. Data collection must be retrospective in such cases.

This discussion also implies that, in emotionally hot research, response rates among individuals and organizations are likely to be higher with a retrospective design. Thus, even using the logic of the traditional scientific method, the quality of the sample obtained when using retrospective data may help compensate for the hazards of human recollections. This is not a design consideration in studies of most cold topics. And perhaps more important, it can be unethical or simply rude to invade the privacy of people while they are suffering severe distress.

NONPARTICIPANTS

Our research also revealed that people who *decline* to participate in hot research may provide more useful evidence than can be gathered from nonparticipants in cold research. This lesson is an important by-product of the "initial observation form" we used to summarize initial conversations with potential informants. When potential informants were unable or unwilling to participate in an extended interview, they were often willing to have a short telephone conversation about the closing. These responses were recorded on the observation form. The profound emotion generated by this transition caused many "nonparticipants" to give us detailed information, which taught us additional lessons about organizational death.

Refusals to participate often came from gatekeepers rather than directly from the chosen informant. The comments made by gatekeepers (such as the one described above who told Schurman that her call was an "outrageous" act) also gave us valuable information. As a result, the initial observation form had provisions for recording gatekeeper responses.

DEVIATIONS FROM COMMON FIELD RESEARCH PRACTICES

Standard practices for collecting questionnaire and structured interview data emphasize that the research should *not* be described to the subject in detail. This form of "error from the investigator" (Webb, Campbell, Schwartz, Sechrest, & Grove, 1981) is thought to bias responses during the remainder of the interview. Similarly, consider the instructions given to professional interviewers at the University of Michigan's Institute for Social Research:

> Remember not to be too specific about the interview in introducing yourself and the survey to the respondent. It is important that you avoid introducing a bias into the interview which might predispose the respondent to answer in a particular way. Very general statements such as: "We are interested in how people are getting along these days" or "We're talking to people all over the country to see how they feel things are going in the world today" are usually quite successful. (Interviewer's Manual, Survey Research Center, 1976, pp. 7-8)

We tried to follow these instructions during our pretesting efforts. We soon learned, however, that potential informants would rarely tolerate such vague statements. Because of the attributes of organizational death, many had recently learned to mistrust fellow human beings greatly. They responded to vague descriptions of the study with pointed questions such as "Exactly what are you going to do with this information?" and "Exactly what is in this project for you?" Thus, we found it was necessary to give them a relatively detailed summary of our research design. While such information probably biased the interviews, it was better than conducting no interviews at all.

The stress and paranoia generated by hot topics requires researchers to make the nature of the exchange relationship more explicit. D'Aunno and Price (1983) suggest that explicit negotiation of all research relationships is desirable because "when this exchange is negotiated openly in a context of mutual respect, the product should be both more scientifically sound and more useful to the community." While explicit negotiation of the exchange relationship may be desirable in emotionally cold or warm research (despite its biasing effects), it is essential when studying topics that evoke profound hostility, depression, guilt, and confusion among informants. Participants in hot research often have more to lose than those in cold research, and demands for information about what they are getting involved with are justified.

Along similar lines, we found that this exchange relationship forced us to reveal more about ourselves than is customary, or deemed desirable, in emotionally cold research. One very nervous informant spent a full hour responding to Sutton's interview questions with his own questions about Sutton's personal life. Sutton gently told him, "I'd rather not answer such personal questions." The informant became angry and said, "You are asking me all these personal questions, why the hell can't I ask you a few?" While such profound pressure for self-disclosure by the interviewer was unusual, our research suggests that there is greater pressure for self-disclosure in red-hot research. This appears necessary because informants need to trust the interviewer more than in cold or warm research, and moderate levels of self-disclosure can encourage such trust.

Hot topics may also force the investigator to abandon widely accepted practices about the use of interview protocols. Common instructions to interviewers include "Ask the questions exactly as they are worded in the questionnaire," "Ask the questions in the order in which they are presented in the questionnaire," and "Ask every question specified in the questionnaire" (Survey Research Center, 1976; Babbie, 1973).

The qualities of the exchange relationship likely to emerge when studying emotionally hot topics conflict with this demand for control over the subjects' behavior. Informants we interviewed would often insist on telling their own story in their own way. In addition, we sometimes did not ask questions from our interview just exactly as they were worded because an informant, we judged, would be offended. We also frequently deviated from the order in which questions were presented in the interview. If an informant talked about the aftermath of the closing before speaking about how the decision was made (especially if he or she was upset about it) we would let him or her talk.

Thus, strong expectations held by informants who participate in emotionally hot research may interfere with or make impossible the use of a highly structured protocol. While deviations from the interview protocol are common in studies that seek to discover hypotheses, such pressures are even stronger when working with distraught informants. Our research calls into question the ethics of using only closed-ended response options (such as Likert scales) when studying hot topics. While we did leave informants with a questionnaire at the end of the interview, this was done after the exchange relationship had been negotiated.

ETHICAL DILEMMAS

Some sticky ethical dilemmas arise in high temperature research. These dilemmas can be separated into two categories, corresponding to a pair of major ethical requirements governing research conducted with human subjects: informed consent and voluntary participation.

INFORMED CONSENT

We have argued that discovering hypotheses requires a flexible research design that can be altered as the study proceeds. We have further argued that informants in our study demand greater knowledge of the research design than is typically encountered in emotionally cold research. The conventional standard of informed consent is difficult to apply in this case because it creates an ethical dilemma. To what exactly is the participant consenting? How much information is necessary for consent to be informed? One practical solution to this problem is to portray the research design to prospective participants with more certainty and specificity than actually exists. The researcher is then faced with the possibility that the research plan will change and the participant will have an inaccurate impression of the study. Sutton, for example, told a number of participants that he planned to use closed-ended survey questions extensively. As the study evolved, these data proved less useful and played a much smaller role than anticipated. Did these participants have informed consent?

A related ethical difficulty concerns whether or not distraught participants can be considered informed and consenting. Consider one interview that Sutton had with an informant who was very angry and upset. Sutton judged that much of what the informant said was confused and distorted, possibly as a result of extreme anxiety. Sutton recalls wondering "Should I end this interview? This guy is really upset." Sutton also wondered how to terminate the interview gracefully. It was difficult to decide which was worse: to continue the interview or try to end it. How does the investigator judge when an informant is too upset? Can prematurely terminating an interview compound the informant's distress?

Sutton's response to the distraught informant in the above example illustrates yet another ethical problem in hot research. After weighing the pros and cons of continuing or ending the interview, Sutton elected to continue. One explanation for this decision is that, despite Sutton's reservations about the impact of the interview on the informant, his role as researcher caused Sutton to make the wrong choice. Conflicting role demands such as this can lead to ethical dilemmas for any research conducted in organizational settings (Mirvis & Seashore, 1979) and are especially likely in emotionally hot research.

VOLUNTARY PARTICIPATION

True voluntary participation may be a rare event in organizational research (Mirvis & Seashore, 1979; Schurman, 1982). Role expectations for organization members reduce or eliminate their freedom to refuse participation. Mirvis and Seashore observe that "researchers are dealing with a social system composed of people who have positions in a hierarchy . . . researchers cannot approach participants in the study as individuals because they behave within an interdependent framework of rights and responsibilities" (p. 79).

The reality of social organization is that, depending on their position in the hierarchy, people can be subtly coerced into "volunteering." Although the effects of such coerced participation are generally acknowledged to be benign, even by many who are critical on ethical grounds (e.g., Wax, 1980), it is not clear that the results of involuntary participation in hot research are benign. Such participation may exacerbate an already distraught person's emotional discomfort. The problem of potential coercion compounds the difficult ethical issue in emotionally hot research previously discussed.

None of the ethical problems described are unique to emotionally hot research, although we have tried to show that they are both more likely and more salient in such research. They are endemic to social research, especially research that relies on qualitative methods. The traditional ethical safeguards are both difficult to apply and relatively meaningless in such research. Some researchers have proposed alterations to the traditional ethical framework governing social research. Wax (1980) has suggested that consent be viewed as a *process* in which the informant and researcher develop a certain relationship within which consent is a progressive development based on shared understanding rather than an *event*. Similarly, Mirvis and Seashore (1979) have argued that the task of the "action-researcher" is to "create ethical relationships" with organization members.

The notion that doing ethical social science stems not from a priori contracts between researchers and subjects, but from the development of ethical relationships between researchers and informants, has a firm basis in both philosophy and practice. Implementation of such a concept in organizational settings on hot research topics is not without serious problems. Few clear guidelines exist about how to form such relationships with multiple organizational actors or how to maintain such relationships with conflicting actors.

We recommend that researchers studying hot topics in organizations turn to the applied organizational change literature for models of developing ethical relationships with informants.

CONCLUSION

The study of hot topics that evoke red-hot emotion creates an arena for the researcher in which both costs and benefits are greater than for cold topics. The advantages are potentially great: Hot topics often concern more pressing social problems, problems of more import to informants, and topics of greater interest to both scholars and the general public. The difficulties associated with hot topics are also greater, however. These include requirements for more resources for the amount of data gathered, more threats to the validity of findings because "tried and true" approaches are less likely to be effective, and greater risk of ethical dilemmas.

This chapter has introduced some guidelines for researchers who choose to face these hazards and opportunities. We proposed a model to help researchers identify conditions that give rise to emotionally hot topics. We specified some attributes of the exchange relationship that emerge when distraught informants expect social support from the researcher in return for the data they provide. Next, it was suggested that hot topics call into question some widely accepted research practices. Finally, we introduced some ethical dilemmas that are exacerbated by the unique demands of hot topics.

We end this article with a suggestion and a comment. First the suggestion. We urge our colleagues to take special care to document the natural history of research on emotionally hot topics. Little is known about conducting it in nontherapeutic settings, and documentation of both successful and unsuccessful approaches is needed to improve the quality of future research. We are especially concerned that those who conduct hypothesis testing research on hot topics will hesitate to be open about natural history since, as Van Maanen observes, "coming clean" is less common in this variety of research (Van Maanen, Dabbs, & Faulkner, 1982).

And now the comment. In exploring the peculiarities of emotionally hot research we have questioned the unqualified value of the traditional scientific method as a guiding force for all organizational research. We do not, however, believe that assumptions and methods that stem from the traditional approach are flawed. On the contrary, they are valuable and appropriate for many (but not all) research problems.

Along these lines, we contend that a wide range of methods must be used in parallel to best discover the qualities of organizations and of life within them. This call may sound trite, as it is repeated often in the literature. We are concerned, however, by how widely it is ignored by those who study organizations. We worry about some harsh battles we have recently witnessed between colleagues of different perspectives. Nasty exchanges have been observed about the relative virtues, for example, of applied versus basic, quantitative versus qualitative, and macro versus micro views of organizations.

Disagreement is valuable when it enhances knowledge. Yet, much of what we have observed can only be described as poorly disguised warfare over the value of one's "turf" rather than sincere efforts to enhance knowledge. In the spirit of seeking enhanced knowledge about organizations, it is our hope that research on emotionally hot topics continues and grows because it is an important *addition* to the organizational studies literature.

18

ASSESSING LOCAL CAUSALITY IN QUALITATIVE RESEARCH

A. Michael Huberman and Matthew B. Miles

"Causality" has a bad name these days among social scientific researchers. Mention the term and you can expect most of your colleagues, to borrow the surrealists' dictum, to reach for their epistemological pistols. Logically enough, the quickest draws are those of action theorists, phenomenologists, ethnomethodologists, and interpretive sociologists, for whom exercises in causal deduction or causal inference represent the worst sort of neopositivism.

Our own work during the past few years has been to reinstate the legitimacy and power of causal analysis in empirical research, and to reinstate it, in particular, in the type of clinical or qualitative research described in this volume. We argue that the determination of causal influence is both appropriate and feasible in social research, and that it need not be done solely with the algorithms of structural equations, covariance matrices, or confirmatory factor analysis.

For us to claim that the determination of causal relationships is both legitimate and feasible in qualitative research has a tantalizing shock value in such a volume as this. It is a strong claim, smacking of hubris; how can it be justified, both conceptually and operationally? That is the agenda for this chapter. First, we shall examine some of the epistemological issues rumbling away beneath the issue of causality. Then we identify the types of causal determination one is called upon to make in social research, and describe the kinds of clinical knowledge enabling a researcher to do this. We draw from past work in analytic induction, social judgment, and qualitative studies to define the requirements of a good methodology for causal analysis.

Having grounded these procedures conceptually, we then ground them operationally, by illustrating at the nuts-and-bolts level just how one can work with qualitative data, incrementally and analytically, to build causal "maps" of local settings and events.

Finally, in covering this terrain, we shall be attentive to the stream of meaning-communicating and meaning-negotiating transactions between the researcher and informants in the field, and how those transactions affect the determination of causality.

We have approached this chapter—and our work—in a systematic, cognitive way, believing that drawing valid conclusions about causality is the product of thoughtful or sense-making activity, both on our part and the part of the people whose lives we are studying. We state our views crisply for clarity, and hope they will not be mistaken for smugness or dogma.

CAUSAL REALISM AND CAUSAL IDEALISM: FINDING THE MIDDLE GROUND

Arguing about the epistemological bases of causal deduction and inference has become so elaborate, passionate, and discipline-specific that it is more straightforward to state a stance and flesh it out, than to erect the ritual conceptual scaffold that will justify one's preferences and elegantly cut opponents' throats. The epistemological litmus test here is how one responds to Hume's classic dilemma: How can one postulate unobservable *connections* among events? The events themselves can be observed, as can the recurring associations between those events, but the *relationships* between these events require our adding more than we can observe.

For a causal idealist, whatever we choose to add—latent variables, constructs, propositions, laws, theories—involves an *arbitrary decision* as to how, conceptually, we prefer to carve up the social universe. Some regularities may be there to be observed, at least temporarily, and the links we postulate between them may be plausible. So, too, are the theories we generate to coordinate those plausible links into a meaningful set—but it is *we* who put the meaning there. The world, as Hanson (1958, p. 14) has put it, is not held together by cosmic glue. Or, more brutally, as Wittgenstein wrote in the *Tractatus,* "causes are superstitions."

For a causal realist, on the other hand, the belief is that the constants or regularities observable in the social world can be expressed in the form of *lawful statements* whose validity is independent of individual cognition. There are lawful patterns out there to be discovered, whether or not we are aware of them or can articulate them. By specifying the conditions under which these processes obtain, by accurately predicting their presence or absence, and by progressively correcting the extant bodies of explanation, we can get a progressively better fix on the laws undergirding events in the world.

It is important to say that causal idealism and causal realism represent a *continuum* more than a dichotomy. There are few people operating at the conceptual extremes, apart from the epistemologists still trying to sharpen distinctions. Scratch those epistemologists, however, and you will find many of them taking a personal stance nearer the middle than at the poles. Virtually no one contends that social processes are wholly solipsistic, nor will anyone claim that such processes correspond to Kantian categories. More important, there are virtually *no* working researchers at the extremes. For example, the social phenomenological research derived from Husserl and Schutz has invariably contained some systematic, inferential procedures for determining such lawful constructs as indexality, et cetera rules, typification, or reflexivity. Conversely, most major neopositivist (i.e., realist) methodologists (see Snow, 1974; Cronbach, 1975; Cook & Campbell, 1979) have shifted toward more perceptual, context-embedded, and interpretive inquiry.

As with all continua, there are middle points—the ones that disappear when militant conceptual partitioning tries to force us into one camp or the other. In the middle lie several, conceptually coherent epistemologies, of which perhaps the best known is "transcendental realism" (Bhaskar, 1975, 1982; Harré, 1972; Manicas & Secord, 1982). Since our own stance is largely reflected here, let us briefly review the basic tenets.

As causal realists, these authors postulate a social patterning that exists independently of cognizing experience. This patterning is not a description of classes of events, but rather an expression of the *causal properties* of structures operating in the world. In that sense, theoretical entities are not hypothetical, but real. This is the operative passage in Manicas and Secord:

Scientific explanation is not subsumption. Rather, it is causal explanation, and it demands that we show how in each particular case a particular causal configuration occurred that had just the achieved result. . . . Explanation thus requires knowledge of the causal properties of the configured structures *and* a historical grasp of the particular and changing configuration. (p. 403)

Such terms as "historical grasp" and "changing configuration" reflect the middle-groundedness of this theory. Transcendental realists assume that social patterns will change—and that social theory, as a social and historical product, has to chase after those changes. They also assume that while we can *explain* social phenomena, we cannot really *predict* them. There will always be an enormous range of co-determining variables, forming complex, shifting configurations.

The consistencies we seek are, in effect, idiosyncratically organized. There is neither full determination nor complete closure, but there are recurrent contingencies and causal tendencies that can be identified and mapped, so as to render some explanations more powerful, more fully saturated, than others. Finally, social behaviors and structures arise in part from motivated human acts—understandings, meanings, intentions—so that the phenomenological dimension is a necessary, although not sufficient, component of those lawful processes we seek to explain.

A positivist epistemology that makes short shrift of correspondence theory, empirical probabilism, and predictive validity, while still making coherent claims to verifiable explanation, is an interesting one. It is especially interesting because it incorporates some of the core components of the idealist position as well—socially generated meanings, intentionality and reflexivity, historicism. In doing this, transcendental realism, like other middle-ground epistemologies (e.g., Campbell, 1975), enables us to draw methods from both the psychometric and phenomenological traditions—to wed clinical/qualitative approaches to actuarial/quantitative techniques.

But its more immediate interest is reflected in the excerpt just cited. The stress is on *causal*, rather than on purely *functional*, explanations. One is not talking about "interdependencies" or "functional relations" among variables—the customary way of sidestepping the issue of causal inference—but about *directional* influences exerted among patterned interactions.

At the same time, transcendental realists are demanding that the governing patterns be continuously connected to the empirical relationships from which they are derived. That is, causal analysis must be *contextualized*, case by case. Thus we cannot translate events and processes into equations "representing" them, as one would routinely in mathematical modeling. We have to stay with the "real" world, and build up to a smaller number of more-inclusive properties that actually function as causal agents in that world. We can identify, perhaps even determine, "local" causality, and can overlay two or more local cause maps, but cannot determine "general" causality—because there is none.

Just *how* we should go about this is not yet clear, but some of the contours are there. We shall need to stay close to the settings themselves. We must define the "variables" we observe there in contextually meaningful ways, listening closely to how actors in the setting define them. We must avoid context-stripping data transformations (e.g., converting descriptors to numbers). And we must ground the inferred causal patterns in the specific events and processes constituting them, not plaster existing theoretical constructs onto them. From this initial list, it is already clear that the methodologies we shall need derive more from a qualitative research paradigm than from a correlational or experimental one.

CLINICAL KNOWLEDGE AND CAUSAL INFERENCE

First things first: What is local causality knowledge *of*? It is knowledge, we have said, of recurring, patterned social phenomena whose recurrence and pattern we infer from concrete empirical instances. We infer it post hoc: We can explain it (the past is determined), but cannot really predict it (the future is not). Such knowledge is often awesomely complex and multilayered. It is unstable, as are any sociohistorical phenomena, so that we must periodically unbundle and reassemble our explanations, unless we work at the most superordinate or general level of theory—which is typically too general to pack much explanatory power for the relatively specific and contingent nature of local determinisms. If we choose to work descriptively, as an ethnographer would, we might agree easily on *what* constitutes an account of local events and processes. But we are shooting higher here, for the *why* and *how* of the what, and there will be several plausible—and contending—explanations in play at that level. The higher the level of inference, the more uncertain and multiple become the truth estimates.

So how will we know when our causal explanations are correct? No metaphysical buzzer is going to go off. Credible analysts will always find legitimate points of disagreement. We are solving neither puzzles nor crimes, which have straightforward algorithms for finding unequivocal solutions. On the other hand—and this is important—some explanations *are* likely to be more compelling than others: They will get more agreement from credible judges; they provide a closer fit with the complete (albeit imperfect, forcibly ambiguous) set of data. It may be that no single explanation is unequivocally correct; but some are better than others, and not anything goes.

Cognitive psychologists and artificial intelligence analysts would say that in the issue of local causality we have an "ill-structured" (Simon, 1977) or "wicked" (Churchman, 1971) problem on our hands, and that this has important consequences for the ways in which the problem can be solved. We are in a propositional "problem space" that is closer to resolving real-world issues like alcoholism or pollution than to determining chemical reactions and physical laws. That is, we *can* resolve the chemistry of alcoholism and the physics of pollution, but we will not have solved the problem of how to deal with either. Worse, if we try to force the situation into one in which the problem *can* be solved by the rules, algorithms, and classical analytic techniques that we use for "well-structured" problems, we will, at best, have resolved only the well-structured part of the ill-structured problem—without knowing exactly which part that was.

In other words, problem spaces for which there exists a single, correct solution usually have either the solution contained in the formulation of the problem (as, for example, in logical deductions) or have preestablished rules—axioms, symbol strings, symbolic transformations—that, when correctly applied, produce the correct solution. Those well-structured problems are amenable to solution by these sets of rules and procedures, but this is not the case for ill-structured problems—like those of determining local causality. That tells us, for instance, that path analysis is not the appropriate solution to the problem of determining local causality. Nor would the formal procedures of logical and inductive inference be useful: They have not traditionally contended with real-world problems in a real-world problem space. We may be able to use some statistics and some procedures of inductive inference—indeed, we shall want to—but we cannot use them *conventionally* if our aim is to generate or to verify causal explanations of naturally-occurring social phenomena.

In short, the resolution of ill-structured problems is not well worked out. Churchman (1971) and others (e.g., Mitroff & Sagasti, 1973; Wood, 1983) have outlined appropriate "inquiry systems" for wicked problems— a "Kantian" approach to partly wicked problems and a "Hegelian" approach to very wicked ones. Unfortunately, the procedures are not well operationalized, and the guarantor of validity is the classic one: the degree of fit between, on the one hand, extant theory and theoretical predictions and, on the other, the data collected under the presumptions of the theory. There are real problems with this line of thought, especially if one subscribes to the middle-ground epistemologies. The "theory" is usually too broad-gauged to be "fitted" to local determinisms; local phenomena easily lend themselves to competing theoretical explanations; more contingent or condition-specific theories often trail far behind the sociohistorical shifts that best account for the data; and "prediction" is, as we said before, a dicey business. So while we are conceptually grateful to the wicked problem/inquiry system approach for indicating what kind of methodology is appropriate to the study of local causal determinism, we are still, technically speaking, naked.

Where does one look? There are a multitude of technologies contending for our minds, but few that claim to take on (1) multifaceted, context-specific social phenomena, *without* the use of (2) preestablished algorithmic or standardized transformations of those phenomena, and *still* come up with (3) causal or deterministic explanations.

Overall, we have borrowed from three methodological traditions. First, we have looked to standard procedures of analytic induction. Next, we have borrowed from the literature on clinical and social judgment. Finally, we have adapted various qualitative methodologies, both in the ethnographic and interpretive traditions. Let us briefly list what we have taken from each.

COMPONENTS OF AN ECLECTIC METHODOLOGY

Analytic induction. The general procedures of analytic induction (e.g., Swinburne, 1974; Hesse, 1974) are iterative; they follow a succession of question-and-answer cycles that entail examining a given set of cases, then modifying and refining that examination on the basis of subsequent cases. Progressively, the analyst scans the data for clusters of similar appearing or similarly functioning variables, and for the relationships among these phenomena. From these, working typologies and hypotheses are drawn, then tested during the next cycle of scanning, clustering and patterning. This requires an "investigative" approach (Douglas, 1976) to the conduct of fieldwork, if one adapts this model to social research.

Inductively derived conclusions are valid in the relaxed sense that they are probable, reasonable, or likely to be true. The premises and the evidence make the conclusions more compelling than any equally detailed rival. "Compelling" can be defined in a number of ways: as best-fitting to the rest of one's current knowledge of an issue; as functionally efficient when applied the next time; as internally complete and cohesive; as more consonant with the regnant constructs or pieces of theory. These alternatives are not mutually exclusive, and taken cumulatively they make for increasingly stronger claims. One can also add to this list. For example, we have looked for "phenomenological compellingness" in our conclusions—that is, conclusions with which several informants at a given field site concur independently. Such conclusions correspond to, although they are *not* necessarily formulated identically with, respondents' own explanations. While this list is a hybrid, there are a few inductivists who have systematized such criteria when the analyst is working with real-life, wicked data gathered from imperfect sources (see Rescher, 1976, 1980, on inductive plausibility).

So analytic induction can provide a general investigative approach for conducting qualitative research, along with some workable criteria for assessing the trustworthiness of conclusions. It can also offer some criteria for determining causal influence: the standard canons of temporal succession, constant conjunction, and directional influence. We shall be illustrating them shortly. Note for now, however, that these three are obviously weak criteria, necessary but nowhere near sufficient for the kinds of multilayered, interactive processes we are trying to pin down in the field. But when one combines them with some of the other criteria we have listed—conceptual consonance, fittingness, functional efficiency, and corroboration from local informants—they can make causal claims much weightier.

Clinical and social judgment. Theoretically, analysts using analytic induction procedures and criteria with complex, real-life data sets would generate more "valid" conclusions. The closest empirical analogue we have found is that of the "exceptional clinician" (Dunn, 1982), "connoisseur," or "expert." Overall, the analytic induction literature has described *general* procedures for essentially nonclinical or noninteractive investigations, while the clinical and connoisseurship literature has been more domain specific and much of it has focused on whether and how an individual can outperform standardized instruments and machine-generated diagnoses. Furthermore, much of it focuses more on how people *learn* to do things than on how much they *know* about what they are doing. But there may be useful insights here. Let's see.

If we start with the notion of the researcher as a qualitative judge (much like a clinician) applying techniques of analytic induction to complex, real-life data sets in order to explain the underlying patterns, the prognosis is a poor one. There is a long stream of research (e.g., Meehl, 1954, 1965; Goldberg, 1970; Dawes, 1971; Faust, 1982) showing that clinical judgments,[1] whether in medical or lay settings, are consistently less accurate than statistical/actuarial ones.

Some of the related studies are hair-raising. For example, Taft (1955) demonstrated that "expert" judges can be wrong more often than untrained ones. Oskamp (1965) showed how clinicians came to feel increasingly confident of their initially *erroneous* judgments as they got more and more *accurate* information. Tversky and Kahneman (1971) were easily able to catch mathematical psychologists in the act of making biased inferences from samples to populations. Mahoney and De Monbreun (1977) found conservative ministers outperforming psychologists, physicists, and engineers on hypothesis-testing skills. Closer to our specific topic, Sherman and Titus (1982) showed how causal inferences are made in the very process of taking in information. Cognitively, comprehension brings into play the causal explanations needed to bind together meaningfully the bits of information being encoded. Finally, Read (1982) has shown how, in complex stimulus situations, one often engages in causal reasoning based on no more than a single instance.

The cognitive processes underlying the biases in clinical reasoning have been well studied (see Nisbett & Ross, 1980). Essentially, they turn around faulty heuristics for *selecting information* from a complex stimulus field (over-reliance on vivid data), for *judging the frequency and probability* of an event (overdependence on cognitively "available" information), for *classifying* persons and objects (ignoring base-rate information), and for *revising initial judgments* (succumbing to an "anchoring" effect). Typically, the clinical or qualitative judge scans the environment more readily for confirmatory rather than for disconfirmatory information—the so-called "cognitive confirmation effect." Alternatively, human judges will generate correct strategies but then fail to use them consistently. Oftentimes, the more complex the stimulus situation, the more primitive the cognitive processing.

Where does this leave us? It suggests, for starters, that the shift from predesigned instrumentation to human judgments combining scientific and experiential knowledge is fraught with danger if one is making claims to validity. Any "clinical" researcher operating in a natural setting had best be well armed with the safeguards against bias described in the social judgment literature.

Qualitative methodology. Let's consider the situation from a causal realist's perspective. Most qualitative researchers work alone in the field. Each is a one-person research machine: defining the problem, drawing the sample of informants and subsettings, designing the instruments, collecting the information, then reducing, analyzing, interpreting, and writing up that information. A vertical monopoly, overseen by a Promethean entrepreneur.

How do we know whether the resulting account is surreal or real? By "real" let us simply mean for now that another researcher, working independently at the same site, would not come up with wholly contradictory findings. Since the published report usually contains few methodological details, we cannot look there. Nor can we blindly accept the robustness of the field researcher's customary tools of the trade for avoiding biases—for example, "bracketing," extensive time on site, thorough description of the setting. These are all desirable procedures, but there seems to be no empirical confirmation that (1) these procedures do, in fact, yield bias-free data and (2) a given field researcher was actually using them rigorously. What we need are specific indications of how the researcher got to the principal conclusions and verified them in such a way as to address the main biases in making social judgments that we have just reviewed.

Still, the qualitative research tradition, as exemplified by ethnographic and phenomenological studies, is a promising one for a causal realist working in ill-structured problem spaces. For one thing, qualitative researchers contend with complex, contextualized social facts, whereas the clinical and problem-solving literature has dealt largely with impersonal, contrived, simplified, or decontextualized settings. Checkmating strategies and simulated clinical folders are pallid proxies for real-life problem resolutions and explanations.

For another thing, careful documentation of naturally occurring events is the basis for making case study inferences. Still another appealing trait is that informants' accounts provide the basis for making sense, at least initially, of the analyst's observations. The notion that informants are *local connoisseurs*—that they have potentially a far more differentiated and complex representation of their surroundings than the analysts is likely to acquire in the time available on site—is a compelling one, provided one can sort out the more from the less plausible versions offered by local informants.

Finally, the social anthropological tradition has a potentially powerful blend of analytic detachment (usually through theory testing) and extensive local acquaintance (usually through vicarious or real social participation)[2] that approximates some of the "confirmatory" procedures of analytic induction, clinical diagnosis, and complex problem-solving found in the empirical research literature. In short, if an analyst of local causality can pluck selectively from the storehouse of methods used in qualitative field studies, he or she will find tools allowing for (1) the study of intact social settings, (2) flexible access to people best able to reflect on the determinants of these local environments, and (3) direct observation coupled with continuous testing of the emerging data against diverse explanations drawn from comparable settings. Such selective plucking, we have argued, is conceptually coherent and legitimate from a causal realist's stance. And if it is combined with some standard procedures for making analytic and causal inferences, together with safeguards against the prevalent biases in clinical and social reasoning, we may have a basic repertoire for doing qualitatively derived causal analyses.

OPERATIONAL APPROACHES TO ASSESSING LOCAL CAUSALITY

Like others, we have wrestled with these epistemological and methodological issues for several years. About ten years ago, each of us moved independently from small-scale, exploratory work into a multi-year venture with qualitative research, and did some subsequent reflection on our learnings and frustrations (Huberman, 1981; Miles, 1979). We then collaborated on a three-year, multiple-setting field study keyed to a national survey (Huberman & Miles, 1983b, 1984). In the course of that project, we undertook a separate study of the procedures actually used in the analysis of qualitative data (Miles & Huberman, 1981).

The task was to document in detail the successive analytical steps taken during single-case and across-case analyses, all the way from the initial coding of field notes to the more explanatory cross-site analyses. Each of the analyses fed into a detailed self-documentation form on which we recorded the successive steps in data-reduction and analysis, the decision rules used, the bases for drawing conclusions, the confidence held in the conclusions, and the strengths and weaknesses of the analysis. These inquiry episodes were then de-bugged, refined, and extended into a sourcebook (Miles & Huberman, 1984) which also incorporated recent work of other qualitative researchers. The examples shown below come from the sourcebook (for a rapid overview, see Huberman & Miles, 1983a). Through training sessions, dissertations, additional studies, and peer critiques, the methodology has been refined further.

Let us now draw selectively from the sourcebook to illustrate how a field researcher can assess local causality through the use of analytic induction, including inferential procedures for determining causal influence, in combination with field ethnographic and phenomenological techniques, and with some simple verification devices to control for the most common clinical biases listed above.

QUALITATIVE DATA ANALYSIS

First, however, a map of the general terrain. We consider that qualitative analysis consists of three concurrent flows of activity: data reduction, data display, and conclusion-drawing/verification. *Data reduction* is the process of selecting, focusing, simplifying, abstracting, and transforming the raw information appearing in field notes. The process occurs continuously throughout the life of the study, *not* only at the end. In fact, even before the data are collected, the researcher is deciding, often without full awareness, which conceptual framework, which settings, which research issues, which data collection approaches will be pursued, and which not. As data collection proceeds, there are further episodes of reduction—for example, writing interim summaries, coding, teasing out leitmotifs, making clusters and partitions, writing memos. In short, data reduction is not separate from analysis; it *is* analysis, which entails a progressive sharpening, sorting, and organizing of the data as the study unfolds.

A second component is *data display*. Most qualitative data are displayed as narrative text, a format we find cumbersome, dispersed, sequential rather than simultaneous, poorly structured, and prone to selective, hasty, oftentimes poorly justified conclusion-drawing. We have come to understand that such displays as matrices, graphs, networks, charts, and figures are more economical and rigorous devices. They force further analysis and ordering; they oblige the analyst to look at *all* the data, not just an alluring segment. They open up avenues of further analysis otherwise masked in the welter of raw field notes, and they force the analyst to peel away the decorative from the jugular.

The third stream of analysis activity is *conclusion-drawing and verification*. This is the basic inductive cycle, whereby the researcher notes relationships, regularities, covariations, and configurations and begins to piece them together into larger, more data-encompassing units. These Gestalts become working typologies and hypotheses that are progressively modified and refined as they get used in the next pass at the setting.

It is the verification part of the cycle that modifies the emerging conclusions. It may be as brief as a fleeting second thought crossing the analyst's mind during coding, followed by a short excursion back to the original field notes. Or it may be thoroughgoing and elaborate, with an analytic "audit" being performed by a critical analyst or with an attempt to replicate the finding in another setting or subsetting.

In this view the three types of analysis activity form an interactive, iterative cycle. The researcher moves steadily among these nodes during and after the data collection, generating, then verifying the main findings. Progressively, the core explanatory issues emerge, are sharpened, checked out, and amended, and then checked out again until they resist the combined assault of several verification devices.

We shall see shortly that the mechanics of generating a local causal analysis follow the same sequence, except that it is the *last* such exercise, building hierarchically from the previous, more fragmentary cycles of collecting, reducing, displaying, and verifying information from the field. For now, however, one should note that the general analytic strategy is consonant with other inductive approaches on the market, be they "constructive," "generative," or "grounded" (Goetz & LeCompte, 1981; Becker, 1958; Zelditch, 1962; Glaser, 1978). What all have in common is the notion of continuous analysis during data collection, in a gradual funneling, focusing sequence. What is distinctive about our version, perhaps, is that it is thoroughly *operationalized*. While other qualitative researchers may well have used similar methods, they have, as a rule, given few indications of how they were actually derived and how they are used.

THE RESEARCHER AND THE RESEARCHED

One more preliminary note. All such analytic approaches, operationalized or not, share a common characteristic of creating cognitive distance between the researcher and the setting. To conduct interim analyses, the field researcher steps back or out, sifts the data, then steps back in. The "stepping back" is consequential. Actually getting the data, of course, can imply any point on the *verstehen* continuum from intersubjective resonance to nonparticipant observation, and the field notes from most points on the continuum will reflect the world view of informants as that view is habitually expressed and made coherent. But during the stepping-back analysis cycle, those notes are *translated*—analytically metabolized into investigative hunches, constructs, propositions, questions, presumed relationships. Analytic induction as a research act inexorably pushes the "emic" toward the "etic" and, thereby, tilts in the direction of the neopositivism exemplified in transcendental realism and other middle-ground epistemologies. No matter how "grounded" or phenomenologically sensitive the fieldwork, the resulting analytic transpositions will redefine and abstract the context into other units, imperfectly isomorphic with those used by local actors to define and explain their setting.

Similarly, when one speaks of "verification," as we have just done, one infers that informants' accounts can be misleading, contradictory, or self-deceptive, and will need to be "checked out." Of the dozen tactics for testing or confirming findings that we have elaborated (see below), about a third entail double-checking accounts furnished by local informants. Here again, the researcher is in an ambivalent stance vis-à-vis the informant, vacillating between a trusting/mistrusting and a partner/suspect relationship. Once again, the investigative or forensic metaphor comes to mind: the qualitative researcher as intellectual detective in a social sphere in which informants are unlikely to volunteer the conflictual or affectively loaded information that the researcher needs in order to piece together the setting. There is, of course, a continuum of investigative stances within the inductive mode, the most extreme being that of Douglas (1976), for whom the informant is invariably a source of mistrust, deceit, or self-delusion, presenting various "fronts" that the researcher then seeks to penetrate. But even the gentler, more phenomenological stances put distance between researcher and researched; the difference is one of degree, not of nature.

That distance is not necessarily to be deplored, and it may even make the validity of causal inference stronger. As we will note later, treating respondents as colleagues, and inviting confirmation/disconfirmation of a researcher-generated causal map can lend much confidence— exactly because of the researcher-researched difference in perspectives.

BUILDING A CAUSAL MAP OF THE LOCAL SETTING

While transcendental realists can legitimate nonstatistical causal analysis on epistemological grounds, they do not show how it is done. We have taken a cut at operationalizing the procedures through the elaboration of what we have called *causal networks*. A causal network is a visual rendering of the most important independent and dependent variables in a field study and of the relationships among them. The plot of these relationships is *deterministic* rather than solely correlational. It is assumed that some factors exert a directional influence on others (X brings Y into being or makes Y larger or smaller) and that the web of these relationships can be mapped. In addition, a causal network has associated text (the causal narrative), describing the meaning of the connections among factors.

Getting started.[3] In the approach we generally favor, the first building blocks of causal analysis are the—deliberately general—conceptual framework and research questions, when these are available, along with the codes that the researcher uses to label various chunks of the field notes. Next come the reflective remarks and added marginal remarks made during the transcription of field notes. These are typically modest, data-shaping exercises. They alert the analyst to variables that go together and that contrast with other variables, and they invite a closer look at something that might be an underlying theme or pattern. All this means that *discrete* variables are getting clumped into *tentative families*. If they can stay in that family through successive data-gathering, -analyzing, and -verification cycles, they are good candidates for a "box" in the causal network.

Finding patterns. Marginal and reflective remarks often translate into what we have called *pattern codes*. These are in effect meta-codes, still bigger bites of data; they often turn into candidates for inclusion in a causal network. In essence, they signal a theme or pattern that makes a local difference. For example, in one study we came up with a pattern code, "TEAMS," which described a conflict between two administrative factions in a school district. The code stuck; it recurred and eventually got amalgamated into a stream of variables on the causal network ("career advancement motivation" and "climate in district office") that, in turn, determined the key outcomes.

Moving up a notch, pattern codes are extended into memos—written comments on emerging descriptive or explanatory concepts that cluster events and processes in the field, keeping them anchored to the context in which they appear (see Glaser, 1978). Memos, in turn, are combined with reflective remarks and pattern codes to generate *interim summaries* and *site analysis meetings* between researchers. These are intended to force out the emerging thematic and explanatory pieces—to move carefully from description to inference.

How, specifically, one moves up the inferential chain is something we have tried to document and then operationalize in the form of "tactics" for generating meaning. The tactics progress from elementary clustering and partitioning exercises (counting, noting patterns, making plausible associations, clustering, making metaphors, splitting variables, subsuming particulars into the general) to more inductively ambitious exercises (factoring, noting relations between variables, finding intervening variables, building a logical chain of evidence, making conceptual/ theoretical coherence). The latter devices, with results checked against the properties of the setting, then modified and refined, combine discrete pieces of data into the evidential chain that has a beginning causal logic.

One notes, approximately at first, which variables are present or absent together in the setting and which appear unconnected to those. Then, more systematically, the analyst begins to plot the variables that are coming regularly into play *before* others, are varying concomitantly *with* others, or are having a directional *influence* on others, with that influence changing when *other* variables are taken into account. In conducting these analyses, the researcher is simply applying the standard canons of inductive inference: temporal precedence, concomitant variation, and directional influence. He or she is also constructing the rudiments of a causal map that contains assumptions about the *directions* of influence among *sets* of variables. These assumptions, of course, will need to be made explicit and checked out during the next time on site—or, if one is off the site, checked out within the available data set. More on this verification process shortly.

Generating causal fragments. It is at this point that the analyst assembles the fragments of the emerging causal map. Here is a specimen list of decision rules for doing this:

- Translate the pattern codes into variables—that is, something that can be scaled (high to low, big to little, more to less).

- Rate the variable (e.g., high, moderate, low). How much of it is there in the site?

- Draw a line between pairs of variables that covary—that appear together consistently at the site or have some kind of relationship (e.g., more of one variable goes with less of another).

- Draw a directional arrow between each variable that comes first (temporally) and those later ones it appears to influence. *Influence* here means that more or less of one variable determines to some extent the rating on another. The rating of the second variable might have been different had the first one not been there.

- If two variables covary and are related but seem only to have a tepid or oblique influence on one another, there is probably another, latent variable that needs to be invented to join the two. Review the full list of codes to see if one fits here. (The analytic tactic here, listed earlier, is *finding intervening variables.*)

Figure 18.1 is an example of a causal fragment. The figure puts together themes having to do with the mastery of a new educational practice. The story can be told quickly. A demanding project with high implementation requirements (1) began with inadequate preparation (2) and was bailed out by high levels of assistance (3), which increased local efforts (4) and facilitated practice mastery (5). The (–) sign indicates reverse causal influence: Low preparation leads to high assistance.

The intent here is to stimulate thinking, not to get closure. The analyst should try to assemble a few such fragments without necessarily connecting one to another—should play around, do some causal

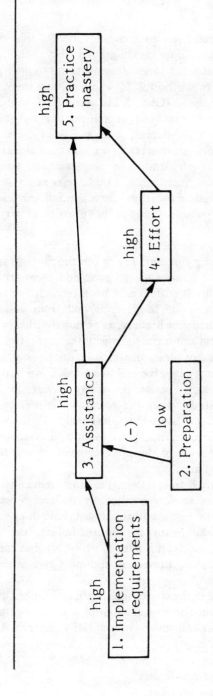

Figure 18.1 Causal Fragment: Mastery of a New Educational Practice

noodling—yet be careful not to connect variables that do not go together *empirically*, even if on logical grounds they should.

A useful next step is to take these fragments out to the field during later data collection to see how, and whether, they work. This can include some *member checks* (Guba & Lincoln, 1981)—that is, submitting the diagram to an informant to get confirmation and qualification (e.g., *some* preparation was decent, some assistance did not have an effect on levels of effort, some users were competent and experienced enough to do without preparation or assistance and still get high practice mastery). That might suggest that the next iteration of the network should have an arrow from a new box labeled "user competence" to the "effort" variable (4) and to the "practice mastery" variable (5).

Testing or confirming findings. Trying out the causal fragments on those being researched is, we suggest, good and necessary medicine. Good medicine, because it buffers each progressive inductive cycle as one moves from particulars to generals and from description to inference. Necessary medicine because, as we noted earlier in reviewing the literature on clinical and social judgment, the qualitative researcher is vulnerable to a pack of biases of which he or she is often, at best, remotely aware. In most cases, these biases break down into a series of "faulty heuristics," which operate, perversely enough, at the crucial moments in a field study: when the researcher is making inductive inferences or generalizing. Since the causal analysis is the hierarchical queen of these lower-level conclusions, its validity and reliability live or die by the trustworthiness of the more elementary and fragmented exercises in generating meaning.

The obvious remedy is to catalogue the most frequently appearing biases, and work out some operationally defined procedures for correcting each of them. Social anthropologists have done some of this work already (e.g., by addressing the "holistic fallacy," the "elite bias," and the "cooptation" or "going native" problem), but many of the solutions are not well operationalized, and most assume that one has several months on site.

In our research and in the sourcebook, we have chipped away at this issue and have reframed it by working out a dozen operationalized techniques for verifying conclusions in qualitative research. A simple list gives the flavor of these tactics:

- Checking for representativeness
- Checking for researcher effects

- Triangulating (by sources, methods, levels, and researchers)
- Weighting the evidence
- Making contrasts/comparisons
- Checking the meaning of outliers
- Using extreme cases
- Ruling out spurious relations
- Replicating a finding
- Checking out rival explanations
- Looking for negative evidence
- Getting feedback from informants
- Documenting and auditing conclusions.

For example, the representativeness problem addresses the faulty heuristics of generalizing abusively from instances to sets of instances. In this case, as in the others, we advise that the qualitative researcher *assume* that he or she is selectively sampling and drawing inferences from a weak or nonrepresentative sample of cases—be they people, events, or processes. In other words, you are guilty until you prove yourself innocent. You can prove your innocence in at least one of four ways: (1) simply increase the number of cases, (2) look *purposively* for contrasting (negative, extreme, countervailing) cases, (3) sort the cases systematically and fill out weakly sampled case types, and (4) sample randomly within the universe or people and phenomena under study.

The last two procedures, not coincidentally, correspond to the stratification and randomization conventions used by experimentalists to enhance internal validity. But, whereas the experimental researcher uses these procedures *early*, as anticipatory controls against sampling and measurement error, the qualitative researcher uses them *later*, as verification devices. That allows one to let all the candidate people and data in, so that the most influential ones will have an equal chance of emerging. But you *still* have to carry the burden of proof that the patterns you ultimately discover are, in fact, representative.

Generating a causal network variable list. About three-quarters of the way through data collection, the researcher should be ready to assemble the remaining pieces of the causal network. A useful first step is to generate the full set of network variables. This, too, is an exercise in playful brainstorming. The idea is to list all the events, factors, outcomes, processes, and so forth that seem to be important, then to turn them into variables. For instance, several fights between employees will become "organizational conflict." The first pass should be exhaus-

TABLE 18.1   List of Antecedent, Mediating, and Outcome Variables

Antecedent or Start Variables	Mediating Variables	Outcomes
Internal funds	External funds	Stabilization of use
Career advancement motivation	Program adoption (NDN)	Percentage of use
Assessed adequacy of local performance	Program concept initiative (IV-C)	Student impact
Environmental turbulence	Program development (IV-C)	User capacity change
	District endorsement	Institutionalization
	Building endorsement	Job mobility
	Influence of innovation advocate	
	Implementation requirements	
	Adequacy of initial user preparation	
	Program-district fit	
	Program-building fit	
	Program-user fit	
	Assistance	
	User commitment	
	User skill	
	Program transformation	
	Teacher-administrator harmony	
	Validation effort (IV-C)	
	Stability of program leadership	
	Stability of program staff	
	Organizational transformation	

tive, the next one more selective. That is, once a full set of variables is down, the list should be combed for redundancies and overdifferentiation (e.g., three types of fighting between employees). As a rough rule of thumb, fifteen variables are probably too few and forty too many. As an illustration, Table 18.1 is a list of core variables generated in a school improvement study we conducted (Huberman & Miles, 1984).

In a single-site study, the variable list is a straightforward procedure. In a multiple-site study, by contrast, we are at a decisive moment. For cross-site comparisons, the same variables are going to be used to analyze five, ten, or twenty sites. For this to happen, theoretically *each* of the variables has to be empirically meaningful at *all* the sites. Of course one should leave slack for the probability that there will be a handful of *site-specific* variables in addition. They are of two types: those that are influential at only one site and those that are influential at most but not all sites. In the former case, the final causal network will contain a site-specific variable, labeled as such. In the latter case, some network variables will be dropped (with an explanation) from the sites at which they contribute little to the analysis.

Drawing the causal network. In principle, most of the items on the variable list will have been prefigured, explicitly or implicitly, in the pattern codes, interim summaries, and memos we reviewed earlier. They will also have emerged during the progressively multivariate displays we have alluded to. Analyzing *conceptual clusters* in the setting, for example, allows the analyst to tease out the relationships within one of the variable families. *Effects matrices* are exercises that identify incipient cause-effect relations. Then, *both* clustering and cause-effect inferencing are combined in *site dynamics matrices.* In other words, the causal analysis is being done incrementally; one is testing individual paths more rigorously and, at the same time, building an integrated map.

Finally, the *event-state* network get us almost there; let us illustrate how. Figure 18.2 is an excerpt from an event-state network for one of the field sites in a twelve-site study we conducted. As the figure indicates, *events* are key, observable, or verifiable actions whose influence is judged to be decisive, and *states* are the consequences of those (and sometimes of other) events. The double-numbering (for number 4 and number 7) indicates that these items are thematically or functionally similar. This sets up the final causal network. Figure 18.3 is an excerpt, with the variable numbers keyed to the corresponding "variables" in the event-state network.

Let us now take a look at a fully drawn causal network (Figure 18.4). It will look initially overwhelming to the reader because it condenses mountains of inferential data into one, integrated display. But stay with us for some simplifying explication.

Drawing the network is probably done best the same way one should analyze it: stream by stream. Some streams—unbroken chains of variables—are long: Look at the one that runs directly from box 1 through boxes 8, 9, 10, to 30, even to 32. Others are, conveniently, shorter; the bottom stream from 5 to 35 and 33 is a short one. Within an unbroken stream, there are usually eddies leading in different directions or ending up at the same place via a different route. They should also be drawn in.

Streams can be most easily drawn—especially if the event-state network is used as the semi-final cut—from antecedents forward in time. It is also possible to take a dependent variable and work backward, but then it is important to run it forward again to be sure the links are coherent and empirically justified. One will usually find that there are cross-stream connections, and they can be drawn in as the network evolves.

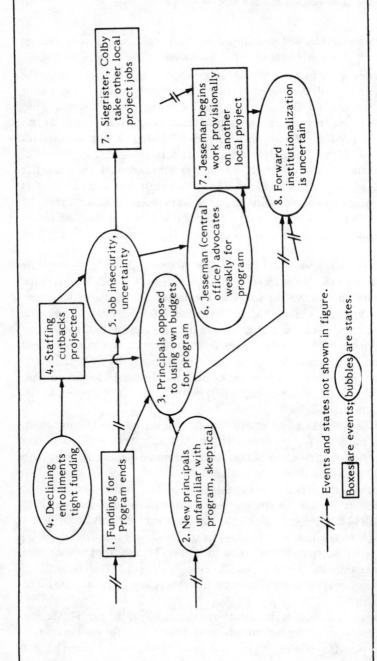

Figure 18.2 Excerpt from an Event-State Network

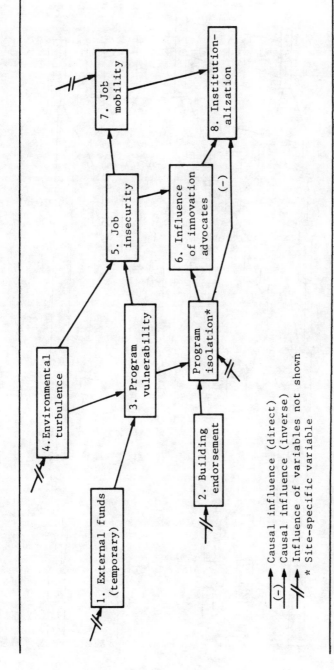

Figure 18.3 Excerpt from a Causal Network

1. External funds (temporary)

2. Building endorsement

3. Program vulnerability

4. Environmental turbulence

5. Job insecurity

6. Influence of innovation advocates

7. Job mobility

8. Institution-alization

➤ Causal influence (direct)
(-) Causal influence (inverse)
⊬ Influence of variables not shown
* Site-specific variable

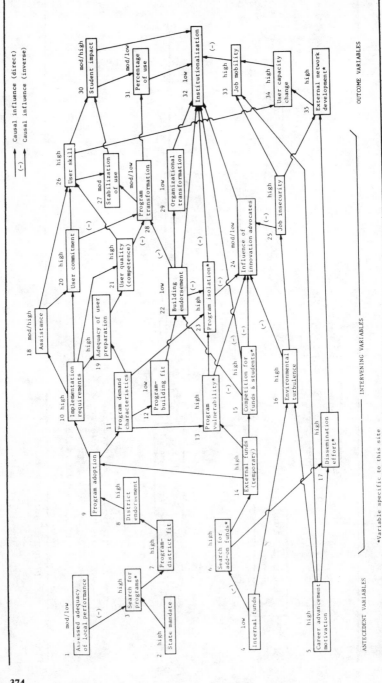

Figure 18.4 Causal Network for Perry-Parkdale CARED Program

Often, these streams and eddies have a name—a scenario or theme—and this makes them easier both to analyze and to render. For example, along the bottom stream variables 5, 17, 35, and 34 have a "cosmopoliz-ing" theme: People go outside their environments in connection with a new project and the experience both stretches them and sets up possible career shifts. Or, again, staying along the bottom of the network, boxes 4, 16, 25 and 33 add up to a "casualty" stream: low money, high turbulence (usually in the form of budget cuts), staff instability, and ultimate staff reassignments.

Alternatively, the streams can be labeled according to the level of dependent variables (e.g., high student impact scenarios, low institution-alization scenarios, high job mobility scenarios). These similarly named scenarios can be very different. For instance, as we just saw, one high job mobility scenario involves a promotion or desirable transfer, whereas another involves an unwanted reassignment or even a layoff.

Causal network narratives. Drawing conclusions from the network should wait until the analyst has a more coherent sense of what is on it. Like all time-related representations, this one tells a story—really, several stories. One should write out a chronological narrative for each of the major streams. In this case, one starts at the beginning. Here is an excerpt from the narrative for the causal network shown in Figure 18.4:

The first three antecedent variables (1, 2, and 4) worked out this way: The state mandate (2) for well-planned career education programs, together with assessment of local performance as less than adequate (1), led to a search for new programs (3), which proved to be a good fit (7) with district characteristics, and hence to district endorsement (8), and to adoption of the program (9).

But these were not sufficent causes of adoption. Inadequate local funds (4) to cover existing programs led to a ceaseless search for add-on funds (6) as almost a "way of life" for the district. That search led to getting temporary external funds (14) for a three-year period; they were the other basic cause of adoption (9).

The program, when adopted, proved to have substantial implementation requirements (10), which dictated the need for assistance (18), and also exerted a good deal of pressure for careful selection of high-quality staff (21), and for careful preparation (19) of them to carry out the program. The heavy implementation requirements (10), and to some degree the assistance provided (18), induced a good deal of user commitment (20), and in turn user skill (26), which was also high because of staff quality (21). High user skill, in conjunction with the fact that the program was quite well stabilized (27) by late 1980, brought about a reasonable degree of student impact (30).

That stream of causality refers essentially to internal program dynamics. What was happening at the *district and building* level?

Moving back to program demand characteristics (11), we note that certain aspects of the program (such as its removing students from high school control, and from high school courses and activities) caused poor fit between the program and the sending buildings (12). That poor fit led to lack of endorsement (22) from building principals, counselors and teachers. Poor endorsement was further weakened by the presence of competition for funds and for students (15), induced by the fact that the external funds (14) were temporary in nature.

Writing the narrative usually does several things. It forces the analyst to be less mechanistic and more coherent: Turning a network into clear text requires one to be fully explicit about what is causing what. Corrections and revisions are likely. Second, it provides an opportunity for expansion: The analyst can explain why variables are related, why they are rated differently, why some precede others, which ones matter more, and so on.

In the same vein, the narrative brings back the *context*, pinning down the conditions and contingencies under which the abstracted variables actually play out. As transcendental realists emphasize, our task is to show how *in each particular case* the causal configurations occurred, then to provide a theoretical redescription of the case that is isomorphic to its components.

Auditing and verification. Finally, both the network and the narrative constitute materials that can be handed to a colleague, to a critic, and to site informants for auditing and verification.

By *auditing,* we mean that a second reader goes carefully over the conclusions to check their robustness.[4] The auditor's task is *not* to generate another network or narrative, but to go through the original one with the kind of fine-grained, nitpicky review that secondary analysts visit on their peers in statistical studies. One of the important assumptions here, which we derive directly from the work on ill-structured problems and appropriate inquiry systems, is that *more than one* causal network may be valid, that there is no single solution to the exclusion of the others but that some solutions are more compelling and robust than others. It is the auditing process that keeps the orginal analyst inferentially honest and, at the same time, informs the reader of the credibility of the analysis.

There is no simple answer to the question of what to do when you and your auditor disagree sharply about some aspect of the analysis procedures or conclusions. Here are some responses we have found ourselves making:

(1) Arguing, "explaining," clarifying one's point of view until both agree that the original cut was right, or that some revision is needed.

(2) Going back to the original data to see if they really support the conclusions drawn; more often than not, an auditor can usually suggest some *new* data that could be used to verify or disprove the conclusions. The familiar technique of *triangulation*—using other data sources, methods, or analysts—is relevant here.

(3) Jointly recasting the particular procedure used (for example, drawing a new network with revised paths and some new variables, together).

(4) Turning the tables and inviting the auditor to become the analyst, with the analyst taking a look at the product. This is, naturally, most labor intensive, and useful only when heavy disagreements exist. (We have found, by the way, that heavy disagreements are in fact rare—and that when they do exist, there is often a social-psychological underpinning involved: The auditor and analyst belong to different subgroups, are uneasy with each other, etc. It pays to work on the real relationship issue, and not to camouflage it as a "data" issue.)

Finally, here are some reponses we do NOT ever recall having made:

(1) Giving the problem to the local authority figure (research director, principal investigator, etc.).

(2) Finding a third, fourth or fifth party, and going by majority rule.

(3) Saying to the original analyst, "Ok, it's your baby. Do it any way you like."

What these responses have in common is a sort of mechanical, disengaged quality, along with the assumption that important substantive issues can be managed by nose-counting or pulling rank.

Feeding the network *and* narrative back to the site is very useful; it serves as a verification device and as an opportunity for the analyst to learn more. Both the graphics of the network and the details of the narrative have in our experience turned out to be helpful decoding and sense-making tools for site informants. The causal networks provide information at macro-analytic levels of inference that most informants initially either discount or swallow whole for their esoteric, "scientific" appearance. But the narratives bring the local actors back into their own surround—and then deepen their understanding and critique of the network. As the symbolic interactionists have shown well, people do not act towards social structures or roles or constructs; they act toward *situations* and *events*, and are likely to understand meta-situational language only to the extent that it is directly plugged into the events and situations described in the narratives.

We have worked up feedback forms for verifying causal networks and narratives through local informants' reactions. Generally speaking, we have tried to pick people from a particular site who (1) are reasonably knowledgeable about the phenomena we are studying, non-defensive, and articulate; (2) come from several different roles and perspectives; (3) are themselves of an inquiring, curious turn of mind. (Naturally, all these criteria cannot usually be met—and probably should not be, lest we merely recreate an ideal image of ourselves in the guise of site informants.)

The forms we have used are described in a previous work (Miles & Huberman, 1984, pp. 142-143). In brief, they present the network and the narrative, then ask the respondent for comments on its accuracy, and to cross out or add boxes, cross out or add arrows, change box weights—and to explain the rationale for doing this. Since we consider this professional work, we offered site people a modest reader's fee ($25-50).

People seem to enjoy doing this work. It lets them see rapidly how the researcher has put the pieces together, and they then run that view against their own perspective. When that perspective is different, informants can quite easily re-draw parts of the network or re-draft parts of the narrative.

Our experience has been that site informants do not differ sharply from our analyses, suggesting only marginal changes—which are, however, often illuminating. Sharp differences would suggest a great deal either about the quality of our field work or some real or perceived danger to the informant.

To illustrate the latter, we should cite an experience where one of us, in an earlier project, fed back *complete case studies* to site personnel. Almost everyone found things in the detail of the cases that either upset them, or could genuinely damage their careers; we were threatened with suit in four of five sites. Such concerns were in fact valid, we judged, and the relevant material was deleted or disguised.

Causal networks, however, are far less likely to tread such dangerous ground. They are abstracted analyses, general maps of what happened and why, and they do not identify specific actors who are blameworthy, misguided, incompetent, or the like.

FROM LOCAL TO MULTIPLE-SETTING CAUSALITY:
A BRIEF NOTE

A case is more than a case. It has components found in other cases; it is, after all, an aggregate of instances that we could simply not comprehend if we did not have, in our own experience, corresponding instances taken from elsewhere. The problem, of course, is that these instances are idiosyncratically organized within each case, and being so organized, they may *mean* different things from one context to another. The Bible probably has it right: Each case is like *no* other, like *some* other, and like *all* others.

Given the current growth in multisite qualitative studies (see Smith & Louis, 1982), we badly need approaches to drawing coherent, valid meaning from more than one case. However, even middle-range epistemologists have made a strong argument for determining local causality, case by case, and an equally strong argument against any such thing as "general" causality. Others, too, have been wary of moving from the idiographic to the nomothetic—or, as Lewin had it, from the Galilean laws obtaining in single cases to the Aristotelian laws affecting *classes* of objects. But there may well be a middle ground here: finding causal determinisms in more than one context, with similar events and processes coming into play. Is there a way of plotting them without recourse to multivariate statistics and without erasing the setting-specific configurations and thereby rendering each case, literally, meaning-less?[5] We think there may be, and have enjoyed tinkering with the mechanics of bringing it off. Given space constraints, we will provide only a brief summary here; the interested reader should consult Miles and Huberman (1984, pp. 197-209).

Essentially, the analyst looks at each of n causal networks (and their associated narratives when needed). For each network, one extracts the *sub*network of boxes and arrows that lead directly to the dependent variable being analyzed. Variables that have no path from them to the outcomes—even through other variables—are ignored. Within each subnetwork, there is a careful effort to isolate and name the streams involved (for example, the "casualty" and "cosmopolizing" streams already mentioned).

The next step is that of matching the variable streams to those in other cases that have similar outcomes. There are two approaches to this: (1) general "pattern matching" at a global level; and (2) in a more detailed analytic mode, putting the variables in an "antecedents matrix" (Miles & Huberman, 1984, pp. 203-205) showing, for the full set of sites, the immediate and remotely causal variables.

Either of these approaches helps the analyst to cluster the streams and to develop scenarios that are more general for sites as wholes. The work then moves up a notch, by clustering *sites* into families (for example, in twelve sites, we found one family of two sites we called "win-lose" because they included both successful and unsuccessful job mobility streams).

The final step involves verifying the scenarios within families: Are the variables the same? Do they have the same value? Are the outcomes at the same level? Do the narratives support the "familyness"? And do families with *different* levels of outcome show different, or differently loaded, variables?

Such a description is rather abstract. We have found, however, that using these procedures does permit one to produce *generalized* causal networks reflecting the shared and the idiosyncratic elements of sites within the same family. We typically found from two to four sites in a family within our set of twelve sites.

CONCLUDING COMMENT

In this chapter, we have tried to spell out a coherent and manageable approach to nonstatistical research that allows for the analysis of local causal influence without disfiguring the configuration of context-specific phenomena. In developing that approach, we have also tried to include some components that many analysts tend to obscure or omit, in particular the epistemic bases for the methodologies proposed *and* the nuts and bolts of the methodologies themselves. Until we can get some agreement on those issues, taken *together*, we will continue to talk past one another in a dialogue of the deaf about clinical qualitative research, like the more comic characters in a Chekhov play or the more tragic characters in a Pinter play. And this, in turn, will put us researchers in the incongruous position of being unsure of what we mean when we pretend to "explain" why our informants behave as they do—they who have worked out consensual and functional ways of going about *their* business and of making perfectly good sense of it.

NOTES

1. These studies use a considerably narrower, simpler, definition of *clinical* than that used elsewhere in this book. But there is no guarantee that clinical judgment more broadly or complexly defined will necessarily produce valid knowledge—which is what we are after.

2. Scriven (1979, p. 69) puts it well in remarking that cause-hunting, like lion-hunting, "is only likely to be successful if we have a considerable amount of relevant background knowledge."

3. This account, with its step-by-step detail, is only possible because we repeatedly carried out self-documentation of our analytic moves, as described above. Reviewing our documentation forms both taught us something about our own fallability as analysts and showed us the usefulness of the procedures as they gradually emerged in an iterative fashion. For more detail see Miles and Huberman (1984, pp. 243-248).

4. This auditing will be much deeper and better if the analyst also has kept some form of documentation of the procedures followed and has recorded the ideas and feelings that surfaced during the process. Even if that has not been done, it is useful to have an auditor do some retrospective interviewing: "What led you to decide on *that* variable as an antecedent?" "Where were your doubts at that point?" "Why do you feel so sure about that stream's name?"

5. In *The End of the Road*, John Barth captures the dilemma nicely when he has his protagonist observe that the authors of (medical) textbooks, like everyone else, can read generality only by ignoring enough particularity.

Commentary

As Helen Swick Perry delved into the biographical details of Harry Stack Sullivan's life she found herself thinking about her father. There were many similarities in the early lives of these two men and, as Perry reported, on occasion she found it hard to keep separate her reflections on each of them. Her relationship with Sullivan's history made salient her relationship with her father, stirring contemporary emotions. The past and the present, other and self all came together in a caldron of fused thoughts and feelings. It would have been understandable if Perry had put aside this overwhelming experience, but her work as investigator turned to the task of drawing new distinctions, separating father from Sullivan, present from past, self from other. At the conclusion she writes, "the very similarities underscored their differences."

This concept, the relationship of similarities and differences, is the essence of the scientific method. It is not possible to have "information" without distinctions. It is difference that creates data. The task of science is to distinguish and to link together that which has been distinguished. It must be noted that the concept of difference is likewise dependent on the concept of similarity. If not for similarity there would be no difference. Without darkness we could not know light. Darkness allows us to have the concept of light. The concepts of darkness and light give meaning to each other because they have a critical similarity.

In many ways the description of science in the preceding paragraph is like the process of identity development in a child or an adolescent. Only as distinctions are made can relationships develop. Only as the two-year-old learns how to say no does the concept of yes have real psychological meaning. Only as we separate from our parents can we know who we are. Significantly, these differentiations can occur only if there are meaningful connections in the first place. The process of becoming fully integrated, both internally and with the external world, depends on clear distinctions being drawn. This enables new similarities and connections to develop. The analogy between the activities of the scientific method and the process of individual identity development underscores the truly human character of scientific work.

At the collective level, too, distinctions play a role in enabling us to identify similarities. In the same way that individuals cannot be understood apart from the groups and organizations to which they belong, science must be understood in terms of its context. If, as Reinharz points out in Section III, the evolution of a community of scientists has been an attempt to formulate an authority system capable of combating the tyranny of political rulers, the distinction between the authority of science and the authority of the king affirms their *similarity* as systems of authority.

Each of the chapters in this section struggles with issues of similarity, differentiation, and integration. Simmons, as she introjected the discrepancies in the archives, confronted a choice: Should she search for what caused the discrepancies or should she search for what the discrepancies might tell about the system's prehistory. Taking the debate inside, she fused the past and the present, outside and inside, system and person, and as she lived with these contradictions was able to draw distinctions that informed her about the past and the present. She *created* new perspectives, new insights, and new theories through the process of incorporation, fusion, differentiation, and integration.

Gillette, by describing the distinction between history and social science shows the presence of history in the here-and-now of social research. Sutton and Schurman struggled with the fact that they were unable to carry out interviews on certain topics using the detached method their training demanded. In the process they realized that those highly structured methods needed to be understood and used differently in different contexts. Their attempts to act similarly in very different settings taught them about the ways they needed to act differently.

This same topic undergirds the chapter by Huberman and Miles. They argue that distinctions are always being made and that these choices should be recorded as they are made. At the same time Huberman and Miles suggest that clustering—delineation by similarity—is an important part of the data reduction process. Distinguishing and clustering are the key processes in the analysis of causal chains and they are the foundation of validity in the clinical side of research.

In conclusion, we would like to point out that the purpose of this volume has been to make finer distinctions, to draw lines not previously drawn, and to make links among that which is now distinguished. We do not believe that this is in opposition to science. It is intended to affirm that the application of the activities of science to science itself is what nourishes science, keeping it vital and expanding its capacity to respond to the demands of the social world of which it is a part.

REFERENCES

Abrahamson, M. (1983). *Social research methods.* Englewood Cliffs, NJ: Prentice-Hall.

Alderfer, Charlene Hareven, J. (1982). Freud, a potential family theorist. *Network, 2,* 9-10.

Alderfer, C.P. (1968). Explorations in consulting-client relationships. *Human Organizations, 27,* 260-265.

Alderfer, C.P. (1977). Group and intergroup relations. In J.R. Hackman & J.L. Suttle (Eds.), *Improving life at work.* Santa Monica, CA: Goodyear.

Alderfer, C.P. (1980a). The methodology of organizational diagnosis. *Professional Psychology, 11,* 459-468.

Alderfer, C.P. (1980b). Consulting to underbounded systems. In C.P. Alderfer & C.L. Cooper (Eds.), *Advances in experiential social processes* (Vol. 2). New York: John Wiley.

Alderfer, C.P. (1984). An intergroup perspective on group dynamics. In J. Lorsch (Ed.), *Handbook of organizational behavior.* Englewood Cliffs, NJ: Prentice-Hall.

Alderfer, C.P., & Berg, D.N. (1977). Organization development: The profession and the practitioner. In P.H. Mirvis & D.N. Berg (Eds.), *Failures in organization development and change* (pp. 89-110). New York: John Wiley.

Alderfer, C.P. & Brown, L.D. (1975). *Learning from changing.* Beverly Hills, CA: Sage.

Alderfer, C.P., Brown, L.D., Kaplan, R.E., & Smith, K.K. (in press). *Group relations and organizational diagnosis.* New York: John Wiley.

Alderfer, C.P., Kaplan, R.E., & Smith, K.K. (1974). The effect of variations in relatedness need satisfaction on learning desires. *Administrative Science Quarterly, 19,* 507-532.

Alderfer, C.P., & Smith, K.K. (1982). Studying intergroup relations embedded in organizations. *Administrative Science Quarterly, 27,* 35-65.

Alexander, J. (1982). *Theoretical logic in sociology: Positivism, presuppositions, and current controversies.* Berkeley: University of California Press.

Andersen, M. (1983). *Thinking about women: Sociological and feminist perspectives.* New York: Macmillan.

Argyris, C. (1952). Diagnosing defenses against the outsider. *Journal of Social Issues, 80,* 24-34.

Argyris, C. (1968). Some unintended consequences of rigorous research. *Psychological Bulletin, 70,* 185-197.

Aronson, E. (1980). Persuasion via self-justification: Large commitments for small rewards. In L. Festinger (Ed.), *Retrospections on social psychology* (pp. 3-21). New York: Oxford University Press.

Aronson, E. (1984). A missionary for social psychology. *Psychology Today, 18,* 40-45.

Aronson, E., & Mills, J. (1959). The effect of severity of initiation on liking for a group. *Journal of Abnormal and Social Psychology 59,* 177-181.

ASA (American Sociological Association). (1980). Sexist biases in sociological research: Problems and issues. *Footnotes.* Status of women in sociology.

Babad, E.Y., Birnbaum, M., & Benne, K.D. (1983). *The social self.* Beverly Hills, CA: Sage.

Babbie, E.R. (1973). *Survey research methods.* Belmont, CA: Wadsworth.

Babbie, E.R. (1983). *The practice of social research* (3rd ed.). Belmont, CA: Wadsworth.

Bacharach, S.B., & Lawler, E.J. (1980). *Power and politics in organizations.* San Francisco: Jossey-Bass.

Bailar, J., Louis, T., Lavori, P., & Polansky, M. (1984). Studies without internal controls. *New England Journal of Medicine, 311,* 156-162.

Baker-Miller, J. (1976). *Toward a new psychology of women.* Boston, MA: Beacon Press.

Balmary, M. (1979). *Psychoanalyzing psychoanalysis: Freud and the hidden fault of the father.* Baltimore, MD: Johns Hopkins Press.

Barlow, D.H., Hayes, S.C., & Nelson, R.C. (1984). *The scientist practitioner.* New York: Pergamon Press.

Bart, P. (1971). Sexism in social science: From the iron cage to the gilded cage—the perils of Pauline. *Journal of Marriage and the Family, 33,* 742.

Barzun, A., & Graff, H.F. (1957). *The modern researcher.* New York: Harcourt Brace Jovanovich.

Bateson, G. (1972). *Steps to an ecology of mind.* New York: Ballantine.

Bateson, G. (1979). *Mind and nature.* New York: Bantam.

Becker, E. (1973). *The denial of death.* New York: Free Press.

Becker, H.S. (1958). Problems of inference and proof in participant observation. *American Sociological Review, 23,* 652-660.

Becker, H.S. (1974). Whose side are we on? In G. Riley (Ed.), *Values, objectivity, and the social sciences* (pp. 107-121). Reading, MA: Addison-Wesley.

Benne, K.D. (1959). Some ethical problems in group and organizational consultation. *Journal of Social Issues, 15,* 60-67.

Bennis, W.G., & Shepard, H.A. (1956). A theory of group development. *Human Relations, 9,* 415-457.

Berg, D.N. (1980). Developing clinical field skills: An apprenticeship model. In C.P. Alderfer & C.L. Cooper (Eds.), *Advances in experiential social processes* (Vol. 2). New York: John Wiley.

Berg, D.N. (1984). Objectivity and prejudice. *American Behavioral Scientist 27,* 387-402.

Berger, P. (1963). *Invitation to sociology: A humanistic perspective.* Garden City, NY: Doubleday.

Berger, P., & Luckman, T. (1967). *The social construction of reality: A treatise in the sociology of knowledge.* Garden City, NY: Doubleday.

Bernard, J. (1973). My four revolutions: An autobiographical history of the American Sociological Association. *American Journal of Sociology, 78,* 773-791.

Bernard, J. (1981). *The female world.* New York: Free Press.

Bhaskar, R. (1975). *A realist theory of science.* Leeds, UK: Leeds Books.

Bhaskar, R. (1982). Emergence, explanation and emancipation. In P. Secord (Ed.), *Explaining social behavior: Consciousness, behavior and social structure.* Beverly Hills, CA: Sage.

Bierce, A. (1911). *The devil's dictionary.* New York: Albert and Charles Boni Inc.

Biographical Directory of the American Psychological Association. (1975). Washington, DC: American Psychological Association.

Bion, W.R. (1961). *Experiences in groups.* London: Tavistock.

Bowen, E.S. (Bohanan, L.) (1954). *Return to laughter.* New York: Harper & Row.

Bowles, G., & Duelli-Klein, R. (Eds.) (1983). *Theories of women's studies.* London: Routledge & Kegan Paul.

Boykin, A.W., Anderson, J.F., & Yates, J.F. (Eds.). (1979). *Research directions of black psychologists.* New York: Russell Sage Foundation.

Brandwein, R. (1984). Feminist thought-structure: An alternative paradigm of social change for social justice. Paper presented at a conference, Toward social and economic justice, Brandeis University, Waltham, MA, March 23-25.

Brown, R.W., & Lennenberg, E.H. (1954). A study in language and cognition. *Journal of Abnormal and Social Psychology 49*: 454-462.

Buraway, M. (1979). *Manufacturing consent.* Chicago: University of Chicago Press.

Campbell, D.T. (1975). Degrees of freedom and the case study. *Comparative Political Studies, 8*(2), 178-193.

Campbell, D.T. (1977). Descriptive epistemology: Psychological, sociological and evolutionary. Unpublished paper, William James Lectures, Harvard University, Cambridge, MA.

Campbell, D.T., & Stanley, J.C. (1963). *Experimental and quasi-experimental designs for research.* Chicago: Rand McNally.

Carlsmith, J.M., Ellsworth, P.C., & Aronson, E. (1976). *Methods of research in social psychology.* Reading, MA: Addison-Wesley.

Cassell, J. (1980). Ethical principles for conducting fieldwork. *American Anthropologist, 82*(1), 28-41.

Chassan, J. (1979). *Research design in clinical psychology and psychiatry* (2nd ed.). New York: Irvington.

Chomsky, N. (1971). *Problems of knowledge and freedom.* New York: Pantheon.

Christians, C.G., & Carey, J.W. (1981). The logic and aims of qualitative research. In G.H. Stempel & B.H. Westley (Eds.), *Research methods in mass communication.* Englewood Cliffs, NJ: Prentice-Hall.

Churchman, C.W. (1971). *The design of inquiring systems: Basic concepts of systems and organization.* New York: Basic Books.

Cicourel, A. V. (1982). Interviews, surveys, and the problem of ecological validity. *American Sociologist, 17*(1), 11-20.

Clawson, D. (1980). *Bureaucracy and the labor process.* New York: Monthly Review Press.

Clawson, J. (1980). Mentoring in managerial careers. In C.B. Derr (Ed.), *Work, family and the career.* New York: Praeger.

Cobb, S. (1976). Social support as a moderator of life stress. *Psychosomatic Medicine. 38*(5), 330-344.

Cobb, S., & Kasl, S.V. (1977). *Termination: The consequences of job loss* (HEW Publications No. NIOSH 77-224). Washington, DC: U.S. Department of Health, Education and Welfare.

Committee to Study the Status of Women in Graduate Education and Later Careers (1974, March). *The higher the fewer.* University of Michigan.

Conklin, H. C. (1955). Haununóo color categories. *Southwestern Journal of Anthropology 11*, 339-344.

Cook, T.D., & Campbell, D.T. (1979). *Quasi-experimentation: Design and analysis issues for field settings.* Chicago: Rand McNally.

Coser, L. (1975). Presidential address: Two methods in search of a substance. *American Sociological Review, 40*, 691-700.

Cousins, N. (1979). *Anatomy of an illness as perceived by the patient: Reflections on health and regeneration.* New York: Norton.

Cronbach, L. (1975). Beyond the two disciplines of scientific psychology. *American Psychologist, 30*, 116-127.

Culler, J. (1977). *Ferdinand de Saussure.* New York: Viking.

Dalton, M. (1959). *Men who manage.* New York: John Wiley.

Daly, M. (1978). *Gyn/ecology: The metaethics of radical feminism.* Boston, MA: Beacon Press.

Daniels, A.K. (1967). The low-caste stranger in social research, In G. Sjoberg (Ed.), *Ethics, politics, and social research* (pp. 267-296). Cambridge, MA: Schenkman.

Daniels, A.K. (1975). Feminist perspectives in sociological research. In M. Millman & R.M. Kanter (Eds.), *Another voice: Feminist perspectives on social life and social science* (pp. 340-380). Garden City, NY: Doubleday.

D'Annuo, T., & Price, R. (1983). Methodology in community research I: Context and objectives. In K. Heller, R.H. Price, S. Reinhart, S. Riger, & A. Wandersman (Eds.), *Psychology and community change.* Homewood, IL: Dorsey.

Davidson, J. W., & Lytle, M. H. (1983). *After the fact: The art of historical detection.* New York: Random House.

Dawes, R. (1971). A case study of graduate admissions: applications of three principles of human decision-making. *American Psychologist, 26*(2): 180-188.

Deegan, M. J. (1981). Early women sociologists and the American Sociological Society: The patterns of exclusion and participation. *The American Sociologist, 16*(1),: 14-24.

Dentler, R.A., & Erikson, K.T. (1959). The functions of deviance in groups. *Social Problems, 7,* 98-107.

Devereux, G. (1967). *From anxiety to method in the behavioral sciences.* Paris: Mouton.

Diesing, P. (1971). *Patterns of discovery in the social sciences.* New York: Aldine.

Dimaggio, P., & Powell, W. (1983). The iron cage revisted: Institutional isomorphism and collective rationality in organizational fields. *American Sociology Review, 48,* 147-160.

Douglas, J. (1976). *Investigative social research: Investigative and team research.* Beverly Hills, CA: Sage.

Dunn, W. (1982). *The theory of exceptional clinicians.* Pittsburgh: University of Pittsburgh, Program for the Study of Knowledge Use.

Durkheim, E. (1895/1938). *The rules of sociological method.* Chicago: University of Chicago Press.

Durkheim, E. (1933/1964) *The division of labor in society.* New York: Free Press.

Durkheim, E. (1951). *Suicide.* New York: Free Press.

Dyer, R. (1983). *Her father's daughter: The work of Anna Freud.* New York: Jason Aronson.

Eagly, A.H., & Carli, L.L. (1981). Sex of researchers and sex-typed communications as determinants of sex differences in influenceability: A meta-analysis of social influence studies. *Psychological Bulletin, 90,* 1-20.

Edelson, M. (1972). Language and dreams. In R. Eissler et al. (Eds.), *Psychoanalytic study of the child* Vol. 27. (pp. 203-282). New York: Quadrangle Books.

Edelson, M. (1975). *Language and interpretation in psychoanalysis.* Chicago: University of Chicago Press.

Edelson, M. (1984). *Hypothesis and evidence in psychoanalysis.* Chicago: University of Chicago Press.

Ehrenreich, B., & Stallard, K. (1982, August). The nouveau Pon. *Ms.,* p. 220.

Eisenstein, Z. (1982). Comment. *The American Sociologist, 17*(1), 29-35.

Eisner, E. (1983). Anastasia might still be alive, but the monarchy is dead. *Educational Researcher 5,* 13-14, 23-24.

Ekstein, R., & Wallerstein, R.S. (1958). *The teaching and learning of psychotherapy.* New York: International Universities Press.

Erikson, E.H. (1956). The problem of ego identity. *Journal of American Psychoanalytical Association, 4,* 56-121.

Erikson, E.H. (1968). *Identity, youth and crisis.* New York: W.W. Norton.

Evered, R., & Louis, M.R. (1981). Alternative perspectives in the organizational sciences: Inquiry from the inside and inquiry from the outside. *Academy of Management Review, 6*, 385-395.

Faust, D. (1982). A needed component in prescriptions for science: Empirical knowledge of human cognitive limitations. *Knowledge, 3*, 555-570.

Festinger, L. (Ed.). (1980). *Retrospections on social psychology*. New York: Oxford University Press.

Filstead, W. (1970). *Qualitative methodology*. Chicago: Markham.

Firestone, S. (1970). *The dialectic of sex: The case for feminist revolution*. New York: William Morrow.

Fischhoff, B. (1982). For those condemned to study the past: Heuristics and biases in hindsight. In D. Kahneman, P. Slovic, & A. Tversky (Eds.), *Judgment under uncertainty: Heuristics and biases* (pp. 335-353). Cambridge: Cambridge University Press.

Fiske, E. (1981, November 23). Scholars face a challenge by feminists. *The New York Times*, pp. 1, 12.

Frake, C.D. (1969). The ethnographic study of cognitive systems. In S.A. Tyler (Ed.), *Cognitive Anthropology*. New York: Holt, Rhinehart & Winston,

Freeman, D. (1983). *Margaret Mead and Samoa: The making and unmaking of an anthropological myth*. Cambridge, MA: Harvard University Press.

Freeman, J. (1979). The feminist scholar. *Quest, 5*, 26-36.

Freilich, M. (1970). Toward a formalization of field work. In M. Freilich (Ed.), *Marginal natives* (pp. 485-585). New York: Harper & Row.

French, M. (1977). *The women's room*. New York: Jove.

Freud, S. (1900). The interpretation of dreams. *Standard edition of the complete psychological works of Sigmund Freud*. London: Hogarth Press.

Freud, S. (1933). *New introductory lectures on psychoanalysis*. New York: W.W. Norton.

Friedan, B. (1963). *The feminine mystique*. New York: Dell.

Friedlander, P. (1975). *The emergence of a UAW local, 1936-1939: A study in class and culture*. Pittsburgh: University of Pittsburgh Press.

Friedman, N. (1967). *The social nature of psychological research: The psychological experiment as a social interaction*. New York: Basic Books.

Gans, H.J. (1968). The participant observer as a human being: Observations on the personal aspects of field work. In H. Becker et al. (Eds.), *Institutions and the person* (pp. 300-317). Chicago: Aldine.

Gappa, J.M., & Pearce, J. (1982). *Sex and gender in the social sciences: Reassessing the introductory course*. Washington, DC: American Sociological Association.

Gardner, H. (1983). *Frames of mind: The theory of multiple intelligences*. New York: Basic Books.

Geertz, C. (1973). *The interpretation of cultures*. New York: Basic Books.

Gelinas, D.J. (1983). The persisting negative effects of incest. *Psychiatry, 46*, 312-332.

Gerard, H. B., & Matthewson, G. C. (1966). The effects of severity of initiation on liking for a group: A replication. *Journal of Experimental Social Psychology, 2*, 278-287.

Gergen, K. (1971). *The concept of self*. New York: Holt, Rinehart & Winston.

Gergen, K.J. (1973). Social psychology as history. *Journal of Personality and Social Psychology, 26*, 309-320.

Geuss, R. (1981). *The idea of a critical theory*. Cambridge: Cambridge University Press.

Giddens, A. (Ed.). (1974). *Positivism and sociology*. Portsmouth, NH: Heinemann Educational Books.

Gillette, J. (1983). *Ethnic workers in New Haven*. Unpublished manuscript, Yale University.

Gilligan, C. (1982). *In a different voice*. Cambridge, MA: Harvard University Press.

Glaser, B.G. (1978). *Theoretical sensitivity*. Mill Valley, CA: Sociology Press.

Glaser, B.G., & Strauss, A.L. (1967). *The discovery of grounded theory: Strategies for qualitative research*. Chicago: Aldine.

Glassner, B., & Moreno, J.D. (1982). Clinical sociology and social research. *Sociology and Social Research, 66*(2), 115-126.

Glymour, C. (1980). *Theory and evidence*. Princeton, NJ: Princeton University Press.

Goetz, J.P., & LeCompte, M.D. (1981). Ethnographic research and the problem of data reduction. *Anthropology and Education Quarterly, 12*(1), 51-70.

Goffman, E. (1959). *The presentation of self in everyday life*. Garden City, NY: Doubleday.

Goffman, E. (1961). *Asylums*. Garden City, NY: Doubleday.

Goldberg, L. (1970). Man versus model of man: A rationale, plus some evidence, for a method of improving on clinical inferences. *Psychological Bulletin, 73*(4), 422-432.

Gordon, M.E., Kleiman, L.S., & Hanie, C.A. (1978). Industrial-organizational psychology: Open thy ears o house of Israel. *American Psychologist, 33*, 893-903.

Gornick, V., & Moran, B. K. (1971). *Woman in sexist society: Studies in power and powerlessness*. New York: Ballantine Books.

Greenson, R.R. (1967). *The technique and practice of psychoanalysis* (Vol. 1). New York: International Universities Press.

Grunbaum, A. (1984). *The foundation of psychoanalysis*. Berkeley: University of California Press.

Guba, E.G., & Lincoln, Y.S. (1981). *Effective evaluation*. San Francisco: Jossey-Bass.

Gurney, J. (in press). Not one of the group: The problem of sexism in field work. *Qualitative Sociology*.

Gutman, H., (1976). *Work, culture and society in industrializing America, 1815-1919*. New York: Knopf.

Haley, J. (1973). *Uncommon therapy: The psychiatric techniques of Milton H. Erickson*. New York: Ballantine.

Hamilton, E. (1940). *Mythology*. New York: New American Library.

Hannah, B. (1976). *Jung: His life and work*. New York: G.P. Putnam's Sons.

Hanson, N. (1958). *Patterns of discovery*. Cambridge, U.K.: Cambridge University Press.

Hareven, T.K. (Ed.). (1977). *Family and kin in American urban communities, 1700-1930*. New York: Franklin Watts, New Viewpoints Press.

Hareven, T.K. (1978). *Transitions: The family and the life course in historical perspective*. New York: Academic Press.

Hareven, T.K. (1982). *Family time and industrial time*. Cambridge, U.K.: Cambridge University Press.

Hareven, T.K., & Langenback, R. (1978). *Amoskeag: Life and work in an American factory city*. New York: Pantheon.

Harre, R. (1970). *The principles of scientific thinking*. Chicago: University of Chicago Press.

Harre, R. (1972). *Philosophies of science*. Oxford: Oxford University Press.

Harris, M. (1979). *Cultural materialism*. New York: Random House.

Heider, F. (1958). *The psychology of interpersonal relations*. New York: John Wiley.

Heider, F. (1983). *The life of a psychologist: An autobiography*. Lawrence: University of Kansas Press.

Henry, J. (1963). *Culture against man*. New York: Random House.

Herma, J.L. (1968). The therapeutic act. In E.F. Hammer, (Ed.), *Use of interpretation in treatment technique and art*. New York: Grune & Stratton.

Herman, J.L. (1981). *Father-daughter incest*. Cambridge, MA: Harvard University Press.

Heron, J. (1981). Philosophical basis for a new paradigm. In P. Reason & J. Rowan (Eds.), *Human inquiry: A sourcebook of new paradigm research*. New York: John Wiley.

Hesse, M. (1974). *The structure of scientific inference*. London: Macmillan.

Hirsch, P.M. (1980). Ambushes, shootouts, and Knights of the Roundtable: The language of corporate takeovers. Presentation to the Academy of Management, Detroit.

Hofstadter, D.R. (1979). *Gödel, Escher, Bach: An eternal golden braid*. New York: Vintage.

Holland, J. (1973). *Making vocational choices*. Englewood Cliffs, NJ: Prentice-Hall.

Holling, C.S. (1976). Resilience and stability of ecosystems. In E. Jantsch & C.H. Waddington (Eds.), *Evolution and consciousness*. Reading, MA: Addison-Wesley.

Holt, R. (1962). Individuality and generalization in the psychology of personality. *Journal of Personality, 30*, 377-402.

House, J.S. (1981). *Work stress and social support*. Reading, MA: Addison-Wesley.

Howe, F. (1982). Feminist scholarship: The extent of the revolution. *Change*, April, 12-20.

Huberman, A.M. (1981). Splendeurs, miseres et promesses de la recherche qualitative. *Education et Recherche, 3*(3), 233-249.

Huberman, A.M., & Miles, M.B. (1983a). Drawing valid meaning from qualitative data: Some techniques of data reduction and display. *Quality and Quantity, 17*, 281-339.

Huberman, A.M., & Miles, M.B. (1983b) *Innovation up close: A field study in 12 school settings: Vol. 4. People, policies and practices: Examining the chain of school improvement* (D.P. Crandall and associates). Andover, MA: The Network, Inc.

Huberman, A.M. & Miles, M.B. (1984). *Innovation up close: How school improvement works*. New York: Plenum.

Hu-DeHart, E. (1982). Women and minority academics in the United States: Academic freedom or academic repression in the 1980s? Paper presented at the National Emergency Civil Liberties Committee Foundation Conference on Academic Freedom in the 1980s, New York, May 21-22.

Ingle, D.J. (1985). The goldfish as a retinex animal. *Science, 227* (4687), 651-654.

Inkeles, A. (1964). *What is sociology? An introduction to the discipline and profession*. Englewood Cliffs, NJ: Prentice-Hall.

Isabella, L. (1983). *Evaluating qualitative research: Five criteria*. Paper presented at the Academy of Management Meetings, August.

Jakobson, R., & Halle, M. (1956). *Fundamentals of language*. The Hague: Mouton.

Jantsch, E. (1980). *The self-organizing universe*. New York: Pergamon.

Jantsch, E., & Waddington, C.H. (Eds.). (1976). *Evolution and consciousness*. Reading, MA: Addison-Wesley.

Jaques, E. (1952). *The changing culture of a factory*. New York: The Dryden Press.

Jaques, E. (1955). Social systems as a defense against persecutory and depressive anxiety. In M. Klein, P. Heimann, & R.E. Money-Kyrle (Eds.), *New dimensions in psychoanalysis*. London: Tavistock.

Jaynes, J. (1976). *The origin of consciousness in the breakdown of the bicameral mind*. Boston, MA: Houghton Mifflin.

Jones, E. (1953). *The life and work of Sigmund Freud*. Garden City, NY: Doubleday.

Jung, C. G. (1931). The stages of life. In J. Campbell (Ed.), *The portable Jung* (pp. 3-22). New York: Viking.

Jung, C.G. (1933). *Modern man in search of a soul.* New York: Harcourt Brace Jovanovich.

Jung, C.G. (1963). *Memories, dreams, reflections.* New York: Pantheon Books.

Kanter, R.M. (1977). *Men and women of the corporation.* New York: Basic Books.

Kaplan, A. (1964). *The conduct of inquiry.* Scranton, PA: Chandler.

Katz, D., & Kahn, R.L. (1978). *The social psychology of organizations* (2nd ed.). New York: John Wiley.

Katz, M.B. (1971). *Class, bureaucracy and schools.* New York: Praeger.

Kazdin, A. (1980). *Research design in clinical psychology.* New York: Harper & Row.

Kazdin, A. (1982). *Single-case research designs.* New York: Oxford University Press.

Keller, E. F. (1982). Science and gender. *Signs: Journal of Women in Culture and Society, 7*(3): 589-602.

Kelley, H.H. (1984). The impractical theorist. *Contemporary Psychology, 29,* 455-456.

Kendrigan, M. L. (1984). *Political equality in a democratic society: Women in the United States.* Westport, CT: Greenwood Press.

Kimberly, J.R., & Miles, R.H., & associates (1980). *The organizational life cycle.* San Francisco: Jossey-Bass.

Kohn, M.H., & Schooler, C. (1983). *Work and personality.* Norwood, NJ: Ablex.

Kohut, H. (1977). *The restoration of self.* New York: International Universities Press.

Kohut, H. (1984). *How does analysis cure?* Chicago: University of Chicago Press.

Kolawowski, L. (1969). *The alienation of reason: A history of positivist thought.* Garden City, NY: Doubleday.

Kram, K.E. (1983). Phases of the mentor relationship. *Academy of Management Journal, 26,*(4), 608-625.

Kram, K.E. (1985). *Mentoring at work.* Glenview, IL: Scott, Foresman.

Kram, K.E., & Isabella, L.A. (1985). Mentoring alternatives: The role of peer relationships in career development. *Academy of Management Journal,* forthcoming.

Krawiec, T.S. (Ed.) (1972). *The psychologists* (Vols. 1-2). New York: Oxford University Press.

Kuhn, T.S. (1962). *The structure of scientific revolutions.* Chicago: University of Chicago Press.

Ladner, J. (Ed.). (1973). *The death of white sociology.* New York: Vintage.

Lasagna, L. (1982). Historical controls. *New England Journal of Medicine.* 307, 1339-1340.

Lawler, E.E., Nadler, D.N., & Cammann, C. (1980). *Organizational assessment: Perspectives on the measurement of organizational behavior and quality of work life.* New York: John Wiley.

Lawrence, P., & Dyer, D. (1983). *Renewing American industry.* New York: Free Press.

Levine, R.A., & Campbell, D.T. (1972). *Ethnocentrism.* New York: John Wiley.

Levinson, D.J., Darrow, C.N., Klein, E.B., Levinson, M.H., & McKee, B. (1978). *The seasons of a man's life.* New York: Ballantine.

Levinson, H. (1972). *Organizational diagnosis.* Cambridge, MA: Harvard University Press.

Levinson, H. (1983). Consulting with family businesses. What to look for, what to look out for. *Organizational Dynamics, 12*(1), 71-80.

Lidz, T. (1968). *The person.* New York: Basic Books.

Lifton, R.J. (1967). *Death in life: Survivors of Hiroshima.* New York: Basic Books.

Lifton, R.J. (1974). *Explorations in psychohistory: The Wellfleet papers.* New York: Simon & Schuster.

Lippitt, R., Watson, J., & Westley, B. (1958). *The dynamics of planned change.* New York: Harcourt Brace Jovanovich.

Lipset, S., & Hofstadter, R. (1968). *Sociology and history: Methods.* New York: Basic Books.

Lopata, H. L. (1976). Sociology. *Signs: Journal of Women in Culture and Society, 2*(1), 165-176.

Louis, M.R. (1980). Surprise and sense making: What newcomers experience in entering unfamiliar organizational settings. *Administrative Science Quarterly, 25,* 226-251.

Lowman, R.L. (1982a). Clinical psychology at work. *The Clinical Psychologist, 35*(3), 19-20.

Lowman, R.L. (1982b). Parallel processes in conducting organizational research. Paper presented at the meeting of the American Psychological Association, Washington, DC (ERIC Document Reproduction Service N. ED 223712).

Luborsky, L. (1967). Momentary forgetting during psychotherapy and psychoanalysis. In R. Holt (Ed.), *Motives and thought* (Psychological issues monograph 18/19, pp. 177-217). New York: International Universities Press.

Luborsky, L. (1973). Forgetting and remembering (momentary forgetting) during psychotherapy. In M. Mayman (Ed.), *Psychoanalytic research* (Psychological issues monograph 30, pp. 29-55). New York: International Universities Press.

Luborsky, L., & Mintz, J. (1974). What sets off momentary forgetting during psycho-analysis? *Psychoanalysis and Contemporary Science, 3,* 233-268.

Lugones, M.C., & Spellman, E.V. (1983). Have we got a theory for you: Feminist theory, cultural imperialism and the demand for "the woman's voice." *Women's Studies International Forum, 6,* 573-581.

MacKinnon, C. A. (1982). Feminism, Marxism, method and the state: An agenda for theory. *Journal of Women in Culture and Society, 7*(3), 515-44.

Madan, T.N. (1975). On living intimately with strangers. In A. Beteille & T.N. Madan (Eds.), *Encounter and response* (pp. 131-156). Delhi: Vikas.

Mahoney, M., & De Monbreun, B. (1977). Psychology of the scientist: An analysis of problem-solving bias. *Cognitive Therapy and Research, 1*(3), 229-238.

Malan, D.H. (1979). *Individual psychotherapy and the science of psychodynamics.* London: Butterworth.

Malcolm, J. (1981). *Psychoanalysis: The impossible profession.* New York: Knopf.

Mandler, G., & Watson, D.L. (1966). Anxiety and the interruption of behavior. In C.D. Spielberger (Ed.), *Anxiety and behavior.* New York: Academic Press.

Manicas, P.T., & Secord, P.F. (1982). Implications for psychology of the new philosophy of science. *American Psychologist, 38*(4), 390-413.

Mannheim, K. (1936). *Ideology and utopia.* Translated by L. Wirth and E. Shills. New York: Harcourt Brace Jovanovich.

Manning, P.K. (1979). Metaphors on the field: Varieties of organizational discourse. *Administrative Science Quarterly, 24*(4), 660-671.

Marrow, A.J. (1969). *The practical theorist: The life and work of Kurt Lewin.* New York: Basic Books.

Marshall, J. (1981). Making sense as a personal process. In P. Reason & J. Rowan (Eds.), *Human inquiry: A sourcebook of new paradigm research.* Chichester, England: John Wiley.

Masson, J.M. (1984). *The assault on truth: Freud's suppression of the seduction theory.* New York: Farrar, Straus & Giroux.

May, R. (1975). *The courage to create.* New York: W.W. Norton.

May, R. (1977). *The meaning of anxiety* (rev. ed.). New York: Washington Square Press.

May, W.F. (1980). Doing ethics: The bearing of ethical theories on fieldwork. *Social Problems, 27*(3), 358-370.

McGoldrick, M., Pearce, J.K., & Giordano, J. (1982). *Ethnicity and family therapy.* New York: The Oxford Press.

Mead, M. (1973). *Blackberry winter.* New York: William Morrow.

Meehl, P. (1954). *Clinical versus statistical prediction.* Minneapolis: University of Minnesota Press.

Meehl, P. (1965). Clinical versus statistical prediction. *Journal of Experimental Research in Personality, 63*(1), 81-97.

Meehl, P. (1983). Subjectivity in psychoanalytic inference. In J. Earman (Ed.), *Testing scientific theories.* Minneapolis: University of Minnesota Press, 349-412.

Merton, R.K. (1957). *Social theory and social structure.* New York: Free Press.

Metz, M.H. (1981). The impact of ethnographer's roles on the research process. Paper presented at the annual meeting of the American Educational Research Association, April, Los Angeles.

Meyer, A. (1952). *The collected papers of Adolf Meyer, Vol. 3: Medical teaching* (E.E. Winters, Ed.). Baltimore, MD: Johns Hopkins Press.

Meyer, S. (1981). *The five dollar day: Labor, management and social control in the Ford Motor Company, 1908-1921.* Albany: SUNY Press.

Miles, M.B. (1979). Qualitative data as an attractive nuisance: The problem of analysis. *Administrative Science Quarterly, 24*(4), 590-601.

Miles, M.B., & Huberman, A.M. (1981). *The realities of school improvement: Analysis of qualitative data* (NIE grant G-81-0018). New York: Center for Policy Research.

Miles, M.B., & Huberman, A.M. (1984). *Qualitative data analysis: A sourcebook of new methods.* Beverly Hills, CA: Sage.

Miller, C., & Swift, K. (1980). *The handbook of nonsexist writing.* New York: Lippincott and Crowell.

Millett, K. (1969). *Sexual Politics.* New York: Ballantine.

Millman, M., & Kanter, R.M. (1975). *Another voice: Feminist perspectives on social life and social science.* Garden City, NY: Doubleday.

Miner, J. (1984). The unpaved road over the mountains: From theory to applications. *The Industrial-Organizational Psychologist 21*(2), 9-20.

Minuchin, S. (1974). *Families and family therapy.* Cambridge, MA: Harvard University Press.

Mirvis, P.H. (1980). The art of assessing the quality of life at work. In E.E. Lawler, D. Nadler, & C. Cammann (Eds.), *Organizational assessment.* New York: John Wiley.

Mirvis, P.H. (1982). Know thyself and what thou art doing. *American Behavioral Scientist, 26,* 177-197.

Mirvis, P.H., & Seashore, S.E. (1979). Being ethical in organizational research. *American Psychologist, 34,* 766-780.

Mishler, E. (1979). Meaning in context: Is there any other kind? *Harvard Educational Review, 49*(1), 1-19.

Missirian, A.K. (1982). *The corporate connection: Why executive women need mentors to reach the top.* Englewood Cliffs, NJ: Prentice-Hall.

Mitroff, I., & Sagasti, F. (1973). Epistemology as general systems theory: An approach to the design of complex decision-making experiments. *Philosophy of Social Science, 3,* 117-134.

Montgomery, D. (1979). *Worker's control in America.* Cambridge: Cambridge University Press.

Morgan, D. (1984). Some thoughts on the etiology and meaning of the clinical demands of research methods. Unpublished notes, Yale University.

Morgan, G. (Ed.). (1983). *Beyond method: Strategies for social research.* Beverly Hills, CA: Sage.

Myrdal, G. (1969). Biases in social research. In A. Tiselius & S. Nilsson (Eds.), *The plan of values in a world of facts.* New York: John Wiley.

Nadel, S.F. (1951). *Foundations of social anthropology.* New York: Free Press.

Nebraska Feminist Collective (1983). A feminist ethic for social science research. *Women's Studies International Forum, 6*(5), 535-544.

Neumann, E. (1979). Freud and the father image. In E. Neuman (Ed.), *Creative man* (pp. 232-245). Princeton: Princeton University Press.

Newhouse, J. (1982, June 14). A sporty game: I. betting the Company. *The New Yorker,* 48-105.

Nisbett, R.E., & Ross, L. (1980). *Human inference: Strategies and shortcomings of social judgment.* Englewood Cliffs, NJ: Prentice-Hall.

Noble, D. (1977). *American by design.* New York: Knopf.

Northrup, F.S.C. (1947). *The logic of the sciences and the humanities.* New York: Meridian Books.

On Campus with Women. (1982). Vol. 34, pp. 1-2, 5. Washington, DC: Project on Status and Education of Women.

Orne, M.T. (1962). On the social psychology of the psychological experiment. *American Psychologist, 17,* 776-783.

Osipow, S.H. (1973). *Theories of career development* (2nd ed.) Englewood Cliffs, NJ: Prentice-Hall.

Oskamp, S. (1965). Overconfidence in case-study judgments. *Journal of Counseling Psychology, 29*(3), 261-265.

Patai, D. (1983). Beyond defensiveness: Feminist research strategies. *Women's Studies International Quarterly, 6*(2), 177-189.

Paul, I.H. (1973). *Letters to Simon on the conduct of psychotherapy.* New York: International Universities Press.

Perrow, C. (1973). *Complex organizations.* Glenview, IL: Scott Foresman.

Perry, H.S. (1970). *The human be-in.* New York: Basic Books.

Perry, H.S. (1982). *Psychiatrist of America: The life of Harry Stack Sullivan.* Cambridge, MA: Belknap Press.

Perry, S.E. (1966). *The human nature of science: Research psychiatrists at work.* New York: Free Press.

Peshkin, A. (1978). *Growing up American: Schooling and the survival of community.* Chicago: University of Chicago Press.

Peshkin, A. (1982a). The researcher and subjectivity: Reflections on an ethnography of school and community. In G. Spindler (Ed.), *Doing the ethnography of schooling* (pp. 20-47). New York: Holt, Rinehart & Winston.

Peshkin, A. (1982b). *The imperfect union: School consolidation and community conflict.* Chicago: University of Chicago Press.

Peshkin, A. (1983). *Fundamentalist Christian schooling: Truth and consequences.* Paper presented at the Annual Meeting of the American Educational Research Association, April, Montreal, Canada.

Peters, D.P., & Ceci, S.J. (1982). Peer-review practices of psychological journals: The fate of published articles submitted again. *The Behavioral and Brain Sciences, 5,* 187-255.

Phillips, D.C. (1973). *Abandoning method.* San Francisco: Jossey-Bass.

Phillips, D.C. (1983). After the wake: Postpositivistic educational thought. *Educational Researcher, 5*, 4-12.

Phillips-Jones, L. (1982). *Mentors and proteges.* New York: Arbor House.

Piaget, J. (1970). *Genetic epistemology* (E. Duckworth, Trans.). New York: Columbia University Press.

Pirsig, R.M. (1974). *Zen and the art of motorcycle maintenance.* New York: William Morrow.

Polanyi, M. (1958). *Personal knowledge.* London: Routledge & Kegan Paul.

Polkinghorne, D. (1983). *Methodology for the human sciences.* Albany: SUNY Press.

Project on the Status and Education of Women (1982). *On campus with women, 34*, 1-12.

Putnam, L.L., & Pacanowsky, M.E. (Eds.). (1983). *Communication and organizations: An interpretive approach.* Beverly Hills, CA: Sage.

Read, S. (1982). Once is enough: Causal reasoning from a single instance. *Journal of Personality and Social Psychology, 45*, 2, 323-334.

Reason, P., & Rowan, J. (Eds.). (1981). *Human inquiry: A sourcebook of new paradigm research.* Chichester, England: John Wiley.

Register, C. (1979). Brief, a-mazing movements: Dealing with despair in the women's studies classroom. *Women's Studies Newsletter, 7*(4), 7-10.

Reicken, H.W. (1962). A program for research on experiments in social psychology. In N.F. Washburne (Ed.), *Decisions, values, and groups* (pp. 25-41). Elmsford, NY: Pergamon Press.

Reinharz, S. (1979). *On becoming a social scientist: From survey research and participant observation to experiential analysis.* San Francisco: Jossey-Bass.

Reinharz, S. (1981). *Dimensions of the feminist methodological debate.* Paper presented at the American Psychological Association annual meetings, Los Angeles.

Reinharz, S. (1983). Feminist research methodology groups: Origins, forms, functions. In V. Peraka & L. A. Tilly (Eds.), *Feminist re-visions: What has been and might be* (pp. 197-228). Ann Arbor: University of Michigan Press.

Reinharz, S., Bombyk, M., & Wright, J. (1983). Methodological issues in feminist research: A bibliography of literature in women's studies, sociology and psychology. *Women's studies international forum, 6*(4), 437-454.

Reisman, D. (1979). Ethical and practical dilemmas of fieldwork in academic settings: A personal memoir. In R.K. Merton et al. (Eds.), *Qualitative and quantitative research: Papers in honor of Paul Lazarsfeld* (pp. 210-231). New York: Free Press.

Rescher, N. (1976). *Plausible reasoning.* Amsterdam: Van Gorcum.

Rescher, N. (1980). *Induction.* Pittsburgh: University of Pittsburgh.

Rice, A.K. (1969). Individual, group, and intergroup processes. *Human Relations, 22*, 565-584.

Rich, A. (1979). Toward a woman-centered university. In *On lies, secrets and silences* (pp. 125-155). New York: W.W. Norton.

Rieff, P. (1974). Freud and the authority of the past. In R.J. Lifton (Ed.), *Explorations in psychohistory: The Wellfleet papers.* New York: Simon & Schuster.

Riley, G. (Ed.) (1974). *Values, objectivity, and the social sciences.* Reading, MA: Addison-Wesley.

Roberts, H. (Ed.) (1981). *Doing feminist research.* London: Routledge & Kegan Paul.

Roe, A. (1961). The psychology of the scientist. *Science, 134*, 456-459.

Roethlisberger, F.J. (1977). *The elusive phenomena.* Cambridge, MA: Harvard University Press.

Rosenthal, R. (1966). *Experimenter effects in behavioral research*. New York: Appleton-Century Crofts.

Rosenthal, R., & Rosnow, R.L. (Eds.). (1969). *Artifact in behavioral research*. New York: Academic Press.

Rosnow, R.L., & Rosenthal, R. (1984). *Understanding behavioral science*. New York: McGraw-Hill.

Runkel, P. J., Harrison, R., & Runkel, M. (Eds.). (1969). *The changing college classroom*. San Francisco: Jossey-Bass.

Russell, B. (1960). *Our knowledge of the external world*. New York: Mentor Books.

Sachs, D.M., & Shapiro, S.H. (1976). On parallel processes in therapy and teaching. *Psychoanalytic Quarterly 45*, 394-415.

Saint-Simon, Henri de (1964). *Social organization, the science of man, and other writings*. (F. Markham, Ed. and Trans.). New York: Harper & Row.

Sarason, S.B. (1972). *The creation of settings and the future societies*. San Francisco: Jossey-Bass.

Schachtel, E.G. (1947). On memory and childhood amnesia. *Psychiatry, 10*, 1-26.

Schein, E.H. (1984). *Organizational culture*. Unpublished manuscript, Sloan School of Management, MIT.

Schlenker, B. (1974). Social psychology and science. *Journal of Personality and Social Psychology, 29*, 1-15.

Schurman, S.J. (1982). *Political realities of conducting evaluation research in the public sector*. Paper presented at the American Psychological Association Annual Meeting, Washington, DC.

Schwartz, C. G., & Kahne, M. J. (1983). Medical help as negotiated achievement. *Psychiatry, 46*, 33-350.

Schwendinger, H., & Schwendinger, J. (1974). *The sociologists of the chair*. New York: Basic Books.

Scriven, M. (1979). Maximizing the power of causal investigations: The modus operandi method. In W. Popham (Ed.), *Evaluation in education: Current applications*. Berkeley, CA: McCutchan.

Searle, J. (1983). *Intentionality*. Cambridge: Cambridge University Press.

Searles, H.F. (1955). The informational value of the supervisor's emotional experiences. *Psychiatry, 18*, 135-146.

Selvini Palazzoli, M., Boscolo, L., Cecchin, G., & Prata, G. (1978). *Paradox and counterparadox*. New York: Jason Aronson.

Shapiro, M. (1963). A clinical approach to fundamental research with special reference to the study of the single patient. In P. Sainsbury & N. Kreitman (eds.), *Methods of psychiatric research*. New York: Oxford University Press.

Shaskolsky, L. (1970). The development of sociological theory in America: A sociology of knowledge interpretation. In L.T. Reynolds & J. M. Reynolds (Eds.), *The sociology of sociology*. New York: David McKay.

Sherif, M., & Sherif, C. (1969). *Social psychology*. New York: Harper & Row.

Sherman, J. A., & Beck, E.T. (1979). *The prism of sex: Essays in the sociology of knowledge*. Madison, WI: University of Wisconsin Press.

Sherman, R., & Titus, W. (1982). Covariation information and cognitive processing: Effects of causal implications on memory. *Journal of Personality and Social Psychology, 42*(6), 989-1000.

Sherwood, M. (1969). *The logic of explanation in psychoanalysis*. New York: Academic Press.

Shope, R. (1973). Freud's concept of meaning. In B. Rubinstein (ed.), *Psychoanalysis and contemporary science* (Vol. 2, pp. 276-303). New York: Macmillan.

Silverman, L.H. (1976). Psychoanalytic theory: "The reports of my death are greatly exaggerated." *American Psychologist, 31*(9), 621-637.

Simmel, G. (1955). *Conflict and the web of group-affiliations.* (K.H. Wolff & R. Bendix, Trans.). New York: Free Press.

Simmons, V.M. (1983). Conflict in open systems: Planning for a new organization. Unpublished doctoral dissertation. College Park, MD: University of Maryland.

Simon, H., (1977). *Models of discovery.* Boston, MA: D. Reidel.

Singer, J.E. (1980). Social comparison: The process of self-evaluation. In L. Festinger (Ed.), *Retrospections on social psychology.* New York: Oxford.

Smith, A.G., & Louis, K.S. (1982). Multimethod policy research: Issues and applications. *American Behavioral Scientist, 26*(1).

Smith, D. E. (1974.) Women's perspective as a radical critique of sociology. *Sociological Inquiry, 44*(1), 7-15.

Smith, K.K. (1977). Some notes for O.D. consultants: Learning how to interact with client systems. *Australian Psychologist, 11*(3), 281-289.

Smith, K.K. (1982a). *Groups in conflict: Prisons in disguise.* Dubuque, IA: Kendall-Hunt.

Smith, K.K. (1982b). Philosophical problems in thinking about organizational change. In P.S. Goodman et al (Eds.), *Change in organizations* (pp. 316-374). San Francisco: Jossey-Bass.

Smith, K.K. (1983a). Social comparison processes and dynamic conservatism in intergroup relations. In L.L. Cummings & B. M. Staw (Eds.), *Research in organizational behavior* (Vol. 5, pp. 199-233). Greenwich, CT: JAI Press.

Smith, K.K. (1983b). A role for community psychologists: As participant-conceptualizers. *Austrialian Psychologist, 18*(2).

Smith, K.K. (1984a). Rabbits, lynxes and organizational transitions. In J.R. Kimberly & R.E. Quinn (Eds.), *Managing organizational transitions* (pp. 267-294). Homewood, IL: Irwin.

Smith, K.K. (1984b). Toward a conception of organizational currents. *Group and organization studies, 9*(2), 285-312.

Smith, K.K., & Berg, D.N. (1984). *Paradoxes of group life.* Unpublished manuscript, University of Pennsylvania.

Smith, K.K., & Crandell, S.D. (1984). Exploring collective emotion. *American Behavioral Scientist, 27*(6), 813-828.

Smith, K. K., & Simmons, V. M. (1983). A Rumpelstiltskin organization: Metaphors on metaphors in field research. *Administrative Science Quarterly, 28*(3), 377-392.

Snow, R., (1974). Representative and quasi-representative designs for research in teaching. *Review of Educational Research 44,* 265-292.

Sofer, C. (1961). *The organization from within.* Chicago: Quadrangle.

Somers, A. (1982). Sexual harassment in academe: Legal issues and definitions. *Journal of Social Issues, 38*(4), 23-32.

Stacey, J., & Thorne, B. (1984). *The missing feminist revolution in sociology.* Paper presented at the Annual Meeting of the American Sociological Association, San Antonio, TX, August 27-31.

Stanley, L., & Wise, S. (1983). *Breaking out: Feminist consciousness and feminist research.* London: Routledge & Kegan Paul.

Stark, W. (1958). *The sociology of knowledge: An essay in aid of a deeper understanding of the history of ideas.* London: Routledge & Kegan Paul.

Stein, M.R. (1971). The eclipse of community: Some glances at the education of a sociologist. In A.J. Vidich et al. (Eds.), *Reflections on community studies* (pp. 207-232). New York: Harper & Row.

Stevens, S.S. (1939). Operationalism and logical positivism, *Psychological Bulletin, 36*, 221-263.

Sullivan, H.S. (1943). *Conceptions of modern psychiatry,* Lecture 1 from 1943-1944 series of unpublished lectures, Washington School of Psychiatry.

Sullivan, H.S. (1947). Review of R. Benedict's *The chrysanthemum and the sword. Psychiatry 10*, 214-216.

Sullivan, H.S. (1948). Towards a psychiatry of peoples. *Psychiatry, 11*, 105-116.

Sullivan, H.S. (1953a). *Conceptions of modern psychiatry.* New York: W.W. Norton.

Sullivan, H.S. (1953b). *The interpersonal theory of psychiatry.* New York: W.W. Norton.

Sumner, N.G. (1906). *Folkways.* New York: Ginn.

Suppe, F. (Ed.). (1977). *The structure of scientific theories* (2nd ed.). Urbana, IL: University of Illinois Press.

Survey Research Center. (1976). *Interviewer's manual* (rev. ed.). Ann Arbor, MI: Institute for Social Research.

Sutton, R.I. (1983). Managing organizational death. *Human Resources Management, 22*(4), 391-412.

Swinburne, R. (Ed.). (1974). *The justification of induction.* London: Oxford University Press.

Szafran, R.F. (1984). *Universities and women faculty: Why some organizations discriminate more than others.* New York: Praeger.

Taft, R. (1955). The ability to judge people. *Psychological Bulletin, 52*(1), 1-23.

Thomas, D. L. & Edmondson, J. E. (in press). The rise of family theory and critiques from philosophy of science and hermeneutics. In M.B. Sussman & S. K. Steinmetz (Eds.). *Handbook of marriage and the family.* New York: Plenum Press.

Thompson, J.D. (1967). *Organizations in action.* New York: McGraw-Hill.

Thorne, B. (1982). Guidelines for introductory sociology. In J. M. Gappa & J. Pearce (Eds.), *Sex and gender in the social sciences: Reassessing the introductory course.* Washington, D.C. American Sociological Association.

Toby, J. (1955). Undermining the student's faith in the validity of personal experience. *American Sociological Review, 20*, 717-718.

Torbert, W. (1983). Initiating collaborative inquiry. In G. Morgan (Ed.), *Beyond Method.* Beverly Hills, CA: Sage.

Trotsky, L. (1932). *The history of the Russian revolution.* New York: Simon & Schuster.

Tuchman, B. (1981). *Practicing history.* New York: Ballantine.

Tucker, R.C. (1984). *Towards a philosophy of social science for black-white studies.* New Haven, CT: Yale University.

Tversky, A., & Kahneman, D. (1971). The belief in the law of small numbers. *Psychological Bulletin, 76*(2), 105-110.

Tyack, D. (1974). The one best system. Cambridge, MA: Harvard University Press.

United States Department of Labor Statistics. (1979).

Van Maanen, J., Dabbs, J.M., Jr., & Faulkner, R.R. (1982). *Varieties of qualitative research.* Beverly Hills, CA: Sage.

Verba, S., with DiNunzio, J. & Spaulding, C. (1983, September). *Unwanted attention: Report on a sexual harassment survey.* Report to the Faculty Council of the Faculty of Arts and Sciences, Harvard University. (mimeo)

Vickers, J. M. (1982). Memoirs of an ontological exile: The methodological rebellions of feminist research. In G. Finn & A. Miles (Eds.), *Feminism in Canada*. Montreal: Black Rose Books.

Vidmar, N. & Hackman, J.R. (1971). Interlaboratory generalizability of small group research: An experimental study. *Journal of Social Psychology, 83*, 129-139.

Von Eckhardt, B. (1982). Why Freud's research methodology was unscientific. *Psychoanalysis and contemporary thought, 5*, 549-574.

Von Laue, T.H. (1975). Transubstantiation in the study of African reality. *African Affairs, 4*, (10), 401-419.

Wallis, R. (1977). The moral career of a research project. In C. Bell & H. Newby (Eds.), *Doing sociological research* (pp. 146-169). New York: Free Press.

Watzlawick, P. (1978). *The language of change*. New York: Basic Books.

Watzlawick, P., Weakland, T., & Fisch, R. (1974). *Change*. New York: W.W. Norton.

Wax, M.L. (1980). Paradoxes of "consent" to the practice of fieldwork. *Social Problems, 27*, (3).

Webb, E.S., Campbell, D.T., Schwartz, R.D., Sechrest, L., & Grove, J.B. (1981). *Nonreactive measures in the social sciences* (2nd ed.). Boston: Houghton Mifflin.

Weber, M. (1926). *Max Weber: A biography*. New York: John Wiley.

Weick, K. (1976). Educational organizations as loosely coupled systems. *Administrative Science Quarterly, 21*(1), 1-19.

Welch, M., & Lewis, S. (1980). A mid-decade assessment of sex biases in placement of sociology Ph.D.'s: Evidence for contextual variation. *American Sociologist, 15*(3), 120-127.

Westhues, K. (1982). *First sociology*. New York: McGraw-Hill.

Westkott, M. (1979). Feminist criticism of the social sciences. *Harvard Educational Review, 49*(4), 422-430.

White, W.A. (1938). *William Alanson White: The autobiography of a purpose*. Garden City, NY: Doubleday.

Whorf, B.L. (1950). *Four articles on metalinguistics*. Washington: Foreign Services Institute, Department of State.

Whyte, W.F. (1948). Status in the kitchen. In W.F. Whyte (Ed.). *Human relations in the restaurant industry* (pp. 33-46). New York: McGraw-Hill.

Whyte, W.F. (1955). *Streetcorner society* (2nd ed.). Chicago: University of Chicago Press.

Wilden, A. (1980). *Systems and structure* (2nd ed). London: Tavistock.

Wittig, M. (in press). Metatheoretical dilemmas in the psychology of gender. *American Psychologist*.

Wolman, C., & Frank H. H. (1975). The solo woman in a professional peer group. *American Journal of Orthopsychiatry, 45*(1).

Wood, P., (1983). Inquiring systems and problem structure: Implications for cognitive development. *Human Development, 26*, 249-265.

Wortman, C.B., Abbey, A., Holland, E.A., Silver, R.L., & Janoff- Bulman, R. (1980). Transitions from the laboratory to the field. In L. Bickman (Ed.), *Applied Social Psychology Annual, 1*. Beverly Hills, CA: Sage.

Wuebben, P.L., Straits, B.C., & Shulman, G.I. (1974). *The experiment as a social occasion*. Berkeley, CA: Glendessary Press.

Wylie, R. C. (1961). *The self concept*. Lincoln: University of Nebraska Press.

Wylie, R.C. (1968). The present status of self theory. In E.F. Borgatta & W.W. Lambert (eds.), *Handbook of personality theory and research* (pp. 728-787). Chicago: Rand-McNally.

Zelditch, M. (1962). Some methodological problems of field studies. *American Journal of Sociology 67*, 566-576.

The self in social inquiry

"This book is an important step toward clarifying what we mean by clinical research and toward illuminating the complexities of the clinical relationship."

EDGAR H. SCHEIN
Sloan School of Management, MIT

"A valuable collection of essays and ideas that will prove of great use to researchers interested in exploring the relationships between researcher and researched."

GARETH MORGAN
York University

"The book will be of considerable interest to those concerned with the problems and the potential of applied qualitative research. . . (and) to organizational interventionists interested in qualitative methodology."

CONTEMPORARY PSYCHOLOGY

"Extraordinarily useful for Ph.D. students in education. It provides a fresh, essential per-spective that helps students tighten research designs through a careful examination of the too often neglected investigator variable."

GEORGE I. BROWN
University of California, Santa Barbara

"This is one of the most stimulating collections of experiences with clinical thinking and methodology that I have seen in a long time. What gives it its innovativeness and instructiveness is that, with one or two exceptions, all of the contributors come from outside of the clinical area. My graduate students in clinical psychology found the book truly provocative."

SEYMOUR SARASON
Yale University .

ISBN 0-8039-2432-1